AMERICAN KNIGHTS

AMERICAN KNIGHTS

KNIGHTS

THE UNTOLD STORY OF THE MEN OF THE LEGENDARY
601ST TANK DESTROYER BATTALION

VICTOR FAILMEZGER

OSPREY PUBLISHING
Bloomsbury Publishing Plc
PO Box 883, Oxford, OX1 9PL, UK
1385 Broadway, 5th Floor, New York, NY 10018, USA
E-mail: info@ospreypublishing.com
www.ospreypublishing.com

OSPREY is a trademark of Osprey Publishing Ltd

First published in Great Britain in 2015

This paperback edition was first published in Great Britain in 2018 by Osprey Publishing.

ISBN: HB 978 1 4728 0935 3; PB 978 1 4728 2487 5; eBook 978 1 4728 0937 7; ePDF 978 1 4728 0936 0; XML 978 1 4728 3175 0

18 19 20 21 22   10 9 8 7 6 5 4 3 2 1

33614080657207

Maps by Peter Bull Map Studio

Index by Zoe Ross

Originated by PDQ Digital Media Solutions, Bungay, UK

Printed and bound in Great Britain by CPI (Group) UK Ltd, Croydon CR0 4YY

Front cover and title page: Lieutenant Welch of the 601st mounted on an M-10 tank destroyer at Calvi Risorta, December 1943. (Author's collection)

Back cover (left to right): Captain Paulick and First Lieutenant Gioia of the 601st consult a map, Tunisia, March 1943. (Courtesy of US Army Heritage and Education Center); M-10 tank destroyers at the Coliseum, Rome in June 1944. (NARA); A Company 601st enters Berchtesgaden, May 1945. (NARA)

Editor's note on the photographs
To illustrate this personal story of the men of the 601st, the author has eschewed official, staged images and provided instead photographs taken by the troops, often in adverse conditions or combat. The size and quality of the images is balanced therefore by their authenticity.

Editor's note on the quoted material
Much of the quoted material is the diaries and letters of soldiers and as such contains idiosyncrasies of spelling and language. These have been left intact wherever possible in order to present the true "voices" of the men. Additionally, the reader will note that US military style of the time gives dates in the reverse of the usual order of month followed by day, and these, as well as the unaccented or varied spellings of European place names, have been retained in the quotes.

Osprey Publishing supports the Woodland Trust, the UK's leading woodland conservation charity. Between 2014 and 2018 our donations are being spent on their Centenary Woods project in the UK.

To find out more about our authors and books visit **www.ospreypublishing.com**. Here you will find extracts, author interviews, details of forthcoming events and the option to sign up for our newsletter.

CONTENTS

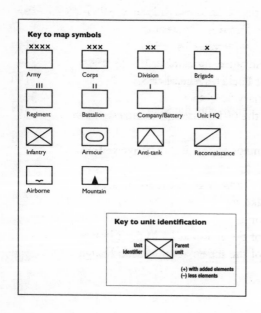

Key to map symbols

XXXX Army

XXX Corps

XX Division

X Brigade

III Regiment

II Battalion

I Company/Battery

Unit HQ

Infantry

Armour

Anti-tank

Reconnaissance

Airborne

Mountain

Key to unit identification

Unit identifier — Parent unit

(+) with added elements
(−) less elements

MAPS

The following maps appear in the image section:

General Crane's battle map of the Anzio area
The Anzio breakout
The race for Rome
Sketch map 1 of the action at La Maison Rouge
Sketch map 2 of the action at La Maison Rouge

ACKNOWLEDGMENTS

When I began transcribing the more than 150 letters my uncle wrote during World War II, I had no idea it would turn into a book, let alone two books. I got to know my uncle, Thomas Peter (Tommy) Welch, during my time as an undergraduate at Southern Methodist University (SMU 1965–69). Because he didn't talk about the war, I remained curious about his experiences. I knew of course Welch was a war hero as one night he showed me his medals without explanation. Also I knew the war was responsible for his having moved to Texas. In 1998 I finished a transcription of the letters from 1942 and it was apparent there was a great story here.

After my mother died, my sister went through all of her papers and provided even more raw material. Cold winters and early retirement motivated me to finish the transcripts. As I did, I went through Welch's US Army records as saved by my grandmother and started to match dull, and some not so dull, military records with events mentioned in the letters. It became obvious to me that I could probably track my uncle's movements and actions during the war in significant detail and that it would be worth doing. The result was the 2012 book

An American Knight, a Tank Destroyer Story. Osprey Publishing was intrigued with the book and invited me to expand the work and tell more of the 601st story. In the process, I was amazed how much more there was to learn.

As with the first book, since the principals are mostly gone now, I wanted to let their words and words of their contemporaries speak for them. Where possible I have traveled to the exact locations where events took place, both in Europe and the United States. Italy is a country I know well, having spent ten years of my life there. Special thanks here to my wife, Patricia, not only for editing help but also for helping navigate modern Italian roads and highways while looking for telltale remains of World War II. In 2011, we made a five-day dash across France following, as she put it, the "Tommy Trail." We even attacked the Siegfried Line, stopping for a beer and a glass of wine along the way in what would have been the middle of it.

In Germany, we visited our friend and former next-door neighbor Dr Rolf Wirtgen, curator for the German Armed Forces Weapons Collection (the *Wehrtechnische Studiensammlung* at the *Bundesamt für Wehrtechnik und Beschaffung*) at Koblenz. Rolf gave me an exhaustive tour of the collection and made sure I had correct information on the German weapons described here.

Thanks also to my first line reviewer and longtime friend, Chief Petty Officer Peter R. Knight, Royal Navy (Retired). Pete and I were stationed together in Castel Volturno, outside Naples (45 years ago), and he still lives in the area. Of special note, Pete's dad, Ronald Orton Knight, served with the Royal Air Force (RAF), attached to the British Eighth Army. He too was a World War II hero and had been in many of the same places in North Africa and Italy where the 601st Tank Destroyer Battalion fought.

Thanks to Mr Howard Klein, formerly a critic for the *New York Times* (who acted as my amanuensis and kept me from "burying the lead") and Mr Malcolm Barr, a veteran of The

ACKNOWLEDGMENTS

Associated Press. Howard served in the USAF and Malcolm the RAF. They read early drafts of the book and made significant comments on the manuscript and earned my gratitude.

As a retired naval officer, I also found I had to be careful about unfamiliar Army expressions and give thanks to two retired US Army reviewers, LTC Tim Stoy and COL Lars Larson. Both helped immensely. Tim is a historian for both the 3rd Infantry Division and the 15th Infantry Regiment. Lars' uncle was one of Welch's sergeants and he contributed more than 40 pages of letters and many photographs.

A special thanks to CPT Monika Stoy, US Army (Retired) and Tim's wife. Monika is a one-lady whirlwind in recognizing the towns and villages the 3rd Infantry Division liberated in France. She also organized seminars on Operation *Dragoon* and the Colmar Pocket. At one of the seminars, I met Mr Joseph Borriello. Joe was a corporal and later first sergeant with the 10th Engineer Battalion. He was assigned to the 3rd Infantry Division and followed the same route as the battalion. Many of his memoirs are included in this work and I enjoyed talking with this very active 92-year-old.

The Stoys introduced me to Mr Jeff Danby who conducted exhaustive research on the combat experience of his grandfather for an amazing book, *Day of the Panzer*. As part of his research in the early 2000s he interviewed surviving members of the 601st Tank Destroyer Battalion. These previously unpublished interviews with those who knew and fought with the battalion were incredible and have made the story come to life. I cannot thank Jeff enough for passing them on to me.

Extensive use has also been made of the unpublished memoirs of Sergeant Charles W. Colprit, Staff Sergeant Bill R. Harper, Private Harold E. Lundquist, Private Thomas E. Morrison, and Sergeant John Nowak, all of the 601st Tank Destroyer Battalion. Mr Bill Nowak allowed me to see and copy his father's photos and scrapbooks, for which I am most grateful.

I am also thankful to the following organizations:

The 3rd Infantry Division Museum, Fort Steward, Georgia
The Third Cavalry Museum at Fort Hood, Texas
Individuals of the Texas and Georgia National Guards who
    sit on former World War II Army Posts
The Geneva Historical Society
The National Archives, Maryland (NARA)
The National Archives, St Louis
The US Army Military Heritage and Education Center
    (USA M H & E C)
The US Military Postal History Society

Finally special thanks to Ms Kate Moore, editor and publisher at Osprey Publishing, Oxford, United Kingdom for seeing the potential of my earlier work and Laura Callaghan for being such a terrific editor. Also thanks to Gemma Gardner for her prompt replies and help with this paperback edition.

Any errors, omissions or other mistakes are mine and mine alone. I mostly took everyone's suggestions, but not all.

Victor "Tory" Failmezger
Commander USN (Retired)
Front Royal, Virginia

Nota bene:
To lessen confusion, I have picked a rank for each soldier who features in the book and stuck with it during the whole narrative. For example, Corporal Borriello rose from corporal to first sergeant during the war; others also increased their rank. I have made an exception to this for the commanding officer of the 601st Tank Destroyer Battalion, Major, later Lieutenant Colonel, Walter E. Tardy. He, by the way, retired with more than 30 years' service with the rank of colonel.

INTRODUCTION

LTC Tim Stoy, US Army (Retired)

Tory Failmezger's *American Knights* is an outstanding review of the combat service of the US Army's first tank destroyer battalion. It is a human view of that battalion's World War II experience, based on the personal accounts of numerous members of this illustrious unit. This book's strength resides in its focus on the individual soldier and his actions in combat in North Africa, Sicily, Italy, Southern France, and Germany. The reader learns of the challenges faced by the soldier, is given insights into each soldier's frame of mind and the book is unsentimental in evaluating the impact of the death and destruction these men encountered. At 70 years' distance it is not easy for anyone not combat experienced to fully understand the tremendous achievement it was for men to go through the hell these men did and still remain combat effective, and to contribute substantially to the Allies' final victory.

The 601st Tank Destroyer Battalion served with two of the Army's greatest combat divisions, the 1st Infantry Division (the Big Red One) and the 3rd Infantry Division (the Rock of the Marne). These divisions are well known because they saw the most combat and succeeded in every mission they were assigned. The partnering of the battalion with both of these great divisions was of great advantage to both the battalion and the divisions – the 601st received first-rate leadership and tough missions from the divisions, while the divisions benefited from the Army's most experienced tank destroyer outfit. As the historian for the Society of the 3rd Infantry Division and the 15th Infantry Regiment Association, I am fully aware of the critical role the 601st TD Battalion played in each of the division's campaigns from Italy to Austria.

The past 20 years my wife, Monika, and I have traveled to Provence, the Vosges, Alsace, Germany, and Austria to participate in ceremonies honoring our veterans. We have experienced the August heat in Provence and the January cold in the Colmar Pocket. We have covered the entire 3rd Infantry Division's route in France, Germany, and Austria trying to understand the flow of the fighting and the challenges of the terrain. Thanks to Tory's well-written narrative I can see in my mind's eye the men of the 601st Tank Destroyer Battalion and the rest of the 3rd Infantry Division maneuvering on it and through it. What they achieved is a truly impressive feat of arms.

Reading the letters the veterans sent home and the interviews they gave in the years after the war one cannot but be awed by their humility. The strength of character of this generation of men is impressive and inspiring. As young men they experienced horrendous things on a regular basis for protracted periods of combat, and after the war returned home to establish families, work, and live ordinary lives. Of course they had their demons and their nightmares, and many of them fought lonely battles in the dark against these demons the rest of their lives. Some, like Tommy Welch, couldn't find the adrenaline rush of combat in any other activity and never fully adjusted to civilian life, but it is amazing how many of the Greatest Generation did.

INTRODUCTION

Tory's book is a great tribute to the men of the 601st Tank Destroyer Battalion – men who served well in battle and helped win World War II. It is a reminder to all readers that war brings out not only the worst but also the best in men. Most of all, it reminds us war is a very human endeavor, and *American Knights* admirably portrays the men of the 601st – not saints, not sinners, just ordinary men serving honorably and sometimes doing the extraordinary under tremendously difficult circumstances.

Tim Stoy
Lieutenant Colonel US Army (Retired)
Springfield, Virginia, September 2014

LTC Stoy is a graduate of the US Military Academy at West Point and a 30-year veteran of the US Army. He and his wife Monika (CPT US Army (Retired)) reside in Springfield, Virginia when they are not traveling to Europe and Korea to place plaques to honor US forces.

FOREWORD

COL Lars Larson, US Army (Retired)

As the second decade of the 21st century continues, participants and witnesses to the events of World War II are quickly disappearing. Many, even now, have remained silent on their roles and personal experiences of the traumatic period that shaped their lives and changed the course of history. Growing up, I was surrounded by heroes, often not aware of them or their deeds until reading their obituaries. At an early age I learned my favorite uncle, Rudolph (Rudy) Larson, had been wounded in combat while serving in Europe. Years later, when telling him of my impending reassignment to Germany to the 3rd Infantry Division as an infantry officer, he remarked "I served with them once," nothing more.

Over time I learned a bit more of Rudy's military service. He had been with a tank destroyer battalion and his unit wore an interesting shoulder patch. Rudy enjoyed life, was a jokester and incessant pipe smoker who did not speak of his many months of combat. This constant teaser and upbeat veteran of World War II had a distinguished record of service and combat experiences that were nearly lost to history. Upon his death and without immediate heirs, my father obtained and saved his brother's letters, photos and military items. Only more recently were they rediscovered with my father's memorabilia. An interest in this collection led to trying to learn more of Rudy's service and the circumstances of his wounding.

This book presents the personal accounts of the men, their combat experiences and campaigns from the soldiers who daily lived with fear, personal losses and hardships that were only shared with their comrades and their close family members. Letters served as the almost exclusive means to communicate between families whose service members were often overseas for years, facing uncertain futures and hoping to return home safely. In an age before copy machines, letters were passed to others or were retyped to be circulated amongst family members, some serving elsewhere around the globe. Rudy's letters written to my father were full of lessons learned. They were obviously deemed important to both men as my father was preparing to deploy to Europe with a tank division. In these letters Rudy described combat engagements without glamor or bravado, simply as they happened without exaggeration. These were the often vivid accounts of events and were remarkable in clarity as he tried to describe his world to those who had not experienced war on the front lines.

The 601st Tank Destroyer Battalion was only one unit in the European Theater of Operations during World War II. What made it exceptional was the men who filled its ranks and their dedication to a common cause, putting their comrades and the mission ahead of their personal fears. It has been my honor and privilege to be a small part of this effort to share with future generations their lives and their distinguished service to our Nation.

Lars E. Larson
Colonel US Army (Retired)

Lars E. Larson grew up in Iowa, and attended the University of Iowa where he received a regular army commission as an infantry officer. He served as a rifle platoon leader and company commander in Vietnam, with further service in Europe and stateside assignments to include the Pentagon. He retired after 26 years of service and resides in northern Virginia.

PROLOGUE

At Berchtesgaden Adolf Hitler had often gazed out on his Alpine world from a huge picture window in his chalet and dreamt of his 1,000-year Reich of triumphal architecture and world-class museums stuffed with looted art from all over Europe.

To set the mood, the overture to Richard Wagner's *Die Meistersinger von Nüremburg* would be played on a phonograph. In the afternoon, the Nazi elite would sip cups of English tea or Brazilian coffees served by Aryan SS waiters and consume Munich *Bienenstich* off swastika-embossed Dresden china. They would pass the time in mindless conversation with their Führer, who sat with his German shepherd Blondie and Eva Braun.

In the room with this picture window, Il Duce, Count Ciano, Sir Neville Chamberlain and others had gathered for conferences which divided Europe and led to six years of war, death, famine and unprecedented destruction.

By mid-summer 1945 the guests were different. The three relaxed sergeants in neatly pressed uniforms had not been invited by the owner. Standing in the frame of that huge window, surrounded by graffiti from previous uninvited soldiers from places like Mine, Pennsylvania and Chester, Montana, the sergeants each wore .45-caliber pistols on utility belts over their Ike jackets.

These jackets were adorned with the 3rd Infantry Division patch and their awards for bravery, Purple Hearts and campaign ribbons. Gone were the hated leggings they had been required to wear when they started back in 1939, replaced by over-the-ankle combat boots, and they wore overseas caps set at jaunty angles. Still in their 20s and early 30s, they would always seem older after having accomplished so much in the war years.

This book is their story, the story of the men of the 601st Tank Destroyer Battalion and a combat engineer who supported them through almost 550 days of combat. Those 550 days required four D-Day amphibious landings, took them through the deserts and hills of North Africa, the "great withdrawal" at Kasserine, the payback at El Guettar, Salerno, the Volturno, Cassino, Anzio, the liberation of Rome, the landing at Ramatuelle (St Tropez), the Vosges Mountains, the Colmar Pocket, the breaking of the Siegfried Line (the West Wall), Nuremburg, Munich, Salzburg and finally to that picture window at Berchtesgaden.

They came from across all America, and they reflected their times. Some had enlisted in the army to escape the doldrums of the Great Depression; others enlisted after the Japanese attack at Pearl Harbor; others were drafted. All put their lives on hold.

Nine soldiers will help tell the story in their own words. Their accounts will differ but all are reliable witnesses. As Sergeant (later Major) Max Altschuld, B Company 601st (Brooklyn, New York) wrote: "Accounts written of the war are not fully accurate, only the soldiers who were there can attest to the accuracy of events at a given time or place."

Joseph F. Borriello, born in 1923, Meriden, Connecticut, enlisted in the US Army in September 1942 and joined the 10th Engineer Battalion in March 1943.

Charles W. Colprit, born 1920, Dover, New Hampshire, joined the Army in August 1942 and the 601st in the spring of 1943.

Bill R. Harper, born 1920, Titus County, Texas, enlisted in the Army in December 1939 in Dallas, Texas. He transferred with his whole battery to the 601st Provisional Antitank Battalion in the fall of 1941.

Edward L. Josowitz, born 1912, New York, New York, enlisted in June 1942; he joined the 601st in 1943. He was the author of the 601st Battalion's *Informal History* (1945).

Rudy Larson, born 1909, Lansing, Iowa, enlisted in the US Army in August 1942 and joined the 601st on October 1, 1943.

Harold E. Lundquist, born August 1923, Minneapolis, Minnesota, drafted into the army in January 1943 and assigned to the 601st, Reconnaissance Company in October 1943.

Thomas E. Morrison, born 1918, Brewster, Ohio, drafted in the Army in April 1942 and joined the 601st in time to ride the *Queen Mary* to Scotland the summer of 1942.

John Nowak, born 1918, Ludlow, Massachusetts, enlisted in the regular army of the United States in October 1940 and was assigned to the 32nd Field Artillery Battalion. He was among the first to be assigned to the 601st Provisional Antitank Battalion.

Thomas Peter Welch, born 1920, Geneva, New York, enlisted in the US Army in May 1942 and was commissioned Second Lieutenant in January 1943; he joined the 601st in October 1943.

On the following pages are some of their exploits, adventures, terror and heroism. All survived the war while many of their buddies did not. Along the way I will introduce other men of this exceptional unit. I hope that by the end, the reader will appreciate these men as I do.

Seek, Strike, Destroy

CHAPTER 1

SEEK, STRIKE AND DESTROY

"An ordeal of dust, cold, rain, no sleep and no rest"

The United States by all accounts was unprepared for World War II, although senior military officers watched what was going on in Europe and worried about what they saw. In 1939, when the German Army invaded Poland, the US Army's ground and air strength stood at about 600,000 men: fewer men under arms than in Bulgaria, Sweden or Turkey!

The Germans had perfected a new kind of war: blitzkrieg, lightning war. Blitzkrieg employed highly mobile forces supported by newly designed *Panzers* (tanks). There was no doubt about the reason for its success, as Lieutenant Jean DuPont, a French artillery officer later declared: "For me the tanks were responsible, more than any other weapon, for the lightning success of the German armies in France."

The Polish cavalry had bravely charged the invading Germans, lancers against Panzers. The results were disastrous: Poland surrendered in three weeks. After a considerable delay, the German Wehrmacht turned west and circumvented the fixed battlements of the Maginot Line.[1] Using glider troops, the Wehrmacht captured the Belgian Fort Eben-Emael and then swept through Belgium and across the unprotected French border. The French could not believe Germany would violate Belgian neutrality and bypass the impregnable Maginot Line, but bypass they did.

Fearing that war was inevitable, the US Congress passed a draft law in October 1940 which required all men, citizens or not, between the ages of 21 and 31, to register for a draft in the event of war. Initially the Army started drafting men for one year in order to build up a pool of trained soldiers, but with the possibility of extension should a war be declared. A popular song of the period was "I'll be back in a year, little darlin'," by "Texas" Jim Robertson. With war clouds gathering in mid-1941, a hold was put on separations from the service. Many soldiers were unhappy with this situation and protested, declaring their intention to go to OHIO, which meant "over the hill in October," the one-year anniversary of the law, although very few men actually carried through on that threat and deserted. Before the Japanese attack on Pearl Harbor, life in the Army for a draftee was not very challenging. There was not much to do and the Army was short on everything. It would take a while for modern arms and uniforms to reach the troops. In the summer of 1941, an extension to the draft registration law was passed requiring men to register who had turned 21 since the first draft law went into effect.

Meanwhile, to the watching US military commanders, not yet in the war, it was obvious the only way to stop the German blitzkrieg was to destroy its Panzers. The concept of a fixed defense that had given birth to the Maginot Line was gone forever. The United States may have been neutral but its military leaders knew the Panzer problem would someday have to be confronted.

To that end, Army maneuvers were held in Tennessee in June of 1941 and George S. Patton, then a major general, took charge. In confronting the Panzer problem, he deployed his 2nd Armored Division in a head-on, rapid attack against US tanks. Agreeing the maneuver had worked, the Army then tested the idea of having independent antitank units that could go against Panzers. The Army decided to organize three provisional antitank regiments. Each was to have three antitank batteries, A, B and C.

In August, at Fort Devens in Massachusetts, the 1st Provisional Antitank Regiment was activated. Battery A was staffed with men pulled from the 1st Infantry Division's (nicknamed the Big Red One) attached field artillery batteries. In September, Battery B was formed with three officers and 65 men, also from the 1st Infantry Division. Soon after, the division's Fifth Field Artillery Battery D was transferred intact to become the new Battery C. This historic battery traced its history back to Alexander Hamilton, its sponsor during the American Revolution.[2]

All this was organized under its first commanding officer, an old-school US Army professional. About him, Edward Josowitz wrote in the battalion's *Informal History*:

> Kind chance sent the 601st a commanding officer in the person of Major [later Lieutenant Colonel] Hershel D. Baker, a two hundred and twenty pound, roly-poly, cherubic looking, foghorn-voiced, ball of fire. The Old Man was a battle wise veteran of World War I, a showman, something of a martinet with his officers but proud as hell of his outfit and 100 percent for his men. From the first day, the 601st was "Baker's Outfit" and it was not long before it had taken on much of the Old Man's hell-for-leather personality. It may or may not be significant that on the very first day of its existence Colonel Baker scheduled a battalion beer-party at the expense of "D" Battery of the 5th.

Maneuvers are the means of building a fighting force, of molding men into units. The first antitank regiment had been formed. Now it needed to learn how to function in the war that many thought was coming to the US.

The regiment left Fort Devens in October for Fort Bragg, North Carolina, for the Carolina Maneuvers, the largest US Army maneuvers ever held to date. General George C. Marshall, then US Army Chief of Staff, based these maneuvers on his World War I experiences, which was the last time US forces of this aggregate size had operated together, some 23 years earlier. General Marshall wanted realistic training with large unit movements so as to give practice to senior commanders and staffs in operational elements of combat. These war games included live-fire exercises. Extended time was spent in the field teaching tactics, fieldcraft and techniques to small-unit officers and soldiers. The maneuvers also functioned as a laboratory to test new methods in the field, to apply tactical principles and to experiment with new equipment. The results were sobering. Had this been real combat, entire divisions would have been annihilated or captured, so ill-prepared was the Army for war, but it learned from mistakes, replaced ineffective leaders and developed new skills.

For the personnel involved, Josowitz said the maneuvers were "an ordeal of dust, cold, rain, no sleep and no rest." Much was improvised: orange flags signaled a gun was "firing." Umpires clanged cowbells to indicate that a unit was under fire. Bags of flour were dropped from Piper Cub aircraft to simulate bombs. Soldiers still wore World War I "silly-looking old type soup bowl helmets." Traffic jams clogged the roads. The men enjoyed their first taste of "C" rations, if enjoy is the right word. They heated this new concoction of cooked meat and beans on the engines of their vehicles; if the mixture slopped onto the engine, it stuck like glue. There needed to be changes all around.

However ad-libbed the maneuver may have been, the new regiment of antitankers "destroyed," with their imaginary shells from their towed 37mm guns, an astonishing number of tanks. Josowitz called them "our super-duper antitank guns." Improvisation ruled: one antitank vehicle was simulated by a jeep with a pole sticking out of the back.

The maneuvers tested General Marshall's hypothesis that mobile antitank gun units, offensively deployed, could in fact defeat Wehrmacht armor. The war game pitted infantry divisions equipped with 4,300 mobile, antitank cannon of varying calibers against armored divisions with motorized infantry in support. The armored divisions had 865 tanks and armored scout cars in all. The results showed the antitank units were promisingly effective and the War Department, at the conclusion of the maneuvers, established a separate antitank command. Its mandate was to set up a training center, later named the Tank Destroyer Tactical and Firing Center. Its mission was to train crews to "Seek, Strike and Destroy" enemy tanks, a phrase that became its motto.

However, the antitank regiments still did not have the right weapons. Even before the formation of the new regiments, the search for effective weaponry led, in mid-1940, to the development of two mobile self-propelled ad hoc antitank weapons. The first was designated the M-3, built on a General Motors Corporation half-track. It was originally a personnel carrier and it mounted a 75mm French-made gun, which faced forward. This gun had been scavenged from leftover World War I barrels that some unnamed Army clerk had stored instead of sold as surplus steel. The half-track's top speed was 45mph and it accommodated a five-man crew. The gun, with a muzzle velocity of 1,900 feet per second, was ineffectual, however, against any target more than 500 yards away. Still, it was the best the Army could devise at such short notice.

The next weapon to be developed was the M-6, a self-propelled antitank weapon that mounted a 37mm gun barrel on the bed of a Dodge ¾-ton weapons carrier named Fargo. In theory, its line of fire encompassed 360 degrees but in practice if its gun fired over the carrier's cab, it shattered the windshield thereby endangering the crew of four. The M-6 could reach 55mph; although it was fast, it was less than lethal. A second version of the M-6 towed a 37mm gun but it needed a larger crew and, since the gun had to be set up to be fired, it was even less mobile. And, as both the British and US Army found, the 37mm gun was simply not effective against heavily armed German Panzers. By March of 1943, the Army scrapped the M-6, in favor of the still inadequate M-3.

In late 1941, these first self-propelled antitank guns were ready. Some were rushed to the Philippines. The remaining guns were assigned to the new provisional antitank regiments. A basic allotment of vehicles for each regiment consisted of 24 M-3s and 12 M-6s. Then began a furious program to design and build a new, self-propelled tank destroyer based on the M-4 Sherman tank. The result was designated the M-10, but it was not ready until September 1942, too late for initial Army deployments to Europe and Asia.

After December 7, 1941 and the Japanese attack on Pearl Harbor, life in the US Army took on new seriousness. Hitler's declaration of war on the United States came a few days later and President Franklin D. Roosevelt and Prime Minister Winston Churchill announced their strategic decision declaring that Europe "must be defeated first." Final victory over the Japanese would take place only after the Nazi menace was eliminated. At the highest level, there was fear the Germans might be working on an atomic bomb, and that contributed to the "Germany first" decision.

In early December, in order to make them sound more aggressive, antitank guns were re-designated tank destroyers. Shortly thereafter, the Army re-designated the 1st Provisional Antitank Regiment as the 601st Tank Destroyer Battalion.

Although there were many changes in weapons and troop allotments, that name remained the unit's designation until the end of the war.

A tank destroyer insignia was adopted at this time although not formally approved by the Heraldic Section, Office of the Quartermaster General United States Army until November 1942. It was described as follows: "On a disc of golden orange 2 13/16 inches in diameter, a full faced cougar's face in black with markings in red, eyes, whiskers, and teeth in white, crunching a black tank with wheels of golden orange, all within a black border 3/32 of an inch in width."

The buildup of men and weapons accelerated apace. During the winter of 1941/42, those units that were deemed reasonably ready, including the US 1st Infantry Division and the attached 601st Tank Destroyer Battalion, were prepared for overseas deployment, "destination unknown." In February 1942, the 601st traveled in convoy along single-lane US highways to Camp Blanding, Florida. The trip from Massachusetts that winter was rough. There were no blankets in the vehicles and during stops the men would run in place to warm up. They arrived in Florida for training in cold but milder weather, towing their 37mm guns through swamps. Departing Florida, they returned to Fort Bragg. Bad weather followed them. Fort Bragg experienced its first snowfall "in about 1,000 years." There, on March 27, battalion companies were brought up to strength. For example, B Company received an additional 78 enlisted men, which brought it to 180 men. In April, the battalion made a road march to Fort Benning, Georgia, home of the 1st Infantry Division, to which they were then attached.

A month later, they were at Indiantown Gap, Pennsylvania, the first staging area for US troops going to England. Time was running out for stateside training but they were finally issued their full complement of M-3, 75mm half-tracks. Here, too, the men got multiple injections for a wide variety of diseases that gave no indication of where they were going; secrecy kept them in ignorance. They had no idea where they would end up, when they would get there, and when they would see home again. Unsurprisingly discipline became a problem.

The battalion's authorized strength was 38 officers and 860 enlisted men. It was organized with a Headquarters Company (HQ); a Reconnaissance Company (Recon); three gun companies (A, B, and C); and a 16-man medical detachment. The company was the basic unit of the battalion and was commanded by a captain and divided into platoons, each commanded by a lieutenant platoon leader. Once a man was assigned to a company he normally stayed with that company until transferred out of the battalion. That did not mean, however, he stayed in the same platoon. Men were moved about as the situation dictated.

The HQ Company had an authorized strength of 14 officers and 155 men assigned, plus an additional 100 men who were used as drivers and laborers as needed. HQ Company contained the service elements whose job it was to maintain and supply the rest of the battalion. Although HQ Company was not assigned any antitank guns, it was equipped with five armored cars, eight motorcycles, eight jeeps, 14 ¾-ton trucks, 20 2½-ton trucks (often referred to as a deuce and a half), and 17 1-ton trailers. The trucks and trailers hauled the battalion's ammunition, gas and supplies. Rounding out the company was a heavy wrecker (T-2) used for retrieving damaged, but salvageable, tank destroyers from the battlefield. Indeed, the battalion was entirely self-sufficient. It sent its own supply vehicles to ammunition dumps and supply depots for the unit.

The Recon Company was authorized six officers and 139 men. It was equipped with 11 armored cars, 22 jeeps (some equipped with machine guns), and one 2½-ton truck. It did not have any antitank guns. Recon used stealth and speed to its advantage in advance of the gun companies and would probe enemy positions and report back on strength and disposition.

All three gun companies were similarly organized with an authorized strength of five officers and 181 men. Each company had four platoons, a headquarters platoon and three gun platoons numbered 1st, 2nd and 3rd. The headquarters platoon had two officers: the company commander and his executive officer. There were 37 enlisted men: 28 in the command section and nine in the maintenance section. Each company had five armored cars, 18 jeeps, eight M-3s and four M-6s. The assignment and employment of each platoon depended on the circumstances and the discretion of the company commander.

Many of the men who would later call the 601st home for the duration started their training at this time. Among those were some of the book's main characters: Borriello, Colprit, Josowitz, Larson, Lundquist and Welch. Welch's training experience will serve as an example of what a 601st soldier experienced during basic training.

"So far it's been grand"

Thomas Welch's army career started on May 5, 1942, at a busy induction center in Rochester, New York. That first day was a blur of activity. The first thing the Army gave Welch was a serial number.[3] He had already passed a physical in his hometown but at the induction center he was subjected to another. There was a flurry of papers to sign. Finally he raised his hand and gave the oath of allegiance to defend the United States and obey the orders of all officers appointed above him. From Rochester he was sent to a reception center at Fort Niagara, Youngstown, New York. There he underwent mental testing and was given training in very basic soldiering. Volunteers received better treatment than draftees, as he noted in the obligatory postcards to his mother, excerpted here:

> Well, here I am a soldier. Oath, uniform, & all – so far it's been grand. The fellows are all good guys, and very friendly. We enlisted men are treated much better than the draftees; we stay in barracks, the draftees in tents. I'll only be here three or four days and then I shove off. The food is good and lots of it. We go to bed at eleven o'clock and get up at 0615, real healthy. I took out $5,000.00 worth of [life] insurance. What a day and what sunburn. We drilled for seven hours today and then had a full dress parade tonight, and it really was inspiring, all the men in full uniform and a military band. Tomorrow I go on KP ["kitchen police"] duty, washing dishes etc. for the first time. It's a little out of my line. At night my buddies and I go down to the service club and dance and listen to jam sessions. Good fun. I've had exactly one glass of beer since I've been here (no money), we have a bar right here on the post where beer only is served. I've gained about five pounds and feel swell. Well I'm going to bed.

A week later Welch was transferred to Camp Wheeler near Macon, Georgia for basic training.[4] Camp Wheeler was built as an infantry replacement center. During the course of the war, more than 218,000 soldiers were trained there both for basic infantry training and in the Non-Commissioned Officer (NCO) School. During the first few weeks of a recruit's service, there was a lot of testing and sorting so after basic training the soldiers could be sent on for further training or directly to a unit. The enlisted infantry training lasted about 16 weeks. Welch describes basic training camp life in the mail he sent home:

Today was a mighty tough and hot day, the sun boiled down all day, what a sunburn! We had bayonet practice and it really was strenuous, lunging and pushing. The food is gradually getting better and I'm putting on weight with it, regular hours, hard work and no drinking. I have no taste for beer or liquor any more, my standby is Coca-Cola. We get up at 0545, breakfast at 0615, clean up the barracks, make our beds and then go to classes or drill. We eat at 1200 then back to work at 1300. We work all afternoon until 1700, dinner at 1730. Then we have until 2300 to ourselves. I'm usually in bed by 2130. We've taken so many shots in the arm they look like sieves and my vaccination is swollen like a baseball. Saturday will be the first time we will be able to leave camp, so I think I'll go swimming.

Things have been happening fast and furiously here. Last Tuesday eve we were told to pack up our things, we were moving out. Rumors started flying fast and furiously, everyone had a different idea where we were going. Of course everyone that told you swore you to secrecy. Well we finally moved next door to the eighth battalion. What a move! The heat here averages 110 degrees and boy that's plenty hot. We took a 12-mile hike the other day with full field equipment. Our equipment weighs about 55 pounds and to top it off we walked two hours with gas masks on. You can imagine what it was like. We've been on the rifle range for the last ten days and it really has been tough. I got a marksman's medal, which was a lot, more than I could reasonably expect. We got paid, but after all the deductions I was practically broke five minutes later.

During evaluation, Welch was selected for Officer Candidate School (OCS), which required him to complete a four-week non-commissioned officers' course. He wrote home that he had signed up for the tank destroyer outfit and if he went there he would be "Deep in the Heart of Texas," referring to the newly established Tank Destroyer School at Camp Hood, Texas.

The Tank Destroyer Tactical and Firing Center was the War Department's answer to counter Nazi Panzers. The center, northwest of Killeen, Texas, was vast and empty and crossed by two railway lines which allowed large numbers of vehicles and materials to be shipped in and out of the post. On June 8, nine TD battalions, re-designated from artillery units, arrived at Camp Hood for training. They lived in tents in the middle of a wilderness. The camp was officially opened on September 8, 1942.

Innovative training at Camp Hood was standard. It was the first US Army post where trainees experienced live ammunition fire while undergoing the obstacle course (using 22-caliber long rounds to stand in for more lethal ammunition). A model Nazi village with pop-up targets was where troops underwent commando-style training.

Welch arrived at Camp Hood late on October 24, a Saturday. He didn't get much time to write, as his first postcard noted: "Well I'm now on my way to a commission. We got here yesterday and have been constantly on the go ever since. We don't walk a step we double-time, all the time. We eat out of mess kits every meal and have to walk a mile to get it. Sunday is just another day here."

According to *The Army Ground Force Tank Destroyer History* (1946):

The graduation requirement of the school stressed leadership. The leadership rating of a candidate was determined chiefly by his company commander and platoon leader based upon their observation of his conduct of command and physical training exercise, his weekly assignments as a student officer or non-commissioned officer, and his execution of practical work in classes.

"Tea and trumpets"

Meanwhile high-level decisions were being made that would guide the entire conduct of the European war, and therefore affect the lives of ordinary Americans who would have to do the fighting. The decisions were controversial and those who made them took risks.

British Prime Minister Winston Churchill's relief in late 1941 was such that when Germany declared war on the United States following the Japanese attack on Pearl Harbor, he claimed to have slept well for the first time since the war started. He had had good reasons for not sleeping. The British Eighth Army had been fighting in North Africa, first against the Italians and later the Germans when Hitler sent the Afrika Korps to help Mussolini after a series of setbacks.

President Roosevelt, prior to Pearl Harbor, had contrived ways to aid Britain without violating US neutrality, famously with Lend-Lease, but that was all over now. One of the first things the President did was to strip the 1st US Armored Division of 300 of its new Sherman M-4 tanks. They were sent to the British Eighth Army in Egypt via the Horn of Africa. The tanks were immediately pressed into service and helped turn the tide against the Afrika Korps. While this infusion of materiel was critical for the British, its effect on the 1st Armored was disastrous; their stateside training was severely curtailed because of the lack of tanks, a factor that was to have a negative effect on the division later when it went into combat in North Africa.

Although it would delay the invasion of France and the subsequent invasion of Germany, President Roosevelt, against the advice of General Marshall, informed both Churchill and his US senior military leaders that he would support Churchill's proposal to invade North Africa. This decision, announced on July 25, 1942, eventually sent more than one million US troops and millions of tons of supplies to the Mediterranean. The Soviet allies clamored for a second front, not willing to believe that US forces and landing craft did not yet exist in sufficient numbers for an invasion of Europe. There were, however, enough troops and amphibious craft for a landing in North Africa, and for now that could be the second front. It would show the Soviets that the Americans were fully committed to the alliance in the European Theater.

Roosevelt reasoned that invading North Africa was one way to bring French North African troops and the French Navy into active service in the Allied cause. The North African campaign would also season new American troops who badly needed combat experience while the US built up the men and materiel required for an invasion of France which, it was argued, could not take place for at least another year. A success in this theater would also shorten the supply lines to India and Burma.

As the 601st Tank Destroyer Battalion made final preparations for departure, and realizing he needed every last one of his men, Lieutenant Colonel Baker declared an amnesty for all of the 601st men who had gone absent without leave (AWOL) during their three months in Indiantown. The men had wanted one last stateside fling. Deeming them irreplaceable, Baker pragmatically looked the other way.

When the men arrived in New York City at the end of July, they boarded Her Majesty's Troop Ship (HMTS) *Queen Mary*; it was increasingly obvious they were headed for England. Each man was loaded down with equipment. One bag for combat gear ("A" bag) and one for class "A" uniforms and personal gear ("B" bag). In addition they carried overcoats, weapons, musette bag (a little bag with hygiene items and cigarettes, etc.), steel helmets and prophylaxis kits. For the most part, the men sailing had come into the army before the war.

Fortunately for the men of the 601st, the run-up to World War II was the period of the great transatlantic ocean liners, large ships of British, French, Dutch, German and American steamship lines. These ships were fast, crossing from the Port of New York to England in five days. Not required to sail in slow-moving convoys with warships as guards, their speed helped them to outrun deadly German U-boats. Importantly, the ship's public spaces could be converted to troop berthing in a relatively short time.[5] These accommodations were Spartan and Private Morrison had this to say about his berthing aboard the *Queen Mary*:

> They had bunks built everywhere, and our bunks were in the swimming pool on a promenade deck. They had these bunks built in; there were five of them, and they were just about 18 inches space in between. You get down to move in, that's the way you stay. You wanted to turn over on your belly, you had to get out and move back in again. So, first we laid our barracks bags and everything on the floor, and the lieutenant comes through and says, "Get those barrack bags out of the aisle." Said we "What are we going to do with them?" He said: "That's your problem son, all I'm doing is telling you." So we took those in [the bunk] with us. We put the barrack bags in and put our foot over the top of it and then moved in, straddling the barracks bags. So, that's the way we traveled.

Another US soldier, sailing later on the USS *West Point*, also noted how amenities had been sacrificed for military practicality:

> We were directed to an entrance that still had one of the original fancy room signs over the entrance that indicated we were entering the Men's Lounge. Now the lounge was a congested living compartment. Pipe type racks were fastened to the beautiful wood paneled walls left over from the SS *America* cruise ship. The pipe framework was fitted to the deck and ceiling, supporting the five-tier "standee" bunks that provided barely 16 inches of vertical space between the bunks. The bunks could pivot up out of the way when not

being used. Adding to the congestion of the compartment, there was no provision to stow our barracks bags and personal items so they normally were stowed on the bunks. Troops lay in their bunks or sat on the deck playing cards, chess or reading books. It was like an obstacle course navigating around the compartment. Even with the congestion of the living quarters there was little complaining, we didn't know how long the voyage was or where we were bound.[6]

After being kept on board for several days, at 1000 on August 2, 1942, the men departed the United States, some never to return. The entire 1st Infantry Division with all attached units was on board the HMTS *Queen Mary*. The packed ship carried a total of 15,125 troops and a crew of 863. According to Staff Sergeant Harper, "men slept in shifts, spending one night in a bunk, the next night in the open on the deck. No one would ever forget how crowded it was." There were long lines for chow and at the onboard Post Exchange. Dice and card games were everywhere. Reportedly the officers ate well, several sit-down meals a day, while the enlisted men ate only twice a day. Most of the men in the 601st drew duty manning the ship's ack-ack (antiaircraft) guns. Staff Sergeant Harper added:

The trip was not too rough after the first day or so, but it was sure rough in the North Atlantic. Some of the fellows who were in the crow's nest manning a machine gun had to stay put until the weather calmed down. The machine guns were British and the British soldiers gave instructions on how the machine gun worked. One fellow in one of the crow's nests didn't remember whether he was told the gun was loaded or that he would have to load a cartridge in before firing so, as the tug boat was moving the *Queen Mary* away from the dock, he decided to check and pulled the trigger, it was loaded and we gave him credit for firing the first shot that the 601st fired during the war.

Five days later, on August 7, 1942 the *Queen Mary* arrived at Gourock, Scotland. The ship did not pull into the pier but rather stood offshore in the protected anchorage and unloaded the troops and their personal gear into small boats. Disembarking on the quay, they marched to the rail station where they boarded special troop trains and transferred to Wishaw, Scotland, ten miles southeast of Glasgow.

Their stay at Wishaw was short. Staff Sergeant Harper recalled the next day when they left their overnight barracks for the train station:

> When it was time to march to the train station for our trip to Tidworth Barracks in England, the Scottish were to supply the marching music. When they came down the street, it was a group of bag pipers. There was no drumbeat to keep pace to. My captain was next to me in the front row and he told me to set the pace. There was not much marching for by the time we arrived at the train station, there were girls marching with the soldiers they had met the night before. We were treated really grand while in Scotland.

Tidworth Barracks was located only 60 miles west of London. The train made frequent stops along the way and Staff Sergeant Harper remembers being given hot tea and meat pies by uniformed British volunteer women. The men, after all that time at sea, especially remembered the warm welcome given by these tea service ladies. One of the 601st sergeants reminded the men to watch their manners as they accepted the "tea and trumpets" offered. Of course he meant crumpets, the English griddle cake.

Arriving at Tidworth Barracks, the men tasted British Army life for the first time. They were billeted in a former British cavalry barracks, an old stone dormitory, and two stories high with outside staircases. There was an ablution room regally equipped with "cold and colder water." According to Staff Sergeant Harper the bunks were made of wood with corn shucks (or some such) for mattresses. The latrine was a two-holed outhouse with buckets that had to be emptied. The battalion ate together in two sittings. The rations were strictly British. Breakfast usually consisted of some type of a very strong marmalade, hard bread and cheese. In the evenings there was lots of oxtail soup, a hitherto unknown British delicacy.

The battalion's first blackout on August 10 made a lasting impression on the men. Now they knew they were in a country under Luftwaffe attack. In Britain space was limited and therefore not ideal for combat training. The battalion made do on the nearby Salisbury Plain. During their maneuvers, the 601st commanding officer Lieutenant Colonel Baker's constant cry was "Where's your alternate position?" The answer to that was usually a pub. There were frequent passes and the most popular destinations, despite the Luftwaffe, were London, Brighton and Dover.

Staff Sergeant Harper experienced his first real air raid of the war on October 12. Selected as Lieutenant Colonel Baker's driver, he drove Baker to a division meeting. Along the way, a German Luftwaffe fighter plane flew directly overhead. Stopping the vehicle, both men scrambled for cover. They were uninjured, but a British farmer working in his field was not so lucky. He was strafed and killed. The other highlight of the day, as reported by Harper, was that they spent the night in the empty home of American movie star Douglas Fairbanks, Jr, which was being used as a US billet.

Meanwhile planning for the North Africa invasion proceeded at a rapid pace. British and American staffs hoped the Vichy French forces in North Africa might be convinced to join the allies without too much difficulty. There were formidable French naval ships in the area and eight French army divisions made up of French, French Colonial and Foreign Legion troops, more than 120,000 troops in all. It was feared the French forces might still harbor resentment against the British for attacks against the French Navy in which as many as 1,500 French sailors had been killed. The British had launched their attacks in July, 1940 following France's armistice with Germany, to sink French ships to keep them from being added to the German and Italian navies.

Allied planners expected to control Tunisia within two weeks of landing in North Africa. They needed to prevent German and Italian troops from reinforcing Field Marshal (Generalfeldmarschall) Erwin Rommel in North Africa. If they succeeded, the British Eighth Army from the east and the Allied troops from the west could crush the Axis troops between them. This would relieve the British island fortress at Malta and protect the supply route to the Middle East and Asia. Up to then, Malta had been heroically resupplied at great cost by the British Merchant Marine and the Royal Navy.

Under the name Operation *Torch*, the North African invasion was elaborate. There were to be three simultaneous attacks by western, central and eastern task forces along the coast of North Africa. The Western Task Force, under Major General George S. Patton, was to land at three places along Morocco's Atlantic coast and surround Casablanca where there were 50,000 French troops. The Center Task Force was under Major General Lloyd R. Fredendall, US Army. He was to land at Oran in Algeria. As the third and most easterly attack, the Eastern Task Force was to land on either side of the capital of Algeria, Algiers. This task force was under the command of Major General Charles W. Ryer, US Army, and was a combined US/British attack. It was headed by a US Army general, a gesture to convince the French that the Americans, and not the British, were in charge. After the success of the landing, command would be assumed by Lieutenant General Kenneth A.N. Anderson, British Army.

The landing at Casablanca would establish a fully protected logistical supply port along the western coast of Morocco. It was feared that if Spain allowed the Wehrmacht to roll into Gibraltar it would close the Mediterranean. Hence an Atlantic safe port from which to supply the troops was required. The aim of the other two amphibious landings was to move Allied troops as far to the east along the coast of North Africa as possible, then to spring into Tunisia. There was the real threat that Axis airpower from Sicily and Italy could destroy any Allied landing force that tried to disembark in Tunis. The Allies would not have air cover until they could establish airfields to support the ground forces.

In total Operation *Torch* would involve 300 warships, 400 troop transports and 100,000 men. The entire operation was so huge it necessitated two fleets in separate sailings. One fleet launched from British ports and was to land at Oran and Algiers, a voyage of over 2,800 miles. Prior to entering the Mediterranean it split into two assault forces, one trailing the other so that both would arrive at their landing simultaneously. Meanwhile the second fleet, US Task Force 34, sailed 4,500 miles from Norfolk, Virginia to Morocco across the U-boat infested Atlantic. This task force of 100 ships had 34,000 troops on board.

As a kind of insurance policy, Major General Mark W. Clark, US Army and General Dwight D. Eisenhower's deputy commander-in-chief, departed on October 21 under orders for Algiers by submarine. His mission was to contact friendly French forces and enlist their promise not to oppose the Allied landings. This was an unusual assignment for a senior American Army general and the debate continues whether his mission was a success or a farce. That same day, the 601st Reconnaissance Company with Captain Michael Paulick (Cloverdale, Pennsylvania and a 1940 graduate of the US Military Academy at West Point) as company commander, detached from the battalion and sailed as part of the US 1st Infantry Division. For the first time the battalion would be split up for combat operations. It was to become the norm.

CHAPTER 2
NORTH AFRICA

"The Carolina maneuvers with live ammunition"

The invasion plan for North Africa in three simultaneous attacks was sound. As was the sub-plan for the taking of the Algerian port city of Oran by the Center Task Force under General Fredendall, again in three simultaneous landings: one at the small port of Arzew, east of Oran, and two at beaches to the west of the city. The overriding concern was to capture the port intact so supplies for the overland move to Tunisia could be unloaded quickly. Under the code name Operation *Reservist* a small British team was to augment the three beach assaults. The British were to sail into the port and seize the facilities to prevent them from being destroyed. Things became messy when the men of Operation *Reservist* were spotted and attacked by French forces with the loss of many lives. It was a disaster. The rest of the Oran invasion, however, was a success.

Captain Paulick, commanding Recon Company, embarked with the company on the SS *Latina* on October 23, 1942, and made the transit with the fleet which sailed from England into the North Atlantic and down to the Straits of Gibraltar.

They passed directly into the Mediterranean unmolested. That they went undetected was nothing short of a miracle.

First in, on November 8, was the 1st Ranger Battalion (Darby's Rangers), which secured two key forts at Arzew with coastal artillery batteries and then captured the Arzew port facilities. The 1st Division troops started to land at 0600. Recon, the only company of the 601st to land on this, the first of the battalion's four D-days, was assigned to Combat Command B's Task Force Red. Recon landed at the most easterly portion of the beach at Arzew, designated "Z" beach. Its armored cars and other vehicles may not have been on the same ship, for when the men reached their landing beach they had to climb down cargo nets, transferring from the SS *Latina* into assault boats. The landing was unopposed and they were ashore by 0800. According to Thomas N. Carmichael in his book, *The Ninety Days*: "Tank landing craft for the bigger Sherman tanks had been improvised for the invasion by cutting away the bows from some oil tankers of very shallow draft used in peacetime on Lake Maracaibo in Venezuela."[7] It is likely Recon's vehicles were on this type of ship.

After getting its vehicles, Task Force Red proceeded southeast and moved through Sainte-Barbe-du-Tlélat and onto Tafaraoui airfield, about 25 miles inland. According to Brigadier General Monro MacCloskey, USAF (Retired):

> [Task Force Red] reached the airfield at 1112 and deployed for the attack. The [US] airborne troops had not yet arrived. To prevent escapes, the roads north and northeast of the airfield were blocked. A vigorous tank assault captured the airfield and took 300 prisoners, and an ammunition train from Oran was seized as it neared the field. At 1215 Tafaraoui airfield was ready to receive Allied planes from Gibraltar.[8]

Tech Five James R. Stevens (McKeesport, Pennsylvania), who was with Recon at Arzew, noted in a US Army Heritage and Education survey: "there was small arms fire. But it was a good invasion because we didn't lose a soldier." That was not the case for the rest of the 1st Division, which suffered 418 battle casualties, including 94 killed. That evening Recon set up its bivouac in the town square of the small village of St Lucien, just south of Oran.[9]

That first morning, November 9, locals in St Lucien dropped oranges from second-floor balconies onto the troops for breakfast. Josowitz noted the soldiers were quickly surrounded by prowling, vino-peddling and cigarette-begging natives and howling dogs. The port of Oran was captured on November 10 and all hostilities ceased. Recon Company then spent most of its time serving as guards for the Allied II Corps Headquarters. No surviving documents make much fuss over their activities. It now remained for Captain Paulick to make preparations to receive the rest of the battalion to join him at St Lucien.

As hoped for by the invasion planners, all French resistance in North Africa ceased by November 13. Algiers and Casablanca had been captured and, after a great deal of discussion and arm waving, all North Africa Vichy Forces had joined the Allies. They would now fight to liberate France from Germany. Making this decision easier was the German invasion of the rest of France several days after the Allied landing and the dissolution of the Vichy government. Together the new allies prepared for a long, 800-mile trek from Algeria to Tunisia where they would join French units already stationed there and expel German and Italian forces.

The new alliance called for the Allied command structure to change. Some British troops were immediately sent to Tunisia and British Lieutenant General Sir Kenneth Anderson was placed in charge of the ground war, commanding the Allied XIX Corps. French General Henri Giraud, overall commander of French forces in North Africa, added his forces to the army corps. General Allen's 1st Infantry Division was parceled out to various French and British units to counter the Axis buildup in Tunisia.

But Recon Company of the 601st, ready to go, was going nowhere fast. There was no detailed plan to get the Army to Tunisia: ground logistic planning had not been fully developed. When the invasion had been planned, men and ammunition were crammed onto ships at the expense of vehicles and fuel. Trucks were at a premium. There were not enough to bring materiel and personnel forward. The inadequate single-track railroad was overtaxed. Making matters worse, air support was minimal since the Allied runways were dirt, unlike the concrete ones the Germans had in Tunisia. Additionally, the Germans introduced a new front-line fighter aircraft, the Focke-Wulf 190. It was better than anything the Allies had. Time was critical as the German and Italian reinforcements in Tunisia grew hourly.

The rest of the battalion, still back in England, was staged to be part of the second wave of US forces to deploy to North Africa. At Liverpool on November 27, companies were assigned to different ships: A Company embarked aboard the armed merchant cruiser HMS *Derbyshire*; B Company (168 men and four officers) boarded the SS *Duchess of Bedford*; and C Company boarded a converted Dutch liner MV *Dempo*. The convoy's voyage lasted about ten days. With little to do on the crowded ships, there was the usual litany of fouled heads (toilets), poor food, seasickness and boredom. Staff Sergeant Harper recalled on-board talent shows eased the passage of time; there was even a piano. The men were anxious. Information from the battlefields of North Africa was nil. They knew that they were going into their first combat against the highly regarded Wehrmacht.

The convoy passed through the Straits of Gibraltar on December 6, almost a year after Pearl Harbor. To the south were the well-lit cities of Spanish Morocco with the darkened Rock of Gibraltar to the north. On schedule, most of the battalion disembarked at Oran, but B Company woke up to find it was in the wrong port. The SS *Duchess of Bedford* had taken it to Algiers. After two days, the *Duchess* sailed back along the coast to the west and called at Oran to disembark its delayed passengers. By December 9, after having retrieved its vehicles, the entire battalion was reunited at the village of St Lucien. It was time to head east.

Josowitz called the rough, 800-mile road trek from Oran to Tunisia "the Carolina maneuvers with live ammunition." The battalion left St Lucien on December 17 for a country that was vast and uninviting. Treacherous roads meandered through the foothills of the Atlas Mountains. The battalion traveled at night to avoid the Luftwaffe. Often, the convoy took roads that hugged the sides of mountains with long drops to the bottom and scant guardrails. It was exhausting if uneventful.

December is the start of winter in North Africa. It was freezing cold and it rained or snowed at least once a day. Everywhere the battalion stopped, little Berber children appeared begging for bonbons (candy), cigarettes (*pour ma père*) and "choo-gom." Every three-year-old knew enough to accompany his begging by making Churchill's "V" for victory sign with his little fingers.

Acting like an Oregon Trail wagon boss, Lieutenant Colonel Baker continuously motored up and down the column, perhaps adding four times the total distance of the trip on his jeep. Cajoling, ordering and terrifying the men, he "chewed ass" of any who violated one of his many rules for road convoy discipline. Baker was heard to bark: "Anyone who passes this convoy does so over my dead body!" Josowitz wrote that at least one sergeant was "promoted" to private and second lieutenants wished they had never been born. This merry outing to the east lasted about five days.

Its first evening in Tunisia, December 21, the battalion found itself at El Khemis, just over the frontier from Algeria. This was located in "Stuka Valley," so named because German dive-bombers, the Junkers 87 Stuka, a two-seater aircraft, ranged up and down the valley looking for targets of opportunity.

Within hours of sorting itself out, the battalion was under attack for the first time in World War II. A pair of German planes had come in low and fast, Messerschmitt 109s, not Stukas, but that didn't matter as they fired with a raging fury at everything and everyone in the battalion.

Shortly thereafter, the battalion suffered its first KIA (killed in action), Michael Syrko, a Headquarters Company clerk, and farm boy from Pennsylvania. According to Private Morrison, an Italian fighter in the midst of the German planes was responsible. Josowitz said Syrko had wanted nothing more than to return to tend his Pennsylvania farm. He was the first of the 111 men of the battalion who would lose their lives on the battlefield.

Ten minutes after Syrko was hit, the enraged TD men shot down their first aircraft: a British Spitfire. The irate pilot parachuted safely and was "captured" by the battalion. It was clear the men of the 601st had much to learn.

Almost immediately the battalion was split up, and on Christmas Eve A Company was sent to Pichon. Its mission was to train with the troops of the newly reorganized French Forces. That never happened. The corps had no time for training but it desperately needed the company's 37mm and 75mm antitank guns. A Company was ordered to the front lines. The objective was a sandstone ridge held by the Wehrmacht from which the Germans blocked the road to Kairouan where an airfield, needed by the Allies, was held by a crack German paratrooper company.

Morrison related that on Christmas Day, 1st Platoon of A Company and its French artillery comrades fired on the ridge all day. The Germans resisted into the evening. At dusk a group of Arabs called Ghoums, part of the French Army, appeared at the foot of the ridge. Stacking their antique long rifles against a rock, they removed their brown and white striped robes, turned them inside out and put them back on. Now, instead of being striped, they were two shades of grey. Carrying long and sharp knives, silently they disappeared into the bush and slipped unnoticed up the ridge. A short time later Morrison heard screaming and on the crest of the ridge, a few Germans could be seen running from their positions in the dimming light. The Ghoums cut them down with their knives then cut off their ears. The French were said to pay 20 francs (about 25 cents) for each enemy ear the Arabs produced. After this, respect for the Ghoums was high among the 601st.

Morrison wrote that his platoon tried to break through the defenses closer to Kairouan on December 29. Supported by a couple of light tanks and some French infantry, they were repulsed by German paratroopers with the loss of two French tanks. Later the same day, the Germans counterattacked, this time with a full armored division. The Allied defense was limited to eight M-3 and M-6 antitank guns. The Germans were unstoppable and the small Allied force was thrown back toward Pichon. During this attack, Captain Robert N. Steele (Detroit, Michigan) was killed. He had been carrying a shiny new map case, which had reflected the sun and attracted the attention of a German sniper.

"Every tree in the valley turned into a German tank"

During the pull-back, three other 601st officers almost shared Captain Steele's fate. For a few days Captain Benjamin A. J. Fuller, II (Milton, Massachusetts), Lieutenant Lawrence Marcus (Dallas, Texas) and Lieutenant Wilcher C. Stotts (Fayetteville, Arkansas) were cut off behind enemy lines. After days of hiding in the desert and avoiding enemy patrols they rejoined the battalion, hungry, thirsty and having learned a lesson in survival. In later years, Lieutenant Marcus (of the family that started the Dallas chain of department stores, Neiman-Marcus) told the *Dallas Morning News* about his ordeal in the desert:

In a January 1943 battle in southern Tunisia, Marcus, 25, was cut off from his unit but crawled 150 yards under machine-gun fire to reorganize his troops and direct 75mm gunfire at the Germans. The battery was forced back, once again trapping Marcus between the Germans and Allies. "I was afraid I would be captured, so I ripped out sections of my notebook having confidential information and ate them," he said one week after the battle. "They weren't too digestible." He dug a shelter using his mess spoon but decided to attempt to rejoin his unit when the Germans set up a mortar and command post yards from his position. "I decided it was better to die than to be captured, so I decided to walk slowly through their lines, figuring if I went slow they wouldn't suspect I was one of the enemy," he said. "It was an awful temptation to hurry, but I got up and as calmly as I could strolled to a cactus patch and down into a gully." His trek back to his unit took two days. He had no water, only four sugar lumps and two small pieces of candy. "When I got back to my unit everybody was surprised, as one of my men had reported that I was apparently killed," Marcus said. "They told me they were already about to divide up my baggage, but I got there in time to save my cigarettes."[10]

One 601st soldier was not so lucky; on January 2, 1943 the International Red Cross reported that Sergeant James C. Everett (Sackets Harbor, New York) was a prisoner of war (POW); where or when he was captured is not known.

With the Afrika Korps and the Allies jockeying for position in the western hills and mountain passes of Tunisia the situation was fluid. By January 4, 1943, B Company was in bivouac near the town of Fériana, close to an airfield vital to the continued use of Allied fighter aircraft. The Luftwaffe was determined to render the airfield unusable and they bombed it twice a day, at dawn and dusk.

According to Morrison, after a little more than two weeks A Company moved from Pichon to the village of Ousseltia which had a French Foreign Legion outpost with a high wall circling the fort. This place could have been the movie set for *Beau Geste*, except Gary Cooper and the saucy little French-Berber girl were nowhere in sight. One could imagine hearing Brian Donleavy scream at Cooper.

Just before dawn on January 10, the company moved five miles down a road to the east and took up positions on the high ground at the mouth of a valley; 1st Platoon was placed on a hill to the left of the road, while 2nd Platoon, with four M-3 half-tracks and four M-6 light destroyers, was stationed along the road. With first light, they saw a beautiful valley sprinkled with Arab houses and extensive olive groves. The men dug in, worried about air attacks. It was a quiet day, and they passed the time reading or playing cards. The quiet was not to last, however, as Morrison wrote:

> At dusk we saw an enemy tank moving down the road. At about 300 yards everyone fired on it but to no effect. Just as it appeared ready to back up, it fired a flare. Immediately every tree in the valley turned into a German tank. These tanks concentrated their fire on those of us on the road. It got dark and the valley looked like it was filled with fireflies and the hillside burst with explosions. We pulled back to the edge of a wooded area on each side of the road. Later we made for the fort at Ousseltia. Here we were joined by a British antiaircraft unit with "pom-pom" guns. Together we formed a semi-circle of guns pointing outward from the fort.

Morrison went on to estimate that there were at least 47 German tanks and "needless to say they weren't worried about eight obsolete French 75mm guns mounted on half-tracks."

Meanwhile the number of confirmed 601st POWs mounted: two men were reported on January 19, 14 more on January 20 and one each on January 22 and 23. The date and place of capture for these men are not known, but in all, 19 men were now reported as having been captured since arrival in theater on December 21, 1942:

Sgt. James C. Everett, Sackets Harbor, New York, January 2, 1943

Sgt. Joseph A. Gaskin, New York, New York, January 19, 1943

1/Sgt. Concepcion R. Gomez, Telehauq, Oklahoma, January 19, 1943

Pvt. John W. Bond, Hiram, Georgia, January 20, 1943

Sgt. Albert R. Brault, Lynn, Massachusetts, January 20, 1943

Pfc. Stanley W. Ciuk, Adams, Massachusetts, January 20, 1943

Pvt. William T. Cooper, Red Bay, Alabama, January 20, 1943

T/5 Leonard J. Dupcavitch, Wyoming, Pennsylvania, January 20, 1943

T/4 Ernest S. Finstein, Boston, Massachusetts, January 20, 1943

S/Sgt. Anthony J. Gauquier, Kingston, Massachusetts, January 20, 1943

Cpl. Thomas W. Glisson, Claxton, Georgia, January 20, 1943

Pvt. Thomas R. Henderson, Springfield, Ohio, January 20, 1943

T/5 Robbie E. Johnson, Fairmont, North Carolina, January 20, 1943

Pfc. Lionel G. Julian, Sturbridge, Massachusetts, January 20, 1943

Pfc. Herbert L. Maymon, Hoxsie, Rhode Island, January 20, 1943

T/5 Albert E. Sharpe, Syracuse, New York, January 20, 1943

T/5 James W. Strickland, Wells, Maine, January 20, 1943

Pvt. Mike Sturak, Culver, Pennsylvania, January 22, 1943

T/5 James Hardenberg, Brooklyn, New York, January 23, 1943

However, the Afrika Korps was not yet ready for a major offensive. Pressure was kept on the Allies but it wasn't until January 22 that A and B Companies, now both at Ousseltia Fort, went into a more significant action. It was about 0100 when B Company sortied from the fort to join A Company in support of French legionnaires. The legionnaires, under a punishing attack in the valley to the east, needed help getting out of there. Both TD companies covered the retreat, firing as they escorted the French back to the fort. During the action, Morrison's M-3 was hit by a round fired from a Panzer. It lifted his half-track into the air, but, remarkably, when the dust settled he was able to restart the vehicle and joined the others in beating a hasty retreat.

The cost of this three-day action was high. Five 601st soldiers were noted as KIA or missing in action (MIA): on January 22 Private First Class Paul C. Behrendt (Freeport Long Island, New York) was listed as MIA and Private First Class William G. Condos (Courtdale, Pennsylvania) was killed; the next day, Private Albert La Rocca (Union City, New Jersey) was killed; and on January 24, Private First Class Nathan P. Johnson (Valatie, New York) died and Private Paul R. J. Le Blanc (Manchester, New Hampshire) was MIA. The remains of Private First Class Behrendt and Private Le Blanc have never been recovered.

On January 25, after being reinforced by elements of the 26th Infantry Regiment, the combined Franco-American force finally captured Kairouan Pass. The Germans had broken off and moved 15 miles to the north. For a while things became quiet, but the battalion's companies continued to be shuffled around to various French and British units. Although the circumstances are unknown, Private Walter Miller (New York, New York) was killed on January 28.

For the 601st Headquarters Company, communicating with the scattered battalion must have been frustrating. By this time the Germans gave the battalion the nickname the "Black Y Boys" because of the identification markings painted on the side of their vehicles: a yellow square with a black letter Y. At first, because they were so dispersed, the Germans thought the battalion was a full armored division and not just a battalion.

Logistics were a nightmare. Part of the North Africa invasion plan called for control of the three-country railway system that stretched from Morocco across Algeria to Tunisia. The railway was needed to move men and equipment rapidly. Despite best efforts, the 1,400-mile single-track rail system was simply not up to the task. Eight to ten trains departed Oran for the east every day but two of them had to carry coal needed for the other six trains to run. There just was not much capacity.[11]

"They just turned and kept going"

Rommel, although fighting the British Eighth Army in Libya, started to feel threatened by the Allied forces to the west. He wanted to drive the Allies back across the Tunisian border and capture the increasingly well-stocked supply dumps. His plan was to send elements of the Afrika Korps on a three-pronged attack by way of the east–west passes through the Tunisian mountains, which separate Tunisia from the Algerian plain. Called *Storm Tide*, the operation spurred the Allies to a quick if erratic and ineffectual response. B Company moved 160 miles in just 15 hours on January 30 but from exactly where to where was not recorded. Everybody was everywhere, assignments were ad hoc and units were split up seemingly at random. Rommel had another advantage: the Wehrmacht's latest Panzer, the Mark IV, had been added to his inventory.

On January 31, near Faid Pass, US armored forces, in support of the French, ran smack into an Afrika Korps trap. Sherman tanks charged blindly into a valley of death. The Wehrmacht had hidden 88mm antitank guns among the trees and bushes. It was easy pickings for them, destroying one after another of the M-4 Shermans, and a major defeat for the new Sherman tank, which could not stand up to German 88mm guns when used in an antitank mode.

Early February found B Company near the town of Maktar and C Company near Ousseltia. According to the C Company unit journal, the company had eight available M-3s and four M-6s, but was in need of half-track spare parts. On February 4, Lieutenant Richardson headed out to man an observation post in the center of the Ousseltia valley with five men in two jeeps. Moving forward, he halted on a ridge to look for friendly troops when he spotted a German soldier about 200 yards to his left. He said to Corporal Clayton F. Muller (Paul Smiths, New York), "Give him hell Muller, he's German." Corporal Muller swung the .30-caliber machine gun around to shoot but his gun jammed and Muller was killed instantly by enemy rifle fire. In the second jeep, Sergeant William E. Bond (Thomasville, Georgia) and Corporal Abe Rauchwarger (Bronx, New York) were seen heading to the southeast of the lieutenant's position and then were lost from view. Lieutenant Richardson and a Private Moreland (either Merle R. Jr, Kindallville, Indiana, or Walter of Rowlesburg, West Virginia), after burying Corporal Muller, returned on foot to friendly lines because their jeep was too shot up to move. The next day the lieutenant returned to the valley to look for Sergeant Bond and Corporal Rauchwarger but no trace of them or their jeep was ever found. Later both the sergeant and corporal were reported as captured that day, as was Private First Class Edwin C. King (Ellendale, Delaware).

Over the next two weeks, most of the battalion except Recon joined up at Maktar. Recon Company's mission was to screen the 200-mile front held by American forces in southern Tunisia. Josowitz described this as a never-ending series of continuous, wild, wet, cold and blackout night drives from one hotspot to another. Because of German air attacks, they folded down their jeep windshields to avoid the glass reflecting their position. To improve visibility the canvas tops of the vehicles were also removed which exposed the occupants to the wintry weather. The men got no sleep, rest or decent food. At Maktar, the battalion was continuously dive-bombed. Their bivouac was not far from a huge supply and ammunition dump, more than a quarter square mile in area and as such a tempting target for the Luftwaffe.

Realizing the Germans were approaching, General Anderson gave orders Sunday evening, February 14, to evacuate the sprawling airbases at Fériana and Thélepte. More than 3,500 troops decamped and 50,000 gallons of gasoline were destroyed. Thirty-four Allied planes grounded for repairs were burned. Morrison said a call went out for pilots, "any and all," and an unidentified soldier from the 601st said he could fly a plane and flew one out!

Companies A and B moved to the town of Sbeïtla, at the opening to the Kasserine Pass. It was here that Rommel launched a surprise attack. His artillery and Panzers fired on the town, setting it ablaze. The 1st US Armored division counterattacked with a large number of Sherman and older tanks. This badly dispersed formation launched an old-style US Seventh Cavalry charge into the Germans' guns. For the German 21st Panzer Division and its Mark IVs, it was easy to pick off the Americans as they charged blindly. As the Allies had seen two weeks earlier near Faid Pass, Panzers could easily stop and destroy a Sherman. Rommel's attack was a US disaster. Men in the 601st heard that 80 Shermans had been lost, although the actual number may have been something less than 60. The remaining Shermans, knowing they were no match for the Panzers, turned north to escape; not all were successful.

At around 0300, night was turned into day with a terrific roar as the Allied ammunition dump at Sbeïtla was blown up. Whether the explosion was deliberate, the result of sabotage or sloppy ammunition handling was not known to the men of the 601st and it didn't matter. This large store of ammunition, transported across the desert at great effort, was gone

Dawn on February 17 demonstrated again the messiness of war. The 601st was moving in a column to the west when a trigger-happy GI mistakenly fired his .50-caliber machine gun at four friendly aircraft, which then justifiably sprayed the US troops. Next, Germany artillery started to zero in on the column and it was dispersed in a small valley among some Roman ruins. Then US artillery commenced firing on the stopped vehicles. Immediately the Germans ceased firing as they now thought the vehicles to be friendly. According to Morrison:

> Soon we made contact with the enemy so we formed up in two echelons with B Company first. They were to fire three or four rounds and retreat back through A Company. Then while A Company fired off three or four rounds, B Company was to form up and fire while A Company pulled back.
>
> A Company started firing as soon as B Company moved through as planned. This was a good retreat plan except when B Company saw 300 tanks moving down on them, they just turned and kept going. I didn't blame them. They [A Company] hung around long enough to get off about seven or eight rounds but then they took off after B Company. After that no one stopped to fire. Every vehicle that had chemical smoke pots threw them out to conceal their position. This made for a very dramatic situation and certainly added to the chaos.

As recorded in the *Field Artillery Journal*, the 601st S-3, Captain Benjamin A. G. Fuller, II (Milton, Massachusetts) related what happened next when he arrived in the town of Sbeïtla:

> When I got into town I discovered that the road going south was blocked by big rock piles, and an MP in the town shouted to me that the road to the south was mined, and pointed the way traffic was to take through the town. At this time four enemy fighter planes were overhead and two were bombing and strafing the vehicles in Sbeïtla. About 10 or 12 vehicles were temporarily blocking the road, and the men were running for cover in the ruins of buildings.

I ordered my driver to continue by moving around the traffic jam, and instructed the men in my vehicle to fire machine guns, rifles and tommy guns at the attacking planes. As we passed each vehicle I shouted to the men taking cover to get back in their vehicles, fire at the German planes, and keep moving, because they were seriously blocking the road. My track was halted at the edge of town by wires across the road where a telephone pole had been knocked down. At this time two Me 109s approached our vehicle, the first one at 3,000 feet and the second at 1,000. My technical sergeant tried to get the .50 caliber machine gun to fire. I dismounted, went to the rear of the track and assisted him in getting the gun from the rear of the track to the left side. The sergeant fired a few rounds at the first plane but saw that he could not turn the gun around on the cradle. The second plane appeared and the sergeant fired about 100 rounds right in front of the plane. He hit it. It started smoking, dropped to 500 feet, banked away, and was seen to drop over the hills to the east. Two other planes circled the area at high altitude.

I ran to the road, pulled the fallen wires loose, and then proceeded northeast so that the road would be clear and that I might reach the area cross-country. At the first crossroad a major, who an MP told me was provost marshal of the armored division, told me to keep the vehicles moving at 200 yards interval in the direction of Kasserine, and that it was important that the traffic keep moving in that direction. I parked my vehicle off the road and passed the information on to the other vehicles that were still with me.

Later Lieutenant Colonel Baker wrote:

The officers and men under my command engaged a superior force, inflicting heavy damage to the enemy in a brave manner, and we withdrew very skillfully until both gun company commanders had their armored cars destroyed. Platoon commanders did everything they could reasonably be expected in completing the withdrawal without losing all guns, only giving way when outnumbered and outflanked.

After the war, Lieutenant Colonel Baker was awarded an Oak Leaf Cluster to his Silver Star for his direction of the 601st withdrawal on February 17.[12] The citation reads in part:

> The President of the United States of America, authorized by Act of Congress July 9, 1918, takes pleasure in presenting a Bronze Oak Leaf Cluster in lieu of a Second Award of the Silver Star to Colonel (Field Artillery) [then Lieutenant Colonel] Herschel D. Baker, United States Army, for gallantry in action while serving with the 601st Tank Destroyer Battalion near Sbeïtla, Tunisia, on 17 February 1943. When a large number of enemy tanks threatened to complete a double envelopment of his command, Colonel Baker went forward under very heavy tank fire and, standing in an exposed position, coolly supervised the orderly withdrawal of the battalion. Colonel Baker's gallant actions and selfless devotion to duty, without regard for his own safety, were in keeping with the highest traditions of military service and reflect great credit upon himself, his unit, and the United States Army.[13]

Lieutenant Colonel Baker was not the only one to receive a Silver Star that day. Lieutenant Robert A. Luthi (Forest Park, Illinois), B Company and commanding officer of a platoon of TDs received the medal and his citation reads in part "Although his vehicle was destroyed by enemy fire, Lieutenant Luthi continually exposed himself to the enemy and direct effective fire until forced to withdraw. His courage and keen tactical judgment inspired the officers and men of his battalion."

Both companies raced through Sbeïtla toward the pass at Kasserine. According to Morrison everything was on fire. The scene was reminiscent of the burning of Atlanta in the film *Gone with the Wind*. Like the movie, boxcars in the railroad yard were full of ammunition, on fire and about to explode. Disabled tanks and knocked-out trucks and jeeps, some still burning, were scattered in the road and along the wayside. German planes strafed continuously as the two companies moved through the town. Exiting the other side, they saw someone, probably Captain Fuller's sergeant, had gotten in a lucky hit downing a German plane. It burned fiercely just off the side of the road. Along the way both companies picked up as many French soldiers as they could carry, taking them through the pass and to the rear.

Some of the battalion's units were among the last to leave Sbeïtla and were almost overrun by German and Italian soldiers. Reportedly, some of these Axis soldiers wore GI uniforms and drove captured jeeps. At one point, the 601st Command Post radio half-track stalled and the driver stopped to clean the gas filter. German planes strafed up and down the road, guns fired and vehicles dashed madly in every direction. Amid this chaos the soldier was said to have held the filter up to the sun and said to his sergeant: "Look at the dirt in that God damned thing!"

But there was little other humor to be found. Tech Five James R. Stevens (McKeesport, Pennsylvania) wrote the following in a US Army Heritage and Education survey form:

> At the battle of Kasserine Pass, I was in the lead jeep. We were crossing a wadi [dried out river bed] and we could see enemy and artillery fire. We hit a land mine. My driver lost a leg and my machine gunner was killed. I was blown out of the jeep and suffered wounds to the head and left eye; also shrapnel body wounds.

Chaos continued. There was no communication between units, no traffic control, no organization and no order. It was every man for himself and the "Heine takes the hindmost!"*
Half-tracks went sailing by jeeps as if the jeeps were standing still. M-4s tore down the road, three abreast, in chariot racing style. The retreat was a sad day for the new, inexperienced American Army. Sergeant Nowak wrote that by February 18, 1943 it was almost all over. He had heard the front had been pushed back more than 100 miles almost to the border with Algeria and that the Afrika Korps had taken not only Sbeïtla, but also Gafsa to the south and Fériana to the southwest. Rommel's *Storm Tide* offensive was working.

The same day, Morrison noted that 1st Platoon of A Company, now down to three antitank guns, was tasked to work with the Derbyshire Yeomanry (British) reconnaissance unit. He wrote: "Their vehicles were small light armored scout cars with a gun of about .30 caliber and a small machine gun. These scout cars were so fast and maneuverable it was impossible for an artillery piece to follow them."

Once again the cost was high for the battalion. Four soldiers were killed during the retreat: Private Michael J. Cronin (Brooklyn, New York), Sergeant Richard G. Hammond (Northwood, New Hampshire), Private First Class George R. Uhlinger (Lackawanna, New York), and Private First Class Richard Watters (Bridgeport, Pennsylvania). Sergeant Hammond's remains were never recovered and he remains MIA. Although the date is not known it is likely that Private First Class Irving A. Ingram (Duluth, Minnesota) was captured at the time as he was reported as a POW at the end of the month.

Dawn on February 20 found Rommel ready to administer the *coup de grâce*. In true cavalry officer style, he decided to lead his

---

* "Heine" – short for Heinrich – was a derogatory term used for German soldiers that originated in World War I.

61

troops from the front, his only battle order, to "follow me." His tanks were close together, almost bumper to bumper. Rarely pausing to take proper aim, they fired armor-piercing shells and advanced rapidly on the road to Tébessa. The pass at Kasserine was his and soon he would have the supply dumps at Tébessa. Somehow, US Army units stopped him that day within 20 miles of his goal. Although elements of the battalion had retreated almost 100 miles, the Allied supply dump and the open road into Algeria were denied Rommel – a major setback for him.

For the first time, the US Army Air Corps played a major role in stopping the Germans. They appeared on the scene just in time and strafed the Germans. During the main attack, as the 805th Tank Destroyer Battalion was going to be overrun, US planes flew over and by rocking their wings got the TD men to follow them, showing the way up and over a hill where the 805th found a way through the pass. It saved them. On the ground around Kasserine, hundreds of Allied vehicles and tons of supplies brought at great effort from the liberated cities of Algeria were lost. American inexperience was again demonstrated and again lessons were to be learned.

Meanwhile, Rommel, concerned about his deteriorating situation in Libya, tried one more time and attacked north to the town of Thala. For the second time he was stopped by American troops. The timely arrival of American artillery reinforcements made the difference. Although Rommel had forced the Americans to retreat at Kasserine, he could not reach the supplies. With Field Marshal Albert Kesselring's approval, Rommel broke off his attack on February 22 and turned his attention south to confront the British Eighth Army.[14]

By the next day, the Afrika Korps was gone from the Kasserine Pass. The 601st Reconnaissance Company sent out two soldiers, Privates First Class John P. Blake (Nutley, New Jersey) and Rudolph G. Mojsl (Saddle River, New Jersey) to patrol a wadi on the left flank of the company position in a jeep.

According to their joint citation, the two men dismounted their vehicle, and:

> They proceeded up the wadi for a distance of approximately one and a half miles behind enemy lines. By this aggressive action, carried out with disregard for their personal safety, they secured valuable information as to locations of enemy Mark IV tanks and artillery positions. The cool and intelligent manner in which they carried out their mission reflects great credit upon themselves and the military service.[15]

Sergeant Nowak wrote the Germans left behind much broken equipment and took off with many captured US half-tracks and jeeps. The Germans also left behind thousands of Italian troops, who, when the Allies arrived, were eager to surrender, often in whole units. Private Morrison recalled on one occasion an Italian soldier appeared and said:

> Hey, paisan, paisan and then he showed us he wanted to give up. So here come the [Italian] officer down the hill and he had two guys carrying his suitcases and he was carrying a bottle of wine, and he offered the bottle of wine to our captain and of course the Sergeant Hicooley [unknown], he took a shot and said it was anisette wine. First time he ever tasted it and so anyhow it must have been three or four hundred Italians coming down off of the hill to give up.

It was during this period that Second Lieutenant Stotts, temporarily attached to a British reconnaissance unit, disappeared. This was the same lieutenant who in late December had found himself trapped behind enemy lines. This time he had borrowed an Arab robe to go behind the German lines for "a little look see." He was captured and spent the rest of the war in a German prison camp.

PROGRESS OF THE 601st
THROUGH TUNISIA
1942–1943

Mediterranean Sea

Bizerte
15 • Ferryville

Tunis

ALGERIA

1   Stuka Valley
2   Pichon
3   Kairouan
4   Fériana Airfield
5   Thélepte Airfield
6   Ousseltia
7   Faid Pass
8   Maktar
9   Sbeïtla
10 Kasserine
11 Tébessa (Algeria)
12 Bou Chebka Forest
13 Gafsa
14 El Guettar
15 Mateur

Gabès

TUNISIA

0   Miles   200
0   Kilometers   200

The 601st moved to the southeast of the Kasserine Pass to the Bou Chebka forest on March 1. After all that had happened, it needed rest and to repair and replace equipment. Out of the front line did not mean out of the battle. Almost every evening there would be an appearance by what was known as a "Kraut Stuka-flying milkman." His flights were so regular the troops on the ground could set their watches by him. He dropped flares every night and kept everyone on their toes.

The battalion used down time to practice ten-minute alerts, hold classes and other drills. Captain Paulick gave what Josowitz called a "historic lecture on mines" and Lieutenant Richardson beat the Old Man to the tune of $2,500 at a great poker session. Josowitz added the "local citizenry dug up its loot and came to trade. Mattress covers were still worth a thousand francs [$13.00] or two hundred eggs and used, dried, repacked tea leaves had a ready market. Vino, rough, rugged vino, turned up out of nowhere in fabulous quantities." Morrison wrote, "We finally knew that our holiday was over when the chow got exceptionally good and the chaplains started holding special services for those of us who wouldn't be around in the future."

The US forces reoccupied Kasserine and now General George S. Patton was in charge. According to Josowitz; "at this time they called him Necktie Patton and it was rumored the GRO [Graves Registration Organization] wouldn't bury a man who'd been KIA unless he was properly garbed in a necktie and leggings."

Another soldier also wrote about what had happened at Kasserine and how the troops were recovering. He wasn't with the 601st but he soon would be. The soldier was Major Walter E. Tardy (Wichita Falls, Texas). At the time, he was the executive officer of another North African-based tank destroyer battalion: the 701st. His letter of March 6 to his wife Elizabeth and son read in part:

> You know, I'm certain, that we've been in a pretty good scrap. Everyone admits that we took some pretty rough handling and lost heavily in men and material, but it could hardly have been otherwise, what with running into Rommel's two crack Panzer divisions, the 10th and 21st. But we took our toll and this added to what's gone before and will follow, will eventually bring this thing to an end. We are now back in a rest area; re-equipping and getting set for what we think will be the "grand finale" of this campaign. Morale is high and everyone is confident and ready for the word "go."

CHAPTER 3

VINDICATION IN NORTH AFRICA

"We knocked out about 35 tanks"

Only a month after the withdrawal from Kasserine, General Patton was eager to test his new command and demonstrate to the British what he knew they could accomplish. First he would retake the town of Gafsa. As the 601st monthly report stated, during the offensive on March 16 to occupy the town, the battalion saw "no enemy action or active combat." The Germans having already left, General Patton moved into the town.

At this time the 899th Tank Destroyer Battalion arrived in Tunisia with its new M-10 TDs. It was loosely attached to the 601st, as evidenced by the 601st unit journals of mid-March, which occasionally referred to the two battalions as the Tank Destroyer Group.

From Gafsa, the 601st Recon Company and Darby's Rangers pushed the Italian Centauro Division out of El Guettar and further east. There, the Italians occupied a strong defensive position on two ridges: the ridge to the north, called Djebel

Orbata, and the south ridge, called Djebel Bou Rbadja. These ridges looked down on either side of the El Guettar–Bou Hamran Road, an unsurfaced track called Gum Tree Road. The Italians dug in.

The TD men were positioned in open desert at the head of these ridges. Over the next three days, they were pummeled by the Luftwaffe. Staff Sergeant Harper wrote of those days that: "The Germans dive bombed and strafed us with their Stuka dive bombers. These planes had a broken wing design and as they came down for their dive bomb run, the wings would make a loud sound like a siren. They not only tried to kill us but to scare us to death with the sirens."

Apart from the Stukas, there was little action. The only ground forces in the immediate area were Italian and their heart wasn't in the fight anymore. It was a waiting game – waiting for the Germans to make a move to support the Italians and for the Allies to move further east.

The entire 1st Division was ordered to leave El Guettar on March 20. It proceeded southeast on Highway 15, the Gabès Road, with orders to destroy any German forces it encountered.

But first they had to deal with the Italians on the two ridges. The 1st Ranger Battalion was given the job to clear the Djebel Orbata, the northern ridge. That evening, more than 500 of Darby's Rangers silently climbed up and behind the Italians on the ridge.

In the pre-dawn hours of March 21, the rangers surprised the Italians, even capturing the Italian officers' mess already laid out for breakfast. The Italian soldiers fought bravely but a great number surrendered. The ranger action was over by 0900, although sniping continued throughout the day.[16]

The left flank having been secured, the rest of the 1st US Division attacked the remaining Italian line on the southern ridge, the Djebel Bou Rbadja. The attack was formed with infantry in front, followed by tanks from the 756th Tank

Battalion, tank destroyers from 601st and finally the 5th Field Artillery. The Italians saw them coming and, after a brief skirmish, more than 1,000 men from the Italian Centauro Division surrendered en masse. Josowitz wrote: "The white flags looked like snow on the mountains." The attack to gain control of the road and the two ridges had been expected to take three days but took only three hours. It was over around noon. That was the Italians. They were about to hear from the Germans.

Captain Rydal L. Sanders, Recon Company (Palmer, Texas) in a US Army Heritage and Education survey later was to write: "My baptism of fire was at El Guettar in Tunisia, the day that George Patton actually came to the front line, I saw old blood and guts, pearl handle pistols, boots-cavalry, guns and all." General Patton had in fact visited the 601st Headquarters on March 21.

The tank destroyers moved south from Gum Tree Road to the southeast side of the Djebel Bou Rbadja on the evening of March 22. The 18th Infantry Regimental Command Post and General Teddy Roosevelt, Jr (son of President Theodore Roosevelt and the 1st Infantry Division assistant commander) were located on a small rise designated "Wop Hill." It was at the most southwestern point along the ridge and had a clear view of the valley to the east. US heavy artillery moved up into a group of large sand dunes on the lower level of the ridge overlooking Highway 15, the Gafsa–Gabès Road, and the large valley. They spread out and dug in. The valley they faced was ten miles long and about six miles wide. The 601st Battle Operations Report (March 28, 1943) described the terrain as follows:

> East of our defensive position and north of the Gabès Road are wadis and gently rolling ridges with some knolls. It is favorable tank destroyer terrain with dry, sandy soil. South of the Gabès Road the terrain is very flat and around our right flank was at that time very soft and boggy. Previous

reconnaissance had proved that even jeeps could not maneuver out of range around our right flank. This ground condition proved invaluable. No overhead cover existed east of El Guettar.

The Germans were at the other end of the valley, straddling Highway 15. Their artillery was on the high ground and in front, German Panzers and infantry prepared to attack.

To protect against the expected infantry attack, the 601st took up positions in front of the 1st Division artillery. They were unaware of the large number of Panzers accompanying the German infantry. Intelligence reports had estimated there were no more than 20 Panzers. Later it was learned the 10th Panzer Division had more than 100 Panzers, vastly outnumbering the tank destroyers. This was to be a major, even a decisive battle for control of Tunisia but to the men of the 601st it was just the start of another day of fighting.

The battalion had 31 M-3s and five M-6s operational and ready, arranged in a battle line more than two miles long. The TDs were dispersed along a low sand ridge and went into full defile. They even sent back to division for additional shovels. A Company 601st on the extreme right moved just past the artillery to the edge of the sand dunes. There they directly overlooked the road and were right below the Wop Hill command post.

Since the withdrawal at Kasserine, A Company had been reduced from 12 M-3s to four through a combination of battle losses and maintenance issues. At the same time, B Company's 12 M-3s were spread to the left of A Company. C Company moved furthest along the front of the ridge with another 12 M-3s. Further down the valley, and closest to the Germans, the battalion's Reconnaissance Company, reinforced with three M-3s from A Company, was strung out in front across both sides of Highway 15. Its orders were "to report any enemy contact, fight a delaying action if necessary, and retire at daylight to reinforce A Company."

At 0445 on March 23, Recon's Lieutenant Joseph A. Gioia (Rochester, New York) captured a German motorcycle with a sidecar. One German was taken prisoner and another was seriously wounded. Lieutenant Richardson recalled the prisoner had, upon Lieutenant Gioia's men, asked "Are you German?" "Hell no!" was the reply. The German was the point of an advanced guard moving northwest toward the American positions. Under interrogation, the soldier revealed that at 0500 there was to be an attack by the 10th Panzer Division. The German orders were clear: "Cut off the US 1st Infantry Division, retake El Guettar and Gafsa."

On the plain, the Germans were laid out in a square formation of Panzers and self-propelled 88mm guns with infantry-carrying vehicles mixed among them. The 601st had thought its mission was to protect the artillery from an infantry attack, but now realized they were there to fight Panzers. After exchanging a few volleys with the onrushing 10th Panzer, Recon withdrew as planned, to augment A Company and to prepare for the coming Panzer onslaught.

There was sufficient moonlight to see vague outlines and shapes at 0500 but it was still dark when the Germans, with more than 100 Panzers, attacked. The odds were weighted against the Americans, roughly three Panzers to one tank destroyer. German artillery at the end of the valley suddenly opened fire and enemy tanks with the infantry close behind advanced. US artillery, opening up in return, had little effect besides forcing the Panzers to spread out.

Just beyond TD range, the huge group of Panzers split in two. About 30 Panzers broke left and continued up the highway towards El Guettar. Their main objective was to recapture the town. Immediately they found themselves in an awkward position, unable to maneuver between A Company's three M-3s on their right and the soft marshy ground guarded by one M-3 on their left. The supporting German artillery fired a lot of smoke, but when that cleared, A Company opened up. The Panzers had exposed their right flanks to the guns of A Company, now reinforced by Recon. The Germans were still 2,200 yards away, yet eight Panzers were stopped in their tracks and the attack was halted. The Germans withdrew, towing four of the disabled Panzers behind them.

Simultaneously, other Panzers attacked the dug-in tank destroyers of B and C Companies in front of the ridge. The Germans advanced in five lines broken into groups of five or six Panzers with between 15 and 20 tanks in a line. Over 100 Panzers, accompanied by infantry, advanced as though they were on a parade ground. The TDs let the Panzers get close before opening fire with armor-piercing shells. Company forward observers warned when a group of Panzers was on the move and gave the approximate range and direction. Upon receiving this information the destroyers moved to the top of the sand ridge, fired quickly and then went back down the ridge. After a while the Panzers came so rapidly that the destroyers stayed on the ridge and fired as fast as they could. The TDs mutually supported each other while defensively changing positions to make it harder for the German artillery and Panzers to hit them. Men not engaged in moving or firing the TDs fired at the German infantry with small arms and machine guns.

In the *TD Combat in Tunisia* report, Lieutenant Colonel Baker quotes Lieutenant Yowell (Dallas, Texas), commander of 3rd Platoon B Company 601st. His narrative begins just before dawn:

A report came over the radio that an enemy armored force was rolling down the road toward my gun positions. I told Sgt. NeSmith [Willie B., Barney, Georgia] to be especially watchful because he was nearest the road. He reported that a tank was within one thousand yards of him, and, as it was still dark, I told him to fire when he saw fit. Some enemy tanks moved in such a position that neither Sgt. NeSmith nor Cpl. Hamel [Victor T., New Market, New Hampshire] could fire. I moved both these destroyers back to facilitate a more effective field of fire. Sgt. Raymond [Adolph I., West Warwick, Rhode Island] maneuvered his gun and destroyed a Mark VI tank with six rounds, four of which ricocheted off the heavy armor. Sgt. Raymond fired one more round at the same range at a following tank, a Mark IV, and it caught fire immediately. His half-track was destroyed before he could fire another round. The enemy scored at least three hits on the vehicle, burning it up completely. His crew came to my half-track and I told them to make their way to the rear on foot. At that time, daylight was just beginning to break, and Sgt. NeSmith, Cpl. Hamel and Cpl. Meczywor [Longin M., North Adams, Massachusetts] were firing heavily at the enemy tanks. At this position I saw Cpl. Hamel destroy a Mark IV and Sgt. NeSmith knocked the turret off a Mark IV at about 1,000 yards range. Enemy infantry came in very close, and their tanks were laying smoke while they brought up line after line of tanks. I estimated from four to five lines with fifteen to twenty tanks in each line. There were tanks in groups of six and a column of tanks along the southeastern ridge also. There were more than one hundred tanks. I am sure of that.

The first platoon to open fire was 3rd Platoon of B Company, drawing all tanks on the south side of the road. This action left the flank of the enemy tanks exposed to us, and they seemed unable to locate our fire, which was very effective. The enemy's right flank was exposed to us continually until NeSmith's and Raymond's half-tracks were destroyed. When the tanks located us, they turned completely around and came back over the same route. I believe some of them returned because A Company and the Reconnaissance Company had made it too hot for them on our right flank, knocking out about eight tanks. They then decided to put my platoon and adjacent platoons out of action. When the tanks located our position, they fanned out and started toward us.

All this time, Staff Sergeant Stima [Michael W., Troy, New York] was keeping a steady stream of .50 caliber machine-gun bullets on the infantry. He also pointed out tank targets with his tracers. It was quite difficult to see at times due to the sun, smoke, gunpowder, and dust. I sent three guns to the ridge and then followed. Sgt. NeSmith's half-track was hit, one man being killed and the others injured. I sent after the vehicle, as it was still available for movement. Before the men could get to this half-track, it was hit again in the right rear. We fired continuously during this period. Another half-track was hit but no one was hurt, and I had all the ammunition transferred. During the transfer, the half-track receiving the ammunition was also hit. I then moved the two half-tracks to the next ridge.

Sergeant Nowak echoed the official report on B Company's actions in his memoirs:

It was about 1 o'clock in the morning when we arrived in our battle positions. We got our pioneer tools out and dug in our vehicles. We dug until about 4 o'clock when it was reported that tanks and infantry on foot were approaching. We were the closest to the tanks, but it still being dark, it was hard to distinguish anything. Finally the action started and it lasted about four or five hours. During this time, we knocked out about 35 tanks and lost some of our own vehicles. One half-track to the left was hit and one crewman was killed.

The other four crewmen came to our tracks and it was there that I helped Lt. Yowell bandage up the injured and applied sulfanilamide to their wounds. The Lieutenant arranged for an antiaircraft track to take the wounded to an aid station in the rear echelon.

The attack lasted until noon. The German attack was fierce and initial losses in the C Company position were heavy. One M-3 in particular drew an unreasonable amount of attention. The Germans had spotted the pennant at the top of its radio antenna, which gave away its position. When that was understood, the antenna was quickly lowered. At the start of the action, C Company had given control of three of its destroyers to B Company. Luck was against them: one M-3 threw a tread and could not move, two others were hit almost at the start of the action but only after they had taken out several Panzers. Several half-tracks had to be abandoned. Morrison with C Company described his part of the action:

> Just at break of day the 10th Panzer Division attacked, but we managed to fight off their first wave. We sat behind a ridge and when we got the word we pulled up to shoot. We were on the high ground for a change and got to shoot down on them. Then we slipped back down the ridge to get ready for the next shot. We hit the Panzers in their tracks. That disabled them. During this attack a platoon of B Company pulled back and took up a position on the ridge to our right. Between us and the 5th Field Artillery we managed to do a great deal of damage to the Germans.

Around noon, the Germans sent seven soldiers dressed in GI uniforms in an American half-track towing a small German 75mm gun. They could have been Americans, so A Company did not fire upon them. At 400 yards though the Germans got out and set up their gun facing the American positions. It was then that an M-3 opened fire, destroying the half-track and killing five Germans; two others were later captured.

Even so, the Germans' attacks were not yet over for that day. Starting at about 1500, the Luftwaffe bombed and strafed the 601st positions at least three times, but the battalion's .50-caliber machine guns disrupted each attack and they had little effect. Morrison wrote: "After the morning attack, we tried to sleep but the Germans conducted almost continuous bombing raids. Our Lt. Marcus [Dallas, Texas] fired at the Stukas with a .50-caliber machine gun on his half-track but was wounded when one of the bombs dropped very close to him."

Late that afternoon, the Americans intercepted a German radio message ordering an attack at 1640. At first it was thought to be a trick. But the TD men decided to take the intercepted message as a warning and prepared for a possible attack. At 1645 they were attacked by two battalions of German infantry, and Panzers could be seen a great distance away. Now with only limited resources, it was time for the remnants of B and C Companies to make a fighting withdrawal. This is Sergeant Nowak's account of what happened to B Company next, edited by the author:

We had close calls from 88s [German 88mm guns] and machine-gun fire. Sgt. Michael W. Stima fired more than 3,000 rounds at the approaching infantry. As the battle progressed, we steadily withdrew from our original positions, and finally we realized that our platoon was about the only one left. Lt. Yowell then maneuvered us from hill to hill and always in defile. We were the last to leave the area and sought haven in the mountains. We even picked up some half-tracks from other companies. We watched the artillery lay down a barrage on the German tanks and saw the German infantry move up as ours moved back. We made a break for it with

our three remaining half-tracks. The other crews abandoned
theirs and went back on foot. We were machine-gunned but
we hugged the floor and so were not touched. We could only
head west. We decided to continue so as to not to lose our
equipment and bed rolls. We had some food and a little
water but often to keep going we had to move boulders and
fill in ditches. The Lt. and I went out to find our headquarters,
but we could find no one and could raise no one on the
radio. The next day after clearing a 400-yard stretch we got
into a wadi and it was easier going. We even picked up a
wounded man, Cpl. Sauklis [Tech Five John, Kirkwood,
Maine, who sometime later in the war was listed as MIA],
and some medics. We shared our meager supplies and finally
re-joined the rest of B Company [at 1200].

What Sergeant Nowak didn't say in his memoirs was that
both he and Sergeant Stima received Silver Stars for this
action. According to a Ludlow, Massachusetts newspaper
article, Sergeant Stima had allowed a German infantryman
carrying a wounded comrade to cross in front of his machine
gun. Right after they passed came many more Germans, one
carrying a light machine gun. Sergeant Stima let go a burst
and was credited by fellow soldiers with breaking up, almost
single-handed, one part of the major German infantry
attack. According to his citation, Sergeant Nowak "gained
the admiration of the officers and men of his company by his
superior skill and courage in exposing himself to heavy
enemy artillery and machine-gun fire to ensure most effective
fire upon the enemy." Not only did he keep Sergeant Stima
supplied with ammunition, but at the same time cared for
four wounded US soldiers.

These Silver Stars were presented in December 1943. In
addition to Stima and Nowak, five other unidentified members
of the 601st received Silver Stars for valor in North Africa.

One of those might have been Lieutenant Colonel Baker who, according to an excerpt from his citation, was awarded the Silver Star for gallantry in action while serving with the 601st Tank Destroyer Battalion, in the European Theater of Operations during World War II.[17] The wording of the citation is not available. Lieutenant Colonel Baker had this to say about the March 23 Battle of El Guettar:

> The men [Germans] walked upright, moved slowly, and made no attempt at concealment or maneuver. The tank destroyers held their fire and let the infantry come in standing up. Our silence apparently gave them confidence. We cut them down at fifteen hundred yards. It was like mowing hay. The tank destroyers fired rapidly, employing all arms. The heavy-caliber high-explosive shells were the most effective. One gun Sgt. [Stima] bracketed rapidly and fired as fast as he could, making five mil deflective changes. He dropped high-explosive shells at seven-yard intervals across the German lines. Our division artillery also opened up with concentrations from 105 and 155mm guns.

C Company had received the same warning via radio as B Company. They believed that the Germans had them almost surrounded as they readied to repulse the attack. Their few remaining TDs pulled back and headed up into the hills of the Djebel Bou Rbadja. Corporal James E. Markel (Randolph, Massachusetts) made a valiant but doomed effort to rescue his M-3 and he drove off at high speed. He quickly became separated from the rest of his platoon and his TD was later seen on fire with a charred body in the driver's seat. He was posthumously awarded a Silver Star. What remained of C Company eventually was able to get back to the battalion command post that evening but it took much creeping around, mostly on foot. They checked in at 2300, tired, but alive.

Staff Sergeant Harper drove an M-3 that day and therefore had to sit near the barrel. He remarked in later years his hearing was never the same after that battle. He added that the Germans were aggressive and when one of their Panzers took a hit, they took the machine gun off the vehicle and set it up to fire at the enemy.

Late that afternoon, the 899th Tank Destroyer Battalion joined the fight, armed with the new M-10 tank destroyer. It was their very first time in combat. Lieutenant Colonel Baker had requested that they be sent up earlier, but they had been kept in division reserve. After being led across a friendly minefield by B Company's Lieutenant Kenneth B. Stark (Sayre, Pennsylvania), the 899th sent a full platoon of four of the M-10s right in front of the German positions. Staff Sergeant Harper watched as the Germans knocked out all four of them. It happened before they even got off a shot. It was their first encounter with the Germans and a deadly baptism by fire.

This final German attack failed, thanks in no small part to the division artillery. Tech Five Thomas E. Morrison noted that as things got really hot, Lieutenant Frederick C. Miner (Seaford Delaware) and Staff Sergeant Raffaele Igulli (Newton Highlands, Massachusetts) called down friendly artillery on their position and that effectively stopped the German tanks and infantry and caused a lot of damage to the German forces. They had to take this action since the observation post of the 5th Artillery had been knocked out. Staff Sergeant Harper over in A Company added, "before the battle was over, the 5th Field Artillery was firing charge one, the charge that fires the shortest distance, that is how close the Germans got to our artillery." The Germans moved back, their attacks over for that day.

The troops on the ground, gratified at the results, were however unhappy with the Allied Air Corps that day. They felt they had been abandoned, but in fact the Air Corps had been busy flying multiple sorties against the 10th Panzer Division.

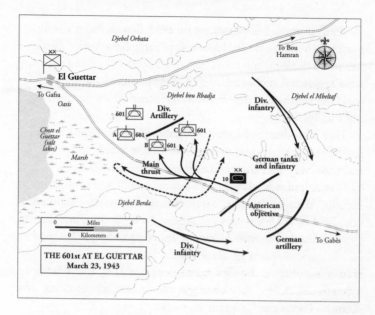

THE 601st AT EL GUETTAR
March 23, 1943

They had concentrated on the rear of the German column, importantly blowing up ammunition and fuel dumps. This may have accounted for the timid German Panzers in the 1645 attack.

The battle at El Guettar had played out General Andrew D. Bruce's dream scenario and doctrine to a tee.[18] Bruce was head of the Tank Destroyer Command in Texas. Despite substantial American losses, concentrated among the now antiquated M-3s, his concept had been sound. Together the tank destroyers and the artillery had wreaked havoc during the day, but at a cost. Twenty-seven of the 601st's 36 guns (31 M-3s and five M-6s) were knocked out. Total casualties were 72, the battalion's worse combat day during World War II; 14 men were killed in action or later died from their wounds. They were:

Pvt. Robert L. Baldwin (Keysville, Virginia)
T/4 Gregory Barone (Worcester, Massachusetts)
Pvt. Robert B. Davis (Arcola, North Carolina)

Pvt. Thomas F. Duggan, (Worcester, Massachusetts)
Pfc. Theodore P. Gelbstein (New York, New York – died May 1943)
Pfc. John A. Gibeau (Lawrence, Massachusetts)
T/4 Austin A. Hritchkewitch (Elizabeth, New Jersey)
Pfc. Henry H. Hunt, Jr (Providence, Rhode Island)
T/5 Theodore S. Kordana (Adams, Massachusetts)
S/Sgt. Kenneth Lynch (Brooklyn, New York)
Cpl. James E. Markel (Randolph, Massachusetts)
Pvt. Charles J. Murphy (Kingston, New York)
Sgt. Alvin L. Pierce, (Elizabethtown, Tennessee – died on May 9, 1943)
T/5 David Rosenfeld (New York, New York)

Ten soldiers were counted as missing in action and were later reported as POWs but the exact date or circumstances are not known. They were:

T/5 Roy M. Blair (Appalachia, Virginia)
Pfc. Anthony Cardone (Providence, Rhode Island)
Pfc. Joseph J. Esposito (Brooklyn, New York)
Cpl. Walter Hammer (Brooklyn, New York)
Pvt. David H. Hobbs (Clinton, North Carolina)
Pfc. Earl C. Lane (Kingsport, Tennessee)
S/Sgt. Harold L. O'Brien (Coeur D'Alene, Idaho)
Pfc. Charles T. Robinson (West Chester, Pennsylvania)
Pvt. Charlie E. Smoot (Mt Airy, North Carolina)
Cpl. James H. Thompson (Canandaigua, New York)

At least 49 soldiers were wounded. Nevertheless, the battalion was able to claim it had destroyed 37 German tanks and damaged an unknown number of others. According to author Rick Atkinson, the battalion had expended more than 3,000 75mm rounds and more than 50,000 machine-gun rounds in a battle that had raged for 12 hours. Losses to the half-tracks were so heavy that the M-3 was nicknamed the "Purple Heart Box." Some declare this was the decisive battle of the Tunisian campaign. Unquestionably it was the US forces' first armored victory of World War II.

What vehicles remained of the battalion went to Fériana on March 24. Of the three half-tracks Lieutenant Yowell and Sergeant Nowak had driven out of the battle and through the mountains, one had a flat tire, one had a broken steering wheel spring (meaning that it couldn't move to the right) and one couldn't back up.

General Terry Allen, commanding officer of the 1st Infantry Division, credited the 601st with the defeat of the Panzers and the preservation of the division defense and supply lines. For its effort the 601st was awarded the Presidential (then called Distinguished) Unit Citation. It may have been the first unit of battalion size independently presented with that award during World War II. The official US Army citation reads:

The 601st Tank Destroyer Battalion is cited for outstanding performance in combat on 23 March 1943, near El Guettar, Tunisia. Filling a two and one-half mile gap in the American Lines, the battalion absorbed the shock of an all-out onslaught by the German 10th Panzer Division, and materially assisted divisional and attached artillery units in definitely stopping two successive determined enemy tank attacks, launched in great strength. Although greatly outnumbered and out gunned, the battalion traded shot for shot with the overwhelming enemy force. Doggedly holding its ground, harassed by enemy dive bombers and long range artillery, with ammunition running dangerously low, the battalion prepared to hold out to the end despite the loss of twenty-seven of its thirty-seven guns. The German tanks approached to within one hundred yards of its positions only to be thrown back with heavy losses. When the enemy reformed for a second assault in their first attack, the battalion placed such intense fire on the advancing German soldiers that the attack was stopped before it could get well under way. The 601st Tank Destroyer Battalion contributed materially to this outstanding victory of the 1st Infantry Division wherein with other units of the division it fought with such ferocity and intense determination that at least 400 enemy casualties were left on the field, thirty-seven enemy tanks and numerous other enemy vehicles were evacuated in a disabled condition.

On reflection, some of the men of the 601st said "We didn't do too well, for although we considered it a victory we only had three guns left by the end of the day."

"A gentleman and a soldier's soldier"

El Guettar had been a victory for the battalion, but now they were short of tank destroyers and without them there wasn't much they could do in combat.[19] On March 26, right after El Guettar, the battalion was assigned to the US 34th Infantry Division as part of the Williams Task Force, a mobile command. The battalion continued to be moved around from place to place and outfit to outfit. First they were ordered to Thélepte; then sent back to Sbeïtla and later to the forest at Morsott. Since the M-3 was being replaced by the M-10 TD, there were not many replacement M-3s available to make up for the losses suffered at El Guettar.

With March turning into April, Josowitz wrote:

Some days later, on April 5, we moved to the Faid Pass where we went into position. We saw our planes returning from a raid and two were on fire. One crashed nearby and burst into flames. We were shelled one day for a little while, but our positions in the wadi were such that the 88s couldn't reach us.

The British Eighth Army captured Gabès on April 9, taking more than 13,000 Axis prisoners. The meeting of US troops from the west with the British Eighth Army coming up from the south foreshadowed the end of the German occupation of Tunisia. Air superiority now rested with the Allied air forces. Resupply and replacement aircraft were making a difference on the battlefield and the airspace above Tunisia was no longer dominated by the Luftwaffe. German aircraft and pilot losses were not being replaced, so at this time there was no concern about air attack and daylight travel on roads was possible.

There was no stopping the British. In the next two days, the Eighth Army took Sfax and the town of Sousse. Things were moving fast and although there was some hard fighting ahead, the US Army found itself left out of the action.

On April 17 the battalion was close to the Mediterranean, having been shifted 200 miles to the north. The land was rugged and unsuitable for tank or antitank warfare. The battalion was therefore sidelined as it waited for a breakthrough to Bizerte and Tunis. The men swam in the Mediterranean and killed time with other recreational activities.

A major shock to the battalion came in the middle of April when Lieutenant Colonel Baker was ordered to return to the States. He had been reassigned to the Tank Destroyer Command at Camp Hood, Texas. The exact reason was not announced – it rarely was – but he was part of an older US Army generation, a World War I veteran. The men of the 601st had conflicting theories for this dismissal. Although Baker had been successful at El Guettar he also commanded during the withdrawal at Kasserine, which had been a severe shock for the US Army. On the other hand, it is known that at some point he was promoted to full colonel and if that had occurred at this time, he would have been too senior for a battalion. Additionally the command at Camp Hood may have felt his expertise was invaluable for their training efforts and wanted him there.

In August 2014, 601st veteran Technical Sergeant Charles W. Phallen (Galion, Ohio) told the author that according to a battalion rumor Lieutenant Colonel Baker was relieved of his command after striking Captain Michael Paulick. The incident occurred in the small hours of the morning at the end of a long, drawn-out poker game during which much alcohol was consumed. A disagreement ensued and Baker reportedly hit the captain. What is not in doubt is that Baker left at about the same time as Generals Allen and Roosevelt in the general housekeeping that ensued toward the end of the Tunisia campaign, at a time when General Patton wanted to ensure discipline was improved.

Lieutenant Colonel Baker had not been popular with all of his men as revealed in the US Army Heritage and Education survey forms. Tech Five Harold A. Snyder (Scranton, Pennsylvania) in describing Lieutenant Colonel Baker, the man who had given a beer bash when he had been given command, said bluntly: "Our first commander was a drunk." This was echoed by then Lieutenant Ambrose G. Salfen, in Headquarters Company, who added: "We went overseas with Lieutenant Colonel Baker. He was an alcoholic and when drunk, a beast." Salfen blamed a decline in morale on: "Col. Baker's rampages." Salfen, a junior officer in charge of moving and setting up Baker's tent, contents and a wood-burning stove, added: "I had to set up the stove and stove pipe whenever we moved. He had a 20 by 20 tent that would have slept 10 or 12 men. The rest of us got into long johns, wrapped in blankets and bedded down in pup tents."

Major Walter E. Tardy (later Lieutenant Colonel) was the new battalion commanding officer of the 601st. He came from the 701st Tank Destroyer Battalion where he had been the executive officer. The 701st was one of the seven tank destroyer battalions then fighting in North Africa. A Texan from Wichita Falls and a member of the Texas A & M (Agricultural and Mechanical) College graduating class of 1936, Tardy had first-hand combat experience when he took over the battalion. He had been promoted rapidly. In April 1942 he was a first lieutenant, by the end of that August a major. His men respected him and later they venerated him as "a gentleman and a soldier's soldier; soft spoken and a great leader." It was clear from the first moment that Major Tardy was the complete opposite of Lieutenant Colonel Baker.

For the final push to Bizerte, elements of the battalion were assigned at last to augment a reconnaissance group, perhaps the 91st Reconnaissance Squadron or the 34th Reconnaissance Troop, it is not known which, with the US 9th Infantry Division. With them, the battalion saw some significant action in the advance on Bizerte. On April 30, one company blasted at an enemy gun observation post that had been peppering them with howitzers and 75mm shells all day. Shrapnel flew around and some men from the Recon Company were injured. Sergeant Nowak wrote:

> The guns shelled us and the shells landed nearby. Sgt. Stima and I went out and tried to locate their positions, but we couldn't spot any muzzle blasts. Some shells landed near where we had our half-tracks, so Stima went back to see if any damage was done while I stood by. He called for me and when I got there the vehicles were gone. We had to walk back to where they had been moved. One shell had landed 6 feet in front of one half-track and it had persuaded them to move without waiting for us.

At this point Recon Company, still attached to the 9th Infantry Division, dismounted and lugged its machine guns through the mountains to fill a gap between the 9th and the French forces on the left. A, B, and C Companies followed the infantry in the hill-to-hill fighting but found little to do. When they had reached the last mountains before the plains of Mateur, Recon Company broke loose and raced toward Bizerte. Halfway there, they returned with the welcome news: "The Krauts are pulling out." The battalion moved forward into the town of Michaud in the valley. By then, all German resistance in Africa had collapsed. Thousands upon thousands of German soldiers, members of the once proud Afrika Korps, came rolling down the road in their trucks looking to surrender.

By May 9, the battle for Tunisia was over. It took less than five months, had taken a heavy toll on the Allied forces, but had critically tipped the scales against the German and Italian forces, which would never regain the territorial offensive success they had previously enjoyed. The Allied troops, now occupiers, again changed their roles to suit conditions.

According to Josowitz one 601st company was employed as guards in a nearby POW camp, which housed almost 38,000 German and Italian prisoners together with hundreds of vehicles of all kinds. In the end approximately 275,000 prisoners had been captured in the final days of Axis resistance in Tunisia. Those experienced troops would never be able to fight again and their vehicles and planes would cost Hitler dear to replace.

With time on their hands, battalion men went sightseeing to the battlefields around the now captured ports. They saw abandoned 88mm guns and in the towns of Ferryville (Menzel Bourguiba) and Tunis not many buildings had escaped the bombs and artillery fire. Bizerte was in ruins, especially the docks and the vital port facilities.

As always, in the face of destruction, soldiers found solace in humor. Josowitz summed up some of the lighter moments of the Tunisian campaign this way:

There were water-buffalo hunts as the uninvited guests of the Bey [traditional ruler] of Tunis. There was a 'Joe-Blow' who drew the entire battalion's rations for a day and then never showed up. There was the scene of the tired and dirty tank destroyer men who went swimming in the ancient Carthaginian sculpture pool at Gafsa with British Spitfires providing overhead cover. The vino filled canteens of the French troops and those poor, beat up, little burros and last because this must end somewhere, the Recon Lieutenant who got lost in the one-street town of Sbeïtla.

Nowak adds that time was spent in training, playing different sports and resting. Their camp was in an olive grove with a creek nearby where they swam and washed vehicles and clothes. Mornings were spent drilling. They were off afternoons and there were nightly open-air movies.

The Moroccan and Algerian railways were essentially undamaged, but the Tunisian railway system required extensive rebuilding; nevertheless, by May 13 the first Allied train arrived in the capital of Tunis, four days after the fall of the city. Equipment from Oran started to flow to Bizerte in great quantities.

During the fighting, 11 hospital trains, improvised from French railway coaches and boxcars, moved wounded men from the front to hospitals in the rear. After the fighting, the US Army Transportation Corps moved more than 172,000 German prisoners of war to the US. Almost half went along the railway system. Later, after Italy had left the war, Italian POWs acted as paid laborers on the railway.

Major Tardy, the new commanding officer of 601st, wrote a letter home to his wife Elizabeth dated May 25, in which he eloquently described the state of the battalion post-battle:

I'm afraid the end of the campaign was the cue for practically everyone to go into a coma as far as writing is concerned.

87

I've never slept so much in all my life. The men are just about worn out with resting so I'm planning to inaugurate some training tomorrow. I held a battalion inspection today and was reasonably pleased with the results.

There was a certain amount of "cleaning up" to be accomplished after the cessation of hostilities. We took a major part in the rounding up of the 40,000 prisoners gathered in this sector.

We've been encouraging athletics, sightseeing trips and beach parties. I've been to Bizerte several times and will probably spend the day on the beach there tomorrow. Tunis is so crowded with British soldiers I didn't spend much time within the city proper but spent the major portion of an enjoyable day browsing about Carthage, La Goulette, and the Tunis Airport. I sat in the amphitheater at Carthage and envisioned Hannibal and Scipio Africanus going through with their harangues and exhortations. Carthage is beautiful, overlooking the prettiest harbor and "bluest" water I've ever seen.

It's certainly strange not to be continuously on the alert for aircraft. This peaceful country is a far cry from the hell it was just a few short weeks ago. The French have welcomed us as long lost brothers and can't seem to do enough for us. My headquarters is in the front yard of a wealthy Frenchman's country home and just a few minutes ago he brought us over a fine brand of cognac. We reciprocate by inviting him and his family in for an occasional meal, taking them to our Catholic services, and furnishing transportation for them to go to Mateur, Ferryville, and Bizerte.

The health of the command is fairly good, although a slight epidemic of dysentery has been making the rounds. I feel fine today after a two-day siege of the stuff.

Within a few days we'll start a long trek back to the vicinity of Casablanca where we hope to be equipped with the "latest" in the tank destroyer line.

Major Tardy and the 601st never made that long trip back to Casablanca. Their replacement tank destroyers were delivered to them in Tunisia. In June, Major Tardy made a five-day trip to Allied Forces Headquarters in Algiers where he probably received briefings and instructions at the Theater Tank Destroyer Command about the employment of the new tank destroyer, the M-10.

The long-awaited new equipment, delivered on June 23, allowed the battalion to rid itself of its remaining M-3s. The M-10 Tank Destroyer was based on the standard M-4 Sherman tank chassis. Built by General Motors Corporation it was lightly armored and not so adept at traveling cross-country. But it was faster, had capacity for a crew of five, an improved antiaircraft .50-caliber machine gun, and 3-inch (76mm) cannon. Importantly, it fired armor-piercing ammunition, which could penetrate 88mm of armor, enabling it to seriously threaten German Panzers from the side and the rear. The gun was so heavy that it required a large counterweight in the rear part of the turret and gave the M-10 a distinctive profile. It had an open turret and it clearly resembled a tank, unlike its two predecessors. Crew members often referred to it as a tank and almost no one used the official nickname, "Wolverine."[20]

While Tunisia was embroiled in the battles just described, at the highest levels of planning, major decisions were taking shape. President Roosevelt agreed with Prime Minister Churchill to continue the attack on the "soft underbelly of Europe," that is the Mediterranean. The American Chief of Staff, George C. Marshall, disagreed, preferring to husband the Allied resources for the planned cross-Channel invasion of France. General Marshall lost the argument and, in early January, at Casablanca, the decision was taken to invade Sicily.

Sicily is the largest island in the Mediterranean, roughly triangular in shape and covers more than 9,000 square miles with some 170 miles of coastline on the south side. The terrain includes mountains (including the 10,000-foot-high Mount

Etna) as well as deep harbors. It occupies an ideal position in the central Mediterranean and possessing it would have further protected the British sea lanes of communications to Egypt, Suez and the Far East. Roosevelt continued to feel that by striking an Axis homeland, Italy, he could bring the war closer to one enemy country, tie down German troops, and hasten an Italian exit from the war.

Although General Eisenhower remained the overall commander, the British were to be in charge of the Sicilian invasion under the command of General Sir Harold Alexander. His British troops were under General Sir (later Viscount) Bernard Montgomery and his Eighth Army. The American troops, formed into the Seventh Army, were under General Patton. The beaches chosen for the invasion were to the south and southeast of the island. The British assumed the principal lead for the invasion with the Americans in support of the British left flank. Patton was not very happy about this but the British remained cautious, mindful of the poor American Army showing at Kasserine Pass. Alexander's plan following the landing lacked detail, but the ultimate goal was to capture the port of Messina, two and a half miles from the toe of mainland Italy. There were roughly 200,000 Italian and 30,000 German soldiers on the island. Half the Germans were replacements and the ill-equipped Italian soldiers just seemed to want out of the war. It was hoped they would not be effective defenders.

Proper equipment was lacking at many levels but fortunately the spirit of improvisation still lived among the Americans. Corporal Joseph Borriello (Meriden, Connecticut), who was with the 3rd Infantry Division's 10th Engineer Battalion wrote about one such occurrence:

> In late June, while still in Bizerte, the 10th was asked to build a flat deck on an LST [Landing Ship Tank]. We were to build this wooden deck over the steel deck of the ship to make it

into an aircraft carrier. It was to carry the planes called LC-1 [here he probably meant the L-4A, Grasshopper]. These were the army version of the Piper Cub used by the artillery to spot targets.

"The prisoners were whooping and hollering"

The Allied invasion of Sicily was called Operation *Husky* and it commenced the night of July 9, 1943. A disastrous airborne assault failed when many paratroopers were dropped into the sea or otherwise crashed ashore. Some of their aircraft were fired upon by the US Navy because they were thought to be German. General Patton, shy and retiring as ever, not only supported Montgomery's left flank, but he ran up the island, capturing the city of Palermo, and then headed east to the port of Messina. General Montgomery had to approach Messina by going up the east side of Mount Etna and there he faced tougher Wehrmacht troops, which slowed his advance. Patton made three leapfrogging amphibious end runs (with the 3rd Infantry Division's 30th Infantry Regiment) around the entrenched German troops along the north coast road of the island from Palermo to Messina, which greatly sped his progress. Patton's successful tactic enabled him to take Messina first and he handed over the city to General Montgomery and the British Eighth Army with great public show. His grandstanding did little to further Anglo-American relations.

Corporal Borriello landed in the first wave with the 10th Engineers at Licata, from where he moved up the western end of the island to Palermo. After the city was taken he headed east and entered Messina with General Patton and later returned to Palermo to prepare for the invasion of mainland Italy.

The 601st however, did not see or experience much of this. Patton chose not to send them as a unit to Sicily. The fact was that the 601st had only just received their new M-10 Tank Destroyers and needed to train with them. The 601st would catch up later.

Although Italian troops were still fighting the Allies in Sicily, the Italian people had had enough of the war and of their dictator. King Victor Emmanuel started looking for a way to get Italy out of the war. On July 25 and with the King's intervention, the Italian Fascist Grand Council voted to oust Benito Mussolini as dictator. He was placed under arrest and spirited out of Rome.

The Sicilian campaign was moving so rapidly there was a need to guard the increasing number of prisoners. On July 28, some men of the 601st interrupted their training with the new M-10 Tank Destroyers and were sent to Sicily to become POW guards. Seventy-nine men and two officers from B Company were thus assigned, some men staying for only a day and others through August and into September. Major Tardy checked on his men during a 10-day inspection tour of the POW camps. One of these men was Sergeant Nowak who later described his POW guard duty as follows:

> We moved out in a convoy for Sicily. The sea was very rough and I got very sick. On the 28th we passed Pantelleria [a small Italian island between Tunisia and Sicily, sometimes referred to as the Italian Malta] and reached Porto Empedocle in western Sicily the same day. We went by truck to the prisoner of war area near Agrigento. There was a ration dump nearby and we lost no time in acquiring cigarettes, rations and can goods. We had the Italian prisoners dig our latrines, fill our water cans, and police up our areas.[*]

*   To "police" an area such as a camp or barracks is a US military term meaning to pick up trash and tidy up.

We traded with the local civilians for melons and grapes but the fresh fruit gave many of us cases of dysentery. We sold cigarettes to the prisoners for 50 lire a pack and we also traded cigarettes for wrist and pocket watches. When we got orders to leave the stockade we had 1,027 prisoners and only seven of us to guard them. We loaded up at Port Empedocle on an LST. It was a rough trip and the prisoners proved to be very unclean and unsanitary.

Sergeant Colprit, who also volunteered for POW duty to see Sicily, went to Agrigento and had this to say:

I was given four men to take 995 prisoners to the harbor, but no one told us that there was a railroad tunnel on the way. We were following the tracks and into the tunnel we went. It became black as pitch. The prisoners were whooping and hollering and strung out for miles when they came out of the tunnel. We loaded them onto an LST and took them down in an elevator to the hold. The elevator was loaded with men as thick as they could stand. One of the four cables broke, it tilted and all fell into the hold like a load of coal. A GI was dug out of the pile and the Italians found his gun and gave it back to him. The prisoners needed water so the cry of "*Acqua! Acqua! Acqua!*" went on till even the ship's skipper was there holding the hose of fresh water into a GI can. They were happy as they thought they were headed for America.

On September 9 when the majority of men from the 601st had returned from Sicily with POWs, many of them moved from one ship directly to a landing ship for the invasion of Italy. Two of the 601st's officers and 108 enlisted men remained in Sicily until September 12.

On August 17, after 38 days of fighting the battle for Sicily was over. The Germans had slowly shrunk their defensive perimeter to the northeast of the island while fighting a rearguard action. They moved troops under the cover of darkness directly from the front lines into waiting transport at Messina for the short trip to the Italian mainland. More than 53,000 German soldiers with more than 9,000 Panzers and other vehicles escaped across the narrow Straits of Messina in this way.

CHAPTER 4
ITALIAN MUD!

"Blasted ships and barges in the water"

Over the summer, the battalion had shuffled personnel and received new replacements as it prepared for what would be a long fall campaign. Private Morrison, who has told much of the story of the 601st during the battle of Tunisia, had his transfer to the Army Medical Corps approved. On July 10, he joined the battalion's medical unit. He later made the landing in Italy where he saw action as a combat medic until, given the choice between a promotion and going home, he opted for home.

Sergeant Charles W. Colprit of Dover, New Hampshire, joined B Company just after the battle of El Guettar and had been integrated into the battalion during the last days of combat in Tunisia. He was among the replacement troops sent to North Africa on a 14-day convoy from New York City to Oran, Algeria, on a Dutch freighter. After a few days in Oran, he boarded an ancient English Channel steamer to the town of Philippeville (now called Skikda), Algeria. The British skipper grimly told the soldiers not to bother with lifejackets since the ship was loaded with bombs and if it was torpedoed they would not need them. As we have seen, soon after joining the battalion, Sergeant Colprit volunteered to go to Sicily as a POW guard.

Over the summer three other soldiers arrived in North Africa who would eventually join the 601st. One of them was Lieutenant Thomas Peter Welch (Geneva, New York). He was on board the USS *West Point* (AP-23) and arrived at Casablanca, Morocco on June 12, 1943. He had a fast, unescorted and uneventful crossing. When he disembarked he was assigned to a replacement battalion at Camp Lyautey, Morocco, just north of Casablanca. Within a week he had contracted malaria.

Malaria was epidemic all over North Africa. Although there was no effective way to protect troops from the disease, reoccurrence could be somewhat controlled with quinine. Since the world's supply of quinine was controlled by Japan, a not very effective chemical called Atabrine was substituted. The nausea and loss of appetite accompanying malaria greatly impaired a soldier's fighting ability. If food could not be kept down, a man was fed intravenously. For several weeks after a bout with malaria a soldier was too weak to fight or do anything else. Lieutenant Tommy Welch, who was out of action for more than a month, described his experience with malaria as well as how he found North Africa in several letters home:

I just got out of the hospital after a 5-week siege of Malaria. I'm as weak as a kitten. This North Africa deal is quite a thing; you have no idea of the poverty over here. The Arabs are sullen. The kids are nothing but beggars. They've picked up slang like, bon-bon, chew-gum, and shoeshine medium polish. The beer and wine, which is all you can get, is like drinking liquid shoe polish. All we've done so far is drill and train under the African sun. The one redeeming feature is the cool breeze and the cold nights. We can get a pass to town every three days, which relieves the monotony, and it's also a relief from the GI food. We can get chicken, pork chops, strawberries and wine very cheaply and it sure tastes good. It is beginning to look like this shindig will be over pretty soon and we can give this damn place back to the Arabs, which suits me fine. I played golf several times and have gone swimming in the ocean. The French babes are OK and my slight knowledge of the language has been a big help. I've ridden on a donkey about the size of Punch [family dog] and also on camels and all that crap. I'm sorry I can't tell you what I'd like to, but I'll have some tales to tell you after the war. I still haven't been assigned to a combat outfit but have hopes of being soon. It's really tough to get in because of light casualties and the fact that there are so many of us over here. If you want to send me something, make it food and a bottle of coke. It's impossible to get any here. The company I'm in is moving out bag and baggage and we're going up close to the front, at least I'm getting close.

With Sicily under Allied control it was time to make the next move, the invasion of mainland Italy. But debate still raged over which way to go. General Marshall and his staff still believed that invading Italy was a sideshow which detracted resources from the crucial invasion of France that was currently being planned. They were willing to consider invading Sardinia, then Corsica and thence into southern France, since that would support a northern France invasion. Prime Minister Churchill and the British continued to favor running up the Italian peninsula in support of the partisans in the Balkans. With airfields in southern Italy, they argued, the Allies could then strike Germany. The British prevailed again but the Americans were able to get the British to agree on a date for the invasion of France – May 1944.

Replacement troops were now consolidated in Tunisia ready for the next campaign. Welch in the next series of letters describes his train trip from Morocco to Tunisia across North Africa:

I've been on the move. I just finished a 1200-mile jaunt in one of those French 4008, which is nothing more than a small boxcar [4008 meant it could carry forty men or eight horses]. It was really rough. So far I've been to some pretty interesting places, Casablanca, Oran, Tunis, Bizerte, Algiers, Mateur and loads of other places and can speak French like a veteran. I've seen a tremendous amount of captured equipment and thousands of prisoners. I talked to quite a few and they are glad the war is over. No action yet, but I've been in some serious air raids. Boy we can sure be glad that the Jerrys aren't bombing Geneva, they can level a city like Geneva in about 15 minutes. I have been swimming in the Mediterranean as well as the Atlantic.

Like Lieutenant Welch, Private Harold E. Lundquist had also arrived in North Africa. His Atlantic crossing had not been as quick as the lieutenant's. Lundquist crossed on a much smaller ship, the *Santa Paula*, leaving New York City on June 10 and arriving at Oran, Algeria on June 21. Private Lundquist made the same trip via rail from Oran to Mateur described by Welch. He noted it took four days and commented: "One tunnel took nine minutes to go through at a rate of about 50 or 60 miles per hour." He also noted that wearing his gas mask in the tunnels allowed him to breathe easier.

Bob Hope, the celebrated British-born American comedian, radio and movie star, and the best-known USO (United Servicemen Organization) entertainer ever, staged several shows for the boys in Tunisia along with movie star Frances Langford. Now in Tunisia, Lundquist wrote he waited several hours to see the Bob Hope Show on August 20 and again on September 2 but both shows had been canceled. The reason for canceling was believable to Lundquist, namely that Hope and his troupe were suffering from what was called the GIs, short for gastrointestinal disorder.[21]

Meanwhile the Germans continued to attack Tunisia. Lundquist wrote on the night of August 27 he saw a lot of lights out at sea and heard that it was a tanker burning after an attack by "Kraut subs." Like Welch, and many others, Private Lundquist also came down with malaria and spent three weeks in the hospital in early September.

Sergeant Rudolph E. Larson of Chicago, Illinois was another soldier destined to join the 601st as a replacement. Rudy, as he was known to his family and friends, trained as a gunner at Fort Campbell, Kentucky. He had arrived in North Africa in April and eventually was sent to a replacement camp near Bizerte, Tunisia, where he would receive orders to the 601st at the end of September. In a letter to his family he shed light on what days were like in Tunisia:

We put on a parade this morning in a nearby town with most of our big vehicles. Pretty French girls lined the streets and threw flowers at us. If I hadn't been driving myself I would have given them more attention. I'm going to Tunis or Bone on a recreation trip tomorrow, a pleasant change from the daily grind. I feel pretty well though malaria is quite common about here. I spent a couple of days in a rest camp this past week. It is located on the Mediterranean in the area where the Germans made their last stand in North Africa. It was quite interesting and told the story without words, blasted ships and barges in the water, trenches and barbed-wire entrapments along the shore, and the vehicles by the hundreds (tanks, trucks, scout cars, etc.). Mostly German, wrecked and burned for miles inland. And those Mark IVs blow apart as well as the rest. We're located along the Mediterranean and we go swimming in it quite often. We work seven days a week over here and don't have a great deal of recreation, probably an outdoor movie about once a week and occasionally an all-day trip to one of the larger cities like

Tunis or Bone. The food isn't bad though naturally there's much we desire, especially fresh foods and sweets. What we get is either canned or dehydrated. Just thinking of those meals we used to eat at your house makes my mouth water.

After the fighting ended in North Africa, discipline sometimes became a problem. Captain Rydal L. Sanders recalled in an US Army Heritage and Education Center survey that while the battalion was bivouacked outside of Tunis one of his 601st men, a Private First Class, not further identified, took a jeep without permission and drove to Tunis. In town he got drunk, picked up two other soldiers and on the way back there was an accident. One of the hitchhikers was killed in the wreck. The unidentified 601st private was court martialed and sentenced to 50 years' imprisonment. Shortly thereafter, while the US Army was disposing of Axis munitions, a fire went out of control and spread rapidly. The private volunteered to man a bulldozer and, at great danger to himself, put out the fire. Because of his heroism, his prison sentence was reduced to one year.

About this time Lieutenant Welch sent a V-mail[22] letter to Bill Delancey, editor of the Seneca Yacht Club newsletter, *Off the Wind*, which was published in the club's October 1943 issue:

Incidentally, here's something, which I think will interest you. After we had cleaned the Ratzies [his term for Nazis] out of Tunisia, I got a three-day leave to rest my weary bones. I went to Bizerte and met some French friends who invited me to sail from Bizerte to Tunis. While en route we were strafed by a sport-loving Jerry. The sail looked like a sieve, so Bill; I recommend that you stick to lake sailing.

The battalion needed to waterproof its tank destroyers and other vehicles for the upcoming Italian landing in case the LST dropped them off in deep water. This was done near Lake

Bizerte and Corporal Borriello described what it entailed:

> We used flexible hosing connected to the tail pipe and routed up above the cab of the vehicle. We also used a putty-like substance and put it around the carburettor and spark plugs to keep them dry. Supposedly, the vehicle would still run even if the engine were in the water. We were told to keep the engine revved up when driving off the ramp of the LST.

On September 3, the British Eighth Army launched Operation *Baytown*, the invasion of mainland Italy. After what was described as an "easy crossing," it landed on a beach just north of Reggio Calabria. Meanwhile, General Mark Clark, the US Fifth Army commander, prepared for the landing at the Gulf of Salerno (code name *Avalanche*). The Germans and the Italians might have been out of Sicily, but they were still able to bomb Tunisia from southern Italy and Sardinia. On September 6, General Clark, in Tunis, inspected the 601st Tank Destroyer Battalion, soon to be part of the invasion. The battalion had been reinforced by 38 men drawn from the 805th, 894th, and 899th Tank Destroyer Battalions. Shortly after the inspection, the Luftwaffe conducted a major air raid on the port of Tunis and the troop concentrations preparing for the invasion.

The loading operation was described in a Texas newspaper article on September 7 by Don Whitehead, dateline: *With the US Navy Invasion Task Force*. Publication was delayed until September 13 for security reasons:

> The port from which our convoy sailed literally bulged with ships loading both American and British troops and supplies. Crews toiled day and night. Lights burned in offices all night long as plans meshed.
>
> Sweating, swearing, over-worked Navy men somehow managed to bring order out of seeming chaos. Truck convoys

rolled up in streams and cargoes disappeared into the bellies of the ships. Tanks, trucks and guns rumbled aboard and troops marched into the hot holds.

Major Walter E. Tardy of Bryan and Wichita Falls, Texas, checked off the last piece of equipment and went up to the ship's wardroom to relax with 2nd Lt. W. W. Emerson of O'Brien, Haskell county, Texas [not with the 601st]. "We fought through the Tunisian campaign and got in the big scrap at El Guettar," Tardy said. "We knocked out 30 tanks in the fight and we only had 75 millimeter guns on half-tracks. Now we are re-equipped with better guns and the morale of the battalion has gone up 100 per cent. I have a great outfit and they are all ready."

The invasion troops were on the way to Salerno on September 8 when General Eisenhower, commander of Allied forces in the Mediterranean, announced the Italians had surrendered and had been ordered to stop fighting. This was a signal for the Germans to put into effect *Plan Asche* (Plan Ash) which was to disarm the Italian armed forces. The former German Axis partners had become adversaries.

"German artillery is bursting about 2,000 yards away"

The next day, Operation *Avalanche* landed the battalion on a beach south of Salerno, near Battipaglia, 50 miles from Naples. The beach was 20 miles wide and was bisected by the Sele River. The British were on the north side closest to Salerno and the Americans on the south side of the river, closest to the ancient Greek city of Paestum.[23]

Staff Sergeant Harper, on board USS LST 378, reported that as the ship approached the shore, it hit a sandbar. Thinking it had reached the beach, the crew let down the loading ramp.

Major Tardy, in his command half-track, raced down the ramp to sink in 8 feet of water. He had to swim for it. He was not alone in the water as he had been followed by US Brigadier General William H. Wilbur, Medal of Honor awardee and deputy commander of the 36th Infantry Division.

Although Field Marshal Kesselring did not know exactly where or when the invasion was to take place, he was ready. He had carefully formulated plans to react quickly upon receiving the reports of any landing. His first act was to dispatch the Luftwaffe. This was all the more impressive since many of his troops were busy disarming his former Italian allies. Sergeant Nowak wrote that they "were constantly bombed and strafed by Kraut planes" as they hit the beach.

The success of the invasion was by no means a sure thing. The British unexpectedly ran into stiff Wehrmacht infantry resistance and US troops had to repulse Panzer and 88mm artillery attacks. Troops were pinned down on the sand dunes and had to be urged forward. General Clark reduced the perimeter of the British sector so their forces were more concentrated and better able to repulse the growing German counterattack. With its high banks restricting movement between the two Allied sectors, the Sele River proved to be the invasion's weak point. The Germans took advantage of this and poured in men and Panzers. Clark considered consolidating all his forces on one beachhead, but instead he rushed in his available reinforcements including the US 82nd Airborne Division which made two successful airdrops.

The line held. At one point General Clark personally directed the defensive action and came under intense German fire, for which he was awarded a Distinguished Service Cross, the second-highest award for valor, second only to the Medal of Honor.

Major Tardy ordered that before being pushed back into the sea, the battalion would head south to meet up with the advancing British Eighth Army, which had been fighting (or as some American historians say, strolling) its way up the Italian boot from Reggio Calabria. That proved not to be necessary. After the initial scare of being pushed back into the sea, and with a lot of help from naval gunfire and Allied air forces, the situation gradually improved.[24]

It was important to secure the three road passes up and over the mountain leading to Naples and to deny them to the Germans as most of their reinforcements were on the Naples plain. Part of the 601st was therefore ordered to re-embark from the beach at Paestum on British LST 422 on September 10. Headed for the town of Maiori on the Amalfi coast, their mission was to support three US Ranger battalions under Lieutenant Colonel Darby. A member of General Clark's staff observed that Darby could use more support, especially armor, so elements of A and B Company were sent to fill a gap between the British and the rangers. The rangers were to seize the Chiunzi Pass at Maiori, the Pimonte Pass at Amalfi and the Amalfi Drive around the Sorrento Peninsula to Castellammare. The British 2nd Commandos landed at Vietri and had to block the Cava Nocera Pass. According to Josowitz, one of their brand new M-10s was driven off the LST at the insistence of a British beach master. It immediately sank in deep water and was retrieved only with difficulty.

On the heights, Lieutenant Colonel Darby was in position to call naval gunfire support down on the Germans as they moved around the great Neapolitan plain. The rangers' biggest problem was getting additional ammunition and chow during the three weeks they were there. It is likely the TDs lobbed shells up and over the mountain in indirect fire support called in by the rangers. They were also there in case of a German armor push. That never materialized and the companies saw no combat action. The rangers were so successful at denying the Germans the ability to reinforce Salerno that they were awarded a Presidential Unit Citation (PUC). A and B Companies of the 601st were later also included in this award. It was their second PUC.[25]

Field Marshal Kesselring ordered a final large-scale attack on the Salerno beachhead on September 15, but by then General Clark had 170,000 troops and 200 tanks ashore. The German attack was suspended. Wehrmacht forces then commenced a slow and orderly movement across the hills to the Volturno River and a loosely coordinated defensive line called the Barbara Line. This was the first of a series of German defensive lines that stretched across the Italian peninsula.

The most important news for the battalion was that after being shuttled around the beachhead for a couple of weeks and having been assigned to various divisions, it received orders on September 20 to join the famous US 3rd Infantry Division. Because of its steadfast defense on the Marne River in France in July 1918 during World War I, the division bore the nickname the "Rock of the Marne." The 601st was to be more or less permanently assigned to 3rd Infantry Division for the rest of the war. At this time the 3rd Infantry Division was commanded by Major General Lucian K. Truscott, who was later to play an important role at the Anzio beachhead and the capture of the city of Rome.[26]

Amazingly, during the whole of Operation *Avalanche*, from September 9 to 20 the battalion reported no battle casualties, "due to the fact that no actual contact with the enemy was gained by any element of the battalion." Staff Sergeant Harper noted that although the battalion saw a lot of action from a distance, they were not in the thick of it. Sergeant Nowak wrote about the almost constant Luftwaffe attacks:

Kraut planes strafed and bombed us but could not stop us. We secured a beachhead and moved inland under heavy resistance. We saw many dogfights and saw P-38s, Spitfires and Kraut planes come down in flames. Enemy planes came into the harbor every night bombing the beaches and trying to get our boats and dumps.

The battalion's luck ran out on September 21, when Private Henry R. Swygert, of Recon Company (Gaston, South Carolina) was killed in unknown circumstances. He was the first of many eventual casualties during the battalion's time in Italy.

From the Sorrento peninsula, the Allies launched their attack on Naples from the pass above Maiori on September 23. They met stiff resistance at every twist and turn of the road. It was slow going. On one 17-mile stretch of highway, the Germans had destroyed 25 bridges: but the rangers and the British commandos were able to break through to the plain and run into Naples.

The British Eighth Army with elements of the 82nd Airborne Division liberated Naples itself on October 1. Lloyd Clark in his book *Anzio, Italy and the Battle for Rome – 1944*, describes what the famous Italian actress, Sophia Loren, living in Pozzuoli (a town west of Naples) had witnessed during the civilian uprising and the final battle for the city of Naples:

> Ragged little boys from the slums finally rebelled against the German oppression and took matters into their own hands. Armed with bottles filled with gasoline they had stolen from the Germans, these boys ignited rags they had stuffed into bottles to serve as wicks, and then darted from side streets and swarmed over the huge German tanks, stuffing the bottles into the gun slits in the tanks just as the gasoline exploded. They attacked tanks and trucks and installations, and no German soldier on the street was immune from their swarming attacks. Their firebombs were exploding everywhere. Many of these boys were shot and killed by the

Germans, their bloody little bodies dotting the streets, but nothing daunted their attacks.[27]

The port of Naples was destroyed but now under Allied control. Ships had been sunk in the harbor, vital infrastructure had been ruined and the buildings along the port blown up. The Germans sabotaged the electric and water works and the city was starving. Thorough in their destruction, the Germans had planted time-delay bombs that went off after the fall of the city, sometimes a couple of weeks later. Just one such bomb killed and wounded hundreds at the Naples Central Post Office.

On Naples Liberation Day, Sergeant Rudy Larson joined the battalion in bivouac near the small town of Volturara, east of the town of Avellino.[28] The battalion and the 3rd Infantry Division crawled through the mountains to the east and northeast of Mount Vesuvius. Encountering twisting narrow roads and blown bridges and constantly under attack by the repositioning Germans, they could advance only in stages, from one destroyed bridge to the next.

Hoping to be in Rome for Christmas, General Mark Clark prepared for the next big push north, an action that Field Marshal Kesselring decided was not going to happen. Originally the plan was to move German forces north of Rome. However, the Field Marshal saw that he could delay the Allied advance up the boot of Italy and he told Hitler that he would make a stand before Cassino on the Gustav Line, which was still under construction. That way, he explained, he could make the Allies fight through the mountains for every mile; Hitler agreed. Not realizing this, on October 2, Major General John P. Lucas, commanding general of VI Corps, ordered the 3rd Infantry Division to push northwest to the Volturno River and right into the mountains and the Gustav Line.

According to the records of the US 7th Replacement Depot, more than 35,000 replacements were sent to Italy that month from North Africa. Among them was Lieutenant Welch, who arrived from Tunis by ship at the port of Salerno. The battalion paperwork states Welch reported at 0630 on October 6 and was assigned to B Company, which was at Paolini, a village northeast of Naples, on the road to Caserta. The palace of Caserta, built as a summer residence by the kings of Naples and rivaling the palace of Versailles outside of Paris, was soon to become the headquarters of General Clark and the US Fifth Army.

The Allied push was going well but, for the men doing the fighting, nothing was certain. What went through Welch's mind as he checked into the battalion we cannot know, but he was probably both scared and excited. Perhaps Major Tardy shared the view expressed by a US Army colonel as reported by Sergeant Ralph G. Martin in *The New York Times Magazine*. The article, "For Them the Men Will Go Through Hell," quotes an infantry colonel as saying:

> My lieutenants die like flies, but they die with their men. Then he pointed to several officers in the distance. Those are three new lieutenants fresh from the replacement depot. We'll know how good they are tomorrow. We are going to attack tonight. The three lieutenants were young, almost too young. One of them had joined up before he was graduated from college; the second had been going to law school and the third had been a soda-jerk in a small town. All three were solid and fit. Their faces were free from strain that comes after days of battle. They were fresh and eager and looked good in their clean coveralls. All of them were excited about the "show" that was coming off that night. Tomorrow one of them might be dead. That's the big thing, really, that brings the junior officer and his men so close together. That's that common nearness to death.[29]

According to Private First Class Arnold Petersen the men "were always thankful that in the 601st we had some of the best officers" and Lieutenant Robert Maynard noted the 601st was made up of "a very competent group of people." At any given time, the battalion had 35 officers and approximately 740 enlisted men assigned to it. The numbered platoons had four M-10s each. The assignment and employment of each platoon depended on the circumstances and the discretion of the company commander.

Lieutenant Welch was lucky in his assignment to the 601st where he became the 1st Platoon Leader of B Company. Platoon leaders were either a first or second lieutenant. Welch was assisted by a staff sergeant, the assistant platoon leader. In his platoon headquarters he had eight enlisted men. The staff sergeant was in charge when the platoon leader was absent and at other times carried out all orders handed down to the platoon by the platoon leader or his superiors. Often the platoon operated in two sections of two tank destroyers each. Each TD had a crew of five: a gun sergeant, a driver, a radio operator (assistant driver), a gunner and a loader. According to Private First Class Arnold Petersen, "I was always in the 1st Platoon, Co B with Lt. Welch in charge of us most of the time. He was a very aggressive lieutenant and was always looking for something to shoot at." The 601st as a whole was a fairly aggressive unit, but Lieutenant Welch had the reputation of being the most aggressive, which was remarkable for a young man in his early twenties.

On the morning that Lieutenant Welch joined the 601st, October 6, Major Tardy held a meeting with the four company commanders. He discussed the fact that the enemy had been reported in strength north of the Volturno River and enemy patrols were still operating on the south bank of the river. He ordered his officers to patrol the road network leading to the high ground overlooking the river for possible avenues of approach. Recon Company made a quick trip to the river. They reported back that the best way for the destroyers to get to their assembly point, the village of Limatola, would be via the village of Maddaloni. Later that day, B Company moved from Paolini to Santa Agata, a town closer to the objective.

On the day he joined the 601st, Welch sent a V-mail to his mother that said in part: "note my change of address, this time it's permanent. I'm sorry I haven't written in so long but things have been happening hot and heavy lately. I'm in Italy and am right in the middle of things; in fact right now German artillery is bursting about 2,000 yards away."

During this period, B Company provided indirect fire support (firing on a target without a direct line of sight) for the 30th Infantry Regiment, near Santa Agata. On October 9, the company moved 11 of its 12 TDs five miles west of Santa Agata to the village of San Felice. This action was part of an operation to chase the Germans from the southern bank of the Volturno, prior to crossing the river in force. The next day they moved 17 miles closer to the river, to the village of Branco. They stayed there through October 13. Originally the attack across the Volturno was to have commenced on the night of October 11/12 but it was postponed to ensure that everything was in place.

German defenses were laid out north of the Volturno in a line running from Castel Volturno, a village on the west coast of Italy, to the mountains of the Abruzzi in the center of the country. Enemy forces numbered approximately 40,000 troops while the Fifth Army had approximately 100,000. Attrition had taken its toll on German air power, but the Luftwaffe still had a large number of planes and they weren't afraid to attack.

The German unit facing the battalion was the Wehrmacht's 29th Panzer Grenadier Regiment. It had been part of the 2nd Division of the Sixth German Army, which had been wiped out at Stalingrad in 1941. Although there were many veterans of other campaigns, this was now a completely reconstituted unit. The regiment had 14 companies divided into three battalions. A company's strength was 165 men divided into three infantry platoons of three squads each. Each squad had two light machine guns. One platoon was more heavily armed, with three heavy machine guns and three 81mm mortars. This company also had eight antitank rifles. Prisoners reported that recently the 3rd Company had been brought back up to strength after losing their company commander and many men during the opposition to the Salerno landing. It had 18 Polish nationals assigned to it, all of whom, it was said, had decided to desert at the first opportunity.

During his early days with the battalion Welch wrote home while near the town of Santa Agata as they were moving to the Volturno River:

I'm with a fighting outfit and seeing lots of action. Since I last wrote, we've been on the move again. If you listen to the news broadcasts, you can pretty well follow my progress. The picture I'm sending you was taken about 20 minutes after we had shelled a fairly large town to the ground. After we had captured it, I saw this old-fashioned box camera in the middle of the street. I stopped the jeep and found the Italian who owned it hiding in a cellar. After he was convinced by my fluent (?) Italian that there would be no more shelling, he consented to snap my picture for four cigarettes. The fellow driving is one of my drivers. The streets are very narrow and my vehicles almost touched the buildings and nothing could pass us, so I held up the war for about 15 minutes while I satisfied my vanity. This is pretty terrible country and the people are dissolute. Mussolini sure did bleed these people. Oh yes, and it rains all the time. Pardon the writing, but I'm writing this on the move.

One can imagine a brand new "shave-tail" second lieutenant joining his first battalion.[30] The old timers probably gave him lots of advice and the immediate result was this request to his mother, written in some haste the same day as the previous letter:

This is just a line to let you know of the things that I need while you can send us Christmas presents. I'd like about three Fox's briar pipes with straight stems and about six packs of Revelation smoking tobacco, you can get them at Fox's tobacco shop, also a couple of cartons of Camels. Also a pair of high-top boots and some waterproofing for them. Don't get them more than 17 inches high. Make them heavy and of oil leather, size 9c and about three pair of heavy wool socks plus a scout scarf, GI color. These are essentials as it going to be cold as hell here.[31]

"Planes came swooping out of the clouds"

The History of the 15th Infantry Regiment in World War II records that patrols returning from probing the enemy lines on the night of October 11/12 reported German resistance was stiffening. There were still some German patrols on the south side of the Volturno. Wehrmacht artillery was very active. It was also at this time that the Germans introduced on a large scale their six-barrel rocket launchers, promptly dubbed "screaming meanies" (sometimes spelled meenies) by the GIs and called screaming "mimis" by the British. The rockets had a terrible whine and hit with a tremendous blast that struck fear into the hearts of the men. The so-called screaming meanie was the German *Nebelwerfer*. The rocket system was originally devised to deliver fog (*Nebel*), smoke, and even poison gas. For this use, it had been modified to deliver a high-explosive shell.

The Fifth Army attacked across the usually shallow Volturno River on October 13. The river varied in width from 150–200 feet and normally was only 3–5 feet deep. However, there had been heavy rain so the river was in flood, overflowing its 5–15-foot-high banks. Members of the 601st Reconnaissance

Company crossed the river in the first wave. *The History of the 15th Infantry* describes the lay of the land:

> Open fields giving no covered approaches to the river, high and steep mud banks often covered with brush and small trees, water waist-to-chest deep, current swift, German patrols equipped with rifles and machine pistols guarding the north bank and German machine gun emplacements all along the river. There was one bright spot in the picture: despite increased depth of the water caused by the continual rains, it was still possible for the infantry to ford the river at points within each regimental sector.[32]

The 3rd Division was assigned the sector north of Caserta. According to Corporal Borriello, the 10th Engineers constructed three bridges to cross the Volturno. The first was a footbridge and the second a light vehicle bridge, nothing more than 3-foot-wide pontoons with 15-foot-long "Irving" grids. This got the jeeps and trailers across. That night Borriello and crew constructed a dummy bridge of pontoons and burlap bags that lured the Wehrmacht to bomb and shell it at first light. This allowed the engineers to complete a third bridge on the site of the destroyed Highway 87 bridge. It was a pontoon treadway bridge built to carry tanks and TDs. Borriello noted the courage of the combat engineers: "There were many, many casualties because the engineers were under direct machine-gun and rifle fire and at times, some artillery fire."

Several of the C Company 601st TDs were waterproofed so they could cross without using a bridge. They were fitted with a large curved funnel device that allowed the engine to breathe, even if briefly submerged. In addition, flotation devices were attached to the sides of the destroyers. According to Staff Sergeant Harper the TDs had to travel almost 20 miles to get to the river crossing but by that time, most of the air intakes were jarred loose and useless. At 1012, British Intelligence reported an intercepted enemy radio message, which revealed the 3rd Battalion of the 29th Panzer Grenadier Regiment was ready to counterattack. Tanks from the 751st Tank Battalion and tank destroyers were ordered to cross the river immediately.

Of course, it didn't happen immediately. The tanks and tank destroyers were to have crossed at daylight but each time bulldozers approached the river to break down the bank for the tanks, they were driven back by German machine-gun and mortar fire. Still the men of the 10th Engineers went forward and, with picks and shovels, tore down the bank sufficiently and allowed the tanks to slither down to the water's edge. Shortly after 1100 the first tank climbed the low sandbank on the north side of the river and, by early afternoon, under enemy artillery fire on the ford, 15 tanks and three tank destroyers had crossed.

In the meantime, artillery and TDs firing from the south bank broke up the enemy counterattack. According to battalion records, A Company fired across the river and accounted for two tanks, a piece of self-propelled artillery, a personnel carrier and "beaucoup Kraut." They expended 418 rounds of ammunition. Nevertheless it was a costly day for A Company. It lost a TD with four of its five-man crew after it toppled off the pontoon bridge while crossing the river. Only Corporal Harold K. Claycomb, (Dawson, Pennsylvania) survived. The men drowned were: Sergeant George L. Bliss (Clyde, New York); Corporal Benjamin J. Markowski (East Norwich, Long Island, New York); Private First Class Cyrus J. Cardosi (Kankakee, Illinois); and Private Joseph A. Auderer (Dubuque, Iowa). According to Technical Sergeant Phallen, who witnessed the incident, the TD had been hit by German artillery in mid-crossing.[33] Another man from the company was also killed that day crossing the Volturno. He was Sergeant George Pollet (Lutcher, Louisiana). The circumstances surrounding his death are not known.

By the end of the day, October 15, the entire battalion was across the Volturno. B Company was the last to cross the river. There were several German air raids during the day. One of them, according to Sergeant Nowak, comprised 30 or 40 Me-109s and Fw-190s. The .50-caliber machine guns mounted on the TD fired but without effect. As usual, the aircraft came out of the sun and the Focke-Wulf 190s dived to the attack. Antiaircraft guns accounted for sending seven aircraft down in flames. Despite the Luftwaffe's onslaught to halt the advance, troops and supplies flowed over the bridges day and night.

By this time, Private Lundquist had joined the 1st Platoon of the Recon Company. He wrote in his diary:

> We moved early in the morning. Soon some planes came swooping out of the clouds, peeled off, and dove for the road. I lay down in a ditch by the front of the half-track and waited until a few were over and gone, then I scrambled into the half-track to get my helmet. Mine was not to be found of course. This taught me to always have the darned thing handy. As I was crossing the road I looked up and saw a bomb peel off one of the planes and come down close by. I learned later it killed all five of the crew of a 441st AA gun behind us on the road. It smashed one fellow against the side of a half-track and blew another right out his boots. That same plane was shot down in flames by another 441st AA crew. Finally we got going and crossed the river on the pontoon bridge. Kraut shells were landing on the shore and in the river about 50 or 60 yards downstream.

During one raid the Luftwaffe damaged several pontoons from the bridge, temporarily putting it out of commission. Some vehicles waiting to cross were also damaged. Field Marshal Harold Alexander, overall commander of Allied forces in Italy, had come to observe the crossing but missed this particular air raid by only 10 minutes.

Just across the river, a small flat plain leads to where 1,000-meter-high hills, part of the Abruzzi mountain chain, rise to the north. Progress there was slow as the roads twist and turn every 30–50 yards. The crews never knew what they would meet coming around a bend. There were casualties. On this day, the unit journal records Captain George E. Stevenson (Buffalo, New York) was severely wounded by enemy artillery fire. He was the battalion S-3, the operations officer, and he was likely with Corporal Rudolph F. Gruneburg (Danbury, Connecticut) who was also severely wounded. Stevenson subsequently died of his wounds on October 17.

On October 19, B Company was in the village of Dragoni, about 15 miles northeast of where they had crossed the river four days earlier. This village is located on the side of a ridge overlooking the Volturno valley to the east. The fight for the village included, for the first time in this sector, some tank-on-Panzer action and the 601st lost a TD. During the afternoon one of the battalion officers reported the location of a "Kraut tank." Upon being challenged if he was sure that it was a German, he replied, "If it isn't, the son of a bitch ought to quit shooting at me!"

The battalion monthly report described the German resistance there as "vigorous." The Germans were adept at using evasion, delay and withdrawing tactics to slow the 3rd Infantry advance. As was to be the case for the duration of the war in Italy, the Wehrmacht used the terrain to strategically place machine-gun nests, antitank positions and observation posts while continuing to reposition their self-propelled artillery. Coupled with terrain that restricted the tank destroyers to roads, German tactics made the use and deployment of the tank destroyers difficult.

On October 20, B and Recon Companies started a six-day operation. Their mission was to move onto the Volturno plain near

Dragoni and to clear the valley to a point north of the two tiny conjoined villages of Baia e Latina so that Allied artillery could move just to the west of the villages in order to support a US 7th Infantry Regiment advance through the mountains. It was slow going for B and Recon Companies as they were pitted against the 1st Battalion of the German 29th Panzer Grenadier Regiment.

Supporting the operation were elements of the 10th Engineer Battalion, which had to clear the roads of mines, rebuild bridges, and cross streams. During this operation B Company entered into a close collaboration with the M-4 Sherman tanks of the 751st Tank Battalion. Together, battalion records indicate that they cleaned out the "Kraut Infantry there."[34] Private Lundquist, still very new to the battalion, noted in his diary what happened on October 20, including the first time he saw a dead 601st comrade:

We left yesterday's position early this morning. It was still dark and misty. We went down the road quite a ways and through a couple of blasted towns. Capt. Paulick found us a spot next to an old Guinea [derogatory slang for Italians used at the time] barn. We put up some camouflage and dug slit trenches immediately. John [Tech Four John V. Rudy, Cleveland, Ohio] found an old Kraut belt, a burp gun and a Garand [M-1 rifle]. I went wandering about and picked tomatoes in a nearby field. Then I inspected an old broken down, shell-scarred house across the road. There were a couple of burned haystacks about 30 or 40 feet away. I picked up an Italian infantry field manual. I saw a Kraut MG with full ammunition about 200 yards away on the shoulder of the road. A Tiger tank was knocked out nearby. T/5 Carl W. Hard [Providence, Rhode Island] was being taken back to the rear by Doc Ostro [Tech Four Stanley J. Ostrobinski, Adams, Massachusetts] and he stopped for John to see him. John had tears in his eyes. He was a good buddy I guess.

117

[During that same action, Private Lloyd J. Prevo (Detroit, Michigan) was also killed.]

On October 23 Lieutenant Welch was first mentioned in the battalion's daily unit journal.[35] At 1210 he reported to the battalion command post that they were under attack and receiving rifle fire. Later that day Welch wrote his mother:

> Well there's nothing much to report, except we're plugging ahead every day and most of the time we're the farthest ahead. I've had plenty of close calls, but I've been lucky so far. This is really very beautiful country here. Yesterday, I pulled my outfit into a town [Baia e Latina] that the Jerrys had pulled out of the same morning. The people were hysterical with joy. About fifty of them mobbed me and started hugging and kissing me. The only thing was they were old, old ladies.

Private Lundquist recorded more of the action in his diary:

> We moved last night again and had a lousy time getting into this area. I dug my slit trench and am writing this in it. Shells are falling thick and fast around here right now. There were tanks (ours) here a short while ago and now I guess the Jerrys are shooting at the spots where they saw them. The tanks that left are throwing much automatic fire around not far away, a half mile or so and I can see them at it. Someone is shooting a big one nearby, from our rear. It sounded like an M-10. Can't see the action around the tanks now and it's only 10 or 15 minutes later.

Fighting continued on October 24. According to Welch's next letter he lost his first man. It was probably Private First Class Chester F. Snowden (Mechan Junction, Mississippi) who died on October 26. The next day, battalion records indicate they were able to get out of the line for a short period and stayed near the village of Roccaromana. Welch wrote:

> Well we finally got pulled out for a few days rest after four of the toughest days I've ever experienced. Yesterday we pulled an attack to clean some Jerrys out of a valley. My platoon of five tank destroyers [he may have meant four] was supporting a company of tanks. Boy we sure raised hell and caught just as much. We got rid of "beaucoup Jerrys." I lost one man but no destroyers. The tanks didn't do as well. How I lived through it I'll never know. Things go pretty slowly here, but it's steady and as soon as we clear the mountain we go like heck.

As the battalion repositioned for the next attack, the famous 601st saluting incident took place. According to the battalion's *Informal History* it was somewhere on the road from Roccaromana to Pietramelara that General Mark Clark had passed by the battalion. Apparently the men did not properly salute the general and "boy did Maj. Tardy get an earful." Later that same day, as the general was heading back to his headquarters at Caserta he passed the battalion again. This time everyone, including the Italian KPs (kitchen police), all came to attention and saluted the general. Not recalling the battalion from his early pass by, the general stopped the last vehicle in the convoy and asked what the name of the outfit was. The 601st Tank Destroyer Battalion was the reply. General Clark then told the driver of the convoy vehicle "Tell your commanding officer that this is the best saluting outfit I've run across in Italy."

Sometime in late October, Welch sent an unusually long letter to his sister Pauline (whom he called Paul) in response to her many questions about combat and Italy. It hints at the personal stresses felt by an officer in command:

This is the long promised letter written on regular stationery. The reason I use v-mail is that it's so handy. I realize my hand is foul. If you'll notice the heading, you'll see that I don't know the day of the week, all I know is that it's pretty late in October. I'll try to answer some of the questions you have asked. I'm sorry to hear about Ted [unknown], but not too sorry, as I see worse things happening every day. When you see your own men, men you work and fight with every day lose their lives, and know that it's your bad or good judgment that means life or death for them; one finds it hard to think about situations at home. Besides, he's better off as he is.

As for the food, it's sketchy, for a couple of days we might get pretty good meals, but most of the time we make our own. We warm a can of beans or stew over a little gasoline fire, make some coffee, without sugar or cream and think we're pretty lucky to be alive. Some nights, I sleep in one of my tank destroyers[36] or in my jeep but most of the time on a pile of straw on the ground. It rains all the time consequently, my blankets and clothes are always wet, but I remember, I'm still alive. If we get a sunny day, our spirits soar, and we think it's the Waldorf [the Waldorf Astoria Hotel in New York City].

I was in a beautiful battle the other day. I was supporting some tanks with my destroyers. It was absolute hell. German artillery was landing so close it practically lifted my destroyer off the ground and remember one of them weighs 32 tons. We lost several tanks, but being lucky, I didn't lose any of mine.

About the souvenirs, most of the stuff Paul is junk, put on the market for the soldier's consumption. However, when I get to Rome, I'll get some good things, and send them along. Well I guess I've answered all your questions. My hand isn't quite as bad as this would seem, but this is an Italian pen and anything Italian won't work. Believe me Paul this is really a rugged life, most of the time we're miles from anywhere. It's pitch black at 1800 so we sit in the destroyer and talk and drink this lousy native wine and listen to the rain beat on the canvass top. Lots of time we don't eat or sleep for two or three days at a time.

It had been tough going and, during a brief respite, Private Lundquist described in his diary what his life was like:

A day of loafing, magazine reading and clothes washing for everyone; I was standing by the supply truck watching the distribution of equipment to those who needed things when we heard planes droning overhead. I looked up to my right and noticed them through a break in the clouds flying high. They were heading in the direction of our rear area but were not recognizable at that great height or from the quick glance we had of them. A minute later we had forgotten them, but two minutes later they again reminded us they were around by peeling down out of the clouds, apparently headed right at us. The group of fellows scattered quickly. Seems the planes were aiming at a bridge near our bivouac but they missed it completely. Don't know if any of the planes were knocked down because we were busy groveling in the ditch.

Lieutenant Welch was still in his first month with his platoon, although by all accounts he was adapting. It must have been difficult as Welch was a "90 day wonder" while the 601st was still a prewar unit with many grizzled veterans. There is always friction between a new officer and the men who are often older and more experienced than the officer who leads them. To be successful, a new lieutenant needed to develop a close bond with his men. Sergeant Martin in *The New York Times Magazine* article mentioned earlier described the relationship between officers and men on the front lines:

Up front the lieutenant and his platoon are a small family and the looey [slang for lieutenant] is mother and father. A good junior officer knows his men well. He not only knows how well they can fight but knows everything they think about and dream about and worry about. He knows that because he has censored their mail, because he plays poker with them, because he stretches out in the dark of night and talks his heart out with them and he always listens hard when they do the talking. They talk about everything that a bunch of men talk about when they are together. And at night the men can't see the gold bar on the lieutenant's shoulder, and he doesn't want them to.[37]

By the end of the month the 601st was near the town of Marzanello, overlooking a three-mile-wide valley that drained into the Volturno river valley to the east. They continued to operate with the 751st Tank Battalion. B Company was now also in direct support of the 15th Infantry Regiment on this branch of the Volturno river plain. It was very slow going and in 15 days they had only advanced about 20 kilometers north to the town of Presenzano, which spills down from a hilltop overlooking the Volturno River as the crow flies. It was like that all along the Italian front. Field Marshal Kesselring's plan to delay the Allies moving up the Italian peninsula had exceeded his expectations.

CHAPTER 5
STALEMATE AT CASSINO

"God, they were so close"

On November 1, Welch and a section of his tank destroyers moved along the principal east–west road in the Volturno valley. They were before the town of Presenzano which spills down from a hilltop overlooking the valley. The 15th Infantry Regiment had been ordered to move up the hill to take Presenzano and Welch was there to provide support. Key to this action was securing a crossroads by establishing a roadblock where a road branched north from the main road and climbed into the town. Welch positioned his two TDs at the roadblock. Immediately, the Germans concentrated 88mm fire on them. At least 75 rounds fell on the crossroads. It was going to be a hard fight.

The first volley of enemy artillery fire hit one of Welch's tank destroyers, wounding three men. Welch, hearing the cries of "Medic," leaped from his tank destroyer to render first aid. Tech Five John C. O'Donnell (Summit Hill, Pennsylvania) climbed out of the crippled tank destroyer to assist his lieutenant. Shells zeroed in on the tank destroyer, some landing as close as 10 yards away and many more burst within 20 yards of the five men. A wounded man lying on the ground was hit a second time. Welch and the Tech Five did not abandon the wounded men for the relative safety of their destroyer but stayed for a full half-hour until medics arrived in a jeep and evacuated the wounded to an aid station. For this action, Welch and O'Donnell were both awarded Bronze Stars for "valorous conduct in action against the enemy."

According to the official description of the newly approved award, the Bronze Star medal was awarded to recognize minor acts of heroism in actual combat.[38] Whether the phrase "against the enemy" applied here was a question raised by Sergeant Nowak who said the three men, Private First Class Thomas Davis (Brentwood, Pennsylvania), Private Clarence J. Schwebach (Grandville, Iowa) and Tech Five Louis A. Cardona (Bronx, New York) were wounded not from German artillery but as a result of friendly artillery fire. Tragically Davis and Schwebach subsequently died of their wounds.

Welch wrote his brother-in-law Reg Bushnell: "It's getting so a shot has to land in my back pocket before I'll even look. They are that frequent. I lost a couple of good men last night to a direct hit and it about got yours truly; I'll never understand why it missed me." And Lundquist noted in his diary: "What a life! Saw lots of fires on the mountainside this night as we were travelling to our new bivouac area. They are said to have been caused by Jerry planes which crashed up there." B Company stayed near Presenzano for the next couple of days.

Until two mountains overlooking Highway Six – the main Naples–Rome road – were taken from the Germans, the Fifth Army could not move further north. The mountains, Monte Lungo and Monte Rotondo, concealed well-entrenched German troops. These Germans stopped the battalion at the town of Mignano and Private Wilbur M. Wedell, (Chisago City, Minnesota) of Recon Company was killed outside the town on November 6. The circumstances are not recorded.

Beyond the mountains loomed the mass of the 6th-century Benedictine abbey of Monte Cassino. The Allies suspected the Germans were using it as an observation post as the strongly fortified Gustav Line ran through it. Monte Cassino was to hold up the Allied advance on Rome for six months with tremendous Allied bloodletting.

Welch wrote his mother on November 7 and the local paper published the letter, which gives vivid insights into the soldier's war:

I just happened to be sitting near a typewriter, so I thought I'd try my hand at it. I got a break today, the men in the outfit got paid today, and consequently they all made out money orders to send home. Well, someone had to take them back to the personnel section, which is well back of the front lines. So I managed to get the job which is a decided rest from what I have been doing. You see tonight I'll be able to sleep without keeping one ear open listening for shells flying over and wake up to find myself diving for a shell fox hole. And believe me, this happens quite often, I've finally taken up sleeping in the tank destroyer, which is uncomfortable as hell but is definitely safer.

I'm firmly convinced that someone is looking after me these days, because if there weren't someone, I'd sure be wearing a halo now. Yesterday was really a tough one. It started at six in the morning and kept up continuously until dark that evening. They had us spotted, and there was nothing we could do about it but sweat it out. God, they were so close. But I've decided that a miss is as good as a mile. It was so hot, that I wouldn't let any of the men stick their heads out of the turret of the destroyer to get the rations which we carry as emergency chow on the back of the tank, so we went all day without food and all night without sleep. However, I did smoke three packs of Marvel cigarettes.

Things are going pretty slowly as far as digging the Jerrys out of Italy go. The country here is very mountainous with deep ravines and gullies to worry us all the time. I've taken these 32-ton Buicks places where in civilian life I wouldn't walk. It's just something that has to be done. Don't let anyone kid you about the war being over in a couple of months, there is "beaucoup" more tough and bloody fighting to do yet, and these Germans are tough fighters. I captured a German prisoner the other day as we were moving into the attack. I had no other choice but to take him with me in my tank. As it happened, we ran into some pretty tough shellfire, and if you saw a scared person this was the one. When we fire the gun, the concussion is terrific, and unless you're used to it or have cotton in your ears, it makes you deaf for a while. Well, we forgot all about him in the excitement, and when it was over; he was positively green with fright and stone deaf. Personally, it amused the hell out of me but strangely enough he failed to see any humor in it. He was strictly not a superman, just a scared kid of 21 years. We fed him and gave him cigarettes and when we turned him over to division headquarters, he was all smiles with the world, even though a little deaf.

Progress was slow and extremely tough going, with the tank destroyers restricted to the narrow twisting roads along the mountainsides. According to Josowitz, "It rained all day, every day, and not only rain but bombs, mortars, heavy artillery, tank fire, 20 millimeters, and various and sundry other little items of German manufacture." Mignano was only about ten miles northwest of Presenzano. The Germans were dug in and there were many minefields. Outside of Mignano a Sherman from the 751st Tank Battalion was "blown to smithereens by an antitank mine." Josowitz added: "Rations had to be hauled across the river on a rope and pulley ferry." There were air raids and rocket attacks each day. Emil T. Byke, a soldier in Item Company, 30th Infantry Regiment commented on the use of the "screaming meanie" during this attack:

> To experience the receiving end of one of these weapons is unforgettable. It was used as a psychological weapon and also a killing machine. We were on Mt. Rotondo bombarded by these screaming shells for several days. Slit trenches cut in the rock of the hill were no protection. Lying in my trench I could actually see these six shells slowly rising from the enemy position in the valley below the mountain. And then came this screaming sound which you would think the shell was so close that it would pop into your slit trench. Several days of this bombardment would drive you wacky. No wonder they called it a psychological weapon. After Rotondo I never was fired upon by this weapon. Thank God.[39]

In early November, Lundquist described a tragic accident involving two newly assigned men, unfamiliar with operating in a combat environment. Captain Paulick, Recon Company commander, called the company together to inform them of a serious incident that had happened the previous evening. At about midnight, one of the new men on night guard duty challenged someone approaching his post. He demanded the password but did not hear it given loud and clear. The guard shot the approaching soldier, the other new man. He died of his wounds later that night. Lundquist felt it had been the other soldier's fault. It taught Lundquist, and no doubt others, to sound out when challenged.

Five Bronze Stars were awarded to members of the 601st for a variety of actions which took place between November 8 and 10, a period when the battalion provided direct fire support during the action at Monte Lungo and Monte Rotondo and the assault on Mignano. It was a particularly rough time. According to Staff Sergeant Harper, the Navy fired its 16-inch guns into the mountains to help with the advance.

Battle fatigue became all too common among the men. On the evening of November 9/10 the B Company commander, an otherwise unknown Captain Mitchell, suffered an extreme case. He was replaced by Captain (later Major) Benjamin A. G. Fuller, II (Milton, Massachusetts). According to Sergeant Colprit:

> Captain Mitchell called Colonel Tardy right over the radio and demanded that we be relieved. The colonel refused and Captain Mitchell then said "I'm coming back and getting relieved." He told Sergeant Byrd [Willard C., Morristown, Tennessee] "You are in charge." Off he went with Lt. Card [Jack H. Card, Exeter, California] never to be seen again. He was probably transferred to the States. Leaving your post in the face of the enemy is a most serious offence. At three in the morning Capt. Fuller arrived to take over.

The winter of 1943/44 was one of the coldest in Italian memory. The weather and mud were becoming a real problem for the Fifth Army. Welch's last letter from this period refers to the increasing cold that gripped the mountains. He wrote "Please excuse the writing, but it's so harsh and so cold, I can hardly hold the pen. It's really cold here, and I am looking forward to a cold winter! There just isn't any place to go to get warm. Things are going slow as hell and it gets depressing at times. Well the candle is burning out so I'll close now." And, as Josowitz wrote: "There is no mud in the world like Italian mud! It was the weather against vino, the great Italian antidote! 'Sunny Italy' became a bitter joke to the TD men in the fall and winter of 1943."

Close to Mignano on November 12, Lieutenant Welch, who had avoided injury so far, was blown out of his destroyer. He remained unconscious for three days.[40] He received a Purple

Heart for his wound, and a later recuperation trip to the Fifth Army Rest Camp on the Isle of Capri. Meanwhile the sluggish advance continued. Corporal Borriello described the slow progress to Cassino from the fighting on Highway Six:

> As we got closer to Mt. Cassino, resistance became stiffer. Although the advance was generally along highway number six, the Germans held high ground on both sides of the highway. Before we could get near Mt. Cassino, several smaller mountains had to be taken, namely mountains Rotondo, Lungo, and Camino. Following the taking of Mt. Rotondo, the 3rd Division was relieved by the 36th Division on November 17, 1943. One of the scenes that stuck in my mind was the lack of vegetation. The woods on the sides of the mountains were completely stripped of any living vegetation. Because of the constant artillery fire and bombings, everything was dead. No leaves, no bushes. It was a barren, eerie sight.

Because of the inclement weather and stiff German resistance, General Clark received permission to suspend the attack for two weeks. There was to be a great reshuffling of men and units. Everyone needed a break from almost two months of continuous combat. On the night of November 17/18 the battalion and the entire 3rd Infantry Division were pulled out of the line. The 601st re-formed and regrouped south of Mignano at the village of San Felice. Then it moved to Calvi Risorta, a small village on the right side of Highway Six on the way to Cassino, 14 miles northwest of Caserta and about 40 miles north of Naples. The battalion, although out of the line, was placed in a position to defend the Fifth Army Headquarters at Caserta in the event of a German counterattack.

For 78 days, since September 9, the battalion had been in combat with only short breaks. Lieutenant Welch had been in combat for 43 days. He had been wounded, seen men die and exhibited courage under fire. He was weary and his experiences had changed him. To quote Sergeant Martin in a *New York Times* article, Welch appeared to be fitting into the reporter's idea of the role of a second lieutenant in combat:

> To his men, the looey is a lot of things. He's a young punk who looks as soft as a woman but who tightens up hard when the chips are down; he is the guy the men turn to when they got a pack of personal troubles and want somebody to talk to who will open his heart and understand such things; he's the one they go to when they need money in a hurry for a brand new baby back home (a Pvt.'s base pay is $50, a second looey has $150 and a first looey $166). He is a junior officer to the old man, who may be anything from a captain to a colonel. But in the field he is just the guy who faces the same bullets his men do, who flops in the same mud, eats the same C rations, wears the same fatigues. He is always lieutenant when somebody else is around, but he may be Harry when two of them are alone. To his men, the looey is one of them. [41]

One of the first things battalion members did upon settling in at Calvi Risorta on November 18 was to send V-mail Christmas greetings to their families. Time was short to get these cards home before Christmas. Somebody, probably in Headquarters Company, put together a semi-official 601st card. It was mimeographed and made available to the men who wanted them. The card depicted two GIs in a foxhole with the phrase: "What the Hell is Merry about this? Merry Christmas 1943 from Italy."

Meanwhile, Private Lundquist kept up his diary. The following are highlights from his comments from late November 1943 on daily life in the bivouac at Calvi Risorta:

New bivouac area, set up my tent, lazed around, cleaned rifle for "supposed" inspection, did cross word puzzles, two pals off to Naples "rest camp," three Kraut planes went over at 100 feet, truck dumped tents here, looks like we'll be here for a while, started training program, calisthenics, gun drill, class on terrain north of Cassino, erected pyramidal tents, gas mask inspection, two Jerry planes over low, one spouting lead, dug slit trench, calisthenics, side arm inspection [weapons], prisoner of war talk, calisthenics, gloomy day, rumor of a long hike, Thanksgiving Day, big dinner with all the trimmings, Capt. Paulick married a nurse [Gladys O. Romoke],[42] battalion assembly and they named the KIAs, the majority were from A and Recon Companies, Jerry pounded Naples, the flak[43] was terrific, had shot in each arm [vaccinations], a pal went to Naples on five-day pass, had a hot shower, did sewing on bedroll, Sunday, no reveille, took laundry to Italian woman at nearby house, the Articles of War were read to us today, had short arm [penis] inspection – issued "invasion equipment" [condoms], went on a pass to Naples and got pretty stinking drunk.

Air attacks on the bivouac were so frequent that the battalion kept their M-10s in among the trees, positioning them so they could fire their .50-caliber machine guns on the overflying planes. The Luftwaffe continued to bomb Naples, particularly the port, and Caserta. It was Thanksgiving and the battalion's morale was described as exceptionally good because of "turkey dinner with the usually expected trimmings" although both Sergeants Nowak and Larson recalled having steak. Sergeant Larson wrote in a November 27 letter to his grandma:

We celebrated Thanksgiving by buying an Italian cow and having fresh beef steak for dinner. Boy, it surely tasted good. We also had memorial services for the boys of this outfit who have already given their lives in this struggle. We have a chaplain here who helps the boys in any way he can. Whether we're under shell-fire or safely back of the combat zone you can depend on him carrying out his duties.

At the same time, Sergeant Colprit related a story that occurred during the Thanksgiving break:

Jungle Jim [nickname for Captain Fuller, B Company commanding officer at the time] had the company fall out to give us a pep talk. He said there had been rumors that we might be going back to the States and he was about to set things straight. He said, "You are not going home and you are going to kill and be killed. If you do not want to do that, step forward and I will transfer you out of the company." None of us dared to step forward for fear of ending up in the infantry.

The last major activity of the month occurred on November 29 when the battalion commander, four officers and 144 enlisted men were required to attend a 3rd Infantry Division formation (parade). The next day, Welch wrote his mother and described being wounded back on November 12:

I'm sorry I haven't written lately, but I've been in the hospital again. This time I was wounded, in fact twice in ten days. The first time I got a few shrapnel wounds in the hand, nothing serious. The next day, I was blown out of my tank and was out cold for three days, no wounds. However, I'm O.K. now and set to go again. I got a letter from Joan [his youngest sister] and five from you yesterday, glad to get them.

Now out of the line, the 601st reorganized per the latest US Army Table of Organization and Equipment (TO&E).

They turned in 53 vehicles and thinned their ranks by two officers and 193 enlisted men. The reorganization was completed by December 4. For B Company that meant they had to transfer 35 men. Private Lundquist was clearly worried about how this reorganization would affect him personally and noted: "I moved to 1st Platoon, several others moved to the pioneer platoon. About 30 men were transferred out of the company. I was very lucky to have remained being a rather new member. Thought I would get the hatchet too and wind up footslogging it in the infantry."

At a battalion awards ceremony on December 5, General O'Daniel, assistant 3rd Infantry Division commander, presented seven battalion members with Silver Stars earned in North Africa. This included Sergeant Nowak for his actions at El Guettar, Tunisia. On this day First Lieutenant Ambrose G. Salfen formally assumed command of B Company from Captain Fuller. He was to remain B Company commander for the next 14 months.

Following the medal presentation, a group photo of 601st officers in front of an M-10 was taken. It is the only known group photo of battalion officers taken during the war. The photo was taken by Mr Ollie Atkins of the American Red Cross who wrote on the back of the photo that it was taken south of Monte Cassino (i.e. Calvi Risorta). In the photo five of the officers in the front row wear leggings, others have adopted a high leather boot. Private Lundquist noted he had his shoes made into boots by having leather tops sewed on by an Italian cobbler and these officers may have done the same. All the men are wearing the short tanker jacket, a standard-issue garment and are shown holding their tanker helmets. Only seven of the 35 officers in the photo can be identified with certainty; they include Major Tardy and Lieutenant Welch.

"I saw ships sunk in the harbor"

After receiving his medal, Sergeant Nowak was rewarded with a five-day pass to Naples.[44] He recorded his impressions:

> On the 5th I went to Naples for five days. I had a good time. I did a great deal of walking. Buildings in Naples were mainly five stories tall. The women prostitutes were many, and women were even trying to sell their daughters' souls. The kids bothered me constantly asking "beefsteak? Spaghetti? Champagne?" The city was filthy and the women were not too good-looking. I saw ships sunk in the harbor. One night the civilians spread a rumor that the war was over.

In Naples, overcrowding and poverty became the norm as peasants left the farms in desperate search of a better life. Crime became a way of life. It was calculated one-third of all supplies landed in Naples was instantly stolen, including, according to legend, a 10,000-ton Liberty ship. Prostitution was widespread; boys acted as pimps for their mothers and sisters. For the women of Naples it was either that or watch their families die of starvation. Venereal disease became epidemic. It was the cause of more Allied soldier casualties in the Italian campaign than the fighting. German air raids, time-delay bombs, and a typhus outbreak added to the horrors of life in Naples at this time.

Things began to settle into a routine. Sergeant Nowak recalled that training continued and there were retreat parades, small arms firing, typhoid shots, classes, and occasionally a movie. There is a picture of him at Calvi Risorta lying on straw in a tent opened up to air out. These were not luxurious accommodations. Private Lundquist detailed life in his own unique style:

> Long hike, day full of classes, tent gas chamber, had a shot in the arm, barracks bag showed up, repaired brick wall, rifle range,

10 mile hike, cleaned my rifle, failed rifle inspection when on guard duty – assigned a week of hauling gravel for dirty rifle, hauled rocks, bought and roasted chestnuts, put in gravel walk for "His Exalted Highness" First Sergeant Richards [Ernest N. Richards, Jr, Watertown, New York], hauled rocks, guard duty, got PX rations today [cigarettes, candy, etc.], got some good vino, hauled rocks, calisthenics, class on orientation and the use of binoculars, cleaned vehicles, guard duty, personnel inspection, cleaned Lt. Rogers' [Otis R. Rogers, Pauls Valley, Oklahoma] jeep, lost my helmet, received carbine ammunition, CW [continuous wave] radio practice, visited Italian family, inspection, CW practice, went to pistol range, cleaned guns, guard duty, Maj. Hinman [Daniel S. T. Hinman, Wakefield Rhode Island] made a tent inspection, current affairs talk, drank cognac, visited Italian family, marked clothes, chased Guineas [Italians] all day while on guard duty, CW practice, heard current news summary, watched 37mm firing practice, went to the movies and saw *The Spoilers* with Marlene Dietrich and Randolph Scott, CW practice, heard news summary, long hike, dry-run for a move out, guard duty, rumored we're going to England, South France, North Italy and everywhere but New York which is where we'd all like to be going.

The war north of Naples continued, but the troops at the front were not making much headway. On December 17, after a prolonged battle, the Fifth Army took the key town of San Pietro on the road to Monte Cassino.[45]

Unsure of where they would be sent next, Major Tardy sent two 601st Battalion officers to conduct a route reconnaissance through the valley between Monte Lungo and Monte Maggiori, northwest of Mignano on December 20 – he wanted battalion-level intelligence in case they were sent to the area. About the same time, just before Christmas, Welch sent a letter to his sister, Betty:

I got your Xmas present today. Thanks a million. Nothing could be more useful. There is no better magazine than *Time*. I read every last word. It's really something I appreciate. Things are rather rough over here; don't plan on a quick finish. I don't think I told you, I was wounded. I was blown out of my tank, all I got was a concussion and I'm O.K. I visited Naples on a three-day recuperation pass and had a grand time. I met a girl at an officer's house whose father was a big shot fascist before we took Naples, after we took Naples he was an ardent ally. It all depends on whose winning. We (the gal and I) went out to the Isle of Capri [the location of the officer rest camp] and boy what a spot. It was nothing less than swank. I blew a wad, $85.00 in two days. I got gloriously drunk, not disgustingly so, but happy as all hell.

There was a Christmas stand-down for the battalion. Before a special Christmas dinner, which Lundquist wrote was "swell," the 3rd Division Roman Catholic chaplain, Lieutenant Colonel Father Ralph Smith, held confessions prior to conducting an outdoor mass at Calvi Risorta. Christmas came and went, but mail was slow. Welch wrote to his mother:

I haven't received any mail for three weeks; consequently I've been rather lax about writing. However, I've received two boxes of candy as well as a package with pipe, scarf, socks and tobacco and believe me they were very much appreciated. I'm sure they will all come in very handy. I'm looking forward to the others. It's very cold here now but little snow and I manage to keep warm. Yes I still have the medal [a Saint Christopher's medal] and always wear it.

"Beats the hell out of walking!"

As 1944 dawned, the Fifth Army staff was planning an end run around the entrenched German defenses across Italy by landing at Anzio, a seaside resort south of Rome. The biggest constraint on the timing of any forthcoming operation was the availability of landing craft. These craft needed to be sent to England as early as possible to allow for amphibious training for the planned Allied invasion of Normandy scheduled for that summer. This severely limited the window of opportunity to conduct an amphibious landing in Italy. Therefore the 3rd Infantry Division quickly concentrated its forces and began training in the neighborhood of Pozzuoli, northwest of Naples. Josowitz reports the battalion moved on New Year's Day through a blizzard to its new home at Pianura, just outside of Pozzuoli.

Where the landing was to take place was unknown to the men of the 601st. They practiced disembarking on the beach near the small island of Nisida in the Bay of Pozzuoli. During one such evolution Josowitz reports Major Tardy asked a 3rd Division sergeant:

"How many of these amphibious operations have you been on?"

"Three," said the doughboy.

"How do you like them?" asked Maj. Tardy, expecting an outburst of bitching in reply.

"Beats the hell out of walking!" said the doughboy nonchalantly.

By January 10, 1944, things started moving quickly as preparations for the invasion were put into place. Private Lundquist wrote he was:

Up at 0700 and rolled our blankets right away as we were told we would go on a 24-hour problem today. Lt. Rogers gave a short talk at 1045 on where we were going and a general idea of what we would do. Ate dinner at 1100 and were supposed to be ready to go out at 1150. Went the same route as before but stopped quite a bit farther on.

Training involved risk, and death too. A series of photos of the practice landings in the Gulf of Pozzuoli were taken at Lucrino and Baia, showing men jumping onto the beach from landing craft and amphibious DUKWs.[46] One photo shows the tragic scene of a DUKW on the beach with a hole blown in the side. Next to it is a hole several feet deep in the sand, probably caused by an un-swept teller mine buried in the sand. Several soldiers are standing around and an unidentified body is lying uncovered on the beach.

Sergeant Nowak described some of the final preparations for the landing, recording that there were more classes, clothing and equipment care, and maintenance on the tank destroyers. They practice-fired their 3-inch guns, machine guns, small arms and other weapons. On the 14th they started to waterproof the tank destroyers. That task took three days.

The battalion went on an eight-mile hike on January 18, which ended in a review by General Mark Clark and the awarding of medals. Later, the entire 3rd Infantry Division conducted a practice landing down in the Gulf of Salerno. Men were landed in the wrong place and on the wrong beach. More importantly 43 DUKWs were lost in rough seas, as were 19 precious 105mm howitzers. It was equipment the division could ill afford to lose. Called Operation *Webfeet*, it was a total disaster. So much so that the Navy wanted to postpone the Anzio landing; there was no chance of that.

Just a few days later, the battalion was loaded aboard landing craft at Pozzuoli for the Anzio landing. According to the January

1944 battalion operation report, space on ten ships, three LCTs (Landing Craft Tank, 191 feet long) and seven LSTs (Landing Ship Tank, 327 feet long), were used to carry the battalion's 83 vehicles and 373 officers and men for the first wave. The three gun companies with a total of nine TD platoons were distributed among seven ships. Each of the three LCTs carried one platoon of TDs and a section from Recon Company. Six of the LSTs each carried one TD platoon while other battalion vehicles were carried on the seventh LST. This dispersion allowed protection from complete loss of the battalion's capability should a ship be sunk. Private Lundquist wrote about that day:

> First Call at 0530 for the group I was in and we were told to have bedrolls and "music" [personal item] bags at the CP by 0645. We were taken down to the docks in Naples to LST 384. Our half-track was way in the rear on the "ground floor." The ship was out in the harbor at anchor and there are a half dozen more LSTs nearby all loaded up and ready to shove off. I saw a few fully loaded troop transports too. In a little harbor northwest of Naples [Bagnoli] I counted more than 40 LCIs [Landing Craft Infantry]. There's a whole smear of different types of vessels here in this harbor too. Saw a couple Red Cross ships. Hope I never see the inside of one, though it'd be prettier than the inside of a blanket shroud from six feet under. We are the only Recon men in this tub! The only other 601st men are some fellows in one platoon of B Company, who's M-10 is parked right next to ours. There is a 155 Howitzer from 9th Field Artillery Battalion on the other side of us; also about 8 or 10 "Ducks" in here. A lot of Engineer vehicles up on deck with great rolls of barbed wire. We're going to hit somewhere south of Rome.

CHAPTER 6
ANZIO

"Easy at first but tough as hell now"

"My tank had bogged down four different times"

On January 23, Operation *Shingle*, the large-scale invasion at Anzio/Nettuno was launched. It involved 250 combat-loaded vessels and amphibious ships of all descriptions from six Allied navies. A partial listing of Allied forces included, on the left: the British 1st Infantry Division; British 2nd Special Service Brigade; British 2nd Commando Battalion; and on the right, the US 3rd Infantry Division; US 504th Parachute Infantry Regiment; the US 509th Parachute Infantry Battalion, and the US 6615th Ranger Force (Darby's Rangers). The commandos and the rangers were to go ashore first and secure the landing beaches.

In addition to the amphibious ships, there was Task Force X-Ray under Rear Admiral F. J. Lowry, USN, made up of 74 US Navy warships. Supporting the British half of the invasion were 52 Royal Navy (RN) ships of Task Force Peter under Admiral T. H. Troubridge, RN. Both navies had the same missions: to see their troops safely ashore and to provide naval gunfire support.

To maintain surprise, there was to be no pre-invasion bombardment. At 0200 however, as planned, two British assault ships launched an intense 10-minute barrage firing 1,500 5-inch rockets. Immediately after the barrage, the commandos and rangers landed to take out beach defenses of which there were few. The rangers then took the town of Anzio and moved on to the nearby coastal town of Nettuno, setting up roadblocks and killing the few German sentries who challenged them.

The US 3rd Infantry Division, assigned to Task Force X-Ray, landed on Red and Green beaches running from Nettuno along the coast to the southeast. The 601st, in its third amphibious landing, was in the middle of the division at Beach Red. According to Sergeant Larson, although thousands of mines had been planted along the beach, hardly any exploded, probably because over time the waves had covered them with sand.

Initially there was virtually no resistance. Few Germans were there to oppose the landing. However, at daybreak, as the unloading of tanks and tank destroyers had begun, the Luftwaffe wreaked havoc on a beached LCT in which part of B Company was embarked. The men were sitting ducks as the planes dive-bombed and strafed. Bombs landed abeam of the LCT and an LCI (Landing Craft Infantry) was hit, causing it to burn furiously with heavy casualties among the disembarking soldiers. They waded with full field equipment through water almost over their heads. Sergeant Larson wrote: "a guide rope was stretched from ship to shore for them to hang on to." While waiting to unload from their LST, Larson saw one of the two pontoons put out to unload the tank destroyers was knocked out of service. A minesweeper was also sunk. He noted that although all of the battalion's vehicles had been waterproofed, his M-10 never was in water deeper than 3 feet. Larson added: "We drove in much deeper water during our two weeks of amphibious training down at Naples."

After the TDs were unloaded, the harbor was again attacked by German planes. The terrain was flat and the ground wet and soggy. Many tank destroyers became mired in the mud. As Sergeant Larson recalled:

> When we hit the shore I only got a couple of hundred yards from the water when my tank bogged down. Another M10 hooked on but couldn't get me out so a cat [a Caterpillar tracked bulldozer] hooked on and the two of them got me out. While we were there, bombers again came over but luckily for us they didn't pick us for a target. Before the day was over my tank had bogged down four different times and others had the same experience. At one time three of the four tanks in my platoon were bogged down. We learned that only by staying on the roads could we navigate on the beachhead. If there had been enemy tanks or antitank guns I dread to think of what would have happened to us.

The 601st moved off the beach and drove to their assigned firing positions about four miles inland. The men saw several dead Germans and some abandoned equipment. According to one source, the first German captured had been on his way to pick up bread for breakfast. The invasion at this location had been a complete surprise.

In addition to the beaches, the roads were also heavily mined. Elements of the battalion's Reconnaissance Company moved down the road toward Rome, meeting no resistance. They got within 17 miles of the city before turning back. Rome was not the day's objective. The next day, B Company's 2nd Platoon destroyed a tank and a concealed machine-gun nest hidden in a farmhouse. Because of the continued light resistance, the company was pulled back for maintenance and de-waterproofing the destroyers.

The success of the landing might have been even greater had the leader been more aggressive. Controversy later swirled about Major General John P. Lucas, the commanding general of Operation *Shingle,* and his failure to capture the high ground overlooking Anzio. It was said that the general was haunted by the near failure of the previous landing at Salerno. Indeed, Lucas had been encouraged to be cautious by Fifth Army Commanding General Mark Clark, who almost got pushed off the beach at Salerno. Lucas believed he lacked sufficient troops to move beyond the beachhead and therefore, even though more than 90 percent of his forces had landed (50,000 men and over 5,000 vehicles) by the end of the day, he nevertheless dug in, constructed a defensive perimeter and did not advance. Major General Sir (William) Ronald (Campbell) Penny, commanding general of the British Division at Anzio was later to remark that they could have gotten to Rome in a day – but would have been POWs in two. There simply were not enough Allied troops to seize the high ground, go to Rome and establish a defensive perimeter on the beachhead.

Early that first day, the Luftwaffe began bombing and strafing the landing force without airborne opposition until the arrival of the famous African-American Tuskegee Airmen who were to patrol the sky that day – Josowitz wrote about the encounter: "Dog fights were a dime a dozen and the 99th Fighter Squadron, a colored outfit seeing action for the first time, did a magnificent job of wasting the Germans out of the sky."[47]

The Germans reacted more rapidly than either General Lucas or General Clark had expected. Air and artillery attacks increased over the next couple of days as the Germans brought in more assets. Daytime movement became impossible for the Allies because of Kesselring. Smiling Albert (so nicknamed by the Allies) Kesselring had a series of plans for every contingency. One, called "Case Richard," called for reserve forces north of Rome to be quickly mobilized and dispatched wherever necessary. Some of these forces were first-rate parachute troops and they arrived at the beachhead by dusk. They swarmed to the site; by the start of the next day, January 25, Kesselring had 20,000 troops on the scene and 40,000 by evening.

Private Lundquist recorded the scene on those days, January 24 and 25:

> We could see the fighting between our infantry and the Krauts real good. Watched them shell buildings, exchange machine-gun fire, and toss mortars at each other. Lots of artillery, air bursts too. After arriving at battalion headquarters, there was an air raid. A bomb hit on the other side of a mound of earth about 100 yards from where I was standing. At 0545 I woke up to the crash of AA guns (as everyone did I guess). It's like an icebox in this place. There was a big air raid on. Now in the afternoon there have been six or eight raids. It's quieter at the front lines. There is another big air raid on at the coast where we just left. Shortly after dark I saw big bombers and lots of flares.

On January 25, three days after the landing, General Lucas felt comfortable enough with his defenses to order a gradual increase in the perimeter of the beachhead. The objective was to capture some higher ground to the east. The 3rd Infantry Division was part of that effort and called it simply "Expansion of the Anzio Beachhead." But now the Germans were present in strength and ready for them.

Moving along one of the many roads that crisscrossed the plain near the little settlement of Isola Bella in the southeastern sector of the beachhead, the 15th Infantry Regiment with B Company 601st in support commenced their advance. Leading from the

Above: Sergeants Weir, Larson, and Dykstra pose in Hitler's famous picture window at his retreat at Berchtesgaden, summer 1945. (Sergeant Larson's photo collection as provided by his nephew Colonel Lars Larson, US Army (Retired))

Men of B Company 601st prepare to leave Fort Benning, Georgia for Indiantown, Pennsylvania, June 19, 1942. (Sergeant Nowak's photo collection)

The new regiment of antitankers was judged to have destroyed a tremendous number of tanks with their imaginary shells fired from towed 37mm guns, "our super-duper antitank guns." Training with the 37mm anti-tank gun, fall 1941. (Far right, Sergeant Nowak.) This photo was probably taken during the Carolina Maneuvers. (Nowak collection)

Indiantown, Pennsylvania, where the 601st was finally issued its full complement of M-3, 75mm half-tracks, summer 1942. (Nowak collection)

The Tank Destroyer Center main gate at Camp Hood, Texas, circa 1942. (Courtesy of US Army Third Cavalry Museum, Fort Hood, Texas)

"This week we're finishing up tactics which is really tough." – OCS Candidate Welch, Camp Hood, the M-3 TD Tactics Training, circa 1942. The training took place among the ruins of houses that were destroyed when the US Army established Camp Hood. (US Army, courtesy of Third Cavalry Museum)

"After the morning attack, we tried to sleep but the Germans conducted almost continuous bombing raids." Private Thomas Morrison sketch, On the Open Plains at El Guettar, from the holdings at Third Cavalry Museum.

Captain Paulick and First Lieutenant Gioia, 601st Tank Destroyer Battalion, consult a map, El Guettar, Tunisia, March 23, 1943. The officers are standing in front of their command half-track. Two jeeps and an M-3 are in the background. (Courtesy of US Army Heritage and Education Center)

Some of the approximately 275,000 Afrika Korps prisoners of war captured in the final days of Axis resistance in Tunisia, summer 1943. These soldiers were experienced combat troops who would not be available to fight in Europe. (NARA)

Italian prisoners of war in Palermo, Sicily, July 23, 1943. "When we got orders to leave the stockade we had 1,027 prisoners and only seven of us to guard them." – Sergeant Nowak. (NARA)

Paestum has the three best-preserved Greek temples in mainland Italy. Miraculously the temples emerged largely unscathed after the Allied landing and subsequent German counterattack. Here US soldiers guard the ancient Greek Temple of Hera at Paestum, September 1943. (NARA)

Unloading ships at the port of Naples, October 1943. The destroyed port was now under Allied control. Ships had been sunk in the harbor, vital infrastructure ruined and the buildings along the port blown up as the Germans withdrew from the city. (NARA)

"The picture I'm sending you was taken about 20 minutes after we had shelled a fairly large town to the ground. I stopped the jeep and found the Italian who owned it hiding in a cellar. He consented to snap my picture for four cigarettes. The fellow in the driver's seat is one of my drivers." – Lieutenant Welch, October 9, 1943. (Author's collection)

A 601st TD crossing the Volturno River on a 10th Engineer Battalion-built bridge, October 15, 1943. (Courtesy of the US Army Heritage and Education Center)

A B Company TD near the village of Dragoni, located on the side of a ridge overlooking the Volturno valley. October 19, 1943. (Courtesy of Third Cavalry Museum)

Air reconnaissance photo taken over Cassino, looking south from the monastery. The hill in the center is Monte Lungo, and Monte Rotondo is the small hill on the left. (NARA)

Sergeant Nowak in camp at Calvi Risorta, November/December 1943. (Nowak collection)

A TD Encampment at Calvi Risorta, December 1943. Air attacks were so frequent that the battalion kept their M-10s in among the trees. (Larson collection)

Welch's Christmas card from Italy, dated November 18, 1943. One of the first things that battalion members did upon settling in at Calvi Risorta was to send V-mail Christmas greetings to their families. (Author's collection)

Lieutenant Welch mounted on an M-10 TD at Calvi Risorta, December 1943. (Author's collection)

The only known wartime group photo of the officers of the 601st, taken in front of an M-10 TD at Calvi Risorta, December 5, 1943. Those identified are: Capt. Walter E. Wardwell (front row, second from left); Maj. Walter E. Tardy, CO (front row, sixth from left); Maj. Daniel S. T. Hinman, Exec (front row, seventh from left); Capt. Don Matter, CO, C CO (second row, first on left); Lt. John C. Vargo, Platoon Ldr., B CO (back row, second from left); Lt. Thomas P. Welch, 1st Platoon Ldr., B CO (back row, third from left); Capt. Samuel Richardson, Platoon Ldr., C CO (back row, sixth from left). (Courtesy of Third Cavalry Museum)

The 3rd Division's Roman Catholic Chaplain, Lieutenant Colonel Father Ralph Smith, holding confessions prior to conducting an outdoor Christmas Day mass at Calvi Risorta, 1943. (Courtesy of Third Cavalry Museum)

Practice landing in the Gulf of Pozzuoli at Lucrino, January 10, 1944. (NARA)

Training involved risk. A DUKW with a hole in its side, having struck a buried mine during the Lucrino practice landing, January 10, 1944. An unidentified body lies on the beach. (NARA)

Corporal Spicer, on a waterproofed M-10, in camp at Pozzuoli, January 1944. Spicer would not survive the attempt to rescue the 1st and 3rd Ranger Battalions trapped at Isola Bella. (Larson collection)

"D-Day," Anzio beach, January 23, 1944. This photo was taken just before one of the pontoons put up to unload the tank destroyers was knocked out of service. (NARA)

German prisoners of war being removed from the Anzio beachhead, January 31, 1944. (NARA)

German shells hit US trucks in Anzio, February 7, 1944. (NARA)

The revetted hospital at Anzio, where Lieutenant Welch and Corporal Borriello were taken. "The hospital had long tents, about 100 feet long and about 16 feet wide that were dug in so that when you were on your cot you were below ground level. That way, the shrapnel couldn't get you [from the side]." – Corporal Borriello. (US Army)

A B Company 601st TD moves up to the action on February 29, 1944. (NARA)

Welch's Boneyard showing ruined farmhouses (arrows), destroyed Panzers (two circles to right) and a destroyed M-10 (circle bottom left). This aerial photo was given to Welch to commemorate the February 29, 1944 attack. (Author's collection)

Sergeant Nowak stands on his M-10, inspecting a shell hole in an Anzio farmhouse, March 1944. Note the shrapnel holes on the TD. (Nowak collection)

Sergeants Lombardi, Nowak and Gauthier with some liberated vino on the Anzio beachhead, March 1944. "But then will come a quiet spell, and one of my buddies will dig up a forgotten bottle of vino from some muddy cellar, and the world sits firmly on four legs again." – Corporal Borriello. (Nowak collection)

Welch steps into the jeep in a rare photo of the 1st Platoon preparing to hunt Panzers at dusk. The soldier marked "Johnny" is Sergeant Nowak. Anzio, March 1944. (Nowak collection)

The Girl You Left Behind

To-day she is pulling down 60 bucks......

A German propaganda leaflet sent home by
Welch, part of the anti-Jewish Sam Levy series.
"They know our fondness for comic strips and
often illustrate their leaflets." – Sergeant Bill
Mauldin. (Author's collection)

"We had milk for the first time in a year."
Welch's grandmother saved this photo taken
by Sergeant Nowak of Lieutenant Welch
milking a cow on the Anzio beachhead.
(Author's collection)

"Much of our time is spent just waiting
for something to happen… when it
comes it's usually sudden and
unexpected." – Sergeant Larson. Staff
Sergeants Kindall and Lombardi on
Anzio, March 1944. (Nowak
collection)

Below: M-18s (T-70s) parked at Naples
and ready for testing, April 1944.
(Nowak collection)

A 601st TD test-pulls General O'Daniel infantry battle sleds. The heat, dust and diesel exhaust from the vehicles made for a very unpleasant ride, Anzio May 1944. (Nowak photo)

"We took Cori and Velletri and pushed inland towards Highway Six." – Sergeant Nowak. The 3rd Infantry Division moves on Cori, May 25, 1944. (NARA)

Snap shot of a TD crew. "Like a typical officer of the 601st, Lt. Welch insisted that credit be given his crew for that job; from top left to right Cpl. Irving, Cpl. Macri, T/4 'Snuffy' Callahan and Sgt. Nowak." – *The Beachhead News*, December 17, 1944 edition about an action during the breakout for Rome. (Nowak collection)

A destroyed Panzer Mark V at Cori, May 31, 1944. The Wehrmacht's 508th Heavy Panzer Battalion noted that on May 25th seven Panzers of the third company had to be purposely destroyed in the vicinity of Cori due to a lack of fuel. (NARA)

Sergeant Nowak shows off the hole he got in his TD near Palestrina on June 1, 1944. (Nowak collection)

A Company 601st on Highway Six, June 1, 1944. (Courtesy of Third Cavalry Museum)

Lieutenant Welch was on the way into Rome on the Via Tuscolana when he fired on a concealed German machine gun nest. This action was caught on film and was published in the Army's *Yank Magazine*. June 4, 1944, Porta Furba, Rome. (NARA)

"By the time we got near the center of town the crowds were so large we had difficulty in moving." – Sergeant Larson. Photo taken from Sergeant Nowak's TD, June 5, 1944. (Nowak collection)

Sergeant Nowak is one of the soldiers standing in the lead TD in a famous photo of M-10 tank destroyers driving around the Coliseum the morning of June 5, 1944. (NARA)

General Mark Clark (in the front seat) leads a little convoy of jeeps meandering around city streets, eventually reaching St Peter's Square, June 5, 1944. (NARA)

TDs of the 601st move through a destroyed Anzio to embark on ships for Pozzuoli, June 1944. (Nowak collection)

Every single item of Allied equipment was openly displayed in the street markets of Naples. Guns and ammunition were also available but you had to ask at the open-air black market. November 1944. (NARA)

Above: Naples experienced a major eruption of Mt Vesuvius and smoke from the crater rose thirty or forty thousand feet and stretched for miles. Here unidentified soldiers watch the smoke rise from the town of San Sebastiano, destroyed in the eruption. March 21, 1944. (NARA)

Above: A mine detonates during a practice landing at Mondragone, north of Naples. While clearing the beach of buried mines for the practice, 18 men of the 10th Engineer Battalion had been killed and 43 wounded. August 7, 1944. (NARA)

Above: In late July the battalion positioned their TDs in the Texas Staging Area prior to loading them on to the waiting ships in preparation for the invasion of Southern France. (Nowak collection)

Above: Hundreds of 3rd Division soldiers wait to embark for Operation *Dragoon* near Pozzuoli, August 10, 1944. (NARA)

Left: "From where I am now [a transport ship], the view is terrific. I can see the whole Bay of Naples with Mt Vesuvius as a backdrop." – Lieutenant Welch, August 1944. (NARA)

A 601st M-10 lands in France, August 15, 1944. (Courtesy of 3rd Infantry Division Museum, Fort Stewart, Georgia)

Beyond the beach, the high ground was sparsely vegetated and dry. The 601st loaded up the infantry and pushed inland, August 1944. (NARA)

A 601st TD entered Aix-en-Provence on August 21, 1944. (NARA)

A 601st TD on the road to Le Colunvier, France. In this photo a forest fire can be clearly seen in the background, August 28, 1944. (NARA)

The German 19th Army was destroyed at Montélimar, France, August 30, 1944. According to Captain Sanders, this stretch of road was nicknamed the Avenue of Stenches. (NARA)

"The FFI seized her, shaved her head, informing us that she had kept company with a German soldier." – Sergeant Larson. Montélimar, August 29, 1944, (NARA)

The 3rd Division's Task Force Whirlwind troops ride an M-10 past a dead German soldier on the Road to Mutzig, November 23, 1944. (NARA)

Assault vehicles of the 601st TD Battalion enter Strasbourg, late November 1944. (NARA)

The 601st occupies the town of Molsheim and here Corporal "Shorty" Lees sits in a jeep next to a TD beside a ruined house, late November 1944. (Nowak collection)

Two destroyed French M-4 Sherman tanks in Strasbourg, part of a force that tried to make a run for one of the Rhine bridges before the Germans blew it up. Early December 1944. (Larson collection)

Troops of the 3rd Division prepare to fire a mortar as part of a special harassment program called the "Watch on the Rhine," December 1944. (NARA)

Martha Schneider, a young Alsatian, gave the men language lessons. Sergeant Nowak thought enough of her to have kept her photos. (Nowak collection)

Company B of the 601st moves 72 miles to the town of Ribeauville, northwest of Colmar in the Vosges Mountains, December 1945. (Nowak collection)

One of Welch's white-painted TDs passes through the town of Ostheim, January 23, 1945. (NARA)

The 15th Infantry moves out on January 23, 1945. Sergeant Nowak took this photo from his TD turret. (Nowak collection)

The collapsed bridge at La Maison Rouge. The turret of the camouflaged and sunk Sherman tank can be seen among the bridge debris, and a reconstructed Bailey bridge is in the background. February 1945. (NARA)

The destroyed Brisach Bridge over the Rhine, February, 1945. (NARA)

One of the battalion's new M-36 TDs at Pont-à-Mousson, March 1945. (Nowak collection)

front was a single tank destroyer commanded by Staff Sergeant John C. Ritso (Worcester, Massachusetts), with Private Arvin M. Hanson (Michigamme, Michigan) as one of the crew. They were hunting for Germans about 100 yards ahead of the advancing US infantry. Every few yards, Ritso rose up from the safety of his open turret to have a look for targets of opportunity. He found plenty to shoot at including some Wehrmacht-occupied farmhouses and many machine-gun nests. He was so close to them, he fired from his tank destroyer at almost point-blank range.

According to the *Field Artillery Journal* (October 1944): "Machine pistol fire, enfilading crossfire from machine guns, and sniper fire from right, left, and rear were hitting the sides of the mount and flying within inches of him." Staff Sergeant Ritso, in the midst of this heavy counterattack, continued firing for almost ten minutes while the infantry rushed the enemy positions. Suddenly the odds changed as small-arms fire gave way to heavy artillery. Immediately, Ritso received two direct hits from "a well-concealed antitank gun," probably an 88mm. The tank destroyer was crippled, immobile and on fire. He feared that the onboard ammunition would heat up and explode. Ritso also had other troubles, one of the enemy shells had caused a compound fracture with severe bleeding from his right leg. He needed help.

His situation was not lost on several officers at the battalion command post in a partially destroyed farmhouse. They were following the progress of the attack on the radio and were near the action. The battalion executive officer, Major Hinman, and the 1st Platoon leader of A Company, Lieutenant Lester D. Matter, Jr (Dallas, Texas), became very concerned and decided to act. According to the journal: "When they heard what had happened to S/Sgt. Ritso they left the comparative safety of the house, ran across 25–50 yards of open ground, across a driveway and then along the road, and crawled along a ditch beside the road for 300 yards."

This may sound like a short run, but they were under constant German small-arms fire and it took them almost an hour to get to the destroyer. The two-man rescue party moved from bush to bush. There was hardly any cover. Each time they moved, they were fired on by the Germans from well-concealed positions, some less than 50 yards away. Fortunately the fire in the destroyer had gone out and the ammunition had not exploded.

By the time the officers reached the crippled destroyer the Germans had established a skirmish line in a semicircle around Hinman and Matter. The sniping was continuous. In addition to the German infantry, a mortar in a house only 40 yards away zeroed in on the destroyer.

Crawling into the destroyer, Major Hinman dragged Staff Sergeant Ritso out and hoisted him on his back. Lieutenant Matter extracted Private Hanson who had a smashed foot. Staff Sergeant Ritso died from loss of blood on the way to their lines, but Hanson, with the lieutenant's assistance, crawled back. The private and both officers escaped further injury.

The action by these two officers in saving Hanson from capture or death earned them commendations. On May 15, 1944, Major Hinman was given the Soldier's Medal for trying to save Staff Sergeant Ritso, by the 3rd Division commander, General "Iron Mike" O'Daniel. He also received a Silver Star. Lieutenant Matter too was awarded a Silver Star and Private Hanson a Purple Heart. During the same ceremony, the late Sergeant Ritso was posthumously awarded the Distinguished Service Cross.[48]

"Back to the mud again"

As operations continued on the Anzio beachhead, Welch continued to write home:

I've been sleeping peacefully for the last week or so; between sheets, etc. it was wonderful. I got out [of the hospital with yellow jaundice] just in time to make the recent development that you've probably read about. It was quite a thing, easy at first but tough as hell now. Sometimes it looks as if it will soon be over, but I hardly expect it before next fall and more likely next Christmas. The Germans are still very tough and show no signs of giving up. They have plenty of everything and still think Hitler is tops. So don't go getting optimistic. The bombers are doing a great job, but we, over here, know they can't win it alone. There are still plenty of tough fights ahead and so far we haven't had any casualties compared with what is coming. I'm not being pessimistic, but telling you facts as they are. Back to the mud again.

In an undated letter from this period Sergeant Larson gave an accurate and clear description of the battalion's operations and the comparative merits of US and German equipment:

We were first attached to a ranger battalion, that is, my platoon was. During the first week, we did little more than act as security against an armor counterattack. Our positions are not well back as you might expect of tank destroyers. We usually are in position right next to the front line doughboys. We're usually only a few hundred yards from the Jerry infantry and sometimes we're right among them, so our tommy guns are put into use. Usually a platoon of our TDs goes into position with a platoon of medium tanks. Jerry tankers who have been taken prisoner here say that they have little fear of the M-4 75mm but really dread our 3-inch gun. But don't think that 75mm won't knock out Jerry tanks for I've seen them knock out several Mark IVs myself in our sector and in another sector they stopped a big Jerry tank attack and they gave a very good account of themselves.

The TDs do a lot more shooting than the M-4s though for we can open up at a much longer range and besides we use our gun to knock down buildings with machine-gun nests or observation posts, knock out bridges or just lob harassing fire well back of their front lines.

On January 28, the Tuskegee Airmen downed four enemy aircraft.[49] Private Lundquist, who saw the action, recorded: "Couple of air raids today in which four planes went down, three of them Jerry's for sure. The other one was too far away to see who it was but it was the only one in which the pilot got out." The battalion operation report noted:

> The iron determination of the Germans was demonstrated on 29 January, seven days after the landing, when 60 aircraft; Junkers 88s, Dornier 217s and Heinkel 177s, came down to smash the shipping in Anzio harbor. The fire of our 90mm guns caught the formation far out to sea, forced the aircraft to strike in single harassing attacks and succeed in destroying five planes. By disrupting the mass plan of attack, the antiaircraft saved the vital ships and ammunition dumps. By that night, when the score was taken, the German Air Force had raided the beachhead 53 times. Antiaircraft had destroyed at least 38 planes and probably 10 more.

But the German counteroffensive was working. Sources estimated that by January 29, the German forces outnumbered the Allies almost two to one. About the same time, a German medic who was armed with a P-38 pistol was captured by B Company, according to the battalion operations report. The report, in a somewhat outraged tone, noted: "a medic carrying a weapon contravenes the Geneva Convention of War, signed by Germany." That a German medic carried a pistol was clarified by Lieutenant Colonel John R. Howard, US Army (Retired) who wrote in a 2013 email to the author: "German medics carried pistols for mercy shots due to their experience with the Russians. The intent was not to contravene the Geneva Convention, but to prevent their wounded from being captured and tortured by the Russians."

"An iron ring around the town"

The key to advancing on Rome was the capturing of the German-held town Cisterna di Littoria. Curiously not mentioned in battalion operations reports for January 30, this was a major attack, complicated in its details and quite dangerous. Cisterna was critical to control of Italian State Highway Seven, the ancient Via Appia, which ran through Cisterna to Rome.

Around midnight on the night of January 29/30, the 1st and 3rd Battalions of Darby's Rangers moved out across the fields and followed drainage ditches on to Cisterna. The rangers' mission was to capture the town and cut off the road. The 4th Ranger Battalion, to the left of the other two battalions, was to move up Cannon Company, its integral antitank company equipped with M-3 75mm gun half-tracks. These were the same type of M-3s the 601st had taken into battle in North Africa. Cannon Company stayed on the road running from Conca to Cisterna, crossing into what the rangers called "Jerryland" just south of the settlement of Isola Bella (sometimes called Feminamorta). Cisterna, about two miles north of Isola Bella, was four miles from the 3rd Division lines. The 7th Infantry was to the left and the 15th Infantry was to the right, ready to move as far as the Alban Hills overlooking the beachhead. The 4th Rangers were augmented by several Sherman tanks and Welch's 1st Platoon TDs. Once taken, other elements of the 3rd Infantry Division were to enter Cisterna.

Intelligence reports indicated Cisterna was lightly held and offered the possibility of an easy capture. Unbeknownst to the rangers, that evening the Germans had strongly reinforced the town and its environs. It was to be the staging area for German forces readying for a major attack. The Germans, observing the rangers' infiltration, allowed them to move in unmolested. But suddenly the 4th Ranger Battalion ran into a roadblock and suffered heavy and sustained fire from houses, farm buildings and other concealed locations. Although supported by tanks and TDs the rangers were in a running fight. By 0400 they had still not reached Isola Bella. Sergeant Larson described the Germans' defense as "an iron ring around the town."

The heavy fire and shelling prevented the 4th Ranger Battalion, with Welch's TDs outside of Isola Bella, from coming to the aid of the 1st and 3rd Ranger Battalions. Colonel Darby ordered Lieutenant Otis Davey, acting commander of Cannon Company, to ask for volunteers to take two half-tracks and attempt to break through. According to Larson, Lieutenant Welch volunteered to see if a section of his tank destroyers could break the "iron ring." At 0600, the section made for the German lines. Welch was in the lead tank destroyer with the tank commander, Staff Sergeant Joseph J. Kindall (Southington, Connecticut), Sergeant Larson as driver, Corporal Lynn A. Spicer (Cleveland, Ohio) radio operator, and Lieutenant Davey. Behind the lead tank destroyer were two half-tracks from Cannon Company. The lead half-track was nicknamed "Ace of Diamonds."[50] The last vehicle in the daring convoy was a second tank destroyer driven by Sergeant Nowak. The mission was to break through the enemy lines and give the trapped rangers armor support. If they could get through, additional TDs from B and C Companies and reinforcements from the 4th Ranger Battalion could then render further assistance.

Sergeant Nowak recorded that as they moved down the road to Isola Bella, they shot at farmhouses, outbuildings, haystacks, anything that might conceal an enemy. Larson, in the lead tank destroyer, recalled he was driving totally buttoned up, which meant with all his hatches closed. Later he added:

> Just as we got to the Jerry lines, we came to a roadblock made up of some knocked-out Jerry vehicles. I swung out into the field and got around it, then headed down the road wide open. About a mile back of the Jerry lines I saw through the periscope a bunch of German teller mines thrown across the road. It was too late to stop or avoid them though by yanking the levers I missed one or two. Then there was a deafening explosion right under me, the tank lurched sideways and stopped, and black smoke came pouring up through the tank. I was thrown against the hatch with quite a bit of force and was momentarily dazed. There was then another explosion and I was sure a shell had hit us. Later I found it must have been another mine that went off.

The series of mishaps continued. Larson recalled that the last two vehicles in the review column stopped when the lead tank destroyer was blown up. The two vehicles were slammed in reverse, backing up for about a half-mile. They were constantly under small-arms fire. Meanwhile, the first half-track, following too close, failed to stop in time and rammed the lead, and now disabled, destroyer. Lieutenant Davey leaped from the TD and jumped into the "Ace of Diamonds" half-track. Then it too struck a mine and was hit by a German antitank gun.

Larson came to and grabbed for a thermite grenade that was kept handy by the driver's seat. He was ready to destroy his vehicle to prevent its capture by the Germans. But before doing so he wanted confirmation from either Lieutenant Welch or Staff Sergeant Kindall. They were nowhere to be found. It later turned out that they had been blown out of the vehicle. Larson was the only one still in the tank destroyer. He was in a tight spot and he should have taken it upon himself to destroy the $75,000 tank destroyer, but he just couldn't. He wrote that:

By lucky chance the traverse wheel had been snapped off by the concussion so the gun was useless to the enemy. Otherwise it may have been used against us as there was a tank full of ammunition. Bullets from small arms were whistling over the turret as I prepared to bail out. Just as I was about to go over, a machine gun sprayed the top with lead. So I dropped back in until it let up, then went over the side head first. As I hit the ground everything seemed to open up on me, so I dived into a ditch.

In the ditch, Larson joined a ranger sergeant from the half-track. The ranger had grabbed a light .30-caliber machine gun off his half-track. They had a whole belt of ammunition. With Larson on one side of the machine gun, and the ranger on the other side, they prepared to fire as the Germans emerged from their foxholes and closed in on the Americans. The machine gun jammed. Larson "yanked the bolt back four times before it finally cut loose." The two closest Germans fell; others took cover. The machine gun, after only about 30 rounds, jammed again. Abandoning the gun, the pair sprinted across the road for the opposite ditch and dove in. It looked like the ditch ran a long way back, straight to friendly lines. There they found other men from the rescue convoy.

They started the torturous crawl back. The ditch was shallow, in many places not more than a foot deep. The Germans opened up with everything they had – machine guns, machine pistols, and rifles – each time they saw the slightest movement from inside the ditch. There was little hope of getting back alive but the Americans, fearing that the Germans would just mow them down if they surrendered, kept their heads down and crawled on.

Slowly, they continued down the ditch and after what seemed an eternity they had reason to hope: they were 300 yards closer to their own lines and safety. Larson ran into three more rangers as well as his radio operator and close friend,

Corporal Spicer. The men pulled up short suddenly because the ditch was breached by a driveway. They had to make a crouching sprint for it, die there or be taken prisoner. Larson was the last in the file, right on the tail end. Three rangers held back and motioned to Larson to crawl around them. Corporal Spicer also said to go ahead of him. They could see Germans moving toward them along both sides of the road and Larson said the others had "better hurry or they'll be cut off." As each soldier in turn broke from the safety of the ditch they brought down a hail of fire on themselves from the Germans firing from both sides of the road. Larson later wrote:

> Then I made the dash, and brother, that took more nerve to stand up in the face of that fire than anything I've ever done. As I started across, a Jerry potato-masher grenade landed a few feet in front of me and more were dropping behind me. I can thank the Lord for an 8-second fuse on those grenades for I went right over the top of it and threw myself flat in the ditch on the other side. Though it went off not over five feet from me, the fragments whistled harmlessly over my head.

Those behind Larson were not so fortunate. Completely cut off from escape, they were taken prisoner. It took Larson and the other men three hours to return to friendly lines. Along the way they were surprised by a German sniper who stood up directly in front of the men, blocking the way. Larson wrote:

> One of the Rangers calmly took aim and shot him with a 45 automatic. At another place another Jerry came out of his hole and set up a light machine gun on the side of the road so he covered the ditch we were crawling in. We crawled through a culvert to the opposite side of the road but we still had to expose ourselves when we came out on the other side. However, his back was toward us but he wasn't over 50 feet

away. We didn't want to shoot unless necessary for it would give our position away to other Jerries in the vicinity. I had a Browning automatic rifle that I had picked up from a dead Ranger. I took it and covered the Jerry while the rest crawled safely out of sight. I had never fired a Browning automatic rifle in my life so I just said a prayer that the thing would work if he should turn around.

Larson learned an important lesson that day. He realized he needed to be familiar with every type of weapon, including enemy weapons. By the time he returned to the American lines, his weapon was "a German machine pistol that he took off a dead Jerry." Finally the small group of men, now reduced to eight soldiers, got to a house in no-man's land. It wasn't over yet. Although the house was unoccupied by Germans, friendly GIs thought Larson's group was German and were about to open up on them with a machine gun. The men had the presence of mind to wave a small white cloth. Of the eight men including Larson, only three were not wounded. One had been shot in the shoulder; another had been wounded by a German "potato masher" grenade. Larson said he had to feed him "almost a whole box of sulfa tablets" to get him back. The others had various wounds.

All during this action, Sergeant Nowak was in the remaining tank destroyer; later he wrote:

We were machine-gunned and sniped at. We saw 20 Rangers [4th Battalion] in a ditch who were trying to get back, so we covered their retreat with 3-inch fire. I spotted many Kraut dug in on both sides of the road. At one I fired the .50 caliber and knocked his automatic rifle from his position. At another I fired a tommy gun. There were many dead US and Kraut soldiers lying around the fields and on the roads. An advancing infantryman on our left was hit and we could hear him yell "they got me!" We put him on the rear of our TD and brought him to an aid station. I heard a Ranger yelling to an unseen Kraut. "Are you an American?" We fired 200 rounds of the 3-inch that day and my TD was credited with knocking out several machine-gun nests, an observation post and six Krauts.

For his actions during the rescue attempt Sergeant Nowak was awarded an Oak Leaf Cluster to his Silver Star. The citation reads in part:

> Sgt. Nowak's platoon was advancing in an attempt to wipe out any strong enemy pockets of resistance. Disregarding mortar shells which landed dangerously close to his destroyer as well as bullets from enemy machine guns only 150 yards away which bounced off his destroyer, Sgt. Nowak, standing in an exposed position, directed the fire of his gun so effectively that at least seven enemy machine-gun nests were destroyed and six enemy soldiers killed. When the enemy advanced so close that the three-inch gun was unable to fire, Sgt. Nowak jumped on the breech of the three-inch gun, completely exposing himself, swung the .50 caliber AA machine gun onto the enemy and sprayed them with bullets, silencing their fire. This action caused such confusion that the Rangers were able to reorganize and consolidate their positions.

The remaining 1st and 3rd Rangers, still south of Cisterna, were caught out in the open, about 800 yards from the town. The Germans hit them hard. Both ranger battalions were trapped, completely cut off and could neither advance nor retreat. As a result, the 1st and 3rd Ranger Battalions suffered more than 400 casualties and approximately 600 were taken prisoner. Only six made it back to friendly lines. Darby's Rangers never recovered from this attack and were evacuated from the beachhead. Larson thought the relief convoy would have suffered the same fate as the rangers "for the Jerries were there in force, with plenty of armor. But in spite of the hopeless situation, the rangers fought bravely to the last man, even knocking out tanks from afoot, and took a heavy toll of the enemy. They deserve the greatest respect that can be accorded them."

Staff Sergeant Robert C. McElroy, C Company 601st (Lexington, Virginia) added that B Company was not the only company ready to attempt a rescue of the rangers. In a US Army Heritage and Education survey he wrote: "I remember journalist Ernie Pyle stood by my Tank Destroyer on Anzio and we talked as I awaited orders to try and get in and relieve Darby's Rangers a few hundred yards away. The orders did not come as they were killed."[51]

Sergeant Larson and B Company 601st also suffered a personal loss: Larson's radio operator and friend, Corporal Spicer, was killed during the rescue attempt. When he finally got some time, Larson did a compassionate thing: he wrote Corporal Spicer's mother a long letter. In it he described the events related above and added some new details. Part of that letter is reproduced below:

My name will mean nothing to you for I've never had the pleasure of meeting you folks personally. But I was one of the many friends your son made while overseas and was with him on the morning of January 30th when he met his untimely death. It was sad for us all, but I fully realize that only you with a mother's love can know the deep grief and heartache at a time like that. It may comfort you to know he met his death suddenly and unafraid. And, that he gave it for a cause which all of us are willing to do likewise if it should be necessary.

Spice was next in line to go [the sprint across the road blocking the ditch] and I was directly behind him. But he hesitated so I crawled up to him and asked him if he was alright. He said, "Yes I'm okay, but I'm so winded I have to catch my breath before I go. Go ahead of me and I'll follow right behind." With that he shook my hand and said "Good Luck!" I just then noticed Germans closing in on both sides of us, some not over 10 yards away, so I yelled at him to follow fast, that we were being cut-off and I sprinted across. As I went across the Germans threw a hand grenade in front of me and several more behind me. I just barely got into the ditch when they went off. I glanced back and saw Spice try to throw himself flat before they exploded but I believe he must have been wounded. But now the Germans had cut his escape off and I saw him and three others raise their hands in surrender. It is not clear what happened after that for I didn't see it. But one of the prisoners who later escaped said the Germans had just started marching them to the rear when a bullet hit Spice, killing him instantly. He didn't know where it came from but likely it was some German riflemen who didn't realized they already were prisoners. Spice's grave was found a few days later when our troops took this area.

I have now told you the details of that morning and I hope knowing them may make your burden less hard to bear. For your son gave his life for his country as a brave soldier. If all our soldiers were like him victory would come much quicker. And he also was a true and loyal friend. I'm sure you found him that kind of a son for he spoke to me often of his home and loved ones. If God permits my return after this war, I shall certainly make every effort to visit Cleveland and meet you in person.

Sergeant Larson kept that promise and after the war, he and his wife visited the Spicer family in Cleveland. He never got over the loss of his friend. In later years he still resented the fact that Lieutenant Welch had volunteered his two crews for the fatal rescue mission.

Neither Lieutenant Welch nor Staff Sergeant Kindall who, as previously said, had been in the lead tank destroyer, were able to give the order for Larson to use his thermal grenade because, for the second time in less than three months, Welch had been blown out of the destroyer by one of the two mines they struck. Perhaps Kindall had helped him back to safety. Welch later wrote he had been unconscious for three days. He was treated at the 70th Station Hospital (located on the beachhead) and he was given his second Purple Heart. Later Corporal Borriello of the 10th Engineers joined Welch in the hospital and wrote about his experience:

> The hospital had long tents, about 100 feet long and about 16 feet wide that were dug in so that when you were on your cot you were below ground level. That way, the shrapnel couldn't get you [from the side]. Wouldn't you know, the first day I'm in the hospital, the Germans bombed it. This was inexcusable as the hospital was very plainly marked.[52]

CHAPTER 7

PUSH THEM BACK INTO THE SEA

"Shells are landing within our uncomfortable zone"

The Anzio landing on January 22 had been promising. The battalion's three gun companies racked up impressive totals of destroyed enemy equipment during those first days on the beachhead. This included Panzers, guns and vehicles, including a Volkswagen Beetle. But a junior officer was lost. Second Lieutenant John C. Vargo (Lancaster, Pennsylvania) was last seen January 31 going forward to contact elements of the 15th Infantry. After he didn't return, the unit journal listed him as missing in action (MIA). On February 9, Jerry's Front Radio (the German radio propaganda station) announced that Lieutenant Vargo was a prisoner. For him the war was over. He was sent to Germany and survived the war.

February 1944 started off poorly for the Allies on the beachhead and for B Company 601st in particular. Sergeant Willie B. NeSmith (Barney, Georgia) commanded 3rd Platoon's lone operational tank destroyer. The morning report listed two of their TDs as so damaged they were out of action for 24 hours. A third had run over a mine that damaged the track. It was a difficult repair since the TD was close to the German lines and was under constant sniper fire.

Things only got worse. Field Marshal Kesselring launched a portion of his attack on the beachhead on February 2. This was part of the planned attack that the rangers had stumbled into two days before. The main thrust of the attack was to be against the British sector, but Kesselring could not leave the American sector unengaged. Sergeant NeSmith was located along the line in support of the 15th Infantry Regiment when, late in the day, the enemy attacked with a battalion of infantry and 20 or more Panzers. Sergeant NeSmith's TD was concealed behind a house. Maneuvering from behind the house to attack the advancing Panzers, one of his two motors died. Movement became difficult and he knew he was going to come under fire.

Using his remaining motor, he moved the TD and peeking out from behind the corner of the house, he saw the fast advancing column. The lead Panzer was less than 1,000 yards away. The Germans spotted NeSmith and lobbed a shell at him causing a corner of the house to fall onto the open turret of the tank destroyer. A second shell glanced off the front armor plating. Uninjured, NeSmith got off a shot and then another, two rounds in short order. He knocked out the first Panzer in the column. Knowing he would be meeting Panzers, he had loaded armor-piercing ammunition and hit a brand new *Panzer Kampfwagen VI*, called by the Allies a Tiger I.

Quickly he got off a round at a second Tiger I, which had been covering the first. His shot hit that Panzer, damaging it, but with his one engine he could not maneuver his TD into a position to finish it off. As dusk approached, the enemy tanks started to withdraw and were gone from the field about 45 minutes later. Sergeant NeSmith received a Silver Star during his service but it is not known if it was for this action.[53]

However, his actions on February 2 certainly deserved such recognition.

In early February Private Lundquist wrote:

Cold night too, frost was thick on my blankets in the morning. Dead cattle nearby, everywhere burned haystacks and shattered buildings. Most buildings I saw didn't have a wall left without a shell hole. Some were completely demolished. Just saw an air burst over by the road. Saw a knocked out M-10 (from the 751st Tank Destroyer Battalion) and other Jerry equipment (half-tracks, mobile guns, 75mm and others). Lots of Jerry and GI dead down the road at the next house to the one where we are, lots of German prisoners being taken back on the road the other side of the fields. Saw an air raid on a nearby town by a bunch of P-40s.

Kesselring launched the main part of his offensive against the British sector on the morning of February 3. The attack caused the 3rd Division to pull back from several forward exposed positions to strengthen their defenses. It was a long time before the ground lost in the division's sector was recaptured. Private Lundquist, in the midst of action, again noted conditions during the first ten days of February:

Shells are landing within our uncomfortable zone; a shell landed about 50 or 60 feet away from us as we were sitting here after finishing eating. One fellow in the infantry who was near the same house was in a foxhole and a shell landed almost inside the hole; put a piece of shrapnel through his helmet and badly wounded him. His legs were also sprayed with steel. On guard at 2100 to 2215 and saw a counterattack by the Krauts that was repulsed. What a sight a mortar barrage is. It's really something to see if you're not the receiver, and the machine-gun battles were fierce. Tracers were flying everywhere and explosions were rocking the ground all about as orange flame blossomed out under each shell.

Later they got a bead on our house and dropped mortars all around us though none actually hit the house. A wagon outside, about 15 or 20 feet from where we stood at the time got a shell right in the middle. The axle and one wheel were thrown up on the roof of the chicken house and we scattered right away. Three times big bombers went over this morning and bombed a hill in the distance. It was very unusual for large bombers to work the front. First bunch had 35 [planes], second one 38. They lost one and we could see it burst into flames and go down, looked as though all the men went with it too. Third bunch went over as I was writing here so I didn't see them.

An account of another action that happened about this time appeared in *The Wichita Daily News* in an article titled "Wichita Falls Officer Answers call for Artillery Assistance" by Daniel DeLuce, Associated Press correspondent. Dateline: At the Fifth Army Beachhead, south of Rome, February 3, publication delayed:

Maj. Walter E. Tardy of a tank destroyer outfit was sitting in a cold, flimsy shed which serves as his command post when the field telephone rang. The quiet, blond gunnery expert from Wichita Falls, Texas, recognized the voice of a wartime pal at the other end of the line. "Listen" said the caller, "the Krauts have been giving my boys fits. They've got observers in those towers [church steeples] in Cisterna and they're raising hell with air bursts and mortars. All we've got for cover is prayer. They can count every button on our coats."

Tardy said that was a tough situation. "It looks as if you need some help." He added. The voice on the other end brightened. "We'd sure appreciate a little sniping by those guns of yours." Tardy called one of his young battery commanders, Lieutenant Ambrose G. Salfen of Allon, Missouri, and gave him the assignment. "The enemy," he explained, "probably will lay down return fire immediately – fast ranging will be mighty important." Salfen picked out the likeliest spot in the exposed countryside with two observation towers sticking up out of the plain and rushed forward a couple of mobile field guns [M-10 TDs].

The enemy noticed the American artillery movement almost at once and tried to catch it with box-type firing. Tardy, watching from the low shelter of a stone wall was unhurt when an enemy shell landed on the other side. Salfen's guns were in action. The first American round missed. The second hit a roof to the left of the German observation post. The fourth went squarely through the observation post. In rapid succession five direct hits then were scored.

Switching to the right tower the American gunners poured in two shells. Enemy counter-fire however was increasing and landing near our gun carriers. A German mortar battery also opened up. His mission accomplished, Salfen ordered his men back to more concealed spots. There had been no casualties. "We used high-explosive delayed action stuff," Salfen said. "It's quite a sight. It bursts inside its target and snuffs it out like an egg. Boy the plaster and scrapple ooze out from every crack."

Battalion men continued to make the ultimate sacrifice. Tech Four Paul O. Blumberg (Corona, Long Island, New York) and Private First Class Emmanuel D. Lalla (Brooklyn, New York) from Recon Company were both killed in action on the beachhead on February 4. Two days later, Corporal Clelland C. Call (Valley Falls, Kansas) from C Company also met the same fate.

During most of the first half of February, Welch's platoon was in position in the vicinity of Isola Bella, firing on enemy positions. Welch wrote to his mother on February 10 and enclosed two *Stars and Stripes* articles:

> I just have time to scribble a few lines. I'm enclosing two clippings from the *Stars and Stripes*. The one article about the M-4s and M-10s is about us. Col. Hammack [Blackstone, Virginia] is the commanding officer of a tank battalion we always work with. Maj. Tardy is my battalion commander. Col. Hammack and I went to a rest camp for three days together and he really is a swell guy. Maj. Tardy is as good as they come. The kind of fighting they describe here is the best way to fight. It really is kind of fun.[54]

And the next day, February 11, 1944 he wrote:

> This particular part of the war continues to be very strange, that is hide and seek with both sides feeling each other out. The first few days were terrific. It was very good hunting, and we knocked off lots of Jerry tanks as well as killing lots of square heads [German soldiers]. The other day I lost one of my tank destroyers and unfortunately I was in it, fortunately no one was hurt. We dragged it back that night. I could sure use a Scotch and soda about now. Perhaps the frozen blood could start to course through my veins once again. It seems that I'm not warm unless I'm in my sleeping bag, so every time I get a chance I hit it real quick. It's one of those zipper affairs with three blankets in it. It's waterproof and warm as the devil. Home seems as far away as ever. I sometimes wonder if this thing will ever end.

Welch may have been referring to this same action that was also described in an undated hometown newspaper. It said that recently Welch went sniping for German tanks with armor-piercing ammunition. He had fired the deciding round into a German Panzer that was pointed out by Sergeant Nowak. When no other enemy armored vehicles showed themselves, Welch ordered Private Gilbert Van Elk (Bronx, New York) to reload the 3-inch gun and fire on a farmhouse. "Six Germans ran out of the building and successive rounds were used to kill them, sniper style."

Private Lundquist captured the details of mid-February this way:

> There were large-scale raids by Jerrys at night while I was in the sack; plenty of bombs and ack-ack all around us. Lots of artillery shells came whistling into the field next to us and I counted at least 20 duds. We always say they were "made in France," hinting at possible sabotage. Artillery is incessantly banging away never seems to stop. I started a dugout for shelter from flak at night. There are so many raids at night now that the flak comes down real thick. I dug a pretty good-sized hole though not so very deep. Next day I dug some more right after breakfast; lots of bombers over this morning and I counted 185 in the forenoon alone. All bombs were dropped on front-line targets, such as AA batteries, artillery, etc. The ground sure shook. Finished my digging today, deep enough to be able to sleep in but still not enough to sit up in and enjoy. Put my tent over the entrance to my "rat hole." It's keeping the rain out.

The previously mentioned ancient abbey of Monte Cassino was bombed and destroyed by the Allies on February 15, but this did not accomplish the expected breakthrough along the Gustav Line and it provided no relief for the beachhead. German defenses across Italy were so effective they were able to pull troops from the Cassino area to attack the Allies at Anzio. According to Donald G. Taggart's *History of the Third Infantry Division in World War II*, the 3rd needed more than 2,400 replacements to make up for losses incurred in less than a month on the beach. And the battalion report noted that recurrent cases of malaria were increasing and fatigue was taking its toll on men "constantly in alert positions." The battalion report also noted that:

> The enemy would attempt any trickery which he thought might have even a remote possibility of bagging some of our guns. In several instances he would, under cover of darkness, withdraw a knocked-out tank and substitute a live tank in its place. Close observation on the part of the infantry and our gun crews exposed this trickery and it has become the policy of this unit to set fire by shelling all enemy tanks knocked out. In another such instance it was found that the Kraut would re-man a knocked-out tank which had not been burned and use it as a pillbox.

On February 16, the Germans launched a second major offensive that had been personally approved by Hitler, called *Fischfang (Fish Catch)*. The ambitious plan was to break through the Allied outer defenses and drive a wedge between the two sectors of the beachhead. After recapturing Anzio and destroying the troops there, the Germans would use the town as a springboard to push the Allies back to Naples. By now there were as many as 120,000 German troops surrounding the beachhead. The Panzer forces against the Allies had also been augmented. One of those units, according to Wolfgang Schneider in *Tigers in Combat I*, was Schwere Panzer-Abteilung 508 (Heavy Panzer Battalion 508).[55] But by evening only two days later, Operation *Fischfang* was canceled, the Germans having lost more than 5,000 men killed, wounded, or missing and presumed captured; the Allies lost almost 3,500 men.

At 1000 on February 16, in the midst of this major attack, Welch's 1st Platoon B Company was credited with shooting down a German fighter, according to the unit journal. The next day, the *3rd Division Daily News* reported: "Five enemy tanks are known to have been knocked out by our tanks during the day, and the TDs shot down a Kraut plane." The aircraft was a Focke-Wulf 190. Not a very large target, the platoon downed it with their .50-caliber machine gun.

In the middle of this German offensive, the 601st rotated one officer, Lieutenant Otis R. Rogers, and 26 men back to the States. The Army permitted a limited number of combat-experienced officers and men to be sent back to the States on rotation.[56]

Once it became clear that the German attack had been suspended, members of A Company set out to retrieve their damaged destroyers. This could be accomplished only during the hours of darkness. Heading up this effort was Technical Sergeant Charles Phallen, assisted by Tech Five Willard E. Brooks (Richmond, Virginia). The men spent the night driving the battalion's T-2 tank retriever and successfully brought back four M-10s. It was just starting to get light and they were decoupling the T-2 from the last of the rescued TDs when the two men were hit by a 270mm shell from "Anzio Annie."[57] Tech Five Brooks was killed instantly and Technical Sergeant Phallen was severely injured. Phallen's evacuation trip to Naples was not without incident. Originally he was to have been placed aboard a British hospital ship, but the Luftwaffe bombed the ship and set it on fire. He spent some very uncomfortable time at the water's edge waiting to be carried to another Naples-bound ship.[58]

According to Josowitz, who made only a brief mention of this action, on February 19, two B Company platoons, one commanded by Lieutenant Thomas J. Kelly (Syracuse, New York) and the other by Welch, attacked and knocked out six German Panzers as they tried to take high ground overlooking a broken highway bridge called Ponte Rotto. They were in support of a company of Shermans from the 751st Tank Battalion, which lost two tanks.

Private First Class Robert P. Teff (Dorchester, Iowa) and Corporal Lawrence R. Bickford (Rochester Heights), both from A Company were also in action that day. Both were killed although the circumstances are not known.

A photo of the VI Corps Headquarters entrance at Nettuno shows the troops on the beachhead going underground. The tunnel led to the wine cellars of an *osteria* (tavern), appropriately called the *Osteria dell Artigliere* (Tavern of the Artilleryman). At this point, Private Lundquist was most concerned with his personal real estate as he dug his own underground headquarters. His diary entries from February 21–23 describe this:

I started to dig my hole deeper. Krauts have been throwing lots of shells around this area. There's a lot of our artillery around here so I guess that's what they're aiming at. Here I sat pecking away at the coal and clay floor right by my doorway when an air raid occurred, the third in less than 15 minutes so I just lay back and waited for all to be over. The ground shook when a bomb was dropped in a field next to these woods where the artillery had a battery of guns. I thought that was a little too close for comfort at the time but a second later one landed about 80 feet to the left rear of where I was sitting and all kinds of things were flying around. Matty's scout car [Private First Class Kenneth C. Mathewson, Oswego, New York] had all sorts of rips, tears and gouges in it from the fragments. Trees were sliced in half and one piece went right through a tree over a foot thick. Moved out after dark, [next day] dug this new hole twice as deep, three or four Jerry bombers just went winging over slowly, you'd think you could throw a grenade in the bomb bay. [The day after that] Decided to enlarge my boudoir this morning and put a top on it. Got it a little deeper and slightly longer but didn't get the top on what with all the ten-minute breaks I took. A Kraut ME-109 went over late in the afternoon. It was flying very slow and just lazily looking the country over. Ed Josowitz said "watch the birdie." I'll bet the guy has photos of every square inch of this area.

In a V-mail letter to his wife, Elizabeth, on February 21, Lieutenant Colonel Tardy thanked her for congratulating him on his promotion to lieutenant colonel and told her he "was a guest of one of my company commanders tonight for supper. Menu: soup, creamed chicken, cinnamon rolls, coffee, and Racquet Club Cigars. Hope the folks at home are eating as well." Most of the menu items had been salvaged and saved from C ration meals, except the cinnamon rolls, likely prepared by the company cook, and the cigars from someone's gift package from home.

Changes in command were taking place in the midst of the action. General Clark replaced General Lucas with General Lucian Truscott, the 3rd Infantry Division commander, on February 22 as commander of Operation *Shingle*. General Lucas had been judged to be not aggressive enough in failing to capture the high ground overlooking Anzio, the Alban Hills, after the invasion. He was made a scapegoat for the failure to move off the beachhead, but his performance was exonerated after the war. The US Army conducted an intensive study of Lucas' actions and concluded that by limiting Lucas' command to only two divisions he was not able to establish and maintain the beachhead and simultaneously seize the hills. Lucas died in 1949, never knowing the study's conclusion. General Truscott was succeeded as 3rd Infantry Division commander by an equally outstanding officer, Major General John W. "Iron Mike" O'Daniel.[59]

There were other changes as well. On February 24, Welch wrote home:

I don't know if I told you or not that I made 1st Lt. quite a while ago and am now sweating out my captaincy. If the war lasts until 1965, I'll probably make it. It's terrible weather here now I guess spring rain has set in. Progress is quite slow, but something big is about to break at any moment.

"Every house had been converted into a pillbox"

Despite apprehension concerning the timing of the next big German offensive, by the end of February things were settling into a routine. In anticipation of this German push, the Allies constantly reinforced the Anzio beachhead. It grew stronger every day. B Company, which had been on the front line for the five weeks since the landing, was now permanently assigned to a section of the beachhead at Isola Bella, just south of Cisterna. It was now integrated in direct support of the 15th Infantry Regiment, 3rd Infantry Division.

The beachhead in this section was on reclaimed marshland, one of Mussolini's pet agricultural reform and propaganda projects. These Pontine Marshes, infamous since Roman times as a breeding ground for malaria, had been drained with a series of canals which made the land suitable for farming, but terrible for tanks. Mussolini had settled the drained marshland with poor, northern Italian tenant farmers, giving them ownership of land and houses for the first time. Now these settlers had been transferred by landing craft to Naples, where they were abandoned to their fate, their dialect incomprehensible to most Neapolitans.

Winter rains caused the water table to rise and the marsh reasserted itself. Everything below a thin crust of soil became liquid. The resulting unstable surface restricted both German and Allied armor to the few roads, hemmed in by the canals. Generally flat, this reclaimed land had little natural defilade to conceal anything or anyone. The best cover, which was used by both sides, was provided by the abandoned farmhouses built for

Mussolini's resettlement program. They were built of stone and cement with half-meter thick walls and tile roofs. The houses were serial numbered, regularly spaced, and often had patriotic slogans painted on their walls. Each could be converted into a fortress and it was the tank destroyers' practice to lie in wait behind these houses for a target. The destroyers were used in pairs so they could cover one another's movements and perhaps catch the Germans in crossfire. In his memoir Sergeant Nowak wrote:

> We numbered the houses. We had numbers one, two and three; numbers four and five were in no man's land; and the Germans held houses six and seven. Every house had been converted into a pillbox, manned with machine-guns. One night I was outside the TD leading it out from behind one of our houses to maneuver into a firing position. I got spotted by the Germans who fired a round. It landed very close, but I ducked in time and jumped back into the tank uninjured. On another occasion, one of our houses was hit and ten soldiers were buried in the rubble. When we cleared the debris, one was dead.

The empty shells of these houses continued to be used even after they had been blown up. The Germans dug into the floors and built bunkers. Debris falling on top of them only provided additional protection from the shelling. Outbuildings, large baking ovens, and even straw and manure piles were similarly fortified.

Welch felt things were heating up. Whether or not he had some valid intelligence or had developed a sixth sense, he wrote his mother on February 26: "Things are pretty quiet over here now. I fear too quiet. One of these nights, all hell will break loose, but we're ready for them." He didn't have to wait long. His platoon kept up a constant harassing fire on the Germans. His four TDs lobbed more than 1,400 3-inch shells during the next three days. They shot at anything that moved and at anything they thought could conceal the enemy. Particular attention was focused on those enemy-held houses six and seven, which were being used as forward observation posts. The Wehrmacht was well dug in around them but their protection was limited. Welch reported that after one shelling, 14 enemy casualties were carried out of the rubble of one of the houses.

Opposite the 3rd Infantry Division and unobserved by Welch, Field Marshal Kesselring had been building up his forces for another attack. He had gathered seven under-strength divisions and some other troops ready to fling against this section of the dug-in US front line. The operation was called *Seitensprung (Affair)*.[60] Defending against this enemy force was the US 3rd Infantry Division with attached units.

Welch was part of this defensive force. He had sent one of his four TDs to the rear on February 29 for critical maintenance. The remaining three TDs were parked directly behind three of the ruined farmhouses. Welch was using one of the farmhouses as his forward observation post since it still had a partial second floor with a usable staircase.

Morning dawned cold, but dry: not raining for a change. The early edition of the *3rd Division Daily News* reported the division was experiencing several light attacks at three or four places in its sector, but it was not certain this was the expected major push. The strongest early attack was on the left flank where US paratroopers were supported by A Company of the 601st. Just to the right of the A Company were the 15th Infantry Regiment and B Company. According to Staff Sergeant Harper, the Germans started their attack by destroying the house behind which his TD was concealed.

By 0830 there could be no doubt that the Germans had launched a major offensive. Welch immediately called for the return of his fourth TD from the rear, but it was going to take a while. His other section of two tank destroyers, located some distance away, came under attack by five Mark VI Panzers and two self-propelled 88mm guns. One TD was caught out in front, exposed to the attacking Panzers. Tech Five Otto Aimone (North Bergen, New Jersey) and Private Frank F. Brown, Jr (Buffalo, New York) were in that TD, which took a direct hit. The tank destroyer was crippled, it couldn't move and it just sat there, a sitting duck. But the gun could still fire and so the men bravely made the decision not to abandon it.

Seeing what had happened, Tech Five Orville W. Freed (Ruffsdale, Pennsylvania), Corporal Henry E. Godlewski (Depew, New York), and Private William E. Alexander (Phoenix, Arizona), manning the second TD of the section, immediately maneuvered out from behind their house to cover their buddies in the crippled TD. In this exposed position the two TDs commenced a coordinated counterattack. It wasn't going to be easy. Although the second TD could maneuver, its traversing mechanism was crippled and its gun could be aimed only by moving the entire vehicle. They were in deep trouble and they knew it. To stay alive they needed to work together.

Aggressively, Aimone's immobile TD commenced a rapid and deadly fire. The only way to make the attacking Germans keep their heads down was to fire as many rounds at them as fast as possible. For a change, the radios in both the tanks were working and they talked to each other, carefully and quickly selecting targets.

Alexander, in the second TD, in making up for the crippled traversing mechanism, showed great skill as he maneuvered his TD into position and took multiple, coordinated shots. Luck was with them that day for neither TD was hit again. When it was over, both crews were credited with not only blunting this part of the German attack but knocking out two of the Mark VI Panzers and crippling the other three in the process. The mobile 88s retreated. The two TDs had fired so much during the fight that later they had to account for having expended more than 200 rounds of ammunition in less than two hours!

The Germans were not finished. It was only the end of round one. At 1005 the battalion command post relayed an order from division to Welch: "Enemy tanks [observed] moving south on Cisterna–Isola Bella road. Stop them cold and leave them burning. We are pushing through with some additional armor to regain ground lost."

"Welch's Boneyard"

Welch was in trouble for he still had only his one, very lonely, TD. His other section was too far away to give support and it was still dealing with its own attack. Wisely, he had parked himself behind the house with the usable staircase. The Germans were moving along the only road in the area that was slightly obscured by a continuous small rise running north and south. It was just high enough to shield the German column from ground level.

Welch, upon receipt of the battalion's order, raced up that usable staircase for a better view. This was extremely dangerous. Germany artillery had zeroed in on the house and multiple hits rocked what remained of the building. At the top of the stairs, Welch was astonished to see 16 German Panzers fast approaching the exposed American positions and threatening to overrun the infantry foxholes. He later described the moment in a letter home:

> I had just one of my tanks up front when an attack started. To my front were no less than 16 German tanks. I thought, "Well here goes Welch." Eight of them stayed in reserve and the other eight came on. The German tanks were going in a lateral direction and were about 2,500 yards away. I was pretty scared of the odds, eight against one, but took a chance anyway.

Dashing downstairs he ordered the TD to move out from the relative safety of the house and prepare to fire. He told the gunner where to aim a round and sent Sergeant Larson up the stairs to report the result. Running through the hail of German artillery fire, Larson dashed back down the stairs to report a direct hit on the lead tank. Welch ordered a reload and then ran back up the stairs where he was surprised to see the remaining seven Panzers were backing down the road. He seized the opportunity.

Running back downstairs, he passed Larson on the way back up. Welch ordered another round to be fired at about where he estimated one of the retreating tanks would be. They scored a direct hit on Panzer number five in the retreating German column. While three Panzers were able to back up, three were now trapped between the two knocked-out Panzers. With growing confidence, Welch and Larson kept up their tag team act, up and down the stairs, and directing the TD's firing. Welch's single TD picked off the three trapped Panzers. The result was five heaps of burning Panzer.

Later Welch wrote of his five kills: "4 were 30-ton one a 60-ton job." The 30-ton Panzers were Panzer IVs and the 60-ton a Panzer VI. He added he was "Lucky as hell but very proud" and that he "aged ten years." Later, after giving credit to his crew, he told a reporter for the *Anzio Beachhead News* the following November: "I won't forget running up and down those stairs to watch the shells hit home. Our rounds were clearing the heads of the infantry by about four feet as they sailed up over the rise."

All of this took place in one hour. At 1132 the battalion command post reported back to division that "those tanks at position F-993310 are burning. 1st Platoon B Company fired 40 rounds HE and APC [high-explosive and armour-piercing capped ammunition] at 4,000 yards." By this time Welch, running low on ammunition, was finally joined by his missing

175

TD. It was fortuitous that the second TD returned, as the Germans had not given up their attack for that day.

After a long unnerving lull, battalion radioed Welch at 1540 saying that two live German Panzers had sandwiched themselves in among the five he had knocked out earlier. He was ordered to attack. Together the two TDs, with Welch making use of that same staircase, successfully destroyed both new Panzers. The men, though remaining on alert, were relieved as it seemed the end of the German Panzer attacks for that day. Word went around that Welch's two sections of TDs had knocked out at least nine Panzers and the men dubbed the resultant junk heap "Welch's Boneyard."[61]

Welch's platoon was not the only one kept busy that day. A section of TDs from 3rd Platoon B Company was elsewhere on the road to Cisterna. Two destroyers, one commanded by Sergeant Harry J. Ritchie (Munhall, Pennsylvania), and the other by Sergeant John D. Christian (later promoted to second lieutenant, Sycamore, Georgia) were parked behind some buildings near Isola Bella. According to the "Brassing off Kraut" article, a Ferdinand (88mm assault gun) and a Tiger I attacked Sergeant Ritchie's building, getting within 300 yards. Three more Tiger I tanks 250 yards up the road were in support and another Ferdinand and Tiger I were in a farmyard about 250 yards east of the position. The gunner, Corporal James F. Goldsmith (North Bergen, New Jersey), tells the tale:

> Sgt. Ritchie ordered me to pull into open view around the corner of the building, and from this exposed position directed three hits onto the most exposed tank, it being about 550 yards up the road at that time, and knocked it out. We drew heavy armor-piercing and high-explosive fire from the other tanks, shells barely missing our destroyer by a few feet and fragments hitting us. We were exposed for about five minutes. Then Sgt. Ritchie ducked his head and shoulders below the turret and pulled back behind the house. When enemy fire

had ceased, Sgt. Ritchie had me pull out again, and from the same exposed position directed two rounds of AP shell that hit and bounced off the front armor of the Ferdinand 250 yards east of us. We again received intensive fire from the enemy tanks and shells were landing so close that fragments were coming through the open turret, one slightly wounding our gunner in the head when it hit our tank and damaging the counter-balance and .50 caliber machine gun mounted on the edge of the turret. We were again exposed to enemy fire for about five minutes. He ducked into the tank and we pulled behind the house again. We continued to fight throughout the day with our damaged gun.

As Sergeant Ritchie fired the second time, Sergeant Christian called him on the radio telling Ritchie to cover him. Christian pulled out from behind the house and shot five rounds at one of the Tigers and the Ferdinand that were pinning Ritchie down. He scored two hits on the Tiger and two on the Ferdinand. Only two men were observed getting out of the two Panzers. The building that Christian was behind was hit repeatedly; had they hit the destroyer instead he would have been put out of action. Later Christian pulled out again and scored a direct hit on another Tiger. That stopped the attack at that position. The unique aspect of this counterattack was that it was carried out with damaged equipment:

> Just prior to this action the sight extension bar on Sgt. Christian's gun had been bent and the only means he had to adjust fire was to stand completely exposed above the turret with field glasses. Two teeth were broken off the turret worm gear, and throughout the engagement the gun was traversed by jolting against the gun housing and jerking the traverse handle until the gears would mesh.[62]

Battles are fought incrementally. These two TDs were responsible for four more German Panzers. Between the two platoons on that single day, B Company got credit for 13 Panzers and they were quite justly credited with stopping the entire German Panzer attack. By now the German command realized their attack had stalled. It had been very costly for the Wehrmacht with more than 900 Germans killed, wounded or missing. The next day, the *3rd Division Daily News* reported the previous day's results from the entire division:

> The enemy's successes yesterday were limited to penetration of our left-flank to a depth of about 700 yards on a 1000-yard front, and the capture of our positions on the CISTERNA road immediately north of the ISOLA BELLA crossroad. The enemy lost nearly 200 prisoners, 14 tanks and a great number of killed and wounded, including many elements grouping for attack but unable to get underway due to our artillery fire.

One of the German armored units involved in the attack was the Schwere Panzer-Abteilung 508 (Heavy Panzer Battalion 508). In their February 29 after-action report they acknowledged that they had commenced an offensive against the 3rd Infantry Division at Isola Bella and admitted four Tigers were knocked out by enemy guns as well as reporting that several others were disabled by mines. They said their attack had been brought to a close by Allied heavy artillery, not crediting that M-10s could possibly get so many of their Panzers. They failed to take into account they had come under fire from their exposed under-protected flanks.

It was time for finger pointing and recriminations. Colonel General (Generaloberst) Eberhard von Mackensen, commander of the German 14th Army, was responsible to Kesselring for the attack. He explained to the field marshal the reason his forces failed to break through:

Our troop training was insufficient and these young replacements are not prepared to meet Allied troops in battle. This is the reason that the Army will not be able to wipe out the beachhead with the troops on hand. The tactics that have been employed to reduce the bridgehead gradually by concentrated attacks by several divisions cannot be continued. New tactics must be developed to enable us to meet the eventual large-scale enemy attack from the beachhead. We need adequate number of troops and supplies.[63]

The US Army awarded two Silver and 12 Bronze Stars to Welch's platoon for the day's successful counterattack. It might have even set some kind of battalion record.[64] Referring to this attack, Lloyd Clark wrote:

29 February was not a successful day for Traugott Herr [commanding general of the LXXVI Panzer Corps]. His formations had run themselves into the ground for very little territorial gain. He had no answer to the power of the Allied artillery and, when the weather cleared during the afternoon, Allied close air support. Even so, Herr continued his attacks through the night and during the following day, but he was only reinforcing defeat. By thrashing away at strong defensive positions in open country the Germans were made to pay for their folly.[65]

CHAPTER 8
WORLD WAR I ALL OVER AGAIN

"No rest, no break and no sleep"

The bloodiest day for the Germans on the Anzio beachhead was March 1, when more than 200 Germans were killed, 700 wounded, and 460 went missing, most presumed captured. The Schwere Panzer-Abteilung 508, down to 12 operational Panzers after the previous two days' attack, reported it had been reassigned to the 69th Panzer Regiment. On March 5, it was pulled out of the line and sent to Rome for rest and maintenance.

Private Lundquist recorded that:

Jerry dropped a bomb near the house down the road and later on there was lots of excitement as a troop of people came in. One woman was crying and held a baby that looked like it wasn't more than a few days old. There was mud all over the baby blanket and the mother's coat. People in the house were ordered to evacuate.

Eight Panzers sent down the main road from Cisterna to Isola Bella on March 2 fared poorly. Two were quickly knocked out and the others were halted by artillery strikes and attacked by the 15th Infantry. Welch's platoon was credited with knocking out one of the Panzers. The next morning the *3rd Division Daily News* reported that although "the enemy kicked up a fuss yesterday afternoon they quickly got slugged by our TDs and artillery, and withdrew with the assistance of a smoke screen." This failed action seemed to be the last gasp of Kesselring's February 29 attack. One result of the three-day offensive was the realization that German forces needed to be consolidated. There had been too many ad hoc formations as the result of the rapid buildup of Wehrmacht troops.

Moving Allied personnel back and forth to the beachhead was risky. The battalion's personnel officer, a warrant officer missing for more than a week, suddenly turned up, a victim of a shipwreck on his way back from Naples. Frank Wagner, Warrant Officer Junior Grade (Bronx, New York) had been on his way back to Anzio at the time. He had washed up on Ponza, an island about 18 miles off the coast and six miles behind enemy lines. He might have been captured had a British LCI not picked him up, unharmed, on February 28, after having spent two nights on the island. This story was in the battalion journal for March 4.

Panzer and infantry attacks were down, but the Germans continued to shell the entire area almost constantly during the day. Josowitz described the long siege as follows:

> The beachhead was a flat chunk of filled-in marshland, about ten miles wide and seven miles deep. It had no real harbor and every inch of it could be observed from the Kraut observation posts in the mountains behind Highway Seven. Kraut artillery in the hills around Cori and Velletri was out of the range of Allied guns but nothing was out of range for the

Krauts. There was no rear area or rear echelon on Anzio. Colonel Snyder's [3rd Infantry Division] MPs and their VI Corps brethren took a terrific shellacking. The bakery was hit; the hospitals were hit; the Anzio Express [a German railway artillery gun] had no conscience and showed no mercy! There was no rest, no break and no sleep except the sleep that comes with complete exhaustion. Thousands of rounds were fired at the Division Command Post at Conca and many of them scored direct hits. One 88mm passed clear through the thick stone wall of the castle headquarters and landed in the Division Surgeon's bed, and then it failed to explode. He couldn't speak for three days! If the DUKWs, affectionately known as "The Ducks," hadn't brought supplies into the beachhead in a never-ending flow, the Kraut might have pushed the invaders back into the sea. Those drivers went through hell to get their stuff ashore and they never turned back![66]

Foxholes and dugouts began to show the results of American ingenuity. There were gadgets of all kinds, everywhere. Small stills became the rage and the production of alcohol zoomed. [To supply the 601st, both Lundquist and Private First Class Mack I. Latz, of Recon Company (Atlantic City, New Jersey) admitted to having their own stills on the beachhead.]

Nobody wanted to go to the Rest Camp at Caserta because that involved a trip to the docks and exposure to the Anzio Express, to air raids and to submarines.[67] The 34th Infantry Division relieved the 3rd and then, the 3rd relieved the 34th but the 601st stayed on! There was never a dull moment on Anzio and after a while the horror of the place wore off and life became almost normal, in a gruesome sort of way. Soon there was everything on the beachhead, even a little VD, everything but daylight movement! And another guy got a post malaria telegram from home saying simply,

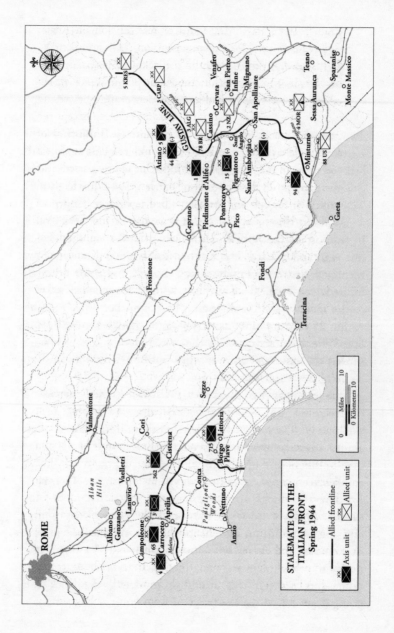

STALEMATE ON THE
ITALIAN FRONT
Spring 1944

Allied frontline

Axis unit

Allied unit

183

"Come home at once. Your health demands it." The weather was terrible but the food was magnificent. The cattle on the beachhead and the chickens and the pigs managed to run into shrapnel at the most opportune places. Fresh meat became a bore!

Two soldiers, Tech Five Eddie F. Buffkin (Fair Bluff, North Carolina) and Private Clarence L. Hamm (Marion, Virginia), both believed to be in A Company were killed in action in unrecorded circumstances on the beachhead on March 5, 1944. It is likely they were cut down by German artillery – an ever-present danger.

At about this time, C Company was in action near Conca in support of the 30th Infantry, when an 88mm shell killed one man and injured several other unidentified destroyer crew members. Staff Sergeant Buckley[68] (Lowell, Indiana), although injured, gave medical aid to the crew chief. He then carried him to the medical station through a hail of artillery fire "landing within 25 yards of him," as read his later citation for the Bronze Star. "He then reorganized the remainder of the crew and moved the destroyer into another position where its mission could be accomplished."

The importance of the ducks (DUKWs) to the entire Anzio operation cannot be overstated because the beach was so shallow. The Beachhead News singled them out, praising their ability to maneuver in an overcrowded harbor, and dodge dive-bombers and shell fire while going through the heavy smokescreen used to hide everything from the Germans. Keeping the ducks operating was the additional job of the drivers. At day's end when the runs between the supply ships and the ammunition and supply dumps on the beach were over, it was the driver who had to clean out the bilges and perform other maintenance. This task took at least three hours but without this attention to detail, the duck was going nowhere.

As time wore on, the beachhead started to resemble the Western Front of World War I. The Allies couldn't break out and the Germans couldn't break in. Field Marshal Kesselring paid a visit on March 23 to his troops surrounding the Anzio beachhead.[69] With the buildup by the Allies, German morale was sagging. Kesselring decided to postpone, and then later canceled, any further offensives.

Deep foxholes with connecting trenches had been dug as protection against the constant daylight bombardment. Up on the front line, the action happened at night so the daytime was the time for rest, sleep and cleaning weapons. There were no showers, little water except for drinking and making coffee and there was little personal hygiene. Letter writing during daylight greatly increased and that is why so many descriptions of the horrors of Anzio survive. In the rear, well there wasn't any rear at Anzio, everything could be seen and was exposed to German shelling.

Sergeant Nowak, who said he went two months without a bath, gave a detailed description of these early days in March:

The first five days of March we were still on the road to Ponte Rotto. The Krauts sent out patrols and tried some small-scale counterattacks, but they were all repulsed. I did some firing at Ferdinands[70] and other tanks, which had gone into hiding behind houses. We witnessed enemy infantry movement on a ridge not far away from a haystack which Stevenson [Sergeant Fred P., Ottawa, Illinois] and I used as an observation post. We must have been spotted because we got shelled. Stevenson got shell fragments in the anklebone and a piece ripped through my shirt and undershirt and stung me but did not pierce the skin. The stinging lasted about a week.

During the second week we did some firing at targets appearing on hillsides and on a bridge. We always drew counter-fire and had to withdraw behind a house. The shells coming in were 150mm; shell fragments pierced our water cans and cut up our tarp; a house was hit and rocks fell on top of the TD. Rain came down and made life miserable. The day before we left, eleven "Anzio Expresses" landed from 20 to 100 yards away. The holes were so big that I stood in one with my hands stretched overhead and still couldn't be seen from the TD.

Wintry weather, Welch noted, was a huge factor in early March, even as the standoff continued. He noted the lack of action in his next several letters:

The weather has been terrible of late rain, sleet and wet snow. I'm half frozen at all times, but don't seem to be any the worse for it. Things are going quite slowly here; it looks like a long war. If they'd empty some of the USO [United Serviceman Organization] clubs back there, it might speed it up. The weather continues miserable, cold and rain and consequently I'm always in the best of humor (joke). Without exaggeration, the mud is eight inches deep, so we don't do much running around with the tanks. Things still go very slowly so don't look for a quick end to this thing.

"The largest self-supporting POW camp in the world"

Welch does not dwell on beachhead conditions in his letters home during the rest of March:

Please excuse the writing, but I had the little fingers of my right hand hit by a shell fragment and it is all bandaged and I find it extremely hard to write. So far, I've knocked out eight German tanks on the beach with my platoon. As for the Purple Heart, it's really nothing to get excited about; you know an awful lot of people have them. I don't think I'll care much about sleeping for a month; my habits are pretty regular now. I'm able to go to bed at two or three and get up at five with no trouble. I've enclosed some leaflets that the Germans send over the lines; we all get quite a kick out of them. I wonder at times what they think of us, expecting us to believe such rot. Things are still quiet and not much action but the usual shelling.

German propaganda efforts were extensive. According to Staff Sergeant Harper, leaflets were shot into the lines by mixing them with real mortar shells. In all Welch sent home nine different leaflets and Sergeant Nowak sent even more. Cartoonist Bill Mauldin had this to say about them:

> Propaganda leaflets are used by both sides. Because we seem to be winning the war, ours are generally more convincing, but I think theirs sometimes show more ingenuity. They know our fondness for comic strips and often illustrate their leaflets. What these pamphlets lack in truth they make up in reader interest. I remember one that arrived in Anzio one morning. It was so well drawn and attractively colored that a lot of guys risked their necks to scramble out and get copies. It has something to do with a profiteer and an infantryman's wife in America. The continuity was awkward, but the pictures were spicy and guys were hard up for reading matter.[71]

Around this time, Axis Sally, the infamous Nazi propaganda radio star, declared that Anzio had become the largest self-supporting prisoner of war camp in the world. Sally was on what the Germans called "Jerry's Front Radio." Because Sally could be picked up on homemade radio receivers, she was more listened to than the Allied broadcasts, which required better radios. Sally often read out the names of those wounded or captured, including Lieutenant Vargo of the 601st. She broadcast four times a day, her big show being at 1830. It featured American records, talk and the latest news. The men really liked the American music she played and paid no attention to the propaganda. Sergeant Allen H. Bowman (McHenry, Maryland) recalled that she often told them to "give up or die." Lieutenant Jack H. Card noted that "We got most of our information from Axis Sally;" but Captain Rydal L. Sanders was more direct. He said that he "listened to that 'Bitch' Axis Sally for the music and didn't pay any attention to what she was saying." Unsurprisingly for Anzio listeners, one of her favorite songs was *Between the Devil and the Deep Blue Sea*.[72]

Replacements continued to be sent to the beachhead and, sometime in March, Lieutenant Robert A. Maynard (Cleveland Heights, Ohio) arrived on the Anzio beachhead to join B Company 601st. He recalled that "on the way from the ship to the battalion at Anzio, the jeep driver was hit. The Lt. [perhaps Lieutenant Welch picking up the new guy for his company] in the jeep took the wheel and drove calmly to the aid station." Sometime shortly later, Maynard was captured by US forces and as he did not know the password, they thought he was a German in a US uniform. He was held for three hours until Lieutenant Colonel Tardy identified him.

In the latter part of March, 601st men continued to die. Private Toney T. Sandoval (Roy, New Mexico) died on March 21 and Private First Class Charles M. Hird (Providence, Rhode Island) on March 23. Details of their sacrifice are not known, but with the amount of German artillery raining down on the beachhead, it is amazing that there were not more casualties.

Private Lundquist noted: "After March 25th the days merge into a fog. We were a reconnaissance outfit so that on Anzio they had no use of us in our normal capacity so they used us on observation post duty." He stopped his diary on that day and his remaining observations used in this book were written later.

The 601st was finally pulled out of the line for a break on March 26 and Welch noted "I'm back for a rest now after 65 days of continuous fighting. It sure feels good." *The History of the 15th Infantry Regiment in World War II* describes the Anzio beachhead and has this to say about the changing conditions:

> The Anzio Beachhead was unique amongst all the battlefields of the world. In this tiny shell-torn strip of land, hemmed in on three sides by the enemy and on the fourth by the sea, things were done with characteristic casualness and abandon. A rest camp was established just a few thousand yards behind the lines where individual men and entire companies were sent for two-day rest periods. They were served hot food and furnished with clean clothing. Showers were available and right under the Kraut's nose the men could listen to their favorite swing music, see a motion picture or play baseball. A daily paper was established well within range of enemy artillery. Many a soldier was baptized in the waters of the Tyrrhenian Sea when chaplains of various units offered to perform these services. At Easter time, services were held in the open fields for our men and broadcast to the enemy in the German language over loudspeakers.

Corporal Borriello also describes the conditions on the beachhead in an open letter he sent to his local USO. His mother saved a copy of it:

> Your letter, or rather paper, was sent to my home address and forwarded to me. I received it two days ago and as this is the first chance I've had to write, I'll let you in on what I can. The radio has informed us that our division is officially on the Anzio beachhead enhancing our glory, I think it said. While

no one could ever accuse the GI of being prima donnish, and nobody here'd ever say, "enhancing glory" is any man's glamour job, we do like to read about ourselves.

The news that we are officially here (with the eyes of the world upon us) first reached us via radio and our division news sheet. Yes, we have an Anzio newspaper. It's just one mimeographed sheet with no pin-up girls or comics, but it brings the outside world into places where it's missed most. Even the Krauts had us on the air one night. According to a guy who knew a guy who hears the nightly snow job from the Nazi propaganda factory, the famous soft-voiced gal in Berlin [actually Rome] welcomed us to Anzio and asked the boys how they liked it here. Well, she's getting her answer, mitt guns on.

Did I say doughnuts? No, but I've been thinking about them all day. Probably the strangest secret weapon buried away in a beachhead hiding spot is our division's battery of three Red Cross doughnut machines. I've never seen them myself and I hope the same goes for the Krauts, but somewhere in the area our three trusty machines are grinding out "holes" for doughboys. We don't get many of them but it's the nearest thing to mother's kitchen that Italy's got to offer.

And speaking of mother's kitchen, the happiest boys of the week were those few fellows who finally took off to the States on rotation for a month's furlough. The percentage is awfully small. There's not much chance of me being on the list for some time to come. But somehow it helps just to touch a guy about to sail west over the Atlantic.

What's it like on our beachhead? Frankly, without revealing any secrets, it's quite often like a night in hell. But then will come a quiet spell, and a flirtatious tank tagged with the name "Fertile Myrtle" will rumble noisily down the road, or one of my buddies will dig up a forgotten bottle of vino from some muddy cellar, and the world sits firmly on four legs again. Then there are those wonderful days when clear skies open up the way for our American big bombers. From our grandstand seats, we watch the show, wave after wave of them, horribly beautiful as they fly over us to pound the Krauts in the rear, where it hurts. Those airmen are never wholly real to us slugging it out with the mud on the ground. They are part of another world, winged angels or devils, depending on whether they're hitting for or against you.

Once out of the line, everyone and everything was checked and double-checked. On March 28, Lieutenant Colonel Tardy and another officer were sent to the 93rd Evacuation Hospital with yellow jaundice. Major Hinman took over the battalion until Lieutenant Colonel Tardy returned in May. In his next several letters, Welch reflected on the quieter conditions on the beachhead:

By comparing dates with the paper and this letter, you can still see it's fairly quiet here. Somebody is waiting for something, what, I've no idea. Long ago I've given up speculation. While in this position, I've had a chance to clean up my tanks as well as wash my clothes, which I haven't done for ages. In fact, I haven't changed for two months. I painted my tanks (inside) a brilliant white with a sickly blue floor, which I had originally intended to be battleship gray. However, not being very familiar with paint mixing, I had to use what came out of my futile attempts to create a perfect blend. I'm seriously considering putting running water, inside toilet and floor lamps in as well as a small fan. In that case, I'm afraid I would have to take the gear and ammunition out, and I heartily like that idea. I hardly think it would appeal to the general.

My record stands, on the beach, at eight German tanks knocked out and one Focke-Wulf 190 shot down, which

I believe is quite an impressive record, at least I'm proud. One other feature, which I enjoy, and is quite novel, is knocking down houses. All houses here are made of stone. Germans have, or had, a habit of putting machine guns in the windows, and this holds our infantry in check. They'd call for help, so I'd send one of my Tank Destroyers or House Destroyers, depending on your point of view, and proceed to demolish it. I've worked out a technique, which works quite well. I put some AP, which is a solid piece of steel, in the corner, which shatters the foundations and then put an APC [steel nose and a high-explosive body], right thru the middle. This shot goes thru the wall and explodes inside. The poor house falls like a deck of cards. It probably took three months for Mussolini to build these quite imposing houses, but I can tear it down in three minutes. I get nothing but the utmost pleasure out of doing this; I suppose it's some sort of a complex. In any event, any sector which I'm placed in these days looks like the ruins of Pompeii, which I've always thought was a poor job of destruction, in comparison.

It's absolutely impossible to stir around here in the daytime. The ground here is like a pool table, it's that flat. You must realize that we hold a piece of ground 8 miles deep by about 14 miles wide. The Kraut, as usual, holds all the high ground, and can see every move we make. This naturally necessitates all movement of supplies and troops to be done at night. It really is a tremendous job. I actually sweat blood trying to move my four tanks into a position on a pitch-black night. Until lately I've been sleeping in a silo. I understand corn liquor is made from the leaving or drainage from a silo. I therefore get a cheap drunk every night and forget about the war. Yes – Yes!

Steven Zaloga wrote that by the end of March, Allied VI Corps had what amounted to six full divisions on the Anzio beachhead and the German 14th Army was significantly outnumbered. There were artillery duels and small raids but no more major attacks and no territory was exchanged. US commanders started to refer to this as "the big war of small battles." It had settled into trench warfare, reminiscent of World War I. In addition to conventional weapons, antipersonnel butterfly bombs were also used. They were bombs that popped open to release many smaller antipersonnel bomblets. From March until the breakout that came in May the Allies and Germans suffered about 10,000 more casualties each. Further, the marshy land bred diseases, recurring malaria and trench foot. The Allies, according to Zaloga, suffered more than 37,000 non-combat-related casualties.

As troop numbers increased, equipment and supplies on the beachhead built up as well. Chaos had to be avoided. Allen described the ingenious and efficient manner of loading and unloading ships that was used:

> The Fifth Army staff devised a unique procedure to increase the amount of supplies unloaded across the Anzio beach. Two-and-a-half-ton trucks were loaded at Naples, and then backed into the LSTs. After they reached the beaches at Anzio, the trucks would simply be driven off and dispatched immediately to the supply dumps. Each LST had been spread loaded in Naples with Class I (food), Class III (fuels) and Class V (ammunition) supplies so the loss of an entire ship would not seriously reduce supplies in any particular category. Each truck carried only one class, so that it needed to go to only one dump in Naples and one dump in Anzio. As soon as the LSTs were unloaded, empty trucks, which had been standing by would be driven back on board the craft head first, after which they would be returned to Naples.[73]

According to Staff Sergeant Harper, the 601st sent its own trucks to Naples and loaded them in the manner described above to ensure the battalion had sufficient ammunition.

Sergeant Larson sent a long letter from the beachhead:

> The Jerries will throw everything, including the kitchen sink at us. These Jerries are determined and shrewd fighters. The biggest mistake one can make is underestimating them. At close range they are very good gunners but at long range we're better. Their weapons and equipment in general are very good. Their machine guns and machine pistols purr almost like a motor, shooting from 900 to 1,000 rounds per minute. Since ours are much slower we have no trouble distinguishing which is which during daylight or darkness. Their artillery isn't very accurate, and in the tanks you have little to worry about from that source anyway unless you get a direct hit, which isn't very likely. One of our tanks suffered a direct hit from about 150 meters. It knocked out the tank, concussion knocking off bolt heads in the tank, shattering the dash, etc., but outside of shock none of the crew was hurt. But it is quite nerve-wracking to have them dropping all around you and you have to fight against your better judgment to keep from moving the tank and exposing yourself. We're under constant artillery fire but suffer little from it. Our worry is direct fire of their 77s and 88s. When their tanks attack they just cover the area ahead with the APs firing as fast as they can. We've learned from them that the one that can get the mostest there with the firstest is the one that's most likely to keep moving. Their Nebelwerfer (rocket) is demoralizing but not very accurate. But they sure can cover an area with it. A mortar shell dropped in the turret of one of our tanks and wrecked things pretty well. That's one way that the M-4s [Shermans] have the advantage over us, with their turret cover. We've had small losses in our battalion here in proportion to the damage we've inflicted.
>
> Much of our time in combat is spent doing nothing, just waiting for something to happen. And when it comes it's

usually sudden and unexpected. When things are real hot it is almost impossible to leave the tank so we eat, sleep, and live in it. During quieter times we get into a house or stable, if habitable or just a dugout. But the tank soon becomes a part of you, and the only place you feel safe is inside it. Here at the front we get two hot meals a day in our outfit. Our commanding officer says if we can sweat it out up here 24 hours a day, the cooks can sweat it out for the short time it takes to bring us hot chow. They come up before daylight in the morning and after dark at night. No traffic can move anywhere within three or four miles of the front during daylight.

April in Italy can bring the best weather and this April was no exception. On April 1, Welch began a series of letters to his mother and older sister over the next ten days, perhaps out of boredom. The men had time to reflect on their conditions, combat and life in general. Welch, now a seasoned professional, reflects in these excerpts the changes that often take place when ordinary citizens become warriors. "Kill or be killed" hardens into a philosophy of death, perhaps disturbing to those at home, but which is presented with innocent candor here. After this spate of letters, Welch was not heard from again for a month!

One day is like the next and March is like April and the other ten are monotonously the same. The weather is really shaping around to be fairly nice. Spring is to be noticed. Flowers, of some kind, are everywhere. The shells gouge into the fields until there is no shape or pattern anywhere. Nowhere can you see a house in good condition, just piles of rubble. I happened to be looking at a big storehouse when it was hit by a big shot. It knocked it completely to the ground. I think that if that happened to a few houses in the States, it might wake a few people up to the fact we're at war. We captured a cow, but no one knew how to milk it. After fooling around awhile old Tom [Welch] got it to work. We had milk for the first time in a year. Every night I take one of my tanks and sneak down to within 400–500 yards of the German lines and shoot the hell out of them with a 50 cal. machine gun. It's the best sport of the war. They don't know what it is, or where it's coming from.

It's now 0500. In 30 minutes I'm going out on a mission to kill some Krauts. I'm taking my four tanks up to within 300 yards of the German lines and fire 25 rounds per gun as fast as we can point blank. This is my specialty only the last time I did it, I walked back. My command tank got hit and I had to burn it up so the Kraut wouldn't get it, Oh Dear! Another $75,000 shot. On the way back we captured a prisoner but we had to shoot him. He pulled a gun, and it's a question of whether I got him with my pistol or one of my men who emptied his tommy gun (50 rounds) into him did. Anyway he looked like a sieve and I got a nice souvenir [a Luger]. A person really gets callous to death here. The other day we were firing on a house full of Kraut and when we had almost knocked it flat, 14 Krauts came out with their hands up. I stopped firing right away, but one of my other guns didn't. One of his shells landed right in the midst of them and killed eleven. We got the other three, and I've never seen anyone so scared. They thought we were going to shoot them. They were half-right cause I almost did.

According to Jeffrey Clarke (one of the authors of *The US Army in WWII*), April 9, Easter Sunday, was a very quiet day. He quotes from a Lieutenant F. Eugene Ligget, a forward observation officer with the 157th Infantry Regiment of the 45th Infantry Division:

On Easter Sunday I was up with the infantry in their trenches next to no-man's land, the Germans were on their side of it, about 300 feet away. A rather unusual thing happened. The Germans were not shooting at us; they were acting a little strange in that they were crawling back and forth to men in other trenches or holes. Before we knew what they were doing, we shot several of them with rifles. After capturing one or two, they told us what was happening and we quit shooting them. Because it was Easter Sunday, they were given a liquor ration and had orders not to shoot at us.[74]

The battalion's monthly report for April, reflecting Welch's attitude in previous letters, goes on to say this:

Morale of personnel remained on a rather low level due to long periods of inactivity. Successful attempts were made to improve these standards by showing movies, [trips to the] Caserta rest camp facilities for a limited number of men, and a regular system of rotation of companies in positions. Due to the regular shifting of positions, equipment has been available for better and more regular maintenance and the condition of vehicles and guns is considered excellent.

"It looked like a Kraut tank on account of the bogey wheels"

In the middle of April, around the 12th, Lieutenant Welch was told to report to battalion headquarters. Generally it is not a good thing for a junior officer to be summoned to the battalion command post: a summons usually imparts bad news. One wonders what went through Welch's mind after hearing the radio operator blare out: "Hey Lieutenant, you're wanted at battalion right away." In this case it was good news.

At the command post Welch was told to take his two best crews to Naples to pick up a new tank destroyer for testing.

One crew was Sergeant Nowak's and it comprised Corporal Joseph L. Irving (Chicago, Illinois), Corporal Vincent J. Macri (Brooklyn, New York) and Tech Four Lloyd E. "Snuffy" Callahan (Montague, California).

Sergeant Nowak later wrote that the evening trip aboard ship on April 17 to Naples was no pleasure cruise. Seasick, he threw up at least five times during the nine-hour voyage. The next morning they disembarked at Pozzuoli and found a temporary bivouac. The new TDs had not yet arrived so the men had to hang around and wait. They made a few trips to Naples and were given $50.00 each "portal pay." Meanwhile Welch tracked down the new TDs and made other arrangements.

After a few days, Welch hopped on a flight to Algiers for a briefing from the 1st Tank Destroyer Group, which was headquartered there. He left Sergeant Nowak in charge, who later wrote "Lt. Welch proved to be a good egg and let us go whenever we wanted to as long as we did not get into trouble."

There was a huge Luftwaffe air raid over Naples on the morning of April 23. That afternoon, two of the new TDs were picked up, experimental models that carried the designation T-70 (when operational, the T-70 designation was changed to M-18, nicknamed "Hellcat"). Nowak recalled during the first five days with the T-70 they got in a lot of firing practice. They tried the gun out on some Italian pillboxes and found it effective, although there was a problem: the gun's recoil knocked the sight off target making it necessary to re-lay (reset) it each time.

The T-70 disappointed Nowak and the others. It was lightly armored and they judged the 76mm gun not as good as the 3-inch gun on the M-10. It traveled too fast and its gasoline engine was a potential fire hazard. Adding insult to injury, Nowak said, "it looked like a Kraut tank on account of the bogey wheels."

After the tests were over, Welch was given a special R & R pass and as he recalled, "I spent ten days on the Isle of Capri.

This is strictly a smooth place. Very continental, with sand beaches, blazing sun, blue sea, ah war is hell. I'm now back in the mines."

For the two crews, their nice break ended May 6 when they transferred to the "Texas Staging Área" for the trip back to Anzio. It was a huge open space near the island of Nisida in the Bay of Pozzuoli, to the northwest of Naples. Sergeant Nowak recalled: "We got to Anzio on the 8th and on the following days we exhibited the T-70s to units of the 3rd Division and fired into the sea for the benefit of generals from VI Corps." Battalion records list a Captain Wilson, likely from the 1st Tank Destroyer Group based in Algiers, accompanied the men and the two T-70s (M-18s) to the beachhead. During this time, the T-70s fired 27 test rounds.

While Welch and his crews were in Naples, the war on the beachhead raged on. B Company rotated in and out of the line, providing direct and indirect fire on a wide range of locations with GI nicknames such as Belleau Woods, Borgo Caruso, the 88 Park, Pink Avenue, Monaco, Kraut, and Pillbox. From April 14 to 30, the company expended more than 4,600 rounds of ammunition. At least one soldier, Corporal Philip J. Turano (Houston, Texas), was killed on April 23, 1944. Like so many others the circumstances were not recorded. Sergeant Colprit with 2nd Platoon B Company described some of the actions in which he and his best friend Tech Four Joseph "Tommy" Thomas (Campbell, Ohio) were involved. He grouped his comments under topic headings:

Rescuing Wounded: Once we were called to rescue two wounded men from a house in no-man's land. Lt. Bell and I entered the house and found the two men plus a German soldier. We put one man into the tank and the other on a mattress across the back of the tank. As we turned down the road Tommy stopped the tank and said to Lt. Bell you had better come down here. In front of the tank was an infantry officer with his 45-pistol out saying "You are not going to leave us." We had to explain to him we had two wounded men aboard and that we would be coming back to support them during the night.

Scavenging Used Parts: The electrical device that fires the 3-inch gun had failed. A Company had a tank that had a track blown out in no man's land and when it was dark Tommy took three or four tools and I took a Thompson machine gun. While Tommy was in the tank with only a screwdriver and wrench, I thought the sound was as if he had a sledgehammer hitting an anvil. No one was as scared as I was. Our own artillery shells were only 20 feet over our heads with that fluttering sound that made you think it had your name on it. They were hitting only about 200 feet beyond us. Our mission was successful.

The General's Orders: We had a position at a large farm called Isola Bella when the enemy attacked across a field and one of their tanks was shooting at our infantry. As I looked through my field glasses all I could see was the turret as the body of the tank was behind a slight hill. I estimated the range as 2,200 yards and started firing. About the third round the tank started burning. Just about that time General "Iron Mike" O'Daniel came running out of the house and ordered us to fire in another direction at two other tanks he had seen. Before I moved the tank I looked through glasses. I said those are ours Sir.

We got a tank: One of our tanks saw an enemy tank about a mile away so I pulled out to fire on it. The German tank turned his gun and fired and the shell sheared the hatch cover hinge right off. It did not take him long to back behind the house and call for help. We were 3,800 yards away. The sight on our

3-inch gun was only graduated to 3,100 yards so I had to raise the gun above that and started firing. We fired 33 rounds and 11 hit and some penetrated. Lt. Salfen (B Company commander) called on the radio and said "Good Going!"

While he was away from Anzio, Welch did not write home. When he returned, he tried to make up for it with a couple of letters. With one of them he enclosed an aerial photograph. Given to him by the US Army Signal Corps, the photograph showed Welch's Boneyard, the hulks of the burned-out Panzers, a destroyed TD and some of the ruined houses. Pockmarked fields show the extent of artillery shell damage. Sergeant Nowak also remembered the photo and remarked on it in his memoirs. Welch added:

I'm back on the beach now, and all set to go again. This next push will be the big one and with a little luck we ought to clear it up before long. We are facing now a great many Italians, who are still loyal to Mussolini, but we can kill them just as easily as Germans, and when we finish with them, they will wish they had quit with the rest of them.

While conditions improved on the beachhead, every day men were still dying. Since the landing, the Allied VI Corps suffered almost 30,000 combat casualties (4,400 killed, 18,000 wounded and 6,800 missing) and 37,000 non-combat casualties. German losses amounted to 27,500 (5,500 killed, 17,500 wounded and 4,500 missing). Spring was now in full bloom and Welch's letters to his mother became more optimistic:

It sure is beautiful here, and I hope it's the same at home. The sun is hot with a fair breeze and I'm sitting on my tank in shorts writing this. We made a crystal set out of razor blades and wire. With the earphones from our tank radio we picked up High Mass from St. Peter's in Rome. It was really quite amazing. If I were home I'd play 27 holes of golf. Things are about to pop over here, so my mail will be pretty slow for a while. So don't worry if you hear from me infrequently.

And things did pop. Operation *Diadem* was launched on May 11, a big day for the Allies and the start of a massive attack on Monte Cassino and the Gustav Line. The honor of taking the ruined abbey was given to the British Eighth Army and the exiled Polish Legion under Lieutenant General Wladyslav Andres, commander 2nd Polish Corps. When Cassino fell on the 17th the Germans fell back to the Hitler Line located in the mountains northwest of the abbey.

In preparation for the breakout from Anzio, General O'Daniel devised an innovative way to move men across the battlefield. In the second week in May, crews from the battalion went to the 3rd Division training area on the beachhead to test the idea of "battle sleds." The sleds consisted of two trains of six sleds, each pulled by tracked vehicles with one man to a sled. The heat, dust and diesel exhaust from the vehicles made for such an unpleasant ride that the concept was abandoned mid-way through the eventual breakout.

Lieutenant Colonel Tardy returned from the hospital on May 13 to reassume command of the 601st. Due to the lack of German activity and his well-trained battalion, he had been given extra time off to recover more fully from yellow jaundice and extreme fatigue. Meanwhile, the 3rd Platoon B Company's four TDs were quite active between May 13 and 16. They expended more than 1,400 rounds of ammunition to soften up the German line prior to the coming breakout. This intense activity was an effort at acclimatizing the Germans to a lot of firing so that when the actual pre-attack shelling took place, it would not seem unusual. According to Zaloga, "A few tanks would rush forward, blast off some ammunition against German positions and then pull back. After a few weeks of this, it became routine and the Germans attributed it to the stir-crazy Americans having nothing better to do with their tanks."[75] One of 601st Recon Company's men, Sergeant Kenneth H. Stone (Groveton, New Hampshire) was killed on May 15, 1944.

The Germans fully expected an Allied breakout. According to Wolfgang Schneider, by May 21 elements of the German 508th were southeast of Latina near Genzano, Velletri, and Cisterna. Two days later they attacked across the Cisterna–Latina railway embankment, claiming they had destroyed 15 Shermans but that Corporal (Feldwebel) Nagel's Tiger was destroyed. The 508th reportedly had at that time 45 Panzers.

As final preparations for the big Allied breakout and subsequent push to Rome were being made, the US 894th Tank Destroyer Battalion was given three of the new T-70s (M-18s), assigning them to its Recon Company to take advantage of their high speed. The remaining two T-70s stayed with B Company 601st. In addition, a spare M-10 destroyer was assigned to each of the 601st companies as a ready replacement.

Sergeant Nowak described the final preparations for the breakout: "On the night of the 21st we moved into position for the attack. Roads were clogged with vehicles, tanks, TDs, and troops. Lieutenant William T. Bowman's TD (Waltham, Massachusetts) struck a mine in a friendly minefield and so did a Sherman tank. Both blew up and burned fiercely."

In the midst of all this, Welch sent letters to his sister and his mother.

By the time you get this, I should be well on the way to Rome. Penny says I'll summer on the Lido di Roma. Needless-to-say I've managed to find some refreshment on the beachhead. Some of it we made ourselves out of canned sweet corn. Lovely stuff, I'm thinking of making it professionally.

CHAPTER 9
BREAKOUT FOR ROME

"It was a weird, terrifying night"

Final preparations were now complete for the long-awaited Anzio breakout. Expectations and hopes were high. But there were complications. General Mark Clark, knowing of the impending invasion of Normandy, wanted to capture Rome before the Allied landing, which would doubtlessly overshadow the liberation of "The Eternal City." But who was to have that honor? There was competition between his Fifth US Army and the British Eighth Army: both wanted to be the first into the city. Suddenly these and other questions became moot as British General Sir Harold Alexander, the theater commander, gave the order: the primary objective was to cut off the German retreat from Cassino along Highway Six; Rome was a secondary objective.

The beachhead breakout, codenamed Operation *Buffalo*, started before dawn on May 23. The troops headed for Highway Seven, the ancient Via Appia, with Cisterna as the first objective. Although two British divisions were assigned to the corps, it was largely an American show. Sergeant Nowak's description of the initial breakout is typically precise: "An artillery barrage started at 0545 in the morning and at 0615 the infantry attacked and jumped off. Chateau Woods was the first objective and was taken the first day. The tanks, TDs and infantry worked nicely together. Highway Seven was cut that evening." Sergeant Colprit added: "On that day with the artillery and the bombs dropped by a fleet of Allied planes, a clear day turned into a misty day. Some of the planes took direct hits; engines, wings, men and gasoline streamed down and were on fire. It was a terrible sight."

It was costly too. The 3rd Infantry Division lost 955 men killed and wounded by the end of the day, the largest number of casualties suffered by any US division in a single day during World War II.[76] Almost 90 tanks and TDs were put out of action. This was despite the fact that Field Marshal Kesselring believed an attack would come from the western edge of the beachhead or perhaps at the mouth of the Tiber River, Rome's port, and had deployed his troops accordingly.

Although the Germans were expecting a breakout, they were largely unprepared for it to come in the Cisterna area; nevertheless, they put up stiff resistance. Tech Five George M. Beal (Highlands, North Carolina) from A Company 601st was killed. One of B Company's T-70s was damaged and over in C Company the acting company commander, Lieutenant Richardson, was injured and had to be replaced. Josowitz describes the harrowing night of May 23/24:

> It was a weird, terrifying night. Everybody fired at anything that moved. Radio communication was out! Ration and gas trucks and jeeps wandered all over the countryside, through minefields and, in many cases, through enemy positions. More than one ration detail got to the destroyers in the morning only to find the water and gas cans full of bullet and shrapnel holes.

According to the unit journal, part of B Company was in support of the 15th Infantry's Task Force Paulick. This was commanded by the same Captain Paulick who had been with the 601st in North Africa and the early days of the Italian campaign before he was transferred to the 15th. Sergeant Colprit described what happened the next day:

> The 24th of May, is a day I shall never forget. We started the day hauling ammunition to an infantry platoon that needed it badly. Our orders were to drive toward Cisterna until we saw two GIs in a ditch and then to give them the ammunition and get out of there. Returning to our position an enemy tank was firing unseen on our infantry from in the woods. I thought that if I could get into the house across the road and upstairs I might be able to see this tank and get the first shot in. In crossing the road the tank fired a tree [level] burst and a small fragment hit me in the butt. A medic put a bandage on it. When I felt pain in my bladder area I knew where that fragment was. Being alone I was afraid that no one would find me so I got up and started walking toward my tank when I started to pass out. On the way to the ground, I hollered to my tank driver Tommy [Tech Four Joseph Thomas].

In the US Army Heritage and Education survey Staff Sergeant Robert C. McElroy, C Company (Lexington, Virginia) commented on an event during the capture of Cisterna:

> I did see one case that sickened and infuriated me; it was on the breakout from Anzio and I was leading my TD platoon as a S/Sgt. (no officer was available) and the infantry I was supporting had been pinned down and shot up etc. When I saw that the problem came from the Cisterna

stronghold we moved in killing men and capturing 120 of them. After disarming them and lining them up to start them on their way to our rear, the infantry commander did not control his men and one came over with a tommy gun and started killing. I turned my gun on him and my men followed my lead and turned all four of our TD 3-inch guns on the infantry which quieted them down and I moved the Germans out to the rear.

La Villa, Ponte Rotto and Cisterna were all captured on May 24. Staff Sergeant Harper wrote he entered a concrete German bunker at Cisterna and it had five underground levels with barracks, bathroom, kitchen and mess.[77] Above ground, there wasn't much left.

The 3rd Infantry Division headed for the hills above the plain on May 25. The B Company commander, Lieutenant Salfen, was wounded when his vehicle struck a mine at 1515 outside of Cori on the road to Artena. He was sent to the 300th General Hospital in Naples. Major Fuller assumed command. Sergeant Nowak wrote: "We took Cori and Velletri and pushed inland towards Highway Six. Many casualties were suffered and many dead bodies were lying around. Tiger tanks were knocked out everywhere, and field pieces, antitank guns, and all kinds of equipment were strewed around." It was here a terrible incident of "involuntary fratricide" (friendly fire) took place, as described by Robert McFarland in *The History of the 15th Infantry Regiment in World War II*:

Shortly after noon, while rounding a sharp curve at the outskirts of Cori, the battalion column was bombed and strafed by five planes, US Army Air Corps P-40 fighter-bombers. The first three planes of the flight dropped their bombs, scoring direct hits on the highway. More than 100 men were killed or wounded, including 70 from the 2nd

Battalion, 15th Infantry and the adjutant and S-3 of the 30th Regiment. A number of jeep trailers loaded with ammunition were hit, and additional casualties were caused by exploding 37mm antitank shells and other small arms ammunition. A considerable number of individual acts of heroism took place during this incident by soldiers who braved the fires and exploding shells to assist wounded comrades. Several jeeps were hit alongside abandoned German tanks in a narrow defile about 300 yards from the curve, tying up traffic for five to six hours.[78]

Josowitz wrote about this tragic incident saying that perhaps it "was due to the fact that the attack moved too quickly once it had got going. Still it was nonetheless heartbreaking to see a battalion of doughboys bombed and strafed by the very planes that they'd been waving at only a moment before. The same sort of snafu occurred twice more before Rome fell."*

Staff Sergeant Harper noted C Company lost two officers in the town of Cori. The first incident occurred shortly after the town was captured when First Lieutenant George Speilberger (Pittsburg, Pennsylvania) set off on foot to check on the whereabouts of one of his TDs. He was never heard from again and is still listed as MIA. A second officer, Second Lieutenant Robert E. Meyers (Tamaqua, Florida), was killed. He had pulled into the center of Cori. He backed his TD up against a building. German artillery shells were still landing inside the town and he reasoned that the TD would be better protected parked next to the building. After positioning his TD, he climbed out and sat on top of the turret. Almost instantly he was killed by an errant piece of shrapnel that bounced off the wall he was counting on to protect him.

---

* "Snafu" is US Army slang for really messed up, standing for Situation Normal, All Fouled Up (snafued).

The breakout tore into the weakened German forces. Wolfgang Schneider's timeline for the Wehrmacht's Schwere Panzer-Abteilung 508 noted on May 25 seven Panzers of the third company had to be destroyed by the Germans in the vicinity of Cori because of a lack of fuel. That same day, there were 11 more Panzer losses near the small village of Giulianello and another outside of Valmontone. These losses were so serious that the German 508th commander was ordered to report to the Führer's Headquarters to explain. He was relieved of command. The 508th, now down to only 24 Panzers, was reorganized to provide defense at Velletri. Subsequently 13 Panzers were returned to Forte Tiburtina in Rome and only 11 operational Panzers remained in the battle line. The 508th crews who now were without Panzers were formed into infantry tank hunter/killer teams under First Lieutenant (Oberleutnant) Junghans.

South of the beachhead, the II Corps broke through the Gustav Line and headed up the west coast of Italy towards Anzio. The same day, US troops moving south from the beachhead met US troops from the 85th Infantry Division moving north. Later that morning, General Clark showed up ten miles south of the Mussolini Canal for a photo shoot with the two conjoined American forces.

Unexpectedly, the Germans withdrew to the Caesar Defensive Line that ran along the front of the Alban Hills. Highway Six and Valmontone were behind that line. At this point, many historians argue that it would have made sense for General Clark to follow British General Sir Harold Alexander's plan to capture Valmontone as soon as possible and cut off the retreating Germans.

However, General Clark was so close to Rome he could smell it. He ordered General Truscott to divide his forces. General Truscott found himself in an unenviable position. He knew General Alexander wanted him to cut Highway Six and trap the Germans. He also knew that General Clark wanted the

Fifth Army to capture Rome as it would be a terrific propaganda coup for the US Army. General Clark instructed General Truscott to see how things went but to remain flexible, ready to exploit any opportunity for Rome.

General Truscott had most of his forces including the 36th and 45th Infantry Divisions turn left towards the north, to the Alban Hills and Rome, but he sent the 3rd Infantry Division with the 1st Special Service Force (a joint Canadian/American unit) straight down the road to Valmontone. Welch's platoon was part of the forces assigned to fast mobile Task Force Howze[79] from May 26 to June 3. They were to spearhead the attack to Valmontone to cut off retreating German forces. Somewhere along the way, 601st Private First Class Francis J. Wasilk (St Paul, Minnesota) was killed on May 26, 1944.

Later Sergeant Nowak with Task Force Howze wrote: "On the 27th we took Artena, two miles from Highway Six. With the 13th Armored Regiment we pushed on towards Highway Six. We finally got stopped and the Kraut threw artillery and 20mm shells at us. We stayed here for a few days and consolidated our position." Things were moving fast, as a determined Welch wrote home:

> I have been in for the last four days a most stupendous attack. It was well planned and executed. We really pushed the Kraut bastard back on his heels. I'm now [blacked out]. The Kraut just doesn't want us to get to Rome, but that's where he's making his big mistake because he's not stopping us. We're about 15 miles from there now and there are about 15,000 Dutchmen [he meant Deutsche men – Germans] between us, but we'll kill them all before we're through.

The day that letter was written, the task force dispersed some German infantry and silenced several machine-gun nests; however, its overall advance was held up. The task force was up against the elite Hermann Göring Parachute Division again and this German division was determined to keep the escape route open for the rest of the German Army.

On May 28, the battalion sustained another KIA: Private First Class Albert M. Babcock, Jr (Brockton, Massachusetts) from Recon Company was killed in unknown circumstances.

A Geneva, New York newspaper published a straightforward press release that described the action on May 28. It stated that platoons commanded by Lieutenants Welch and Bowman were credited with knocking out three German Mark VI Panzers with their antitank guns. They were in the Alban Hills advancing towards the Via Casilina, Highway Six. Apparently the German Panzers, well concealed in the woods, had deliberately let the infantry pass their position. Then they opened up and let the American troops have it from the rear. Welch described what happened in a much later interview with *The Beachhead News* in the December 17, 1944 Sunday supplement:

Long months of campaigning stretch behind but time seemed only to sharpen the excitement of the incident as the lieutenant paced the kitchen floor of the farmhouse and told again how it happened. Scared? I'm still scared every time I think of it. Welch said. I shook for two days afterward. This infantry colonel was right down there beside the TD yelling over and over: G-D it man, can't you see that tank! He's shooting the hell out of my men!

But the smoke of battle blotted out everything in front of us and I couldn't see a thing, not a thing. The colonel kept hollering and I kept trying to pierce the smoke with my field glasses but it was no go. This Kraut was raising hell too. He had let the infantry go through and now was shooting them up from the rear. Then it happened. The smoke rolled away and there he sat as big as life, a Mark VI and about 500 yards away. We both had our field glasses glued on one another because he knew I was around too.

I yelled down to the gunner: shoot man, for God's sake shoot! And WHOOM! – THE ROUND WAS AWAY. That one shot was plenty because it tore the top right off the German. Lt. T. P. Welch, B Company platoon leader of the 601st stopped, waved his hands expressively for a few seconds and then added: The only thing that saved us was having the muzzle pointed almost at the German with a round already in the breech. That gave us the jump to mean curtains for him instead of us; and like a typical officer of the 601st, Lt. Welch insisted that credit be given his crew for that job; T/4 Snuffy Callahan, Cpl. Joe Irving, Sgt. John Nowak and Cpl. Vincent Macri.

Although Welch got that Panzer, it still took two more days to get out of Artena. Meanwhile the Germans were streaming down Highway Six, saved to fight another day.

Panzers weren't the only problem facing the Americans and 15th Infantry Regiment. According to the regiment's unit journal for May 28 more than 200 men were so sickened with ptomaine (food) poisoning, they could not fight. The source was believed to be C rations. The journal recorded the cans had been dented and were bulging; apparently the troops opened and ate them anyway.

That same day Welch sent his last letter home until well after the capture of Rome: "Another short lull before we jump off again. We were really in a pitched battle last night. We got so far in front of our troops we got shelled by both sides. It was about the worst I've been under. I still can't hear a damn thing."

"I didn't know what to do with him"

Sergeant Larson and Corporal Dykstra, both from Welch's platoon, were awarded Silver Stars for saving the life of Richard

L. Reynolds (Jackson, Mississippi), a tanker in the 751st Tank Battalion. At a reunion in 1980, 36 years after the events of May 30, 1944, the two men had an emotional meeting as they recalled the details of the rescue mission.

The action started on the night of May 29. Under the cover of darkness, Larson drove his tank destroyer within 500 yards of some German armor. They were on the road to Valmontone with another TD and a platoon of Shermans. The US armor was positioned on the top of a little hill that overlooked a small village. This unnamed village was to be the morning's objective. They were almost right on top of some German infantry.

At daybreak the Americans attacked, pushing the Germans back a few hundred yards and paying a heavy price for the real estate. The Germans had machine-gun nests scattered among the trees and they were difficult to spot. The infantry took heavy casualties while repeatedly trying to knock out the machine guns and then they called for armor. The decision was that Shermans would push on ahead, covered by the tank destroyers, even though they all knew that the enemy armor in the area was watching for this type of move.

At around 1000 the Shermans moved forward. They had gone less than a hundred yards before two were disabled, hit by a self-propelled German gun. One Sherman was hit in the turret, about 1,000 yards from the tank destroyer containing Sergeant Larson, who watched its crew bail out; during a lull in the fighting Larson thought he heard a call for help.

Heedless of their own safety, Sergeant Larson and Corporal Dykstra, his radio operator, dismounted from their destroyer and ran through heavy enemy small-arms fire to respond. Germans, only 100 yards from the crippled Sherman, were moving in fast. Reaching the tank, Larson crawled up and inside the turret where he found "the driver pinned half in the turret and half in the driver's compartment. The man was quite badly wounded and was almost choking to death. The concussion from the enemy shell had broken the traverse mechanism, causing the gun to swing loose. It had caught the tanker as he tried to crawl out."

As Corporal Dykstra started to climb into the tank, two Germans stood up in the tall grass only 30 feet away and opened up with machine pistols. Dropping to the ground, Dykstra yelled to Larson to keep down and stay inside the tank. Larson shouted back to Dykstra that the tanker was trapped and explained what he needed. The corporal raced back to his TD retrieving a crowbar, metal pincers, and morphine. Running back to the crippled Sherman he threw the tools and morphine to Larson through the hatch.

It took Larson 45 very long minutes with the crowbar to free the tanker from the turret. As he related later, "when I finally did get him free I didn't know what to do with him knowing Jerries were around the tank." All this time he had not heard from Dykstra and he was afraid the Germans had wounded him or worse.

Larson was stuck. How could he leave the tank and get back to his own lines with this severely wounded man? He determined to see if the tank would start so he could drive it out of there. "No one was more surprised than I when it started. I backed it around and drove back to the road a few hundred yards where I got help to unload the wounded man." Medics took the tanker to safety. Dykstra had been wounded, having received several slugs in his neck, but he had been able to get back by concealing himself in the high grass. The medics saw to him as well. As their joint citation stated, Larson and Dykstra "had saved the tanker from certain death."

The Germans continued with their stubborn resistance the following day – June 1. Sergeant Nowak described the fighting this way:

On the 1st we went into position overlooking a railroad station in preparation for an attack. We got one tank in the attack and gained some ground. We took Valmontone and cut Highway Six. We tried to go to Labico [the next town], but no dice. That night we moved towards Palestrina. We tried to advance but were fired upon. A Sherman tank was knocked out and the tank men got shot by snipers.

It was recorded that Tech Five Orland J. Bianconi (Cresson, Pennsylvania), probably wounded during the May breakout, died of his wounds on June 1, 1944. He was most likely in a hospital still operating on the Anzio beachhead.

On the morning of June 2, US armor and infantry pushed out together, and now turned down Highway Six to Rome. A German antitank gun fired but Sergeant Larson, spotting the muzzle blast, lobbed a few rounds at it. Then there was a loud bang. Larson wrote:

My driver came up into the turret and said we'd been hit. Bolts had busted loose in his compartment so his one leg was numb so I had to back it up to a concealed position. When we took inventory we found we were hit in the track suspension but still able to move. I spotted a Mark IV about 600 yards away on our right flank. Evidently he was the one that hit us. So the gunner and I pulled the tank ahead again and let fly three fast ones at him and were rewarded by seeing a flash after our third round. There was so much dust and dirt flying that observation was very poor. But the next day a Mark IV was there knocked out and so we like to feel we did it.

The crew took more fire and worried that next the Germans might use armor-piercing shells. Their limited mobility made them a sitting duck. The crew bailed out, as Larson related: "A Jerry opened up on us with a machine pistol but we got away without a scratch." About a half-hour later, Larson and crew returned to the crippled destroyer and found although the German rounds had been high explosives they hadn't done much damage. The men decided to "let fly three more quick ones just to show we weren't out of action and then pulled back a few hundred yards."

Nowak's M-10 was also knocked out that day and so both crews withdrew. Larson wrote: "As if that wasn't enough action for one day, Jerry planes came over us that night, dropped flares all around us and bombed our area quite heavily. Boy it was sure a full day."

And a successful day, for by its end the German line had collapsed and a major retreat from the Alban Hills towards Rome had begun. Because of the rapid advance, the battalion report noted, the gun companies had become widely separated. Welch, with a TD section and still with Task Force Howze, headed for Frascati and then on the Via Tuscolana toward Rome. Separated from Larson and Nowak, Welch was unaware of what had happened to them.

Nowak and Larson, with their crews, found the battalion command post on June 3, got two new M-10s and drove about 20 miles that night to a position just outside of Rome. There was a full moon that night and the noise of the German withdrawal could be heard all over the city. Thousands of Germans and their confiscated vehicles were leaving. A long line waited to cross the ancient Milvian Bridge on the Via Cassia Antica. The retreat lasted well into the noon hour on June 4, as shown by a series of photographs of the retreating troops taken from the heights near the Villa Borghese, overlooking the city. Robert Katz quotes an Italian Catholic priest, Monsignor Giovannetti, about the German withdrawal:

The soldiers were retreating orderly, but they looked spent and humiliated. They had requisitioned anything with wheels, private cars, horse-drawn taxies, even oxcarts with the oxen. It was an interminable procession. Some were marching with huge, overstuffed backpacks, carrying their weapons in their hands. The people stood by and watched them saying nothing. A few boys offered them something to drink. Soldiers, who for nine months had fought with valor against a superior enemy, passed by, showing all the signs of a terrible battle. How many of them still believed in the promise of Hitler's Thousand-Year Reich?[80]

Uncharacteristically, Hitler gave Field Marshal Kesselring permission to abandon Rome and declared it an open city. Nevertheless Kesselring organized his forces for a fighting withdrawal. To keep the general populace of Rome calm, Lieutenant General Kurt Mälzer (the commandant of Rome) attended as planned an evening gala performance of *Un Ballo in Maschera* at the Rome opera house. He left the city immediately after the performance. The battle for Rome was almost over.

As a last reprisal against Italian resistance, the Gestapo removed 14 Italian prisoners from the infamous Via Tasso prison. Taken along the Via Cassia by retreating Gestapo officers, they were summarily shot at the 14-kilometer post outside the city. These Italian partisans were the last victims on a long list of murders committed by the Germans during their nine-month occupation of Rome.

"With three generals in his crosshairs"

Around noon on June 4, Sergeants Nowak and Larson, just outside the city, found out they were to head into Rome. Because both of the replacement M-10 tank destroyers were new, they got busy removing the cosmolene (rust preventive) material on both the 3-inch gun and the .50-caliber machine gun. They needed to be ready for action.

Katz relates an incident of high drama that took place on the outskirts of the city early in the afternoon of June 4:

General Frederick, like everything else on Highway Six, was standing still when a jeep carrying Mark Clark and II Corps Commander, General Geoffrey Keyes, pulled up beside him. Clark, just down from the Alban Hills, the prize now so close, wanted to know what was holding things up. A welcome distraction then arose as one of the photographers traveling in Clark's entourage drew attention to the reflector-studded blue highway sign just beyond them. It read ROMA. It was in fact a city-limit marker on the Casilina, approximate at best, but if you were reading it you were probably not in Rome, whereas if you were looking at the blank reverse side, you might be. It was awe inspiring, in any event, and, in a flash, so to speak, a famous photo was taken. Then Clark turned to Frederick and said, "Golly Bob, I'd like to have that sign in my command post. Frederick himself went to retrieve what was now a museum-class artifact but at that moment a German sniper, with three generals in his cross hairs, cut loose."[81]

The sniper missed. The three generals were not injured and Frederick handed Clark the sign.

Operations Instructions Number 33 (marked "Secret") from Headquarters 3rd Infantry Division, dated June 4, 1944, was written by General "Iron Mike" O'Daniel. It noted the 3rd had been designated to garrison the City of Rome and set out the following rules:

Troops will refrain from associating with civilians until further instructions are issued on the subject. At this time acceptance of gifts such as alcoholic beverages is prohibited.

While passing through ROME and its suburbs and while occupying ROME care will be taken not to commit overt acts or misunderstanding with the civilian population. Care will be exercised to prevent unnecessary bloodshed.

We are envoys of our country and must endeavor to create a favorable impression. As we act so acts our army in the eyes of the Romans.

The people of this country respect force and dignity. Be firm without being overbearing, be courteous without being too familiar. We are conquerors and must act like conquerors, therefore dignity is necessary. When in doubt as to what action to take, men will be instructed to consult the officer in charge.

Be alert and on the job at all times until the moment comes for relaxation. When that time comes you will be notified.

Sergeant Larson wrote:

Some of our TDs [Lieutenant Welch] encountered some pretty heavy fighting on some roads heading into town but we didn't fire a shot. There were quite a few dead Jerries lying around the streets though, as well as quite a few civilians. Some of those in civilian clothes were Jerry snipers that were rooted out by our advance patrols. Others were Germans that just failed to get out of the road.

Lieutenant Welch encountered fighting on the way into the city. He wrote his mother that he was in the forefront of units going into Rome on June 4th. Late that afternoon, Welch entered Rome on the Via Tuscolana. Shortly after passing through a city gate, the Porta Furba, he was in action. Stopping his destroyer, he opened fire on a concealed German machine-gun nest. This action was caught on film and was published in the Army's *Yank Magazine*, a World War II Army publication. He sent a copy home to his mother, noting on the picture that he was one of the two crewmen visible in the TD's turret. According to a later letter, immediately after the picture was taken a load of dirt was dumped on the machine-gun nest and that was the end of the German defenders.[82]

Sergeant Nowak described their triumphal entrance into Rome on June 5:

…we got up and proceeded slowly towards [the center of] Rome. We entered about 0530 in the morning with no resistance. The city was clean and orderly. I got my picture taken by English and Americans. Many of the burned Kraut vehicles and tanks in the city were put out of action by Allies and partisans.

Sergeant Larson added:

I was one of the first in the city and I won't forget it for a long time. It was in the very early morning hours that we rolled in there. Had little difficulty at that stage and in no time at all people were swarming out of their houses and lining the streets. By the time we got near the center of town the crowds were so large we had difficulty in moving. And being the home of Fascism, these Romans surely gave us a swell reception. Everyone was clapping their hands and cheering and shouting "Bravo Americans!" They swarmed around us trying to shake our hands, and many of the pretty Senorinas were trying to get near the soldiers to kiss them. But we all fought bravely to prevent that, as you can imagine. Many brought us wine until we were as hilarious as the Romans themselves. We probably didn't look much like conquering heroes. I hadn't shaved for about a week, was filthy dirty and bleary-eyed from lack of sleep, for in the two or three days before that I had had only a couple hours' sleep.

Sergeant Nowak was later identified by his son, Bill, as one of the soldiers standing in the lead TD in a famous photo of M-10 tank destroyers driving around the Coliseum the morning of June 5. Sergeant Larson took some personal photos of that morning from atop his tank destroyer.

There were still snipers active elsewhere in the city, including one at the Colosseum. Early that morning Larson silenced it with a burst from the 50 caliber machine gun mounted on his M-10 TD. He was heard to remark, "the Colosseum had so many holes in it, and I figured a few more would not make any difference." Sgt. Larson wrote:

> A fellow just told me yesterday that he saw me in the newsreels in one of the theaters in Naples on Sunday. It was an English newsreel showing the assault on Rome and he said my tank was on the screen for quite a while. He said I was sitting on the turret as clear as could be, stopping the tank every once in a while to get the civilians out of the way. From his description I know it was taken just a couple of blocks before we passed the Coliseum.

Many claimed to be the first soldier to enter Rome after the Germans left. The author has however heard one story directly from the soldier involved, which has the clear ring of truth. Technical Sergeant Charles W. Phallen (Galion, Ohio) was a member of A Company 601st and had been recuperating in Naples after being wounded at Anzio. He was eager to return to the battalion and his company. Released from the hospital, he arrived at battalion headquarters the night of June 4. Phallen was given a jeep and was told to go find his company. They were somewhere up ahead. About dawn, having still not met up with any of his company, he found himself driving through the deserted streets of Rome. He was alone, a single soldier in a jeep. He crossed the Tiber River unmolested and ended up in St Peter's Square.

Fearing that he might never get another chance, he parked the jeep, jumped out and ran up to the huge doors of the basilica. Amazingly, they were unlocked. He took a quick look inside St Peter's; upon exiting two soldiers in strange uniforms called to him from his left. They were members of the papal Swiss Guard dressed in fatigues. As he approached them, they inquired if he were an American. After he replied in the affirmative they announced that the Holy Father, Pope Pius XII, had yet to meet an American soldier and wanted to talk to him. He was then escorted up the stairs into the papal apartments and met with the Pope for about five minutes. He returned under escort, got into his jeep and drove away. Eventually he found his company.

The grand entrance of the American liberators into Rome was anticlimactic. General Clark finally entered the city mid-morning on June 5 to receive the surrender. Not knowing where to go, someone suggested the town hall but his aides and drivers didn't know how to get to the mayor's office at the Campidoglio, the ancient heart of the Roman capital, its piazza designed by Michelangelo. The little convoy of jeeps meandered around city streets, lost, eventually reaching St Peter's Square where they found an American priest from Detroit who pointed the way. Meanwhile a crowd of excited people surrounded General Clark in the lead jeep. Finally, a boy on a bicycle led the convoy back across the Tiber and to the Campidoglio.

The general arrived to find the building locked. Neither the mayor nor anyone else was there to formally surrender the city. Undaunted, Clark held a news conference announcing the US occupation of Rome. His moment of glory did not last long. On June 6, the D-Day invasion of Normandy was launched and completely overshadowed the liberation of Rome in the world's press.

Sergeant Nowak wrote: "We rode around the city nearly all day. I saw the Coliseum; King's Palace, the Tiber River, Vatican City, etc. At evening we bivouacked near a racetrack where we stayed overnight. The occupation of Rome was complete. That night from the outskirts our big guns were firing on retreating Krauts."

H. V. Morton, a well-known English travel writer, heard the following story first hand from Signora Signorelli Cacciatore, the curator of the Keats-Shelley House at the foot of the Spanish Steps in Rome, concerning the night of June 4/5:

> The Signora stood at the window and watched this happening. It was a calm moonlight night. The last Germans had gone; the last bursts of machine-gun fire were over. The silence was unearthly as even the usual sound of *La Baraccia* was stilled, for the conduits had been bombed and, like all the fountains of Rome, it was dry. Suddenly a voice was heard calling from one of the windows in the *Piazza di Spagna* that the Allies were coming! She heard the rumble of approaching tanks. Then two files of armed figures passed silently in the moonlight. People ventured out of their houses and some flashed torches in the faces of the soldiers, who smiled and passed on into the darkness. Then an order was given and a halt was made. The Piazza was crowded. There in the moonlight the soldiers slept: on the pavements, in the dried-up fountain, on the Spanish Steps. For a moment it seemed to Signora Cacciatore that all these men were dead, victims of a silent battle fought in the Piazza.[83]

CHAPTER 10
HERE WE GO AGAIN
Training for the forgotten D-Day

"I made my Headquarters the Grand Hotel"

With Rome liberated and filled with GIs, the *3rd Division Daily News* gave advice to soldiers about spending money in the Eternal City:

> Members of the 3rd Division will soon be on the streets of Rome with money in their pockets. Rome, one of the great cities of the world, will offer most everything possible to spend that money for. After four months on the Anzio Beachhead, the Third's doughboys will have plenty of money to spend and plenty of inclination to spend it. At least those who haven't fallen victim to the poker wolves. Our price standards will be new to the Roman citizens. If we refuse to pay more for anything than we would in the States, we won't have to pay any more for it. Prices, in other words, will be just what we make them. If the dough foots, loose under the bright lights for the first time in months, fail to show restraint

in their spending, prices on everything will sky rocket and black markets will flourish. Don't rob yourself. Remember, the natives wise up fast.

Many men took guided tours of the city. For the first time in months, they could relax. According to Josowitz:

Rome was clean, beautiful, full of lovely girls and it had hardly been touched by the war. Of course, there was at least one jerk in every company who looked at the Coliseum and said, "Boy! We sure bombed the hell out of that place." On the 6th, there came the tremendous, electrifying news of the Normandy Invasion! Hope ran high in Rome that day and the vino flowed freely. There were trips to the Vatican and to less holy places.

Private Lundquist described an experience that happened to him:

When the D-Day landings occurred on June 6th, I was walking down the streets of Rome, sightseeing. I saw a short fellow in ODs [olive drab uniform] coming towards me. I recognized him as "Shorty" Lees [Corporal Donald G. Lees, Canton, Ohio] who I knew in basic training at Camp Hood, talk about a small world. After all the slaps on the back and "how are you doings," we got around to the usual subject GIs everywhere fall back on, namely "What outfit are you in?" It turned out he was in the 601st too but in one of the gun companies [B Company]. We got a big yak out of that and walked around together for some time.

Tech Five William P. Hale (Miami, Florida) missed the liberation of Rome. He died in hospital on June 6, perhaps back at Anzio of wounds. Originally buried in Italy, he now rests at Arlington National Cemetery, one of the few 601st men buried there.[84]

The 601st was billeted in the outskirts of the city and placed in "rehabilitation, rest and equipment care" status. Sergeant Nowak describes the next few days:

> The 601st B Company moved to an assembly point south of Rome where we stayed near a sports stadium for about three days [June 8–10]. We were supposed to go to the Lido [a famous resort town], but it was badly damaged and heavily mined by the Kraut. During our period of inactivity we got re-equipped with new combat boots and other equipment that we needed. We also got attached to the II Corps and the 88th Division along with the 751st Tank Battalion. I went into Rome for a day. It was a beautiful city, untouched by our planes and by German occupation forces. Carfare [transportation] for soldiers was free since the Germans started the practice. The weather was nice, and north of Rome American troops were chasing merrily after disorganized Krauts.

And Larson and Welch recorded their impressions of the Eternal City as well. Larson wrote:

> Rome itself was surely a treat to those of us that had spent those long months at the little Anzio beachhead. There we had experienced almost constant danger, lived like rats in a hole, and saw nothing but dirt and destruction. Now here in Rome we saw a city beautiful beyond all expectation, little touched by war, and streets filled with well-dressed people, pretty girls, flags waving and banners hastily put up, saying "Welcome to the Liberators." And best of all we felt like we had finally accomplished one of the primary jobs that we had been working on for such a long time. And when we heard of

the invasion of France, well you can just about imagine what a boost our morale got with the two events so close together. Wish you were over here to see some of the sights of Rome. There surely is plenty to see in the city, especially if you've studied Roman history. I wish I had remembered more of it. The Coliseum, Baths of Diocletian, Forum, Stadium, St. Peters, the Vatican, etc. are just a few of the many sights one could spend weeks exploring. And besides ancient Rome there also are beautiful modern buildings, memorials, hotels, apartments, business houses, etc. The Average American surely knows little of how the other half of the world lives. It's just a shame that a war is necessary to bring this about.

Welch's letter describes the heady first days of occupation:

Things really ran riot in Rome the first two days. A good time was had by all. I made my Headquarters the Grand Hotel, a really lush spot. I went to the Vatican and saw the Pope as well as St. Peter's, which is really lovely. We met a Baroness Barrocco who was a lass from Boston who threw a cocktail party for Bowman and me at the Rome Country Club where we met the smart set of Rome. They are really very nice people, all speak English. They do nothing but follow the season around.

The Fifth Army forces were at the provincial town of Viterbo, about 45 miles north of Rome, by June 9. The Germans had made a major effort to save their equipment, but the Allies moved too quickly for them. Captured at the port town of Civitavecchia was that nemesis of the Anzio beachhead, the infamous Anzio Annie. During the summer, the huge railway gun was taken to the States for evaluation.

The next day, the battalion turned in its remaining T-70 TD for salvage and the unit was back to an all-M-10 outfit. That same day, the unit journal noted Lieutenant Colonel Tardy called a company commanders' meeting to discuss recreation and general training during the rest period. It noted that enlisted men were encouraged to visit the city and there was to be a special church service at St Peter's, scheduled for Sunday, June 11. The meeting also discussed the shower unit that had been set up, noted movies would be shown in the evenings and that there was to be an inspection on June 13.

After only a week, the battalion was reassigned on June 15 back to the 3rd Infantry Division from the 88th Infantry Division. The higher commanders were not sure how many troops they would need to pursue the retreating Germans into northern Italy or how many would be required for a possible invasion of the south of France. As a result, as estimates varied, units were frequently realigned.

On the 16th, the 601st was transferred from a suburb of Rome to a bivouac eight miles east of Ostia, the ancient port of Rome at the mouth of the Tiber River. There they encamped with the divisions identified for the upcoming invasion of France. Corporal Borriello reported on a rumor that after taking Rome, the Vatican requested US combat troops be quickly moved out so the Germans would not bomb the city.

The battalion's Roman holiday did not last long. Less than two weeks after the liberation of Rome on June 18, the 601st was on the road again. Sergeant Nowak noted the battalion moved out in a motorized column during an early morning rain. They rode south to what had been the British sector of the Anzio beachhead. There they stayed for four days, sorting out who would go by road and who would go on the LSTs. It was decided that to save the treads and maintain speed, tracked vehicles would embark on the ships and the wheeled vehicles would go by road.

The road column left for Pozzuoli (near Naples) on June 22, where they had trained for the Anzio landing. Moving the battalion's vehicles by road required extensive organization. The 133 non-tracked vehicles were organized into a convoy of six elements by company. They were given strict speed limits for the trip, 15 miles per hour in towns and 20 miles per hour on the open road. B Company, for example, left Anzio at 0045 and arrived at 1715 that evening after a trip of almost 120 miles. There were frequent stops but all arrived at Qualiano, near Pozzuoli, without incident.

Sergeant Nowak remained with B Company's 12 TDs, six half-tracks and the battalion T-2 (tank retriever) with the mobile kitchen towed behind. He took photos of the company moving their tank destroyers through Anzio and re-embarking on an LST. On the night of June 24/25 they departed Anzio and disembarked at Pozzuoli about six the next morning. They drove from the port and arrived at Qualiano by 0900. The other gun companies made similar transits and in all a total of 259 enlisted men and 12 officers from the battalion made the trip by sea.

In his book *Naples '44* Norman Lewis wrote about the town of Pozzuoli, the new home of the 601st:

> There may be some hidden significance in the fact that Pozzuoli had endured the experience of our occupation with such indifference and calm. Somehow it seems to have contrived to stand apart from the war, to have been overlooked by raiding planes and by-passed by armies whether attacking or in retreat. Pozzuoli indulges in sedate sea-washed pinks, and hangs green shutters at its windows, many of which come to a point in the Venetian style. The presence of several cupolas heightens a Turkish effect. I remember being told that the natives of Pozzuoli are quite separate by customs, traditions, and probably even blood from the Neapolitans, and that they speak a markedly different dialect. It was at Pozzuoli, and Baia, a couple of miles farther on in the curve of the bay, that all the richest,

the most profligate, and the most terrible of the Romans built their seaside villas and the gay and gracious landscape is steeped in the black legends of their doings. Here, Nero murdered his mother Agrippina. Tiberius was smothered by Macro, his guard commander. Pozzuoli put on extravagant wild beast shows and gladiatorial fights in its amphitheater. In AD 305 San Gennaro [the patron saint of Naples] was thrown to the lions there, after which, being rejected by them, he was beheaded.[85]

"I am not interested in your syphilitic sister"

The battalion was retracing its steps. Since the battalion left Pozzuoli and Naples in January 1944, Naples had undergone significant change. Now the principal port in the Mediterranean for US forces, it swarmed with a huge influx of men and materiel imposed on a starving population. Things there were unsettled.

The men of the 601st came into contact with the Peninsula Base Section (PBS), the rear-echelon command at Naples. This organization provided everything that the US forces required through the Service of Supply (SOS) for MTOUSA (the Mediterranean Theater Operations US Army). Support organizations such as this were the vital mainstay of the US forces abroad. One of them, the 7th Replacement Depot, called the "repo-depot" by the troops, for example, arranged the return of the wounded to their units after convalescence and for replenishing units with replacements.

The official history of the 7th provides many interesting details of what went on behind the front lines. In March 1944, the depot was moved from North Africa to Naples, occupying the large open area at the Agnano Hippodrome (horse-racing stadium). For an idea of what the teeming city of Naples and the town of Pozzuoli were like as the 601st rested, refitted and trained for the invasion of southern France, the monthly depot reports provide slice-of-life insights. Below are some excerpts from those as well as from Norman Lewis's book, *Naples '44*.

Naples was off limits in March, when the depot arrived, because of a typhus epidemic and the high rate of venereal disease. It was estimated that 42,000 women in the greater Naples area were involved in prostitution, approximately one in three of the city's younger women. Conditions were dire and it was the last resort for women who had to feed their families. To curb this high level of prostitution, a leaflet was printed in Italian to be handed to any who offered the services of a prostitute. It said: "I am not interested in your syphilitic sister." This was a bad idea since in southern Italy remarks about family members can easily provoke a duel.[86] And the Army established a prophylaxis station, which the men were encouraged to visit after a night on the town for a scrub down.

According to Lewis, some even thought prostitution was part of a Fascist plan to spread venereal disease among the Allies, it was so prevalent. Taking this seriously, officials hatched a scheme to send 20 prostitutes infected with a particularly virulent strain of VD to German-occupied Italy to spread the disease among German soldiers. Women were actually selected and, after being wined and dined, they were told of the plan. Presumably the women objected and the plan was summarily scrapped.

Throughout the period that the 601st was on the beach at Anzio, Naples was heavily bombed. On March 14, for example, an air raid resulted in 284 known casualties, including 117 deaths. Lewis, after visiting the Santa Lucia port section of Naples, wrote: "I saw a heart-rending scene. A number of tiny children had been dug out of the ruins of a bombed building and lay side by side in the street. Where presentable, their faces were uncovered, and in some cases brand-new dolls had been thrust into their arms to accompany them to the other world."[87]

As if to put man's explosive weapons in perspective, and to make matters worse in Naples, nature put on a demonstration of its power. On March 19, Mount Vesuvius erupted, sending smoke and ash 30,000–40,000 feet in the air, and the ash cloud stretched for miles. The US Army evacuated 6,000 people from the town of San Sebastiano on March 21. The town, directly in the line of lava flow from Vesuvius, was completely destroyed. Staff Sergeant Harper had written in October of 1943 of "some type of volcanic eruption" and it was rumored that Mount Vesuvius had been woken up by the US Army Air Corps by using the crater for bombing practice.

Food is always a vital commodity of war. During March and April of 1944 the 7th Replacement Depot reported critical food shortages. There was even a shortage of C rations! The Allied invasion had disrupted the previous year's harvest so local food supplies were low. The Army declared at the time that "locally grown food was not considered fit for Army consumption" so even had local supplies been available, it would not have helped. The Army's reason for this ban might have been due to the unsanitary storage and handling of food, such as storing meat in the open air. It also may have been that the Army did not want GIs consuming scarce civilian food supplies.

The black market was the principal reason for supply shortages. According to the Allied Psychological Warfare Bureau, 65 percent of the per capita income of Neapolitans was from selling stolen supplies on the black market. Estimates were that as much as one-third of everything that entered the port was stolen before it got to the Army warehouses. Every single item of Allied equipment could be seen openly displayed in the street markets of Naples. Guns and ammunition were also available but you had to ask. Everyone wore GI clothes or clothes made from GI blankets. Only American cigarettes were smoked, bartered or traded.

The depot reported that in a two-month period, May–June, they salvaged almost 60,000 clothing items turned in by soldiers for reissue. This resulted in a monetary saving of $174,389.13. But thievery from American forces continued to be an issue. According to the August 1944 report:

> The Provost Marshal of this depot, having been informed of government property being in the possession of civilians near this depot, made inspections in several houses and found large quantities of government clothing and equipment. The clothing and equipment was seized and brought to this headquarters.[88]

It was thought that this brisk trade was being controlled by the local mafia, La Camorra, and there was a strong US connection. The headman was Vito Genovese. He had been second-in-command of the New York mafia family headed by "Lucky" Luciano. After Luciano was sent to prison, Genovese became the boss and was acknowledged as the head of the American mafia. Just before the war, he returned to Italy to escape a murder trial in the US. He became friendly with Mussolini, but with the coming of the Allies and his American background, Genovese was made an interpreter and liaison officer for the US Army. And from that position, it was thought, he was able to control everything.

In mid-May German planes mined the Naples harbor. That disrupted shipping until the waters were cleared by minesweepers. That same month, the depot reported it was required to supply 50 litter-bearers each day to help handle casualties from the breakout from Anzio and the battle to reach Rome.

It also had to deal with men who went AWOL, a problem that all front-line units, including the 601st, faced. As spring turned into summer, the depot was able to reduce the population in the stockade because the front lines were moving further north and it became harder for AWOL GIs to get lost in Naples. These men were still needed for battle and punishment was lenient. Three courts for Special and Summary Court Martial were set up and, as the depot report noted: "when a man is convicted and sentenced to a period of confinement, if the man can be shipped to his organization at once that confinement is suspended."[89]

Meanwhile troops had to be kept busy and out of trouble. A depot report listed a touring USO show in March that included actor John Garfield and supporting stars Sheila Rogers, Olya Klem, Jean Darling and Eddie Foy. Another on May 12 featured the famous German-born actress Marlene Dietrich and her company including Danny Thomas, Milton Frome and Lynn Mayberry. Under the heading MORALE, the depot listed the following activities that it felt were "conducive to a high state of morale:" nightly moving picture shows with comfortable and unlimited seating; weekly boxing programs in the east grandstand; facilities for baseball, basketball, volley ball, ping-pong and horseshoe pitching; bathing and laundry facilities; opportunity for religious activity; post exchange; special services (engraving of personal items, unit patches and other such details); and postal and supply functions.

By summer the depot had established 13 messes, the menus of which included fresh chicken, eggs, other meats, vegetables, beer and ice cream. It was a significant improvement on the food shortages of a few months earlier. Prices were set so things were affordable to the GIs. Even the official price of a haircut was established. It was set at 25 lire: 50 percent to the barber; 35 percent to the PX Recreation Fund, its only source of income; and 15 percent distributed among other company funds. And there was the American Expeditionary Radio Station on the air, which rebroadcast news from the British and American radio, and played lots of music, including the hugely popular Kate Smith Show. Comedy shows such as Duffy's Tavern and Bob Hope were featured and, in season, baseball and football games were also broadcast.

Even the weather cooperated during the summer that the 601st was in Pozzuoli:

> The superior climatic conditions of the Naples area during the month of July have been most conducive to health and well-being of the thousands of inhabitants of this Depot. In addition to the prescribed training activities much interest has been shown by many of the personnel in taking advantage of the fine weather prevalent here and indulging in informal games on the playing fields provided. While the sun's rays have been steadily growing warmer the nights have been most comfortable for profitable rest.[90]

"Cut your initials on their goddamn faces"

The battalion was reunited. On June 24 the 3rd Infantry Division was formally assigned to the Seventh US Army for the invasion of southern France, which was planned but not yet announced. The Seventh Army patch is a seven-step triangle, referred to by the soldiers as "seven steps to hell."

The battalion was ordered, for the second time in less than a year, to bring itself in line with a new Table of Organization and Equipment (TO&E). This and other issues were discussed at a battalion company commanders' meeting according to the unit journal for June 25. The other issues included the availability of LSTs and LCTs for training in loading and disembarking; calisthenics and road marches; awards; memorial services; the battalion athletic league for softball and volleyball; malaria and venereal disease control; and a daily inspection of quarters.

One result of the meeting was a written request to the 3rd Infantry Division to retain some excess vehicles that the battalion felt were mission essential. Specifically they requested personnel half-tracks be kept in lieu of additional armored cars; the five excess 2½-ton cargo vehicles be retained as 11 proved inadequate; and finally the battalion ambulance retained. This equipment was kept since the monthly summary notes the battalion turned in only seven miscellaneous vehicles.

Five officers and 200 enlisted men attended a 3rd Infantry Division ceremony on June 17, where 76 battalion members were presented with medals. Although the medal was not available until November, Welch was recognized for his Bronze Star at this ceremony.

With the invasion of southern France looming, training for the battalion's fourth amphibious landing commenced on June 29. The battalion practiced on four amphibious landing ships off the island of Nisida, near Pozzuoli in the Bay of Naples. Part of the training involved TD crews cross-training to become proficient and interchangeable as drivers, gunners and radio operators.

A battalion memorial service for fallen comrades was held at the bivouac on July 1. It honored those killed in action, those who died of wounds, and those missing in action. Battalion records do not indicate how many men were honored or who they were. Perhaps not a coincidence but on the same day, Private First Class John W. Kufta (Johnstown, Pennsylvania) was reported as a POW. He had probably been captured in May or June during the breakout from Anzio and was now in Germany.

At 1500, during a training maneuver on July 3, Welch jumped from one of his tank destroyers and broke his lower leg. He was admitted to the 182nd Station Hospital on July 4, and was discharged with a walking cast on July 18. On July 6, he wrote his mother and said "Well this time I have a good excuse for not writing. I got in a tank fight and my tank got hit. I came out with a broken leg and a few cuts. So, I'll be out of the war for six weeks or so." Although Welch wrote he was in a "tank fight" it was not in combat but was a training accident.

Training continued, but the unit journal notes an M-10 firing exercise had to be canceled on July 5 because the DUKWs could not tow the targets in rough water. The next day, Lieutenant Colonel Tardy held officers' call and gave final instructions for a coming night training exercise. Later that day Tardy monitored his M-10s loading on LCTs in the vicinity of Nisida and later visited his men in the hospital. On July 7, the battalion lost an M-10 overboard in the Gulf of Baia (opposite Pozzuoli). The LCT's ramp gave way under the weight of the TD. Battalion records indicate it was quickly recovered.

Sergeant Nowak describes this training, writing "we had amphibious training on LSTs and LCTs. We got replacements from the 3rd Infantry Division. We went on night maneuvering with the TDs and went on hikes nearly every day, sometimes before breakfast. For security reasons we took off division patches from shirts and helmets."

Continued rough seas caused a night exercise scheduled for July 9 at Mondragone, about 25 miles along the coast, north of Naples, to be rescheduled to July 13/14. Although the practice area was desolate it had been mined and was dangerous. While clearing the beach prior to the practice landing, 18 men of the 10th Engineer Battalion had been killed and 43 wounded while removing buried mines. The rescheduled exercise involved marching to a new bivouac area closer to Pozzuoli called the "Iowa Concentration." The eight-mile night move was part of the consolidation effort of the 3rd Infantry Division as it was transferred to the operational control of the Seventh Army. The unit journal noted the move ended with another awards ceremony conducted by General O'Daniel.

Welch wrote his mother on July 11 that "My leg is coming along fine and I'll be back to work shortly." But life for the battalion was not all training, work and formations. Josowitz had this to say about battalion activities and the Naples experience:

There were movies, trips to Naples, where the local Chamber of Commerce representatives now greeted visitors with "Bifsteak! Cognac! Spaghetti! Signorina thirteen years!" trips to the beach, back-breaking speed marches, riots at the officer, non-coms and privates clubs, "unauthorized visitors" to the company areas, night problems, and of course days and days of amphibious training. The 3rd Division patches and vehicles markings were on again and off again and on again and off again and every little three-year-old "gook"[91] knew that the 3rd Division was training for another amphibious operation. Then Sally [now broadcasting from Milan] made that historic crack, "There will always be a 3rd Division so long as the blue and white paint holds out!" Rumor ran riot again but everyone knew that no matter where it was, it would surely be an amphibious landing.

Staff Sergeant Harper remembers that when on a pass to Naples, each man had to assemble at Division Headquarters where the division command duty officer would give the men a little pep talk and tell them to have a good time. On one occasion, the duty officer said his orders were not being carried out and "the only ones who had obeyed his order for a good time was the 601st."

The men had many interactions with locals during this period, some with surprising endings. Corporal Borriello had befriended a nine-year-old Pozzuoli girl. The child showed up almost every day and Joe would give her the candy from his C ration packages. That girl was later to change her name and became a famous actress: Sophia Loren!

Things were coming together for the invasion. Sergeant Nowak relates that "On the 23rd we started waterproofing our TDs, and on those last days we got our PX rations [candy bars, cigarettes]." Coast Guard officers visited the battalion to receive additional information on the coming loading operation. Josowitz remarked later: "The 601st was restricted to the battalion area. Naples harbor became a tightly packed parking lot for ships of every shape, size and description. The MPs began to pull sneak raids in the company areas in search of unauthorized visitors."

The unit journal reports another battalion commander and company commanders' meeting July 24. Some items were similar to previous months' agendas such as awards and venereal disease. But other issues clearly show the battalion gearing up for the invasion of France. For example, the deadline for loading the assault wave vehicles on the LSTs was set for Wednesday night; after that all jeeps would be under the control of Major Fuller. The orders continued:

Vehicles will be sandbagged and numbered and marked uniformly. Company commanders will check on all insignias and uniform regulations will be observed. ... all court martial cases will be completed, shot records must be up to date and men must keep their toe nails cut [to avoid cut toes and infections]. Large tents will be turned in after Wednesday.

Welch seemed keen to get back into action judging by a letter to his mother while invasion preparations went on:

My leg is just about well and I'll soon be all set to go again. Don't plan on my coming home until the war is over. I wouldn't come if I got the chance. There's too much good fighting and places to go yet. This is really a good education in itself. I'm enclosing some pictures taken at Anzio also the citation for the Bronze Star. I don't have the medal yet, but will send it home when I do have it. You can see that you don't get a citation for knocking out tanks. That's part of the job. The news continues well and the war here should not last much longer. Perhaps I can get home for a short time before I tackle the Japs. I have to take a crack at those people.

According to Sergeant Nowak, in late July the battalion positioned its TDs in the "Texas Staging Area," then loaded them onto the waiting ships. With the equipment on board, the men remained ashore and hiked and trained. On August 1, the battalion was ready for the amphibious landing. By this time the Italian Front was not receiving the resources it once commanded. Fifth Army records reveal its strength had been reduced by 50 percent from the forces available to it at the time of the liberation of Rome, two months earlier. That meant a long slow war for those troops remaining in Italy, which no longer included the battalion or the 3rd Division.

On August 3, Sergeant Larson, waiting for the invasion, wrote his brother:

> Mail will be slow reaching me for a while, I fear. For by the time you get this you'll probably hear of new developments over on this side. And you can depend on it that yours truly will be in the midst of it. I'd like to give you some details but there is little to give. General Patch [Alexander McCarrell "Sandy" Patch, commander of the Seventh Army] hasn't taken me into his confidence yet. But I assure you it won't be small-time. As usual, we're still working with our old mother organization, the 3rd Division, on this new expedition. We've worked with others, such as the Rangers, a couple of parachute battalions, the 45th Division, the 34th, but whenever the 3rd goes into the line you can depend on us being with them. And they are a real fighting bunch of men. We've seen certain elements of it wiped out two or three times but they soon have a rugged bunch of replacements to take their place. They seem to take a pride in being a part of the old Marne Division. But being with an outfit like that means always being in the hot spots.

Sergeant Nowak was awarded an Oak Leaf Cluster to his Silver Star during a battalion formation on August 4. It was for his efforts during the ranger rescue attempt on January 30. On the following day the entire battalion was present at a division review held on the Pozzuoli parade field. Josowitz noted the "gooks" took advantage of the occasion and robbed the battalion area. As noted by William B. Breuer in *Operation Dragoon,* Major General Truscott (VI Corps) and Major General O'Daniel (3rd Infantry Division) addressed the troops as follows:

> Truscott spoke first, "Men, I'm not asking you to hate the Germans, I'm only telling you that you've got to win this war! Win it, I tell you! Win it!"
>
> Iron Mike O'Daniel, the firebrand, took the microphone from his boss, shook his fist violently, and roared: "You can take it from me, boys – hate the Germans! Hate the Bastards! Cut your initials on their goddamn faces!"
>
> A mighty roar from fourteen thousand throats echoed across the landscape. "Give 'em hell, Iron Mike," a soldier shouted, "Give 'em hell!"[92]

Excitement was in the air. Expectations were high. These men had liberated Rome, after all, why not the rest of Europe?

Sergeant Nowak, still on shore, recalled the briefing for the invasion. The troops were told they would have air mastery over the battlefield. On the first day, the invasion forces would consist of the 3rd, 36th and 45th Infantry Divisions. The attack would commence at 0730 after US Special Service Forces took a couple of islands overlooking the landing area. The French would follow later. Except for a few British paratroopers this would be a Franco-American show.

At the same time, Josowitz noted:

> By the 8th of August, all the tactical elements of the battalion were on board ships in the Naples harbor. There were ships

everywhere, as far as the eye could see. Some of the commanders permitted the "passengers" to swim. Others did not. Several of the officers sneaked over the side and hitchhiked into Naples every night. Deep-sea melon peddlers came out to swap melons for cigarettes. They tossed the melons up after the GIs tossed their cigarettes down. One peddler had a good-looking gal in his boat and nearly caused a riot. "Throw up the Signorina! Not the melons" was the wolf-cry.

Most of the men took the opportunity to send letters home. Lieutenant Welch wrote:

> My leg is progressing nicely now. I have it taped and can get around with it quite well. I'm all set for our next operation, which promises to be a honey. From where I am now, the view is terrific. I can see the whole Bay of Naples with Mt. Vesuvius as a backdrop. Don't be alarmed if you don't hear from me for a few weeks. Things are looking pretty fair here now, and I don't see how it can last much longer. It really looks as if this thing might end soon, so perhaps I'll be back by spring.

The invasion fleet ships sailed for France the evening of August 12. British Prime Minister Winston Churchill reviewed the fleet, seeing them off while riding around the bay in a speedboat. Josowitz says that "word got around that 'Eleanor' [wife of President Roosevelt] was coming next." Most of the men still had no idea where they were going and would not be told until after the ships departed Naples. *The History of the 15th Infantry Regiment in World War II* says that:

> The broad aims, simply put, were clear, to strike with all the might of the Seventh Army west to the Rhone valley and

then north up its axis to force a junction with the Allied armies pushing east from the Normandy Beachhead now 350 miles away. The invasion had been a poorly kept secret. For weeks, ships, men and materiel had been piling up in Italian ports and the Germans, long before D-Day, had announced that landings on the French Riviera were imminent. The evidence increased as our Air Corps pummeled enemy installations, bridges, and road nets from the coastal areas far inland and up the Rhone valley. Almost every type of plane in the catalog hammered at the Nazi occupation forces. Then, four days before the landings, the Allied air fleets began the unmistakable preparation of the southern coast for the invasion.[93]

CHAPTER 11
FRANCE ISN'T ITALY

"The D-Day landing was less difficult than some of the practices"

Arriving at effective wartime strategies is difficult work at best. Options are set forth, criticized, defended. Tables are pounded. Experienced men oppose each other's ideas and present strong arguments for their positions. In the end, decisions are taken. So it was with this next D-Day.

The long preparations for the second invasion of Europe were over. Operation *Dragoon* was launched August 15, early in the morning. In hindsight one sees the logic of leaving Italy, where the retreating German army would continue to exact a toll for every mile gained by the Allies. And then there would be the Alps to climb. In fact, the invasion was on and off many times as the pros and cons were argued at the highest levels. Prime Minister Churchill insisted on pushing up the Italian peninsula and entering Austria via the Julian Alps. Against this position were General Marshall and his teams of American planners. To them, proceeding up the Rhône valley was the logical and more practical course. After Allied forces had joined those coming from the Normandy invasion, Germany would be attacked.

The southern invasion was to have been simultaneous with Normandy but two realities of war prevented that optimal timing. First, the Allies needed to push the Germans further north in Italy to prevent attacks on their right flank. Second, the time for invading Normandy had come and there simply were not enough amphibious landing craft for two simultaneous invasions. From the beginning, Normandy was the priority. But things had changed: the Allies realized they needed the ports of Toulon and Marseilles as the capture of the port of Antwerp, critical to bringing supplies to the Allied armies on the continent, was a long way off. Another factor was that the French forces involved in the Italian campaign saw no reason to fight in Italy while their own country was still occupied by the Wehrmacht.

When the Allies became bogged down in the hedgerows of Normandy, Churchill and others gave in, realizing that the Americans were now providing most of the personnel and equipment. The plan, originally called Operation *Anvil*, was brought down from the shelf and renamed Operation *Dragoon*. General Patch, commanding the US Seventh Army in Sicily, had not waited but had his staff continue to plan for the southern invasion, especially the naval elements. From the official resurrection of the idea on June 24, it was two months until the invasion was on its way. Anticipating the decision, the 3rd Infantry Division had been pulled out of garrison duty in Rome on June 15 and intensive amphibious planning had begun immediately.

The massive Allied naval forces were under the command of Vice Admiral Henry K. Hewitt, USN, and the veteran commander of the Western Naval Task Force. The fleet was composed of 885 ships and 1,325 landing craft. They were divided into four naval task forces, one for each of the three US divisions and one for the follow-on French forces. There was also a small carrier task force with 224 Seafire and Hellcat aircraft launched from small escort carriers. The Allied ships carried more than 151,000 troops, and 21,400 trucks, tanks, tank destroyers, bulldozers, tractors, and other vehicles. The First French Army, part of the invasion forces, was composed of 41,000 men and 2,600 vehicles. It was made up of mostly colonial troops from French North Africa commanded by French officers and non-commissioned officers. Language would be a problem. The French general, Jean de Lattre de Tassigny, after getting the go-ahead from General de Gaulle, had agreed to be under General Patch's command until the expected linkup with the Normandy invasion forces; then the French would form their own independent command.

One reason for the invasion's success lay in the selection of three US infantry divisions, the 3rd, 36th and 45th, all of which had extensive amphibious experience. Involved in North Africa and Italy, there were no units in the US Army more experienced than these. Most importantly they knew each other and how to work together. In addition to the three US infantry divisions and four French divisions, the other forces of *Dragoon* included the Anglo-American 1st Airborne Task Force (under Major General Robert T. Frederick), the Canadian-American 1st Special Service Force, and some French special assault detachments.

Bill Mauldin, who put a smile on every story he told, understood the need for experience as well. He was probably referring to this invasion when he wrote:

> Invasions are magnificent things to watch but awful things to be in. Evidently the Army likes to pick certain outfits, train them in landing operations, and then use the same men for every invasion. This is undoubtedly an efficient system, but it gets a little rough on the guys who do the invading. My old division [the 45th Infantry Division] was one of several whose only rest seemed to come when they were waiting for

boats to carry them to other lands where the language was different but the war was the same. These amphibious creatures have seen so much action that when they land back in the States they will, just from force of habit, come off shooting and establish a beachhead around Coney Island. There they will probably dig in and fight until demobilization thins their ranks and allows the local partisans to push the survivors back into the sea.[94]

The invasion was a poorly kept secret. During the preceding weeks, German agents and aircraft had consistently reported that ships, men and materiel had been piling up in Italian ports around Naples. In fact the Germans had even announced that landings on the French Riviera were imminent. They just didn't know where. The Army Air Corps pummeled enemy installations along the French coast, bridges, and road nets from the coastal areas far inland and up the Rhône valley. The Germans kept guessing and they positioned their troops away from the Riviera in order to react to the exact landing place when the invasion happened – they lacked sufficient troops to cover the entire coast.

The Allied air forces, under the XII Tactical Air Command, were based on the island of Corsica, 100 miles from the invasion beaches. The Luftwaffe was busy supporting the Wehrmacht in Normandy and was nowhere to be seen. Four days prior to the invasion, the Allies began bombing the southern coast of France. The German 11th Panzer Division, the 19th German Army's most capable and mobile division, was trapped on the wrong side of the Rhône because most bridges along the river had already been destroyed.

Clearly, the German position was untenable. Its 19th Army, severely under strength, could not protect the 400-mile coastline, nor was it supplied with the best equipment and weapons. Its strength had been siphoned off to defend Normandy. Further compromising its effectiveness, its soldiers were largely from the occupied countries, including Russians, Poles, Czechs, Turks, North Africans and Indo-Chinese. Only their officers and non-commissioned officers were German.

While at sea on August 13, Lieutenant Colonel Tardy and his officers briefed the men of the 601st on the invasion. The 601st's A Company once again supported the 7th Infantry Regiment; B Company the 15th Infantry Regiment; and C Company the 30th Infantry Regiment. The invasion was to take place along 30 miles of coastline, roughly from St Tropez to Cannes. The 3rd Infantry Division was assigned the most westerly landing beach near St Tropez.

Close to midnight the next day, Welch wrote his mother:

> It's now 11:30 [2330]. In 5½ hours, we'll go crashing into Southern France. I think that this will be our last one. This should bring the Kraut to his knees within a few months. It's going to be a great show, and I'm glad my leg healed fast enough for me to take part. I was afraid I was going to miss France and speaking the language quite well that would be a blow. I'll write again in a few days.

The 1st Special Service Force attacked the islands of Port Cros and Levant off Toulon. These islands were thought to have some large coastal guns that needed to be eliminated. The guns proved to be dummies. Meanwhile, the 1st Airborne Task Force was to attack in the vicinity of Le Muy, a few miles inland. It was a night assault and although the majority of paratroopers landed within ten miles of their objective, some were scattered over a wide area.

According to the map in the battalion's *Informal History*, the invasion force sailed through the narrow channel between Corsica and Sardinia. This afforded the fleet excellent land-based air cover. Josowitz had this to say about the voyage:

The ships were very crowded, the food "uninteresting," the chow lines fantastically long, the sleeping and toilet facilities practically nil, but the weather was warm and the sea smooth and everybody was too scared and too worried to give a damn about anything. The Navy fired its rockets and its big guns, the bombers dropped their eggs and the assault boats went in. Nothing happened! The D-day landing at Collobrières [the collection point for the battalion], in southern France, was less trouble than some of the practice landings in Naples Harbor. The Krauts had taken off, inland.

The History of the 15th Infantry Regiment in World War II noted:

The operations began with one of the most terrific barrages in modern warfare, first the big guns of the fleet units spoke, hurling tons and tons of high explosives on the coastal positions and installations of the defenders. Then, as the first light of day crept into the overcast skies, hundreds of American and Allied aircraft raked the invasion coast, strafing and bombing. Fourteen thousand airmen flew that day from carriers and land bases, almost a larger army in the air than the enemy had on the ground.

The noise and tempo of the invasion increased to a steady and deafening roar as tiny rocket boats darted in toward shore to plaster the beaches with their murderous cargoes, 6,000 rockets were released in the division sector alone to rip up the underwater barriers, mines, and wire and to pulverize enemy positions. As H-hour approached, TNT boats, each loaded with a half-ton of explosives, were sent in by remote control to rip out whatever underwater barriers remained and these could be heard exploding above the already tremendous din of the mighty concentration of fire.[95]

The beach that the 3rd Infantry Division stormed on August 15 was bordered by pine woods and the Germans had left the coastline as inhospitable as they could. Trees cut down from those woods had been used to construct underwater and anti-glider barriers. The anti-glider barriers were composed of stakes driven into the ground and wired together. They could stop any aircraft and covered every field suitable for landing gliders. Thousands of such obstacles covered acre after acre of land. In addition there were underwater barriers and thousands of mines, many of which had been cleared by French civilians and partisan forces, who had marked the fields as being cleared or mined, which helped the invaders minimize casualties.

The Allies used deception to confuse the enemy. As had been done in Normandy there were three-foot-tall dummy parachutists dropped for the attack. Several small naval units made up of patrol craft raced towards the beaches at several points to simulate an invasion force. One of these was commanded by Lieutenant Commander Douglas Fairbanks, Jr, the popular swashbuckling American film star.

That bright, warm August morning hundreds of Allied aircraft raked, strafed and bombed the Riviera's beaches in advance of the invasion. Once again Corporal Borriello was part of the D-Day landing. He was one of the first men to go ashore from the 10th Engineer Battalion. He drove his jeep off the ramp into the water and it flooded out. To his embarrassment he had to be towed onto the beach by a battalion bulldozer.

By 0930 the invasion force was 2,000 yards inland. The low, flat beaches and pine forest had given way to long, vineyard-covered valleys. After that, the high ground was sparsely vegetated and dry. Since the 601st was among the first units landed, it loaded up the infantry and pushed inland. The Germans commenced a general withdrawal.

Welch wrote his mother later that day, probably while waiting for local guides and for his TDs to be stripped of their waterproofing equipment:

> I just have time to write a few lines and let you know I'm OK. The invasion came off very well, and still moves ahead with good speed. I am point of a task force consisting of some armored cars, light tanks and two of my TDs. We operate well ahead of everybody looking for trouble and killing Kraut. The country here is beautiful, the people nice and quite glad to see us.

As invasions go, it wasn't the worst, but it was not the "champagne campaign" as sometimes described. By 2400 on August 15 all 601st combat vehicles were ashore and operating in their respective sectors. The battalion had suffered no casualties. *The History of the 15th Infantry Regiment in World War II* states:

> The successes scored by our troops on D-Day were tremendous. The War Department called the operation the most successful operation in military history and officials referred to it as a tactician's dream. After months of planning down to the minutest details [the Navy had begun its staff work in February], the action went off without a flaw. The speed was dazzling; seven waves had been put ashore in the corps sector within the first two hours, perhaps 14,000 troops. More battalions were landed on D-Day than in any other operation, Normandy included. The attack made history. It marked the opening of a fourth front against Adolf Hitler. It was the return of the French Army, in strength, to his home soil after four years of banishment. But even more than that, never before in the five long years of fighting had the German Army been so humbled at the hands of the Allies.[96]

The town of Collobrières, the designated collection point for the 601st, was liberated that first day. Collobrières is on a road running east–west, parallel to the coast and weaving around hills. The town lies along a bend of a fast-moving stream. There is an early church, St Pons, now abandoned, on the hill. In recognition of its place in history, the village square was later renamed *Place de la Libération* – August 15, 1944. It is the only town in the area. Lieutenant Henry Anderson (East Rockaway, New York), C Company 601st, recorded these notes on the town's liberation:

> When we entered Collobrières, there was a great ovation; but we knew that the road leading into Collobrières to the north must be secured. We immediately set up a defensive position on the north end of town. We sent a French civilian in a car to inform Colonel McGarr [7th Infantry] of our success. Within an hour a company of German infantry with their small arms rode into view on bicycles. We pulled our armor forward and they quickly surrendered. The infantrymen of the 3rd Infantry Division led them into a local municipal building as prisoners.[97]

The *3rd Division Daily News*, August 16, reported the invasion of southern France under its TODAY'S SITUATION heading:

> The Third Infantry Division (known to the Krauts as the *Sturm* [Storm] Division) made its fourth major landing against a hostile shore yesterday, gaining a beachhead varying in depth from five to ten miles in the first 24 hours, and capturing an estimated 1,200 prisoners, the largest number of men in German uniform ever taken by this Division in a single day.

On the second page it was noted in a box that: TROOPS MAY WRITE HOME THAT THEY ARE IN SOUTHERN

FRANCE, BUT NO MENTION MAY BE MADE OF OPERATIONS OR UNITS INVOLVED.

As if to confirm the invasion's success, Hitler ordered a general withdrawal from southern France that day. Only Marseille, Toulon and several other smaller ports were to be defended. The two ports had only 13,000 and 18,000 German troops respectively. At this time, Sergeant Nowak wrote:

> We moved rapidly and took many towns. On the 17th we picked up two paratroopers and they stayed with us.[98] We moved on the road to Toulon. Near a crossroad we got fired on. A Sherman tank with us was disabled. We ambushed a bicycle patrol, but early firing by a doughboy enabled them to escape on foot. We were relieved that evening by the French while we carried doughs and moved to another sector. In advancing on one town, two doughs were killed by snipers. We went on a roadblock with 3rd Recon[99] and ambushed a 20-man patrol. We went to St. Maximin where we saw a woman paraded around with hair shaved off for dealing with the Nazis. She gave information to the Nazis, which caused the deaths of 27 French Foreign Legion soldiers. The next day she was shot.

Now the casualties started. Tech Four Evan S. Dalrymple (Frenchtown, New Jersey) and Private First Class Melvin F. Freeman (Augusta, Georgia) were both killed on August 17. Freeman was in C Company and it is not known if Dalrymple was with him. Like so many others, including Staff Sergeant Joseph S. Zielewicz (Cleveland, Ohio) and Sergeant Harold B. Jarrett (Salisbury, North Carolina) who died the next day, the details are unrecorded. It is likely they were the men Staff Sergeant Benjamin A. Buckley (Lowell, Indiana) of C Company wrote his parents about. His tank was blown from under him, killing three of the crew, and wounding one, but he escaped without a scratch.

On August 19, Private Burl E. Meeks (Waverley, West Virginia) was reported as missing in action and his remains were never found. The death of Private Eduard A. Dabulas (Scranton, Pennsylvania) on August 22 must also be recorded. He died of his wounds on that day, but when or where he was wounded is unknown.

Sergeant Nowak's section was credited by battalion operations with capturing three prisoners of war, killing 18 Germans, and destroying two trucks and one car. Unfortunately during this action on August 20, Nowak suffered multiple shrapnel wounds from an exploding rifle grenade. He was transferred to Naples and was out of action until early September.

Over in C Company, Staff Sergeant Benjamin A. Buckley was awarded an Oak Leaf Cluster to his Bronze Star while in action against the enemy on August 21. The citation is as follows:

> In action against the enemy on 21 August 1944, at about 1600 hours, in the vicinity of La Begude de Lauzane, France, in an attempt to obtain better observation and thereby give maximum support to our advancing infantry, Sergeant Buckley dismounted from the safety of his M-10. Spying a force of "Kraut" deploying over the top of a knoll, he took an exposed position on the rear of his destroyer and directed 3-inch and machine-gun fire on these enemy soldiers. Despite small-arms fire striking his destroyer and slashing the branches over his head, Sergeant Buckley continued to direct his destroyer's fire for over fifteen minutes with the result that he forced the enemy back over the top of the hill and by deliberate targeting, blasted a mortar observer out of a concrete OP. Upon later investigation, the slope Sergeant Buckley fired on was found to be littered with dead "Kraut."

The French troops that landed in southern France were designated French Army B (French Army A had fought in Italy). They were part of the second wave of Operation *Dragoon*. Their landing was actually pushed up six days because of the lack of German opposition. For political reasons they were the forces that liberated Toulon, Marseille, and eventually Lyon.[100] To allow the French time to capture Toulon, on August 21, General O'Daniel ordered the 3rd Division "take up aggressive defense for a short time."[101] Josowitz made this comment about the invasion:

> After fighting alongside of the FFI [*Forces Françaises de l'Intérieur,* Free French of the Interior] and witnessing the hysterical celebrations, the head shaving, the accidental shootings and even a few hangings, it became easier to understand Napoleon's march from Marseilles to Paris during which his followers grew from a corporal's guard to an army. There were torchlight parades and the Marseillaise and champagne and beautiful girls who insisted on kissing the "Liberators," and volunteer spies and scouts and yellow head-lighted motor patrols. There was a fever about the war in Southern France; a wild, inspiring, patriotic fever; a contagious fever that affected everyone, sooner or later. It made men try harder and push harder. The Kraut didn't stand a chance. They were spied upon and misled and ambushed. And the champagne was wonderful!

When the invasion of southern France took place, the US Seventh Army encountered the irregular forces of the French Forces of the Interior (FFI). This organization was originally made up of French resistance fighters. In southern France they evolved into a force of more than 6,000 men and had the Wehrmacht tied up. In October 1944 when the status of France changed from being an occupied nation to a liberated one, the FFI were organized into light infantry units with the regular French forces.[102]

Although there had been plenty of action and much progress, on August 23, the Germans took a stand at the small village of

Allan south of Montélimar. The 15th Infantry Regiment was supported by the 756th Tank Battalion and B Company 601st Tank Destroyer Battalion. The Germans aggressively stopped the advance for several hours that day and inflicted several US casualties.[103]

No one can predict how a battle will go and it pays to be prudent. The planners may have been overly cautious, however, when they front-loaded the invasion with extra ammunition and artillery at the expense of fuel, replacement vehicles and spare parts. It was a prudent decision as on every other amphibious invasion German resistance had started on the beaches. The Allied advance was initially unexpectedly rapid as the Germans quickly realized they could not defend southern France and retreated. But the American lack of fuel soon slowed everything down and they could not pursue the retreating Germans.

"Avenue of the Stenches"

Despite the lack of fuel, the Allies had much to celebrate. On August 23, Paris was liberated by French and US forces. In the south, regular units of French Army B took the French naval base at Toulon on August 25 and Marseille was taken on August 28.

Captain Rydal L. Sanders, a member of the 601st Recon Company, wrote: "On August 29th an artillery observer spotted a large convoy of heavy cargo vehicles; about 2,000 in all. It included horses and carts and personnel. It stretched out along Highway Seven north of Montelimar for 14 kilometers."[104]

The next day a destroyer from the 2nd Platoon B Company in support of 1st Battalion 15th Infantry scored multiple hits on the convoy. It fired on and destroyed a German gasoline truck, an ammunition truck and a truck carrying personnel, killing several of the enemy. On a larger scale, this attack stopped a retreating Germany convoy of 300 vehicles, and they

Somewhere in Germany, April 1945. The officer to the right is Lieutenant Maynard. (Larson collection)

B Company scout car on the west bank of the Rhine, late March 1945. For most of the men in the 601st this was their third time to the river. (Larson collection)

B Company 601st and the 15th Infantry were the last to cross the Rhine, south of the ancient cathedral city of Worms, March 26, 1945. (NARA)

A white sheet hangs from a window of a German house as a sign of surrender, April 1945. (Nowak collection)

The 601st makes a brief stop along the road, somewhere inside Germany, April 1945. (Larson collection)

Larson and his crew on the outskirts of Nuremburg, April 16, 1945, shortly before he was wounded. (Larson collection)

Nuremburg, Germany taken from a TD, April 1945. (Larson collection)

Sergeant Nowak leaving Strasbourg in a boxcar in the evening, April 28, 1945. (Nowak collection)

A Company 601st enters Berchtesgaden, May 4, 1945. (NARA)

Victory in Europe Day (VE Day) found half the battalion drinking champagne liberated from Hitler's cellars at the Berghof on Obersalzburg, outside Berchtesgaden, May 4, 1945. Photo from the cover of *Yank Magazine* and titled "3rd Division Soldiers drinking Hitler's Champagne at the Berghof."

Above: 601st M-36s lined up at the end of the war, summer 1945. (Larson collection)

Right: Betty Welch Failmezger and her brother, Tommy Welch, June 1945. Betty, the author's mother, was in her Red Cross Volunteer uniform. (Author's collection)

Staff Sergeant Clyde Choate about to be presented the Medal of Honor by President Harry S. Truman, August 23, 1945. (NARA)

The men of the deactivated 601st TD Battalion at Salzburg, Austria, prepare to board trains for the trip home at 1000, August 18, 1945. (Larson collection)

From left, Captain Monika Stoy, US Army (Retired), Mr Joe Borriello (WWII veteran and a contributor to this book) and the author after placing a wreath on the Tomb of the Unknown Soldier, Arlington National Cemetery August, 2011. (Courtesy of Dennis G. Hatchell)

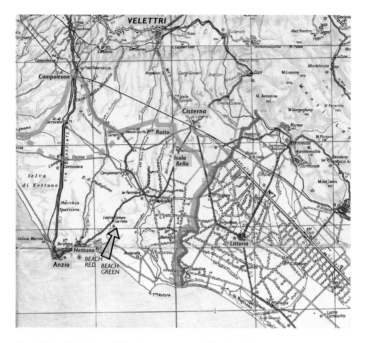

General Crane's battle map of the Anzio area, annotated by the author.

Brigadier General William Carey Crane (1891–1978) was a 1913 graduate of the US Military Academy at West Point. In 1944–1945 he was the Artillery Commander of the US Army IV Corps. Although not marked up, the map retains evidence of use during the period. W. Carey Crane, III of Middleburg, VA, a grandson of the general and a friend of the author's, gave permission for this map to be used in this book. Significant towns and locations like Cisterna, Ponte Rotto and Isola Bella are highlighted. The blue line is the Mussolini Canal, 60 yards wide and 16 feet deep, forming the eastern border of the beachhead. The solid green line shows the approximate extent of the beachhead February 1, 1944 and the dotted green line shows the location of the Allied line on February 12 after German counterattacks. An arrow marks the approximate position where the 601st landed.

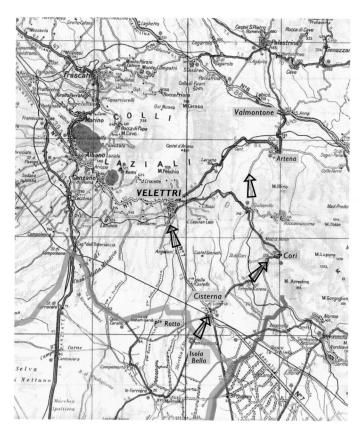

The 3rd Infantry Division's Anzio breakout – General Crane's battle map, annotated by the author. The blue line is the Mussolini Canal, and the blue areas indicate lakes. The green line represents the Allied beachhead.

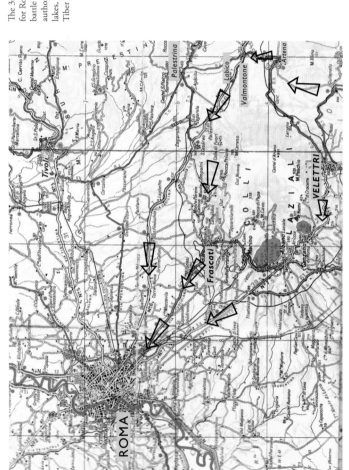

The 3rd Infantry Division's race for Rome – General Crane's battle map, annotated by the author. The blue areas indicate lakes, and the blue line is the Tiber River.

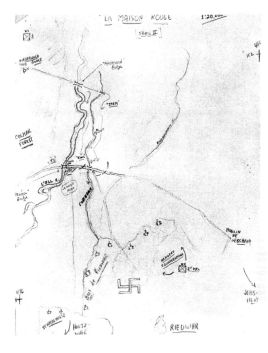

This sketch and the next are from Lieutenant Melvin J. Lasky's report on the action at a small French farmhouse called La Maison Rouge, January 23–24, 1945. The map shows the route of two 15th Infantry companies, Item and King, as they crossed the Ill River at 0400 on the 24th via a reconstructed Niederwald footbridge and took up positions around La Maison Rouge (King) and east of the Orchbach Stream an hour later. The position of Welch's three TDs is clearly marked on the other side of the La Maison Bridge.

Daybreak at La Maison Rouge, showing Item Company overrun by German troops of the 2nd Mountain Division and the King Company line of foxholes about to be overrun. The tanks indicated to the north of the farmhouse are two Shermans (both disabled) and one 601st TD which had crossed the Ill River via a temporary bridge at Niederwald and arrived about 0830 on January 24th. The position of Lieutenant Welch's three TDs across the Ill River is clearly marked. It was from here that the lieutenant kept up a barrage on the advancing German armor approaching from the southeast.

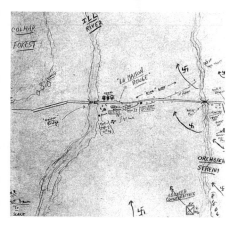

601st Tank Destroyer Battalion Flag showing the unit's ten World War II Battle Stars. The flag is now on display at the 3rd Infantry Division Museum, Fort Stewart, Georgia.

Lieutenant Welch's Tank Destroyer patch.

US 5th Army patch.

US 7th Army patch.

US 3rd Infantry Division patch.

captured the entire convoy. This foreshadowed an even larger attack on a German column at Montélimar just one day later.

Since August 22, Allied forces from the 36th Infantry Division had been following and attacking retreating Germans to the north and east of the town of Montélimar. On August 30, the 3rd Infantry Division arrived from the south and on that day, the 601st was credited with destroying hundreds of retreating German vehicles in the vicinity of Montélimar. Lieutenant Henry Anderson of C Company 601st described the scene:

> As I approached the highest point north of the city, I saw the greatest sight I had ever seen. There were columns of all types of armor, trucks, artillery pieces and personnel of many units on foot. There also were large pieces of artillery on flat cars on the RR line adjoining the highway. This was finally the chance to look down their throat for a change. We fired every piece of ammunition at the enemy scoring direct hits, even knocking out the steam engine pulling the RR cars. The 3-inch naval guns that we were using in our TDs were so hot we could hardly get the shells loaded home due to breech expansion.[105]

Captain Sanders noted: "When the artillery, tank destroyers and air bombing was over (the next day), the three-day action accounted for 485 killed and wounded; 800 enemy prisoners and 1,000 dead horses. The stretch of road was nicknamed the Avenue of Stenches."

Still, many Germans and much equipment made it beyond Montélimar. Welch, who missed this action, wrote about the first two weeks after the invasion in a letter to his mother from the hospital in Naples:

> Well I'm in again. I seem to have a way with hospitals. This time I have malaria, and I feel pretty mean. I don't know how long this takes to cure. I had 15 fast and furious days on the

beach in France, and boy what days they were. We did not have much trouble getting in, but met some resistance at scattered points. We got into quite a number of fights and we managed to kill quite a few Kraut. We were moving all the time through the most delightful country and lovely little French towns. The people in these towns were moved with joy at our arrival. Old men and women would cry and kiss you on both cheeks, we felt like Julius Caesar. The wines here are excellent, the famous Rhone valley. I was evacuated by plane to Naples in 3½ hours, a very pleasant ride despite the fact I was so sick.

Sergeant Larson wrote his brother about pursuing the Germans, just after the action at Montélimar on August 31:

This surely is a type of war that's different from what we experienced in Italy, especially at Anzio. Needless to say it is much more to our liking. Our biggest job is keeping up with Jerry though at times he stops and puts up quite a battle. We have little time for rest; a full night's rest has become a rare luxury. We may push at him all day long, and then when night comes instead of getting some sleep we'll probably take a 30 or 40 mile road march to cut some vital road or maybe move in on some town not previously occupied. One night my lieutenant [Welch], another sergeant, and I went in and took a town by ourselves. A good-sized German garrison had been stationed there previously but fortunately for us they had moved out just before we came in.

The FFI here is doing a swell job. The Germans have snipers and small pockets of resistance behind us as they withdraw and are quite a menace. But usually the FFI rounds them up in short order. And they cause plenty of grief to the retreating Germans by wrecking communications, roads, bridges, etc. In one town we took over we were talking to a beautiful girl when we first entered the town. We all thought she was pretty swell. But while still talking to her, the FFI seized her, shaved her head, informing us that she had kept company with a German soldier.[106] I got myself a nice German Luger pistol a couple of days ago when I took a German sergeant and a German corporal prisoner. Hope I get a chance to bring it home with me. I also got lots of other stuff off of them, including about $140 that I divided among the crew on my tank.

To the officers of the 601st, it was clear that relief was needed by the overworked tank destroyers as pointed out in the "lessons learned" section of the August battalion report of operations:

> In one case a platoon of four M-10s was spread out over a front of 40 miles acting as individual roadblocks. This mission should have been assigned to infantry organic antitank guns. Maintenance has been made difficult and tank crews extremely fatigued by the fact that they continue in the attack with the leading infantry company. They do not get relief when one infantry company is passed through by another. One platoon should always be kept in reserve and rotated in the assault.

Josowitz summed up these early days in France corroborating the reports of constant pressure he and others were under:

> In retrospect, the advance up the Rhone valley seems to have been little more than a rough tactical motor march but it would be rather dangerous to mention that to a guy who was, shall we say, a lead scout or a tank driver. All they heard was "Keep 'em moving all the time! Load up and move! Keep 'em on the run!" No maps, no gas, no tires, no tracks, no spare parts, no ammunition but keep moving! That list should include, NO MAIL.

The success of the invasion was undeniably spectacular. During the first 15 days of the invasion, it is estimated 75,000 men of the German 19th Army were captured, cutting its strength roughly in half. The prisoners added to the strain on the Seventh Army, which had to feed and guard these hordes.

The whole battalion cut to the northeast on September 1, along the Isère River to the town of Voiran, about 20 miles northwest of Grenoble. The 93-mile trek was done in one day. The next day, September 2, the Free French liberated Lyons. After a two-day break, the 601st continued to the northeast to the vicinity of the town of Lons le Saunier, a town about 100 miles northwest of Geneva, Switzerland. The 3rd Division then advanced into position to attack the ancient fortress city of Besançon high on a hill over the river Doubs in the province of the Franche-Comté. The advance was again slowed due to equipment problems. According to Yeide: "At one point in September, almost half of the M10s in the 645th Tank Destroyer Battalion were dead-lined, most because of worn-out tracks."[107]

Welch, out of the hospital, wrote his mother:

> Just a line to inform you that I'm back in France. I flew up from Italy with another officer from the battalion. After we landed here we had to travel 300 miles quick to catch our outfit. So you can see we're really moving here. It looks mighty good, but I've long ago given up all types of speculation on the length or the duration. I've had no mail for two months, we move so fast.

Welch was able to rejoin his platoon on September 8, in the vicinity of Besançon. The city of 80,000 straddled vital land-communications links. After a two-day battle, Besançon was cleared of Germans late on September 8. After the war, Staff Sergeant Buckley over in C Company told about the attack on the town for a local newspaper:

Battering down centuries-old walls of medieval castles proved a tough job even for modern armor and high-velocity guns, a veteran tank destroyer platoon sergeant found out when the cannons of his platoon were turned on the moss-covered ramparts guarding Besançon in France. S/Sgt. Benjamin A. Buckley with his platoon from Company C of the 601st, supporting the 1st Battalion of the 30th United States Infantry Regiment. The retreating Germans, nearing the end of their flight from southern France early in September of last year, determined to make a rearguard stand at Besançon, outpost of the Belfort Gap into the Rhine valley, while their beaten units streamed through the gap. They made the stand for two days.

Our 3-inch guns made more of an impression in that old masonry at 800 yards than did the HE shells of the 155mm [about 6in.] howitzers. But it really was the concussion from the 155s which finally drove the Krauts out. Those walls were of stone three feet thick, backed by six feet of sod. [108]

With the capture of Besançon, the nature of German resistance changed. The September battalion operations report describes it this way:

From the time of initial contact with the enemy south of Besançon until the end of the month, there was close contact with the enemy at all times. His action was a steady withdrawal with an occasional stand in the vicinity of towns or villages. Operating in close support of the infantry at all times, the gun companies knocked out numerous enemy strongpoints, machine-gun nests, and fortified houses, thereby facilitating the more rapid advance of our elements. During the major part of the month the terrain plus the weather was favorable towards moving the destroyers cross-country. However, at the end of this period, mountains and wooded terrain were encountered and the rains set in which forced all vehicles to stay on the roads. Upon seizure of successive objectives, the destroyers were placed on roadblock and flank protection missions to assist in countering enemy infiltrating and repelling counterattacks.

Battalion KIAs continued. Private Walter J. Kielar (Philadelphia, Pennsylvania) was killed in action in the vicinity of Besançon on September 8. He had been a member of A Company.

The US Third Army, coming from western France, and the US Seventh Army, coming from the south of France, joined up at last on September 11. The problem of supply became critical because both armies had long pipelines for materiel and supplies. For the Seventh it was now more than 500 miles. The battalion report noted that throughout the month of September: "the enemy employed antitank guns, roadblocks, mines, artillery, infantry, and snipers in his effort to slow the advance of armor in support of the friendly infantry regiments." The following detailed accounting is adapted from a portion of the summary:

- Antitank guns were usually found on high ground, at the rear of towns, well camouflaged and manned by experienced gunners who tried to pick off any crewmen who showed their heads above the turrets. Our fire often caused the German antitank crews to surrender.
- Roadblocks consisted of felled trees with mined approaches, booby traps and antitank guns.
- Mines were found in greater numbers and they slowed up movement. Even tiny trails were mined. There were also dummy minefields made from wooden crates with tin can tops.
- Artillery prevented TDs advancing when terrain was too soft to allow cross-country movement and restricted road movement.

PROGRESS OF THE 601st
THROUGH FRANCE
1944–1945
→ Route of the 601st

- Infantry and snipers: "The open turret of the M-10 has made movement through towns extremely hazardous to the vehicle's crew because snipers can locate themselves at high points in buildings and shoot down into the tank destroyers. Snipers were found almost any place but most frequently along wooded banks which ran close to the road. No casualties were reported from sniper fire, however. Many snipers were armed with 'bazookas' and ordinarily were found along the roadside at the edges of towns or heavily wooded areas."[109]

"From my tank all were killed"

After Besançon, the battalion moved up from the flat river valley into countryside that became hilly and wooded north of the town of Vesoul and through the village of Espreis. Welch wrote his sister:

I started this [letter] four days ago and we have been moving ever since, and this is the first chance I've had to answer it. Things have been going pretty well here up until a few days ago, and then the Kraut showed a little fight. We have to fight all the time now. I really think that it should be over soon. We're getting really close, and I don't see how he can hold out much longer.

At the village of Colombotte near Espreis, B Company suffered their worst single day in combat in France on September 13. Three TDs were hit and six men from Lieutenant Bell's 2nd Platoon were killed and six others were wounded, two seriously. According to the unit journal, two of the TDs were caught out in the open by a hidden antitank 88mm gun as they moved down a road. The third TD was hit as it maneuvered out of the way and slid down a road embankment. Sergeant Colprit witnessed the deadly aftermath of this day when he returned to the battalion from the hospital on September 14. He had been wounded previously at Anzio on May 24, during the breakout to Rome.

On the way we spotted a sign for the 601st beside the road so in the morning we walked back to join the outfit. As we walked in some of the boys met us with burns on their faces and some bandages. The day before they had lost two tanks and five or six men killed. From my tank all were killed. Tommy was gone [Tech Four Joseph Thomas]. Sergeant Prauman was gone and others. My body turned to jelly and my legs would hardly hold me. The next day I was promoted to sergeant and given command of a tank. The only way I could restore myself was to realize that the enemy were fighting for their country just as I was and that they were using live ammunition and someone was to get hurt or killed.

All those in the first tank destroyer were killed: Staff Sergeant Earl L. Prauman (Manchester, New Hampshire), tank commander; Sergeant James C. Childers (North Bend, Ohio); Tech Four Joseph Thomas (Campbell, Ohio, the Tommy in Colprit's stories at Anzio); Private William B. Brown (Eclectic, Alabama); and Private Richard C. Corthell (Haverhill, Massachusetts). The second and third TDs suffered one killed, Sergeant Alfred Hoffman (East Schodack, New York), the tank commander, and two seriously wounded: Sergeant Robert J. Morvant (New Orleans, Louisiana) and Private Charles G. Upton (Sacramento, California). Four others were wounded but not hospitalized; Sergeant John W. Martell (Pawcatuck, Connecticut); Corporal Howard E. Aldridge (Belton, Missouri); Private Maurice D. Amerine (Great Bend, Indiana) and Private Robert C. Hines (Delhi, Minnesota).[110]

Although it made little difference to the soldiers on the ground, the US Army officially ended the Southern France campaign on September 14, 1944. The Rhineland campaign commenced the next day, September 15. According to Jeff Danby the cost to the Allies had been high:

When the battle for southern France ended on September 15th, more than 2,000 Americans were listed among the killed, captured, or missing, with another 2,500 wounded. Regular Free French forces suffered similar losses, and many other French Resistance irregulars and civilians perished. Estimates of German losses run as high as 7,000 killed and 21,000 wounded. For all of these unfortunate souls, southern France was no Champagne campaign.[111]

CHAPTER 12
CONQUERORS OF THE VOSGES

"Officers are never tired"

At the end of the Southern France campaign the battalion moved to the village of Raddon near the town of Lure, where they stayed until September 24. While still on alert, the troops had a much needed but short break. The mood in the ranks was now less aggressive and this worried the top brass. Complacency at this point could stall efforts and actually lengthen the war. Two letters point out the contrasting views of the war.

Lieutenant Welch's letters, his last for well over a month, describe tourist aspects on the ground:

France is indeed a very beautiful country. It's very much like upstate New York in a lot of respects. Everything is very fertile and green and the people don't seem to have suffered much from the war. The villages especially are very quiet with a decided Swiss influence in the sector in which we have been operating. They consist of 15 or 20 stone houses in a quiet valley. All have red tile roofs and very high gables. The people almost without exception wear the wooden *sabots* [wooden shoe]. The houses are spotless and the people friendly if not exuberant. Each village centers on the church and in most cases it's usually very old. The people ask us in for eggs, potatoes and red wine. The cities, like Marseille, Cannes, Nice, Grenoble, Lyon and such are quite modern and like all cities. Here the people go wild when we come in. We have dances in the street and much singing of the Marseillaise. Everyone but us usually winds up quite drunk.

The Riviera and Monte Carlo are all they are cracked up to be in scenery and such. The gambling houses and hotels are getting quite packed from lots of us. The service there is still excellent despite the war. I pulled my tanks up to the Grand Hotel in Cannes, which is a beaut, and we spent the night in luxury. I'm afraid we didn't make such a big impression on them as we hadn't showered or washed in a week. Nevertheless we barged in, got wonderful rooms, good meals and I had quite a talk with the bartender, who is quite well known in the international set and knew the Prince of Wales, etc. He told some good stories over excellent martinis. Quite an experience.[112]

The day the above letter was written, Lieutenant Colonel Tardy and all commanding officers received a stern letter from Major General John W. "Iron Mike" O'Daniel, US Army, commanding general of the 3rd Infantry Division. The subject is "Fighting to Be Done" and it is reproduced below in its entirety:

There is a noted tendency on the part of some commanders and troops to allow their effort toward vigorous assault to lag. Some explanations are that the men are tired, they are wet, the enemy fire slows them up, the hills are bad, and they believe the war will soon be over, so why subject themselves to possible injury.

This attitude, where prevalent, will be corrected at once. The following points will be brought to the attention of all officers.

The German knows that he is bound to lose by surrender. He also knows that if he holds out by fighting to the last that he will be no worse off than by surrender; in fact, he may gain by holding out in that we may tire of the war and agree to more lenient peace terms. If he does continue to fight, which he doubtless intends to do, and we are not aggressive in our actions, he will regain the advantage and the fighting will become tough or tougher than Anzio.

The country here favors the defender. He will have more artillery and mortars than at Anzio and it will be more active and accurate. Summing this up means that the slackening up of offensive action on our part will play directly into the hands of the enemy and will cause us to bog down, necessitate digging in and then be subjected to intensive fire, which will cause high casualties.

On the other hand, if we are vigorous in our actions, aggressive and relentless in our attack, the enemy will have no opportunity to get the range on us nor will he be able to stop us because we will keep him off balance. Therefore, any remarks concerning being tired, wet, or a mental attitude toward the war's being over soon, must be discouraged.

Officers are never tired. Any indication by an officer that he is tired is epidemic with the men he commands. Therefore that word is taboo. We are never pinned down or stopped because we have the means of overcoming any enemy action.

The war will be over when we, by our action, defeat the German Army. Let's have no more Anzios. Any shirking or neglect of duty by any officer of your command will be reported to me personally by you. You are to take action at once in the form of talks to your officers concerning the subject matter of this letter. Bear down and neglect nothing toward pushing the attack.

And bear down they did. By September 27 the 601st was in the vicinity of the town of Remiremont. It had met, as predicted by "Iron Mike," tough resistance from the Germans through mountainous terrain on the heavily wooded western slopes of the Vosges Mountains. The road had climbed out of Lure through forests and the villages of Rupt and St Amé. The mountains run north–south for 70 miles and are 40 miles wide. Terrain became an enemy. At the end of the month Sergeant Nowak noted:

> On the 27th we moved out towards Remiremont, passed St. Amé, and finally stopped near a sawmill. It rained pretty steadily. We moved out and got into firing positions. We registered on a couple of roads we had good views of. We fired 65 rounds into the town of Vagney. The last day we put on a shoot with a quadruple .50 caliber ack-ack half-track.

The next objective was the town of Gerardmer, about 30 miles west of Colmar. *The History of the 15th Infantry Regiment in World War II* notes:

> It was also the beginning of some of the bitterest and bloodiest fighting in the 15th Regiment's long combat record. Troops of questionable caliber had given way to crack enemy front-line units, or to scores of fanatical Hitler Youth who were preparing to defend their home soil to the last. The regiment was now fighting under tremendously difficult circumstances. The thickly forested hills and mountains gave all the advantages in terrain to the defenders.[113]

Noting their disadvantage, the 601st Battalion report of operations for the month of October described the situation this way:

> Because of the terrain, which afforded the enemy excellent defensive positions, resistance became considerably stronger

and our advance slowed somewhat. The mountainous country allowed only limited maneuvering of enemy armor; consequently, the battalion's main mission became that of direct assault fire in support of the infantry regiments, rather than principally in the role of protection against enemy armored attacks. It was impracticable to employ all of the guns of the battalion because of the limited road net; therefore, many of the gun platoons in the battalion were employed in indirect fire positions on night harassing missions. The wooded and mountainous terrain presented problems that heretofore had not been encountered in France. The movement of the tank destroyers required extensive foot reconnaissance on the part of the platoon commanders and chiefs of section in order to find favorable trails by which the destroyers could keep up with the infantry and give it the necessary supporting fire. However, this movement of the tank destroyers over seemingly impossible routes, through woods and over hill masses, paid big dividends in that it allowed the destroyers to surprise the enemy with devastating flank fire.

The Germans exploited their advantage in the hilly terrain by laying mines, setting roadblocks and manning antitank weapons. Autumn rains kept the TDs on the few roads in the region, providing another advantage to the enemy. Progress was slow, painstaking and fatiguing for the Allies. The battalion report noted that elements of the 601st had been in the line for 77 consecutive days.

The reassignments continued. On October 2, A Company was off on a special assignment and B Company was split up among the 7th and 15th Infantry Regiments. The monthly report notes that October 2 to 20, B Company was active near the villages of Vagney, Sapois, St Amé, Moselle, Le Tholy, and Don Martin, a relatively small area.

At St Amé, the road turns northward following the Cleurie River. Along this road, B Company 601st supported the 15th Infantry Regiment in a six-day battle for the German occupied Cleurie (L'Oment) quarry. The quarry overlooked the main road that the 15th Infantry Regiment needed to move north. This quarry had extensive tunnels, which the German soldiers used for cover during artillery attacks. After the shelling stopped they would pop up and fire at the US infantry. It was a virtually impregnable stronghold from which the enemy guarded a roadblock, preventing any Allied movement. The Germans reinforced their troops in the quarry with a hastily formed emergency company of 100 cooks, butchers and bakers.

Sergeant Colprit describes the 601st's part in a successful action on October 8:

> The infantry had met much resistance in trying to capture a quarry. It faced north and advancing from the south they were not able to bring fire upon the enemy within the quarry. They asked for one of our destroyers to cross the valley and go up on the high ground to bring fire across the valley and into the quarry where the enemy was in buildings there. We took up a position the evening before. I measured on a map, estimated by sight and decided on 2,500 yards. I did not get much sleep that night, knowing our infantry were near the rim of the quarry and any miss on my part would mean death or injury to some of our troops. In the morning we waited for the mist and fog to clear and we fired the first shot. The sound echoed over the valley sounding like a freight train. The first shot went right into the quarry and Lt. Bell gave me the order to fire for effect. As we fired the last shot the infantry stormed in and captured the quarry allowing other troops to advance up the valley.

By 1030 the quarry had been taken. Sergeant Nowak described a frustrated attack further up the valley:

We went to another sector with the 15th Infantry and did some firing from a high hill. In one place were the remains of a medic's jeep that had run over a mine. On the second day of firing we got direct fire in return. They were short and ever so close. I really got scared and got into a ditch. The driver moved our TD into the cover of a wood. Later we went back and one shell had hit exactly where our TD had been, and another hit a tree behind which Larson was hiding [in his TD]. We tried moving ahead, but rain and mud and impossible roads stopped us. We got three out of four tanks and TDs stuck at one time but luckily we got them out.

The buildings along this road were distinctly Alpine in appearance: houses and other structures were hung with flower boxes. The road mounts higher and winds as it moves up the valley to the village of Le Tholy. The World War I memorial and the village church were badly damaged during the defense of this road. The battalion had no Panzers to attack but did shoot at *Flakwagens* (flak wagons: mobile antiaircraft guns), enemy-held houses, hilltops, wooded areas and other strongpoints.

The strain of combat, physical and psychological, was taking a heavy toll on the troops. Skin infections were becoming endemic, largely as the result of constant wet weather and a chronic shortage of bathing facilities. Many veterans of the bitter winter fighting in the Italian mountains had little stomach for winter operations in the French mountains. Morale was further affected by the heavy officer and NCO casualties and the perceived decline in leadership as enlisted men were promoted to fill the void. In addition, replacements were often poorly trained. General O'Daniel's fears were echoed by other senior officers and troop commanders.

Stopgap solutions were tried. At least one division established rest camps for the men. One officer expressed his faith in his troops' ability to bounce back: "You give them three days and they'll be back in shape without any trouble. Just leave them alone, let them sleep and eat the first day, make them clean up the second day, and do whatever they want to do the rest of the time and they'll be ready to go."

Moving supplies to units in the field became even harder as forces moved farther into the mountains. Optimism over the capabilities of Mediterranean ports and the supply lines proved premature. The problem was serious; during two days in October the Seventh Army received only 20 tons of ammunition, while its units were using nearly 1,000 tons per day. Severe rationing was the only immediate answer. In desperation 300 mules were sent from Italy to haul rations and munitions to the troops. Although providing forage for the animals posed another problem there was little or no interference from German artillery or mines on these mule supply trains.

"Did a pretty good imitation of Superman"

Progress had slowed so much that front-line gains were being measured in yards. The reasons were obvious, as McFarland noted: "the enemy made good use of his mortars and 20mm flak wagons to support his well-organized, dug in infantry. Prisoners consistently reported that a special company of SS troops was threatening them from the rear to prevent their withdrawal and to urge them to attack."[114]

Most of the battalion stood down outside Remiremont, beginning on October 10 and for the next ten days remained on alert. It is a small town and must have been very full when occupied by American soldiers. Remiremont was the 3rd Infantry Headquarters from September 27 to October 20. Both equipment and men needed maintenance and rest. According to Josowitz "there were passes to Remiremont, movies, cognac, girls, MPs and delinquency reports."

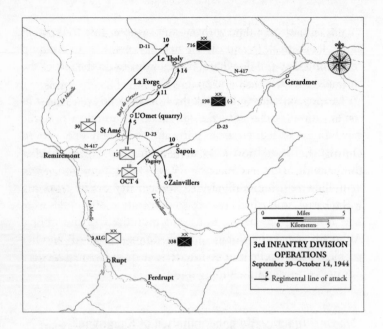

3rd INFANTRY DIVISION
OPERATIONS
September 30–October 14, 1944
→ Regimental line of attack

It may have been at Remiremont that Captain Rydal L. Sanders recalled that during the time out of combat, discipline sometimes became a problem. On one occasion he noted that a drunken 601st Master Sergeant took a swing at him, but his company First Sergeant "cold cocked" him. The next morning the Master Sergeant came by to apologize for his act of the night before, but Captain Sanders said that he "didn't remember the incident, case closed." Further Captain Sanders noted that "the unit was very religious in between crap games, a fling in town and a little bottle of vino."

In a letter to his wife Elizabeth, dated October 11, Lieutenant Colonel Tardy noted the need for rest during this period:

> Maj. Danny Hinman, my executive officer, left yesterday along with two junior officers in the battalion for a 30-day leave in the states. I'll miss him but I'm glad for him to get

this respite, and I think a change of scenery will do all three of them a world of good. We heard all broadcasts of the World Series games, and it surely was an exciting series. And, incidentally, I picked up $30 on a few little friendly wagers. I seem to do better on baseball than on poker. It's been a long time since I got into a poker session.

During the stand down, Lieutenant Colonel Tardy held a company commanders' meeting on October 13 and the agenda items illustrate the disciplinary, equipment and morale problems at the battalion level:

a. Looting, suppression and punishment of offenders
b. Drilling and maintenance when not in actual combat
c. Reporting of shell [usage] reports
d. Stragglers
e. Laxity of aggressive action
f. Illegal confiscation of personal articles from prisoners
g. Unreliable source of FFI information
h. Replacement training
i. Future division offensive action
j. Company grade officers
k. Attitude of men to the "Destructive to the Enemy-Initiative to Drive on"
l. Arrangements for rest and entertainment, showers, etc.
m. Delinquency reports
n. Discussion of overhead cover for M-10 against air bursts
o. Dissemination of orders down to the last man. Enforcement of orders
p. Communications between tanks, tank destroyers and infantry. Various plans discussed. No definite decisions reached
q. Driver and Gunnery School. Each company to send two drivers and two gunners to VI Corps 1st Armored

Group School. A Co to furnish one M-10 with driver and gunner

r. Prospects for combat promotions and commissions

s. BN S-4 [supply] reported that winter clothing available by first of the month. Ammunition shortage still exists; 2,300 rounds 3-inch in battalion reserve

t. General briefing on future division attack

The 601st moved to the town of Grandvilliers and prepared to attack the towns of Bruyères and Verezelle, which were taken by elements of the 3rd Division on October 22. According to Nowak "The Krauts once again counterattacked using American uniforms, and one company of the 7th Infantry Regiment lost many men."

The 601st lost a man too. First Lieutenant Tolbert Hays, Jr (Orland, California) was killed in action on October 23. Originally buried in the American Cemetery at Épinal, France, his family requested his remains be sent to California and he now rests in the Golden Gate National Cemetery, San Francisco.

It was in the vicinity of Bruyères that Staff Sergeant Clyde L. Choate (Anna, Illinois) of C Company according to Josowitz "did a pretty good imitation of Superman" when he singlehandedly knocked out a German Panzer. Sergeant Colprit summed up Staff Sergeant Choate's deed:

> The story is that his tank was knocked out and he ran to an infantryman and took a bazooka, ran through a hail of bullets that nearly tore his jacket off. He disabled the enemy tank but it was still firing so he went back and got another bazooka shell, went back and finished off the tank.

For this action he received the Medal of Honor, the only one awarded to a man from the 601st during the entire war.

Staff Sergeant Choate's official Medal of Honor citation tells the same story but with more detail:

> He commanded a tank destroyer near Bruyeres, France, on October 25, 1944. Our infantry occupied a position on a wooded hill when, at dusk, an enemy Mark IV tank and a company of infantry attacked, threatening to overrun the American position and capture a command post 400 yards to the rear. S/Sgt. Choate's tank destroyer, the only weapon available to oppose the German armor, was set afire by two hits. Ordering his men to abandon the destroyer, S/Sgt. Choate reached comparative safety. He returned to the burning destroyer to search for comrades possibly trapped in the vehicle risking instant death in an explosion which was imminent and braving enemy fire which ripped his jacket and tore the helmet from his head. Completing the search and seeing the tank and its supporting infantry overrunning our infantry in their shallow foxholes, he secured a bazooka and ran after the tank, dodging from tree to tree and passing through the enemy's loose skirmish line. He fired a rocket from a distance of 20 yards, immobilizing the tank but leaving it able to spray the area with cannon and machinegun fire. Running back to our infantry through vicious fire, he secured another rocket, and, advancing against a hail of machinegun and small-arms fire reached a position ten yards from the tank. His second shot shattered the turret. With his pistol he killed two of the crew as they emerged from the tank; and then running to the crippled Mark IV while enemy infantry sniped at him, he dropped a grenade inside the tank and completed its destruction. With their armor gone, the enemy infantry became disorganized and was driven back. S/Sgt. Choate's great daring in assaulting an enemy tank single-handed, his determination to follow the vehicle after it had passed his position, and his skill and crushing

thoroughness in the attack prevented the enemy from capturing a battalion command post and turned a probable defeat into a tactical success.

This small corner of France was witness to yet more extraordinary actions. It was near Bruyères too that the 442nd Regimental Combat Team, made up of Japanese-American soldiers from Hawaii (and detention camps from the western half of America), rescued the Lost Battalion from the 141st Infantry Regiment of the 36th Infantry Division. The Germans had cut off the battalion near Bruyères. Twice the 442nd attempted a rescue but with no success and heavy losses. In the third attempt the 442nd broke through German defenses and rescued about 230 men. In those five days of battle (October 26 to 30), it suffered more than 800 casualties. Item Company went in with 185 men and eight walked out unhurt; King Company began with 186 men and 17 walked out.

Today, on the road to the town of Brouvelieures, a short distance north from Bruyères, there is a spot marked by a 3rd Infantry monument which is called the "Crossroads of Hell," since the fight there was so fierce. The inscription translates as: "To the Valiant Combatants of the 3rd US Division, the liberators of this canton from the 20th of October to the 10th of November 1944. In memory of the courage and sacrifice of the 'Cotton Bailers' of the 148th, the 621st and the 7th Infantry Regiments." The 7th Infantry, supported by A Company 601st, had 152 men killed and 824 wounded at this place.

After the crossroads, the town of Brouvelieures and the villages of Domfaing, Rouges-Faux, and Haute Jacques were attacked and liberated. The battle for the last village was described as particularly bloody by Josowitz who said: "the Kraut kept their mortar-men firing by placing machine guns at their backs." It was there on October 30 that Private Wilburn Ross of Company G, 30th Infantry Regiment received the

Medal of Honor. On that day he manned a machine gun through eight German attacks, killing or wounding 58 of the enemy during the five-hour assault.

On October 30, Welch wrote his family: "Pretty cold here in the mountains and we expect snow soon. Pretty slow going here now. We're in the Vosges Mountains and it is raining and cold most of the time. I doubt very much if it will break this winter. Perhaps I'll get home this spring. I'd like to."

During the next two days B Company knocked out four German Panzers, a towed gun, two flak wagons, two armored cars and killed or wounded an unknown number of the enemy as they retreated towards the Meurthe River. Welch wrote a letter to his mother mentioning this action:

We had quite a full day yesterday, knocking out several tanks and armored cars besides killing 40–50 Kraut. It was just like a shooting gallery. The Germans are terribly dumb at times. I have a new puppy on my TD. He's part German police and collie. Cold as hell here and looks like we'll have a white Xmas.

The battalion occupied the high ground overlooking the Meurthe River at the beginning of November. They were on the west bank in support of their infantry regiments. On November 1, B Company and the 15th Infantry attacked the village of Nompatelize by firing on enemy-occupied houses and enemy infantry from a hill overlooking the town. Welch wrote a couple of letters home that commented in his offhand way on the weather, action and medals and the election of Franklin D. Roosevelt for an unprecedented fourth term as president, all with equal emphasis:

What a day, miserable cold wind accompanied by a driving rain. We're in a town that's all shot to pieces and dead horses and cows are all over the place. I got another medal the other day. It is the Silver Star for some stuff I did at Anzio. I'll give you the details later. Well this is Armistice Day;[115] you'd never know it here. There has been no slacking of the fighting to be noticed. We're all pleased here with the election results. I guess most people are.

Sergeant Larson wrote home about the same time and he too mentioned new medals as well as the effects of the war on the civilians:

I was notified a few days ago that I've been awarded the Silver Star medal and also the Bronze Star medal for a couple of incidents that took place in Italy. I was especially pleased to get the SS for that is the third highest award that the Army has to offer for gallantry in action. I got that for helping get a tanker and his tank out of no-man's land. The Bronze Star was for stopping a counterattack on Anzio beachhead when only my tank was covering a sector where the Krauts made a counterattack with 17 Mark IV tanks and infantry. They'll make nice souvenirs anyway.

The civilian population is now taking a pretty tough beating. Practically every town or village we go thru has to be almost leveled before we can drive the Krauts out. And the few places that escape our guns are usually taken care of by the Kraut guns when we move into them. The people in some places are pretty hostile towards us. Can't blame them much for winter is upon them and they are left without home, food, or anything else and with no prospects of replacing anything for some time to come. Those that aren't hostile toward us treat us OK, more or less an attitude of indifference. If the Krauts came back they would no doubt treat them just as well.

Elements of B Company were in reserve with the 15th Infantry Regiment. They were able to perform some much-needed vehicle maintenance. There was also hot food, showers and movies. The rest didn't last very long as Sergeant Nowak related they had to attack retreating German columns:

> We moved out near La Bourgance and from one position we got three tanks, four personnel carriers, an American jeep, some horse drawn artillery, and a motorcycle. The next town was La Salle, about one mile away. Our four TDs fired more than 600 rounds into the town, and we finally went in with the 15th. We made short gains from there. Going into Biarville with a task force, we pulled off a small-scale, armored attack. After parking behind one house, we got 12 prisoners from its cellar. The house we were behind got part of its roof knocked off, but artillery couldn't get at us in our position. We fired .30 caliber machine guns at the German infantry, but the distance was too great for effective firing. That night our sentry was killed.[116]

The History of the 15th Infantry Regiment in World War II described the unglamorous but necessary fighting:

> The fighting in the western hills and mountain approaches to the Vosges was the unspectacular slugging, bloody type of war that grinds the enemy and also is very costly to us. This period contained little that would cause headlines in the home newspapers, but soldiers know the significance of having to fight in rainswept forested mountains, continually harassed by snipers and bitter battles for stubbornly held villages.[117]

The front was moving to St Dié and Corporal Borriello described the devastation of the town by the enemy:

> As we were getting closer to St. Die, we could hear many explosions in the town. We thought that our artillery was

really doing a job on the town. It was later learned that the Germans had been ordered to destroy St. Die. For no apparent reason, certainly no military reason, and without notice to the population, the Germans set charges all over town. By the time we moved into the town, it was completely gutted and in ruins. The Meurthe River was our next obstacle at St. Die, and now, in November, it seemed to be raining constantly.

"Bullshit we're combat men"

The Vosges Mountains had never been successfully attacked by an invading army. That is why the Germans chose this formidable barrier as the last defense before the mountains opened up onto the Alsatian plain. The Wehrmacht had constructed elaborate fortifications as usual, using Alsatian farm boys, interned French soldiers and others to build them. There were pillboxes, machine-gun placements and defense in depth. Conquering the Vosges would be hard. And before that the Meurthe River had to be crossed. The Germans were no longer relying on troops conscripted from the occupied countries. Too close to home, the troops were now first rate, all German units with determined SS men as backup.

The German defensive line during World War I had been the Meurthe River near Housseras, close to St Michel, and they had returned to fortify it again. Allied operations called for the 3rd Division to launch an assault across the Meurthe River on November 20 in the vicinity of Housseras. The division was to cross the river and establish a bridgehead on the east bank, clear the hills around the town of St Dié, and drive northeast through the Saales Pass. The goal was to get to Strasbourg on the Rhine.

Sergeant Larson's diary of November 1944 spoke of the lack of firing across the river for several days and described the Wehrmacht's activities as well:

French civilians reported that for two months the Krauts have been building fortifications and gun positions on the other side of the river with drafted civilian labor. A special group of SS troops was sent here from Germany and had charge of building the defense line. The people here say that the regular German Wehrmacht was well behaved around here but the SS troops were nothing more than kids and fanatical Nazis and behaved like young gangsters shooting up houses with their pistols if they didn't get what they wanted.

H-hour to cross the Meurthe was set for 0645 on November 21. During the night of November 19/20 the 15th Infantry made five attempts to send patrols across the river. Only one of these patrols reached the east bank because of the swift current. The patrol got their rubber rafts across without tipping over, a major feat in itself. The 10th Engineers were to throw a couple of bridges across the river. Larson, writing this in real time, recorded that:

At 0615 we opened up with one of the heaviest barrages on positions across the river that I've ever heard. Artillery, tanks, mortars, AA and everything else opened up for two hours. We fired about 0700 with several rounds from our two TDs. As soon as daylight came, our planes came over and ever since the sky has been full of planes dive bombing and strafing. And of course our artillery is continuously pounding the whole area. The town of Clairefontaine right across the river from Etival is taking the heaviest beating from the dive bombers. That's the first objective of the battalion we're working with. As soon as they secure the town engineers are to throw a bridge across the river. Then the first vehicles to cross will be the M-4 tanks and next will be our TDs.

Later in the day, Larson recorded: "We're now sitting out in a field from where we fired this morning. And since I started writing this,

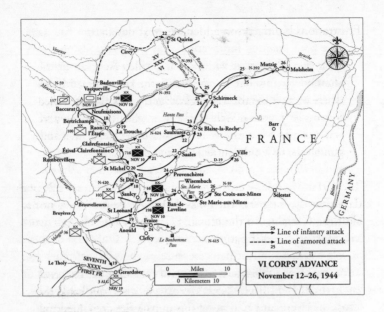

a high wind came up and soon the sky was black. Now it is raining steady so our air support is gone." The men in the open-topped TDs were miserable. They would wait a long time. Work had not yet begun on the heavy vehicle bridge that would be needed to cross the Meurthe. The night before they had commandeered a house; but even though it was only a couple of hundred yards away, they could not return to it because the 1st Battalion medics from the 15th Infantry had taken it over. Larson wrote:

> We could probably have stayed in our house but the executive officer (Maj. Hinman) [back from home leave] of our battalion was talking to Lt. Welch and Lt. Welch told him nobody could have our house. The Maj. told him to say "sir" when talking to him and Lt. Welch said "bullshit we're combat men." So the Maj. got sore and had us booted out of our house. The Lt. also told him if they wanted their "choice of house" to go out and capture them like we have to do.

Frustrations built. Larson added the next day that:

> Well we didn't get to cross the Meurthe yesterday. In the afternoon we set out 5 miles down the river to St. Michel where we were to cross last night. But the first tank that tried to cross got to the middle of the river when the bridge gave way so now all you can see of his tank is the 50 cal. machine gun on the top of the turret sticking out.

The 601st did finally cross the Meurthe on November 22, two days after the infantry. The noisy TDs were delayed so as not to alert the Germans to the crossing. Larson wrote of their work in almost an admiring tone:

> Saw some of the elaborate fortification the Krauts had built and I guess we're lucky we didn't have to fight a full-scale battle for them. Connecting trenches dug about 10 feet deep, beautiful dug-in gun positions etc., were all dug in vain and never used. I have found out our heavy barrage wasn't necessary for the Krauts had almost all pulled out except for a few delaying troops. Our doughboys cleaned them out but in some places lost quite a few doughboys killed. We found out today that a couple days ago the French broke through the Belfort Gap and captured Mulhouse, even reaching the Rhine itself. It also probably accounts for the reason the Krauts had to give up their Meurthe line without a fight for they were in danger of being outflanked by either the Third Army or the French.

Although the Meurthe crossing had not been as fiercely opposed as had been feared, the war continued to exact a high number of casualties. The 601st men saw many dead Germans, destroyed vehicles and abandoned equipment during the next several rainy and miserable days. Often the roads were blocked with fallen logs and were heavily mined. Sergeant Nowak noted:

"We did much pulling of logs, and prisoners were captured wholesale. They seemed dazed at our fast progress." Indeed, the 601st and the infantry units they accompanied could consider themselves lucky that the majority of German defenders had been redeployed elsewhere.

CHAPTER 13
ALSACE

"We can watch the Krauts without glasses"

Things were moving fast. On November 23, the French 2nd Armored Division captured the city of Strasbourg. B Company 601st moved through the mountains mopping up retreating Germans through the towns and ancient villages of the lower Vosges, most of which had seen war many times before.

In Mutzig, the company had trouble moving about the town since the old houses were so close together that there was little space to squeeze through with the TDs. Corporal Borriello recorded that they were assigned to blow a hole in the fort, which guarded the town. They used a German half-track loaded with over 3,000 pounds of TNT. According to Borriello, it made a nice big hole in the fortifications. This idea came from Lieutenant Colonel John Heintges, executive officer of the 30th Infantry Regiment and soon to be the regimental commander of the 7th Infantry Regiment.

The 3rd Division now stood up "Task Force Whirlwind."* Its purpose was to break through the unfinished German

---

* "Stood up" is a US military term for when diverse units are brought together for a specific objective or time period.

Winter Line and move on to Strasbourg and the Rhine. The task force was to move out of the Vosges Mountains and take Saales, the first town on the Alsatian plain beyond the mountains. It was composed of elements from the 15th Infantry, the 756th Tank Battalion, the 601st Tank Destroyer Battalion, the 3rd Reconnaissance Troop, the 10th Engineers and the 93rd Field Artillery Battalion.

Arriving at Saales on November 24, the battalion was moving fast but it wasn't easy. Welch wrote home: "Don't think that this is going to be over soon, because it gets harder every day." Lead elements of both the 3rd and 100th Divisions were now out of the mountains and along the Bruche river valley. They headed down the eastern slopes of the Vosges on the road to Strasbourg. There was a rumor there was a 72-hour pass for the division that reached Strasbourg first and the two divisions became rivals to enter the city. With the 3rd on the right bank of the river and the 100th on the left, the two American forces were often visible to each other as they cleared the remaining German-made obstacles. General O'Daniel of the 3rd Infantry Division actually complained to the corps commander that the 100th Infantry Division was capturing towns in his sector. Unsurprisingly no 72-hour passes were promised.

That same day, several of Hitler's closest military advisers, concerned that the German 19th Army could better be used to defend the Black Forest and Germany itself, recommended it withdraw across the Rhine. Hitler, however, said that Colmar must be defended and he ordered the army to stay put. Hitler then appointed SS-Reichsführer (Commander of the SS) Heinrich Himmler, who had absolutely no military experience, to command the German forces on the west bank of the Rhine. A German general described Himmler's understanding of military matters as childish. The bridgehead was to become known as the Colmar Pocket. The "pocket" was huge, approximately 45 miles long and 25 miles wide, stretching from the Rhine west into the Vosges Mountains.

On Thanksgiving Day, November 25, the battalion had little to be thankful for. Sergeant Nowak reported: "a dinner was brought to us in Marmite cans [a metal container used to ship food to keep it warm], but the driving rain spoiled it all." The exhausted 3rd Infantry Division had to defend Strasbourg and the 601st was assigned to occupy the town of Molsheim, west of the city.

Seventh Army continued to shift the 601st from division to division. On November 30, part of the battalion, including B Company, was reassigned to the 103rd Infantry Division. The battalion's November monthly operations report was openly critical of these frequently shifting assignments:

Tank destroyer battalions should be an integral part of an infantry division rather than corps troops. In this way they would support the division during its operations and rest and train with the division when it is withdrawn from the line. Under the present set-up, a tank destroyer battalion is attached to a division during an offensive and, as soon as the division is withdrawn from the line, the battalion, or parts of it, are attached to another division to carry on a new operation; as a result neither the men nor the tanks are off the line long enough to have the necessary rest or maintenance. Also, by splitting up the battalion amongst various units, neither tactical nor administrative control can be efficiently carried out. At this present writing, the battalion is spread out over a 35-mile front, operating two companies with the 103rd Infantry Division, two platoons with the 3rd Infantry Division, one platoon with the 117th Reconnaissance Squadron, and the Reconnaissance Company with the 3rd Infantry Division.

After another eight days, the battalion was reassigned to the 3rd Infantry Division on December 8. So began a short period of relative quiet for the 601st. As can be gleaned from Welch's letters and the morning reports, not much was happening except the move to the eastern suburbs of Strasbourg. B Company ended up at Königshofen, a suburb on the Rhine. The men were able to look across the Rhine at Germans moving around on the east bank. According to Josowitz: "Strasbourg was a wonderful place: luxurious command posts, plenty of liberated champagne and cognac, beautiful, friendly Alsatians, not too many MPs, and not too much trouble with the Kraut, just a regular exchange of hot lead across the Rhine."

Welch's platoon was billeted only 300 yards from the Rhine. The civilians had deserted the eastern suburbs of Strasbourg where there were only soldiers: French, American and a few remaining German diehards. Because the 601st was so close to the river they were exposed to fire from the German side. Daylight movement was impossible. Both Welch and Sergeant Nowak enjoyed well-furnished private apartments or stayed in finely appointed hotels. Welch's platoon remained in this area for about ten days and he wrote: "this was a beautiful apartment, quite modern and lovely furniture. There is no housing problem here, they're all vacant. Too much noise I guess." Sergeant Nowak in his memoirs noted: "we stayed in fashionable hotels and did much looting, with an abundance of fine furniture, clothing, etc."[118]

The 3rd Division had to play a painful waiting game with the Rhine and Germany so close. It was a tempting target. As Welch wrote to his mother: "It's going to be quite difficult to cross I believe." To his sister he wrote: "We're both waiting for the other to make a move."

Not willing to just sit there, the division commenced a harassment program called the "Watch on the Rhine," the name taken from the German song, *Die Wacht am Rhein*. Written during the 1870–71 Franco-Prussian War, it had been a popular rallying call urging Germans to guard its border against the French along the Rhine. *Die Wacht am Rhein* was also the German codename for what the Allies called the "Battle of the Bulge"[119] although the 3rd Infantry Division planners did not know that when they named their operation.

The "Watch" entailed having various units fire at German soldiers and fortifications in rotation across the Rhine. Welch's platoon was positioned right on the river next to what had been a large, modern girls' school. On a main street in front of the schoolhouse were two destroyed French M-4 Sherman tanks. They were part of a force of five French tanks that had tried to make a run for one of the Rhine bridges before the Germans blew it up. From where they were billeted, the TD men could see three bridges that had been destroyed by the retreating Wehrmacht. Sergeant Larson added:

> From where we sit we can watch the Krauts without glasses as they move around over on the other side. Concrete pillboxes line the river across from us. The Krauts have machine guns zeroed in on the streets around here so in daylight we have to be very careful in moving around or we will be caught in a burst of machine-gun fire. Many doughboys have been killed by it.

Larson also said the Germans had snipers on the Strasbourg side of the river. They were in abandoned apartment houses sitting in windows, waiting until they saw solitary GIs and then letting them have it. The snipers quickly changed buildings and then waited for their next opportunity. Larson noted: "It is impossible to find them for the whole area is a collection of vacated apartment houses, a regular ghost town."

Amazingly, life goes on in a war, even romantic life. And so, on December 14, after four months waiting for the paperwork to go through, Captain Sam G. Richardson married an army nurse, Lieutenant Bette Holmes, of the 59th Station Hospital. He had been recently promoted C Company commander. They were both from Tampa, Florida and had even graduated from the same high school, but first met only when they were stationed in Italy. The wedding took place at the station hospital outside Mutzig, Alsace, with Lieutenant Colonel Tardy as best man.[120]

At daybreak on December 16, Welch's platoon fired into Germany for the first time. The platoon received orders the night before that were clear and simple: fire across the river at dawn and pick your own targets. As Sergeant Larson explained "It was just an experiment to see what we'd draw back." He wrote that before dawn, he moved his TD close to the river. Nowak's TD was a couple of hundred yards back. Larson said: "After looking at the map we noted our two tanks are the most advanced tanks toward the east on the whole Western Front. From where we sit we can see Kehl across the river about 200 yards away."

The TDs moved out from behind the school and proceeded to the bridge embankment. Both TDs chose pillboxes across the river as their targets. Larson was in the lead. They had to move around several burned-out vehicles and go through barbed wire. At this point, Larson dismounted from the tank to lead it through additional obstacles. Antitank Teller mines were scattered all around and he could have been blown sky high had he stood on one, but fortunately he saw them all and disarmed them before the destroyer set them off. He wrote later:

> As soon as it was light enough to see the pillboxes we opened fire with APC and block-buster ammunition, firing at almost point blank range. This one pillbox was so well constructed that when I hit it on the side it only scarred it up a little bit. We fired 20 rounds and then pulled back behind the school again.

Sergeant Nowak also wrote of the ineffectiveness of those rounds: "Later I heard that only eight penetrated to any degree. The cover of darkness was our only protection, so after firing we pulled away fast, but we got no return fire."

That same day, the Wehrmacht launched Hitler's last major offensive in the west, a massive attack in the Ardennes Forest, later called the "Battle of the Bulge" by the Allies. The primary goal was the recapture of Antwerp and the surprise attack caught the Allies completely off guard. Hitler hoped to force a negotiated end to the war. This was to be the largest and bloodiest battle of the war. Its ultimate failure further weakened German forces, ensuring the eventual defeat of Germany.

For the 3rd Infantry Division the peaceful sojourn in Strasbourg was over. Troops were immediately pulled back from the front lines north of Strasbourg and shifted to the west to make up for those forces rushed to the Ardennes. B Company was sent to the north of Strasbourg to the Hagenau sector. There they stayed in the village of Leutenheim, 20 miles northeast of Strasbourg. On temporary assignment with the 117th Reconnaissance Squadron, they were there for about five days. Here they registered their guns for indirect fire support, but nothing came of it. There the men met a young Alsatian girl named Martha Schneider who gave them some basic language lessons. Martha Schneider is otherwise unknown, but Sergeant Nowak thought enough of her to keep two pictures of her in his photo album.[121]

As elsewhere throughout the Allied front, offensive operations continued to be slowed by the increasingly cold, wet, and overcast weather. The 3rd Division was placed directly under the operational control of the First French Army on December 18. Their orders were to assist the French to clear out the Colmar Pocket, which the French had repeatedly tried but failed to eliminate during the first half of December. It was not always a partnership without consequences. Lieutenant Robert

A. Maynard recalled that while working with the French during the Colmar Pocket battle, "one of my men on guard duty challenged a soldier twice. The soldier didn't respond so the guard shot him. He was a French soldier and so I informed the French the next day and they just crossed off his name."

The area was crisscrossed with swollen streams and canals and French armor had not been able to get through. Further, the area had been heavily reinforced by German troops. The 3rd replaced the 36th Infantry Division, which had been with the French since it first began to push through the Vosges in October and was worn out from being in combat for more than two months.

Colmar, the last German city west of the Rhine in this sector, was important for its functioning road bridges across the river and a very critical railroad bridge at Neuf-Brisach. If the Germans could gather enough men and materiel they could attack north along the Alsatian plain and recapture Strasbourg. Meanwhile, because the Germans controlled this pocket, they tied up Allied forces and brought additional troops and supplies across the river without interference.

Welch, although involved in this movement, was ever the tourist. He wrote his sister:

I just spent a few days in Strasbourg. It's quite a nice place. The cathedral there is well worth seeing. There is something I'd like you to do for me. I'm enclosing a check for which I'd like you to buy me a pair of loafers size 9C. Make them good with a fairly heavy sole. I'm sure you can pick them up for me in New York.[122] Cold as hell tonight, pretty tough fighting all over, don't get frightened. I believe it's the last big German effort.

Welch wrote his mother on December 19 with some revealing news:

I got your packages and they showed lots of thought. Everything will come in very handy. The fruitcake is delicious. All my men like it. It arrived in excellent shape. I turned down a promotion last week so I could still fight the war. I've been with my men for so long and we've been through so much together that I couldn't leave them now. I hope you understand why I'm still a Lt. I'm sincerely proud of myself because I've been through the worst there is without lacking. In my job we fight every day, the time passes quickly. It's very exciting flirting with death and spitting in his face. So far I've out-thought and out-fought every German I've met, I know I can continue. The strange thing is that I'm still Tom Welch.[123]

Early on the morning of December 22, B Company of the 601st was released from its temporary assignment to the 117th Reconnaissance Squadron. It had orders to move 72 miles to the town of Ribeauville, northwest of Colmar. According to the 601st unit journal, Welch was assigned to lead the advance billeting party for B Company, in support of the 15th Infantry Regiment.

And Lieutenant Colonel Tardy received Orientation Order Number 106 on the Forthcoming Operation from Headquarters 3rd Infantry Division. It stated that the initial objective was to move the 15th Infantry and 30th Infantry Regiments along the Fecht River, southeast from the village of Ingersheim, to the village of Ostheim. The mission was broken down into two phases. The objective of the first phase was to capture the villages of Sigolsheim and Bennwihr. The next phase was to advance further east and seize and hold two bridges before moving on to eliminate the northern end of the Colmar Pocket. Section I of this operation instruction ends with the following statement: "Of overall importance is the fact that in addition to the operations in which the 3rd Infantry Division will be involved, the entire First French Army, of which we are now a part, will resume the offensive with a view to liquidating the enemy bridgehead west of the Rhine."

"There really is bitter hatred now"

Germany's back was against the wall and there would be no more easy gains for the Allies. *The History of the 15th Infantry Regiment in World War II* records that this attack involved seven days of the "bitterest and bloodiest fighting in its long record." The Wehrmacht had been replaced with crack German SS troops who were ensconced in the villages of Sigolsheim, Mittelwihr and Bennwihr. These men were under oath to hold their ground until death. The history went on to say:

> Germans wounded and later evacuated by our own medical detachment, bluntly told interrogators that should any man leave his post, officers and noncommissioned officers would immediately fire on him. Captured German documents show repeated written orders by Heinrich Himmler, SS Reichsführer, that this last foothold on the southernmost part of the Vosges would be held at all costs.[124]

On December 23, part of B Company 601st moved near Mittelwihr to provide direct fire support to a 15th Infantry Regiment attack. According to Sergeant Larson, the attack failed. Apparently the Germans had got wind of it and attacked first. Many 15th Infantry soldiers were killed. Although the village of Mittelwihr was eventually taken later that morning, it was lost again later that day.

The next day, the 15th Infantry learned of a planned 0700 attack by at least 600 Germans. At 0630 US forces attacked first, catching them off guard. On Christmas Eve, after Mittelwihr had been recaptured, part of the village of Bennwihr was taken – the two villages are so close together it is impossible to know where one starts and the other leaves off. Sergeant Larson's description graphically shows the changed mood toward the enemy:

About 200 Krauts were killed and the rest driven off. Many of the fellows don't even take Kraut wounded in any more. They just finish them off with another bullet. But the same is true of our treatment by them. There really is bitter hatred now, fighting is very close in and we are all mixed together. Even tanks meet face to face on street corners and the one who gets the first shot is the one that keeps going. Bazookas are getting a lot of tanks on both sides. There are more dead laying around on the hills and streets than anyone has ever seen since Anzio.

Krauts are everywhere; even still in the town sniping, so it is very uncertain. And they're training the heaviest concentration of artillery that we've yet had since Anzio as well as using tanks. There is little quarter asked or given now. There have been several instances of Krauts mowing down helpless American prisoners so now our doughboys are doing likewise. They even bayonet them when they come with their hands over their heads to surrender. War of course always means hatred and ruthlessness, but lately over here it is especially evident, as we hit more and more at Germany herself and the fighting becomes more and more violent. Now both sides have had so much combat that they have little patience and when they meet there is hatred written all over their faces. I never thought I'd get to feel that way myself, I always felt that a soldier, regardless of which side, was merely doing a job thrust on him and there was nothing personal about it. But after some of the things we've been experiencing here of late, and knowing that they continue fighting without hope of victory just to inflict as heavy casualties as possible on us, well, I'm no different from the rest of the GIs now.

A plaque in the village of Bennwihr commemorates the liberation as being on December 24, 1944, although there was considerable fighting over the next few days. The Germans were not idle and unleashed one of the heaviest artillery and mortar attacks ever experienced by the regiment, according to the 15th Infantry Regiment's *History*. Veterans of Anzio declared it the worst ever. There was no cover in the bare and frozen mountainside. Progress was slow and laborious. The history describes the action this way:

> Enemy machine guns and snipers, dug in along the crest of the hill in well-prepared dugouts with connecting trenches, peppered the approaching troops and threw up a screen of fire that forced the men of both companies to crawl inch by inch over the frozen ground. With grenades, rifle and machine-gun fire, our men battered at the enemy, but still he held to his advantageous positions.[125]

On Christmas Day, Sigolsheim and Bennwihr received more than 300 rounds of high-explosive shells fired by B Company. Sigolsheim was only a few kilometers southwest of Bennwihr, fewer if you went up and over Hill 351. Welch, writing that day despite the conditions, related:

> Xmas night, it's been terribly hard the last two days, no letup likely, just one more day, closer to home we hope. One of our officers [unknown] was killed today which makes twice as much work for me. I didn't mind the day passed quickly. This has been some of the worst fighting we've seen, we're trying to take Colmar. We're meeting, and beating the best they have, the SS troops. I killed two today with a pistol at about 20 yards. They're terribly fanatical; they still think they're winning the war. Please forgive the writing my hand is cold, it's hard to write, I'm writing by the light of the moon.

Although he didn't mention it, Welch had found a new use for his TD as a rescue vehicle. In a January letter he says: "I suppose you'll be seeing my name in the papers again soon. Some fool correspondent got my name for some work I did Xmas day." The article said:

> First Lt. Thomas P. Welch is not a man to sit around idly with his tank destroyer when there are no tanks to be destroyed, especially when there is an extraordinary call for his services. Two wounded Americans lay in a field dominated by a German machine gun. Every effort at rescue was met with a withering hail of fire. When the situation was grasped by Lt. Welch, he called for volunteers to carry litters. Then, with the litter-bearers shielded between the tank destroyer and the enemy, Welch drove alongside the wounded men while the German machine-gun bullets spattered harmlessly against the side of his vehicle. The men were placed on the litters and the procession returned to the safety of the American lines while the Fritzes grunted in disgust.

German resistance continued to be fierce but the 3rd Infantry Division operations order was realistic and had not made optimistic predictions about capturing the villages mentioned in the order. From December 26 through 29, B Company 601st continued to shell enemy-held houses on Hill 351 and the outskirts of Mittelwihr and Bennwihr. Longer-range shells were fired at Sigolsheim. But the Germans continued to throw in troops, replace lost equipment and reinforce their forces in order to hold Hill 351. By now they had committed a battalion of first-class troops to the action.[126]

Meanwhile, Welch sent an upbeat letter to his mother which remarkably hardly referred to the war at all:

> I don't believe I told you that I flew to Paris for 60 hours. It was wonderful. You'd love it. The women and clothes are *trés*

chic. I met and dined with the Countess de La Salle. She was a Groves from Boston. I met her at the Continental Hotel and when she learned I was from New York she asked if I knew the Fogwills from there. He's the boy I met in N.Y. the last time I was home. I went to her villa, very lush, in the suburbs and got quite drunk on excellent champagne, lovely party. It's still the same here, kill or be killed, I yawn quite frequently now from the monotony.

"I fed seven cows, two calves, ten pigs, 30 or 40 chickens, ten ducks, and ten rabbits"

Private First Class Samuel H. Kelly (Canandaigua, New York) was reported as a prisoner of war on December 27. It is known that he was captured in France and sent to Germany. There are no other details, but at the end of the war he was repatriated.

As the Battle of the Bulge raged on, the new year began and the first phase of the Colmar Pocket operation ended. It had been rough. There were many US and German casualties, and things were still intense as they prepared for phase two: the elimination of the pocket and reaching the Rhine. The battalion's unit journal for December 30 mentions that Welch went to the battalion command post to inquire about the condition of three of his men who had been evacuated to a hospital because of their wounds. This is corroborated by the monthly report, which lists five B Company men as wounded during the second half of December.

After visiting his men on December 31, Welch went to battalion headquarters to report on their status. The morning report for that day has one section of his platoon at Guémar and the other at Ostheim. These villages run north to south along the Fecht River. They were waiting for the next big push. They were not idle and fired 200 rounds of high explosive (HE) in support of the 15th Infantry Regiment in and around

Ostheim and at Hill 351 above Mittelwihr but things had settled down a little. Welch's letter to his mother is again upbeat given how tough it must have been: "New Year's Eve! It's a cold blustery night tonight. It's starting to snow so it'll probably warm up. I've enclosed a propaganda leaflet that the Kraut threw at us the week before Xmas. It looks as if we've finally got him stopped for the present. Let's hope so."

Josowitz, in the informal history, sums up December this way:

Christmas Week, 1944, was cold, miserable, and anything but joyous. The Destroyers were all over the Division area, firing at the Kraut, blocking roads and catching plenty of hell. The news from the north was terrible [the Battle of the Bulge]. There was constant talk of a coming Kraut push. Recon was up in the hills with the French Ghoums. Morale was "Excellent" on the morning reports but nowhere else! One Recon platoon spent New Year's Eve patrolling in front of the barbed wire around the 30th Infantry's machine-gun outposts. The Krauts chased the 3rd Division Officers' Club, waitresses and all, out of Strasbourg. B Company sent a couple of platoons to Orbey and Le Bonhomme to support the French. There were parachutist scares and rear area patrols. A Company had two platoons with the 254th [Infantry Regiment] and one with the French.

The situation looked bad for the Allies, especially to the northwest of Strasbourg. On New Year's Day, the Germans launched what was to be their last offensive west of the Rhine. They intended to take advantage of the weakened forces protecting Strasbourg because so many US units had been sent as reinforcements for the Battle of the Bulge. Code-named Operation *Nordwind* (*North Wind*), it was an all-out German attack on the US Seventh and the First French Armies. The attack was concentrated to the north and northwest of Strasbourg. General Eisenhower authorized a fighting withdrawal from the city. The French, especially General Charles de Gaulle, insisted there be no withdrawal from Strasbourg. Nevertheless, some Allied forces gave up ground in what was described as some of the hardest winter fighting of the war. Casualties were heavy. On New Year's Day, January 1, 1945, Sergeant Larson wrote home:

> I got up for two and ½ hours guard at 0400 this morning. When guard was over I fed seven cows, two calves, ten pigs, 30 or 40 chickens, ten ducks, and ten rabbits. I also milked three of the cows. Then I washed the milk utensils, had some breakfast, did a little house cleaning, and even cooked a turkey for our New Year's dinner. I didn't have a place to roast the turkey so I cut him up and cooked him on top of the stove. The civilians were hastily evacuated, leaving homes, livestock, and everything just as they stood. We hate to see the stuff starve to death so we spend half our time, between shell bursts, running around town feeding the stuff.

During the first days of January, B Company 601st was in the vicinity of Ostheim, Mittelwihr, and Zellenberg, north of Mittelwihr, and still in support of the 15th Infantry. These small villages are all within ten miles of each other and the 601st was moved around where it was most needed. Welch's platoon expended almost 240 rounds of high-explosive shells and almost 30 rounds of armor-piercing shells firing at dug-in enemy positions and strongpoints during these days. On January 4, Welch's company was attached to the 3rd Battalion of the 254th Infantry Regiment. In intense action that day Welch's platoon fired more than 486 rounds of high explosives, an average of 120 rounds per barrel. Later that week they were placed in support of French paratroopers near Louchbach, Habeaurupt and Rudlin.

The Germans launched *Sonnenwende* (*Solstice*) on January 8, with the objective of breaking out from the Colmar Pocket to

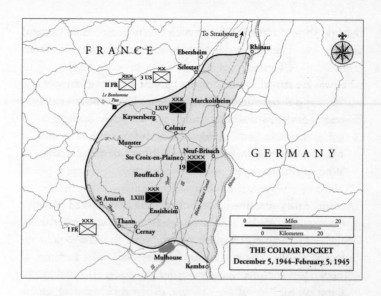

FRANCE
To Strasbourg
Rhinau
Ebersheim
Selestat
II FR   XXX   XX   3 US
Le Bonhomme Pass
LXIV   XXX   Marckolsheim
Kaysersberg
Colmar
Munster
Ste Croix-en-Plaine   XXXX   Neuf-Brisach
19
Rouffach
GERMANY
LXIII   XXX
St Amarin   Ensisheim
Thann   I FR   XXX
Cernay
Mulhouse
Kembs

0   Miles   20
0   Kilometers   20

THE COLMAR POCKET
December 5, 1944–February 5, 1945

the north by crossing the Ill River. It was the Colmar Pocket's part of the German Operation *Nordwind*. On January 10, Welch's platoon was placed in regimental reserve. He took the time to write home, again striking a casual tone:

> Please accept my apologies for not writing sooner, but as you can see by the papers we've been quite busy of late. I'm back in the Vosges Mountains, again and it's breathtakingly beautiful. Deep snow, crystal clear air and cold. There are quite a few winter resorts here and I managed to sandwich a few skiing trips in between fights. I captured a beautiful Great Dane dog from the Krauts. He's black and huge. I hope to get him home with me.[127]

Sergeant Larson wrote his brother January 13 and also confirmed a little ski R&R. The platoon had taken over what had been a ski lodge up in the mountains. The retreating Germans had destroyed the main lodge, but there were some rooms over the garage where the GIs stayed. Downstairs the men found some ski equipment and got in a little skiing. There were no chair lifts. Larson wrote:

> There are resorts up in these mountains and a few days ago we stopped overnight at one of them where there were a bunch of skis. The first morning I was up before daylight & got in a couple hours of good skiing before we had to pull out. It was lots of fun but I sure took some nice spills on these steep mountain slopes.

The Red Army meanwhile launched the Oder River Offensive into central Germany on January 14. In a panicked response, all available German forces were pulled from the Western Front and sent to the Eastern Front. During the early evening of January 15, Welch received the order to relocate his platoon in preparation for Operation *Cheerful*, the final elimination of the Colmar Pocket, later referred to as the "Other Battle of the Bulge." This operation was in direct response to Germany's *Sonnenwende* operation. Hitler had declared the city of Colmar a *Festung* or fortress city which should be held to the last man. But there were not many combat troops in the city itself. The Germans had only two engineer battalions, two construction battalions and two field penal battalions. The better troops were in the suburbs, as the 601st would discover at a cost.

Winter required appropriate camouflage. By January 20 all four of the battalion's companies had painted their vehicles white and drew white jumpsuits or "spook suits" to blend in with the snow-covered terrain. These suits were made locally from bed sheets and anything else that was white. While the paint was drying, Welch sent more letters home. In one he noted: "Look for a new Seventh Army drive two days after this date." This drive was called Operation *Grandslam*, the 3rd Infantry Division portion of *Cheerful*.

Far from being cheerful, things were only going to get worse.

CHAPTER 14

THE OTHER BATTLE OF THE BULGE

"F'Chris' sake! Don't fire our gun"

Operation *Grandslam* started the evening of January 22, exactly one year after the Anzio landing. General O'Daniel, with the 1st French Infantry Division on his left, was confident of a rapid breakthrough and he planned to begin the 3rd Infantry Division's attack with successive assaults by the 7th, 30th and the attached 254th Infantry Regiments. The 15th was held in division reserve. Taking control of rivers and bridges would be critical to Allied success.

Welch's platoon, with elements of the 15th Infantry Regiment, was located on the eastern outskirts of the village of Bennwihr, northwest of Colmar. It was preparing to execute the second phase of General O'Daniel's plan to push to the Rhine and, together with the French, eliminate the Germans from the Colmar Pocket. Its task was to cross the Ill River and the Orchbach Stream, 400 yards to the east of the Ill, then drive south to the village of Holtzwihr, bridging the Colmar Canal before heading southeast to capture the Neuf-Brisach bridge. The Neuf-Brisach bridge, east of the city of Colmar, was the only railroad bridge still intact in this sector across the Rhine. The attack would be difficult because they would have to cross several north–south flowing rivers, streams and man-made canals: all formidable obstacles in the middle of winter.

By January 23, Welch's platoon was repositioned to Ostheim, a village that had been destroyed during the fighting the previous week. The Fecht River divides Ostheim; at the start of the battle the population on the east side had been evacuated by the Germans while those on the west bank had been evacuated by the Americans. During the next day and a half, Welch and his platoon, now reduced to three M-10 tank destroyers, found themselves in the middle of an aggressive German counterattack at a wooden bridge near a farmstead called La Maison Rouge. This bridge was to become the key to US efforts to eliminate the Colmar Pocket.

That morning, far in advance of their supporting armor, five companies of the 30th Infantry crossed the Ill River in the vicinity of Illhaeusern, a few kilometers east of the village of Guémar, north of Colmar. The engineers had constructed a footbridge suitable for troops but not vehicles. The infantry moved to the south along the Ill riverbank before striking out to the southeast. There they crossed the Orchbach and headed in the direction of the villages of Riedwihr and Holtzwihr, largely unopposed as they advanced. They were still without any accompanying armor.

Meanwhile, the engineers trying to bridge the Ill were stymied. At 0928 there is a notation in the 601st unit journal that the battalion command post "could not get confirmation as to whether or not our M-10s have crossed the Ill River." Tanks and tank destroyers were to have crossed a bridge in the vicinity of Illhaeusern that the engineers hoped would be captured intact and prove to be usable. It was not. The Ill River is not wide, perhaps 20 yards across, but it was fast moving at this time of year and had steep banks, making it a small but formidable obstacle.

At 1155 good news came: the wooden bridge at La Maison Rouge downstream from Illhaeusern had been captured intact, making it possible to move armor to support the 30th Infantry. Just a few minutes later Welch was ordered to move east out of Ostheim and join up with several companies of the 3rd Battalion 15th Infantry. The 601st unit journal recorded he was to take positions on the west bank of the river. The 15th, although still in reserve, was to move south from the village of Guémar to Niederwald in the *Forêt Communale de Colmar* (Colmar Forest), lying just west of the Ill River.

By early afternoon, elements of the 15th Infantry completed the move to Niederwald, which was really only a few houses nestled in the middle of the Colmar Forest. They were to cross the Ill River "to protect the rear and flanks of the 30th Infantry companies at the farmhouse at La Maison Rouge." German artillery shelled Niederwald constantly. Between 1300 and 1400, the unit journal notes Lieutenant Bell reported to the battalion command post that three TDs of Lieutenant Welch's platoon were committed to action and firing across the river. He was still on the west side of the Ill River with the 15th, but in a position to support the 30th Infantry companies moving south to the village of Riedwihr.

The German 708th Volksgrenadier Division and the Sturmgeschütz-Brigade 280 (the 280th Assault Battalion) counterattacked the 30th Infantry just north of the village of Riedwihr. The Germans had armor and the GIs started to fall back.

The pressure was on. By mid-afternoon they urgently needed to bring tanks and tank destroyers across the Ill River to support the troops moving south. It was critical. The bridge had to be usable. The engineers decided to overlay treadway sections (iron matting that improved and strengthened the roadway surfaces) on each end of the captured wooden bridge at La Maison Rouge. There was not enough treadway on hand for the whole bridge, but the engineers judged the short center span might take the load of tanks without added support.

Although the center span was still not reinforced, the engineers, after running several towed 57mm antitank guns and a 10-ton truck across the bridge, gambled and sent a Sherman tank across. The tank, from the 756th Tank Battalion, went up the ramp and onto the center span. As they feared, the bridge gave way and the tank plunged into the icy river. Only its main deck and turret remained above water. The tank crew escaped but the bridge was now blocked. Ironically an additional 305 feet of treadway arrived minutes after the bridge collapse.

It was frigid and getting colder. Ice forming in the firing mechanisms rendered three TDs unable to fire, the commanding officer of C Company 601st reported at 1550.

Captain Stuart of Item Company, 15th Infantry, walked across the destroyed bridge at 1800, going as far as the Orchbach. He saw a few GIs running across the field back toward La Maison Rouge; then more. Attempting to stop them, he was told there were two German Mark VIs on the right and two on the left "so we got the hell out." As Captain Stuart moved further east, many more men were on the run, men without packs, weapons and even helmets. No one was making a stand.

Sergeant Nowak described the scene:

German tank fire sprayed our helpless doughs, so they retreated and jumped into the river. Some came across safely and ran across an open field towards woods where we were. We covered their retreat by firing our .50 caliber machine-guns and that was what gave our position away in the darkness. So when the Panzer guns opened up on us, we countered the shooting. After firing five rounds we were going to pull out of our spot and go into another, but we were hit on the move.

Sergeant Nowak and Private Conklin both suffered facial wounds from shell fragments. Sergeant Nowak had shrapnel in both eyes and had to wear glasses for the rest of his life. German tanks moving up to the fight showed up against the snow even as dusk fell. Across the river, Welch saw several Mark VIs and a new *Jägdpanther*, a heavy German TD with an 88mm gun.

In darkness now, the five 30th Infantry companies ran in a blind panic back towards the west and friendly lines. But first the men had to cross the waist-deep Orchbach, run 400 yards, and then plunge into the Ill River, where they were observed by Sergeant Nowak. The exhausted soldiers congregated on the ruined houses at Niederwald. They had suffered 345 casualties and lost approximately 80 percent of their equipment. They were rounded up by officers and NCOs who re-equipped them as best as they could.

At about 1900, the Germans intensified their fire on the retreating troops, stopping the rush across the river. Meanwhile on the west side of the Ill River, Love Company, 15th Infantry, occupied a protective ditch along the road and started to return fire.

Just west of the bridge one of the tank-destroyer officers (Lt. T. Peter Welch) located an emplaced machine-gun. In the darkness the German tanks began moving up and closing in. The white fields of snow made for some visibility in the blackness of an overcast night, and across the river the Wehrmacht's Mark VIs and the new Jägdpanthers could be observed just beyond the Maison. Fire was opened [by Welch] on two men in the turret. In a moment Welch was joined by another man who had apparently leaped out of a nearby shell-hole. "F'Chris' sake!" he shouted, "don't fire our gun! You're going to use up all our ammunition and we've only got 2 boxes left." Welch explained with a little impatience that there were "Kraut Mark sixes" sitting just "over yonder," and won him over to the cause. He fed the belt as Welch fired. The first shell the tank threw in return fell rather short and knocked the gun backward in their laps. It was set up again, and with some small-arms support from adjacent right and left, "six men, holding a defensive line! Only six god-damned men, wet and scared and in no fighting condition," the area around the Maison and to the southeast was sprayed with fire. The second tank shell hit the machine-gun. Welch found himself sprawled in the snow some yards back holding onto a leg of the tripod. His "assistant" who had expressed such tender concern for the gun lay in a ditch with fragments of the barrel through his head.[128]

By 2000 US officers regained control of the retreating troops and re-established discipline. Approximately 600 men had arrived back safely. The call went out for replacement material. They needed everything: food, dry clothing, weapons, helmets and tents and stoves. All of the division supply units responded and soon the material poured in, including rifles, machine guns and ammunition. Informed of the improving situation, General O'Daniel ordered the 15th Infantry Regiment to cross the Ill River, secure the bridgehead, repair the bridge, and be ready to resume the attack.

At midnight, seven US officers were called together to discuss next steps in one of the ruined Niederwald houses. The group included Welch and Captain Stuart. A counterattack was planned to jump off at 0230. The 15th was to send two rifle companies, Item and King, to secure La Maison Rouge farmstead. Welch and his TDs were to provide supporting fire across the river until tanks and TDs could cross the Ill on a bridge being built further upstream.

"He whooped a few rounds"

At 0400 on January 24, two 15th Infantry companies crossed the Ill River east of Niederwald on a US engineer-built footbridge and secured the immediate area then moved south to La Maison Rouge. Difficulty in rounding up the members of the attacking companies delayed their movement by an hour and a half. As King Company moved into the farmstead, they encountered some 30th Infantry stragglers. Item Company of the 15th moved to the east and created a defensive line across the Orchbach.

At 0500 the Germans, seeing that troops had reinforced the farmhouse, reoriented their defenses to the north, away from the river. They placed a Panzer a short distance behind La Maison Rouge farmhouse. Welch was still across the Ill River and parked at the edge of the woods and he observed this movement. To counter the new threat, "he whooped a few rounds" past the house and into the fields beyond. An effective tactic; the German infantry and the Panzer withdrew.

Item Company dug in. They had a tough job in the darkness and the mind-numbing cold, for the ground was frozen solid. It was slow going and the fresh dug earth showed up clearly against the snow, giving away their positions to anyone watching. King Company re-occupied foxholes dug around the farmhouse the previous day by the men of the 30th Infantry and subsequently enlarged by the Germans. By daybreak there were approximately 120 men from King partially concealed around La Maison Rouge.

A half-hour later, troops from the German 2nd Mountain Division, supported by four or more Panzers, attacked the two companies of the 15th in the weak daylight. They quickly overran Item Company and men broke and ran. Many of the men were replacements and it was their first day of combat. Some men found refuge at La Maison Rouge; some made it to the riverbank and others were captured by the Germans.

Shortly thereafter King Company came under an intense German attack. More men fled, casualties were high; but there were many acts of individual heroism in and around the farmhouse. Lasky recorded Welch's description of his actions:

> From the opposite side of the Ill River at the southeast edge of the Colmar Forest Welch at his TD position had almost a panoramic view. He estimated some 13 tanks across the whole battalion line and about a company of infantry. Welch opened fire on the southernmost section of the German armor emerging from the Schmalholtz woods. The tanks (TDs) raked their machine guns over the files of troops coming up behind.[129]

Help appeared at approximately 0830 when two Sherman tanks and a 601st TD arrived. Crossing a temporary bridge erected by the engineers east of Niederwald, they rushed down to La Maison Rouge where they took up positions across the road from the farmstead. Bunched together, the advancing German Panzers fired, disabling the two Shermans. The TD, although hit, withdrew. The men in the farmhouse lost heart watching 30–40 men from Item Company being marched off as German prisoners. German Panzers and infantry pressed the attack on the farmhouse. By this time, only 20–30 men from King Company remained able to defend La Maison Rouge. Their only hope for support for the next assault was Welch's one remaining TD.

The greatly reduced King Company nevertheless fought back with a retrieved 60mm mortar and a .50-caliber machine gun. US infantrymen were being picked off. According to Lasky, "Welch's TD in the woods west of the river was traversing and firing, oftentimes blind hoping to hit something. Nobody believed, however, that the enemy would be stalled for long." Sadly, Welch's lone TD was then hit and silenced.

The intense shelling by Welch's platoon across the river was so effective that Tech Four Lester L. Berner (Amherst, Ohio) and others were awarded Bronze Stars for their efforts. The citations stated that at La Maison Rouge, "despite the fact that their tank destroyer was hit and immobilized twice in succession" Berner and two other soldiers used their 3-inch guns so accurately that "they completely destroyed two enemy tanks and materially aided in stopping an enemy counterattack, paving the way for the infantry to advance."

Then, at 0900, a firestorm hit as the 3rd Division artillery opened up, firing 125 rounds at the Germans in 15 minutes. One Panzer was knocked out and four others retreated across the Orchbach. German infantry became disorganized in the shock and concussion of shelling. The rest of King Company was encouraged, increasing their efforts the rest of the morning and expending a huge amount of ammunition.

A new threat appeared as a 3rd Division artillery spotter reported an unknown number of Panzers moving from the east to the west towards the temporary treadway bridge at Niederwald. This new development was reported in the 601st unit journal, at 1100. US armor on the way to relieve the men at La Maison Rouge was slowed up by this counterattack. Finally after six very long hours, the Germans were stopped.

At 1430, more US armor and infantry were able to cross at Niederwald, ready for a final attack to relieve the tiny garrison at the farmhouse. Four US tanks and three 601st tank destroyers moved down both sides of the Orchbach Stream. They flushed out Germans and some surviving men of the 30th Infantry. A half-hour later, the surviving men at the farmstead were relieved.

At about 1900, Lieutenant Welch arrived at the battalion command post and reported that during the action his platoon had knocked out four Mark Vs and perhaps two more. The 601st unit journal also noted Welch reported all four of his TDs inoperable at this time. Lasky sums up the action this way:

For a few hours enemy tanks had dominated the whole area north of the Maison Rouge road and east of the Ill. Only the small band at the barn and farmhouse had held out. The long chances had been played in river crossings, and tactical gambles risked in committing an infantry attack with armor coming soon. For a period during the morning of the 24th it appeared that nothing could stop the [German] 2nd Mountain Division from completely upsetting the American hopes for "Grand Slam." Whether it could have held its newly won position for long in any event was extremely dubious. In the end they were beaten by superior strength.[130]

Losses on both sides were severe. In addition to Welch's four M-10 tank destroyers, the 756th Tank Battalion lost two Shermans. Item and King Companies of the 15th Infantry Regiment lost 94 men. The Germans lost at least four tanks, a Panzer Mark V (Panther), a Panzer Mark VI (Tiger I), one *Jägdtiger* (a heavy tank destroyer with a 128mm gun), and one Jägdpanther. The battle is thought to have been the last Panzer versus tank destroyer battle in France.

Sergeant Larson wrote a couple of letters that described this action:

You may wonder what I am doing in the mountains in Alsace. Well, I am at our battalion rear getting a new tank and am moving up again in the morning. Got into a rough tank battle a couple of days ago and I cost the Army another $75,000. My tank got hit and burned up so I also lost everything to my name, except the clothes I was wearing. Didn't worry much about that though for I was too glad to get out alive, and also the rest of my crew. My radio operator got burned some in the face and hands for it was a mass of flames the second it was hit. The rest of us got out OK in every way except for some scorched eyebrows and a big scare. A second shot hit our ammunition and then the tank blew up but by that time we were all out. You'd be surprised how fast we can move in a case like that, if you're still able to move.

The tank battle actually started the night before. All night long we battled it out and at only about 500 yards. Naturally both sides suffered some casualties, even at night. But after daybreak it became more vicious. My tank lasted until shortly after noon. Still don't know how I managed to last that long for the shells were zipping into the ground on each side and in front of the tank and others went over the turret so close we could actually feel the wind from the shells. We lost pretty heavy in this engagement but it was by no means one-sided. We accounted for quite a few Kraut tanks. It was quite a unique battle for it was between our tank destroyers and mostly a tank destroyer of theirs called the Panzerjaeger [also called the Jägdtiger]. This Panzerjaeger is a 58-ton tank, low built and very heavily armored and has one of the most powerful guns ever put on a tank. We got several of them.

But then he got his big brother, a monstrous 70-ton tank called the Ferdinand [the Jägdpanther] and his first shot made mine a mass of flames the instant it was hit. So now I'm in the same fix as at Anzio when I lost everything, only this time was even more complete. But have now gotten replacements on most of our clothes and a new radio operator and ready to go again. That's the life of a soldier in a tank. I've always been afraid of losing my third tank, afraid my luck wouldn't hold out that long, but now I'm sure it's not meant for the Krauts to get this Swede.[131]

At 1318 on January 25, a new bridge at La Maison Rouge was opened for vehicle traffic including tanks, according to the 601st unit journal. That same day a shell fragment wounded Lieutenant Salfen, according to a 601st Battalion memo. Private Petersen noted he was evacuated on the hood of a jeep. This left a vacancy in command. According to Lieutenant Maynard, "by seniority and all other rights, Lt. Welch should have become the B Company Commanding Officer and I was very surprised when I was selected over Welch." Lieutenant Maynard explained that Welch was a little brash, did a lot of things on his own, and this is what might have prevented his advancement.

The attack on La Maison Rouge was costly for the men of the 601st. Corporal Charles A. Mitchell (Odessa, Missouri) was killed on January 25, and Corporal Robert H. Moore (Eastville Station, Virginia) together with Private First Class Thomas J. Pruse (Struthers, Ohio) are listed as missing in action according to the MIA Monument at the American Cemetery, Épinal, France. The next day, Private First Class Gilbert J. Van Elk (New York, New York) was also killed in action. The individual circumstances are not known.

The 1st Platoon B Company 601st was in the Riedwihr woods on January 26, near the village of Holtzwihr. Josowitz said that during the next couple of days the woods were "taken, lost and recaptured half a dozen times." And it was in these woods that day that a remarkable American performed acts that not only got him decorated – he was awarded the Medal of Honor – but led to fame and an extensive film career after the war.

First Lieutenant Audie Murphy, acting B Company commander of the 15th Infantry Regiment was in the action; its effective strength at this time was 18 soldiers, down from over a hundred. Murphy was the only surviving company officer.

The basic facts of his well-documented story are that his platoon was under German attack by six Panzers and more than 250 men from the Wehrmacht's 2nd Mountain Division, newly arrived from Norway in white snowsuits. A section of two TDs from Welch's platoon had advanced ahead of Murphy's infantry company and sat astride a dirt road. At the start of the attack one TD was hit by an 88mm cannon. It was disabled and caught on fire. The tank commander and another soldier were killed (their names were not recorded). The second TD went into action. According to Staff Sergeant Harper, the TD commander was Sergeant Joseph Tardif and his gunner was Private Robert Hines. Suddenly the crew lost control of the TD and it slid into a ditch. It was stuck and its gun, now pointing skyward, was useless. There was nothing to do but abandon it. Finding their position untenable, Murphy sent his men to a more protected position several hundred yards deeper in the woods. The surviving TD crews fell back with the 15th Infantrymen.

Murphy planned to follow them when he was sure that they had safely repositioned. He was about to move when he spied the wrecked M-10. He knew possession of the woods was critical to the American advance. The village of Holtzwihr to the south was a German stronghold and the recapture of the road would allow a German counterattack on the entire 3rd Division position. Lieutenant Murphy judged the .50-caliber gun on the burning TD appeared to be serviceable.

Jumping on the burning TD, Murphy opened fire on the advancing German infantry. He had a working portable radio with him and he used it to call in both artillery and friendly air strikes. Murphy could see the enemy quite clearly, but he was concealed by smoke from the burning tank destroyer. With the help of the shelling and bombing, he fired into the advancing enemy without letup. At one point when his radio squawked about the position of the enemy, Murphy is reported to have said "If you hold the phone a minute, I'll let you talk to one of the bastards."

Murphy had stopped the German advance single-handed. Having done all he could and aware that the ammunition in the burning tank destroyer might explode from the fire, he jumped off it and made his way back to his men. He struggled, for he had been wounded and thoroughly shaken up after a couple of German 88mm rounds landed near the TD.[132] But his timing was good: as soon as Murphy got back to his own men, the TD blew up.

Allied efforts to take the Colmar Pocket intensified. Men and materiel kept being thrown against the Wehrmacht and constant battle took its toll. The 15th Infantry Regiment needed a respite; but there was no rest for B Company 601st. It was placed temporarily in support of the 30th Infantry Regiment. Sergeant Larson, who had been equipped with a replacement TD, had a new mission: to push the enemy out of Holtzwihr for good. It was the start of the final drive against the Colmar Pocket called Operation *Kraut Buster*. The attack was vicious. Many Germans were killed or wounded and an enemy antitank gun was destroyed. It took four days until the 30th Infantry Regiment, with the 601st in support, occupied both the villages of Holtzwihr and Wickerschwihr to the east.

"Shells are both going and coming"

Back in support of the 15th Infantry Regiment after a brief respite, B Company was located south of Wickerschwihr on the banks of the Colmar Canal. A major obstacle, the canal is about 50 feet wide with 12-foot banks with freezing cold water running six feet deep. After the engineers erected a temporary bridge, the TDs crossed on January 30. Welch's platoon, divided into two sections, simultaneously attacked the villages of Fortschwihr and Muntzenheim with the 15th Infantry. During the attacks, each TD fired almost 100 rounds of high-explosive ammunition. The next day, January 31, they were in the two villages. This was Hitler's final offensive in the west but it was now clear that their push out of the Colmar Pocket had failed. Although the US 3rd Division did not know it, German forces had started to pull back but they did not completely abandon the field, fighting delaying actions for every yard. It was expensive real estate.

Sergeant Larson described his thoughts and the action in a letter home on February 2:

I am spending tonight [February 2] in some German barracks that yesterday were full of Krauts. They are very nice too, for barracks, even though they did get beaten up a little. I have my tank here tonight getting some maintenance. The radiator on one of the motors was hit with shrapnel yesterday. This is considered the rear for us but actually the Krauts are less than a thousand yards away and as I'm writing shells are both going and coming and I can hear the Kraut machine guns rattling away. Just before the attack started night before last, we brewed up a pot of coffee and ate your cookies with it and they surely tasted good. It also served to keep us occupied and something to enjoy. Always before an attack everyone becomes pretty tense for we never knew just what we'll run into or how we'll come out of it. When the fighting starts we are kept so busy with the job at hand that we don't have time to think of anything else. But after being briefed on an attack and we have nothing to do but wait for zero hour to come, well anyone that says a lot doesn't go thru his mind is just telling a story. Everyone knows that there are some that won't come back, and maybe many of them.

North along the Colmar Canal and in the vicinity of the village of Durrenentzen,[133] just a few kilometers from Muntzenheim, Welch was in an action on February 2 that led to more honors for him: the award of the Oak Leaf Cluster to his Silver Star. His platoon was still in support of the 2nd Battalion, 15th Infantry.

The Wehrmacht threw everything it had at Company G of the 15th Infantry. Many soldiers were cut down by rifle and machine-gun fire, including the G Company commander, the only infantry officer present. Severely wounded, he was evacuated to an aid station. The company was now leaderless and in disarray. Welch immediately recognized the problem. Grabbing his carbine, he jumped down from his TD.

There were German mortar shells bursting as close as twenty yards to him and starting to zero in on the infantry positions. Small-arms fire missed Welch, he later said, by "scant margins." The lieutenant moved from man to man as he reorganized the company. During this time he pointed out enemy targets to both the infantry and his section of tank destroyers. Then he moved to the head of the infantry company and firing his carbine he fearlessly led an infantry charge forward "in a ferocious attack on enemy positions."

The charge broke through the enemy's defensive line and in the process Welch and the infantry captured 35 German soldiers. They had also wounded or killed an unknown number. It was a remarkable action for a tank destroyer officer, deserving of the Oak Leaf Cluster.

Corporal Craig E. Cookson, A Company (Lubec, Maine) was killed in action on February 4. The next day, Private First Class Morris Silverstein (Minneapolis, Minnesota) was also killed. Sometime before the fighting in France ended, Private Oucie Nelson (Elba, Alabama) was killed. Tragically, neither the exact date of his sacrifice or the location of his burial is known. Yet again the exact circumstances of these three deaths remain obscure.

B Company 601st now rapidly moved south along the canal to cut off the German withdrawal from Colmar in the vicinity of the town of Biesheim, east of the city. And by February 6 it was all over. The Colmar Pocket was at last eliminated with a final attack on Fort Mortier and the destruction of the Brisach Bridge over the Rhine. This ended a portion of the war that had been particularly costly for both sides. Hitler belatedly ordered the withdrawal of his forces from Colmar on February 8.

The 601st continued to have casualties. Staff Sergeant Dante Cappiello, A Company (Schenectady, New York) even spent a few hours as a POW in the Colmar Pocket before he was wounded on February 5, 1945.

Sergeant Larson wrote his brother Les, a lieutenant commander in the United States Navy in the Pacific, on February 7. Note the candid tone of this letter to a fellow military man, which differs from other letters home which soft-pedal harsh facts:

Over here things are also looking much brighter now. I seldom give way to optimism but now I do feel the end isn't far off. Oh, it may drag on a few weeks more but on the one hand it could end overnight now. But don't think the Krauts have quit fighting. We've had some of the roughest fighting in the past month that I yet experienced. I had another rough engagement a couple of nights ago. Didn't lose my tank but one of the machine guns on the tank got hit, a radiator got a hole in it, and my gunner got a machine-gun slug in his hand so guess he'll be gone for a while. I also had a close one, just grazing my forehead enough to draw a little blood but not enough to put me out of action. So you see Les, this tanker's life is anything but monotonous. People around here are not overly friendly. Of course practically every building is leveled as we move thru the towns and countryside so their liberation is rather costly individually. But most of them here along the border are pro-German. You can't trust anyone. Some civilians are Kraut soldiers with civilian clothes out to do all the damage they can. And every trick is used by them and regular civilians to inflict casualties, booby traps, sniping, spy work, poisoning, etc.

CHAPTER 15

GERMANY AT LAST

"Soon-to-be-forgotten vows"

After the tremendous victory of the Colmar Pocket there was no time to rest, but history had been made and the heroism of the warriors was being cited and honored. During the destruction of the Colmar Pocket, the 601st was credited with destroying 16 Panzers, six of them by Welch and his platoon. The division, including the 601st, picked up two more awards. The first was a Presidential Unit Citation (PUC) given for the Colmar Pocket operations. This is a unit award on the same level as the individual award, the Distinguished Service Cross. It was the battalion's third award and the complete citation gives important details of the actions undertaken in the Colmar Pocket:

> The 3rd US Infantry Division for outstanding performance in combat during the period 28 January to 6 February 1945. Fighting through heavy snowstorms, across flat land raked by 88mm, 120mm mortar, artillery, tank and machine-gun fire, thru enemy-infested marshes and woods, the 3rd Division breached the German defense on the northern perimeter of the Colmar Bridgehead and drove forward to isolate Colmar

from the Rhine. Crossing the Fecht River from Guemar Alsace, by stealth at 2100 hours on 22 January 1945; assault elements of the 3rd Division fought their way forward against mounting enemy resistance. When a bridge constructed across the Ill River collapsed before supporting armor could arrive on the far side, two heroic battalions of the 30th Infantry Regiment held tenaciously to their small foothold across the stream against furious, tank-supported enemy attack. Driving forward in knee-deep snow, which masked acres of densely sown mines, the men of the 3rd Division fought from house to house and street to street in the fortress towns of the Alsatian Plain. Under furious concentrations of support fire, 3rd Division assault troops crossed the Colmar Canal in rubber boats at 2100 hours on 29 January. They drove relentlessly forward to capture six towns within eight hours, inflict 500 casualties during the day, and capture large quantities of booty. Troops of the 3rd Infantry Division slashed through to the Rhone–Rhine Canal, cutting off the garrison at Colmar and rendering the fall of the city inevitable. Then, shifting the direction of the attack, the Division moved south between the Rhine–Rhone Canal and the Rhine toward Neuf Brisach and the Brisach Bridge. Simultaneously, Neuf Brisach was attacked from the west side of the Rhone–Rhine Canal and the walls scaled by ladder and through the combination of these maneuvers the fortress was captured. In one of the hardest fought and bloodiest campaigns of the war, the 3rd Division annihilated three enemy divisions, mauled three more, captured more than 4,000 prisoners and inflicted a total of approximately 7,500 casualties on the enemy.

The second award was the *Croix de Guerre 1939–1945 avec Palme* (the 1939–1945 War Cross with Palm), a French unit award. This award is actually a *fourragère*, often referred to as a rope, and is worn on the left shoulder. It was given to the entire

3rd Infantry Division. The citation reads in part: "To the Elite Division which remained faithful to the finest traditions of courage and sacrifices which had been its pride during the last war when it acquired the name Rock of the Marne." The award was presented by General Jean de Lattre de Tassigny.

The cost of the battle for Colmar was heavy on both sides. American casualties were estimated at 8,000, French at 16,000. Almost a third of the losses were due to disease and noncombatant injuries. The deep snow, freezing temperatures and numerous water crossings caused a marked increase in trench foot and frostbite. Official German casualties were 22,000 killed or missing and non-battlefield casualties were likely also high. The German *Sonnenwende* operation to preserve the Colmar Pocket succeeded only in tying down German troops in the 130-mile defensive Colmar perimeter. In the end, no more than 10,000 German troops managed to escape across the Rhine, abandoning their combat vehicles as they fled. In effect, the German 19th Army ceased to exist.

The official US Army history by Jeffrey J. Clarke sums up the US 3rd Infantry Division as follows:

> In this area, the US 3rd Infantry Division showed everyone why it was considered one of the finest units in the American Army. Shrugging off the Maison Rouge bridge incident, the division's stellar performance was clearly vital to the First French Army's overall success. Although it was an old division that theoretically had been fought out, exhausted, by the end of its Italian campaigning, its small units, especially the infantry-tank teams, seemed to rise to the occasion as they approached each of the fortified Alsatian towns on their route of advance.[134]

Meanwhile, the war went on. For a couple of days, the battalion remained along the Rhine in the vicinity of the destroyed

Brisach Bridge. Then, on February 6, they were moved to a reserve position near the village of Kunheim, east of Colmar. The battalion's February monthly operations report notes that "For the first time in 185 days the battalion was completely relieved from the line and the utmost effort was being made to bring the men up to top physical and mental condition in anticipation of future operations."

At last there was some time off. According to the morning reports for February 11–14, 1945, Welch and four 601st enlisted men (Tech Four Daniel H. Green, Jr (Ashland, Pennsylvania); Corporal George C. Boyer (Superior, Wisconsin); Private First Class Paul R. Brown (Aurora, Illinois); and Staff Sergeant Angelo P. Morone (Paterson, New Jersey)) were rewarded with a three-day pass to the 3rd Division Rest Camp in Paris. On the way back, Welch wrote home:

> I'm sure you must be quite worried by now, but we've been in the worst fight we've ever had. We finally took Colmar. I lost three of my four destroyers in one day, had quite a few men hurt but I'm OK. I knocked out six Kraut tanks. I collected a couple more medals, which I'll tell you more about later. Rushed for time.

Welch returned to the battalion from Paris early on the 15th. By this time the 601st was billeted near Jebsheim, six miles northeast of Colmar and near the site of Audie Murphy's heroic one-man stand.

On February 19, the battalion made a 120-mile road march across the French countryside to Pont-à-Mousson without incident. The route from Colmar was back through the Vosges Mountains. Among the towns they passed through were Kayserberg, St Dié, Baccorat, Lunéville and Nancy.[135] Pont-à-Mousson was the designated 3rd Infantry Division assembly point where it would prepare for the final push into

Germany. Back in September 1944 it was at this town that the Germans held up General Patton's Third Army for almost two weeks. Lundquist noted that "The town was pretty well blasted with the bridges over the river of its name lying down in the water." And Josowitz said this about the town as well as the upgrades to their equipment:

> The people of that city probably will never forget the 601st, nor will the MPs. A great deal of work was accomplished during that rest period. The M-10s were exchanged for M-36s and the crews had to learn how to use them and to shoot the new 90 [mm]. Maintenance sections worked day and night, cutting, welding, and adjusting. But when the battalion wasn't working, it wasn't wasting any time.

There was much to do and not a lot of time to do it. The battalion commenced an aggressive program of training, rehabilitation and maintenance on February 20. It had been in almost continuous combat since the landing in southern France on August 15, 1944.

Changes were being made. The battalion's 36 M-10 TDs were replaced with 36 new M-36 TDs. Adding these destroyers meant the 601st would be the only US tank destroyer battalion to take all varieties of US Army World War II tank destroyers into combat. Not everyone in the battalion was happy with the change. Research and development had continued during the war, and the M-36 TD was the product of a US Army program to build a tank destroyer designed from the ground up. Many Army officers felt the M-10 had been hastily designed and was a stopgap weapon. The M-10's biggest problem was the shells it fired could not penetrate Panzer frontal armor. The US Army had three similar caliber guns on the battlefield, the 75mm (M-3), 76mm (M-18) and 3-inch (76.20mm, M-10) naval gun. None was effective in a frontal attack. According to

Lieutenant Maynard, up until the M-36 "there was not much difference between the guns used by US forces during the war."

The M-36 was named "the Jackson," after US Civil War Confederate Army General Stonewall Jackson. It was manufactured by the Ford Motor Company. The Army mounted a 90mm antiaircraft gun after observing the success that the Germans had with their 88mm antiaircraft gun in an antitank role. It was thought a tank destroyer equipped with a 90mm barrel could go head to head against German Panzers. Additionally, the M-36 was designed to correct a turret counterbalance problem and to be faster than the M-10. This was accomplished by replacing the GM diesel engines with Ford gasoline engines. This change was the single reason the men of the 601st did not like the M-36. The gasoline engine was dangerous. Sergeant Nowak noted that on at least one occasion "two of the killed burned in their front seats." The unit journal during the rest of the war reported three occasions when the new TD caught fire and burned the crewmen. This was the direct result of substituting gas for diesel engines.

The 776th Tank Destroyer Battalion was already experienced with the new TD, so while the battalion was at Pont-à-Mousson training on the M-36, battalion records note that the S-3, Major Miner, visited the 776th.[136] The purpose of his visit was to understand the field modifications made by the other battalion and to learn about any specific maintenance procedures and operational tactics they had implemented. A technical observer from the Ford Motor Company arrived as well to offer expertise to the battalion officers on the new TD, as noted in the unit journal of February 26.

It wasn't all work and training. On February 21, Welch wrote home: "We're resting now in the vicinity of Nancy. It's beautiful around here. I've visited Metz and Verdun, which are quite interesting. It's spring here now and it sure feels good. Rest easy for a few weeks, as I won't be fighting. OK?"

As part of their training, they conducted experiments to familiarize themselves with the capabilities of the new 90mm gun on the M-36. In one series of tests, they used a captured German Tiger II (Royal Tiger) as a target and fired armor-piercing and high-explosive rounds at it over a couple of days. According to the battalion's March operations report, when they fired the gun at 1,000 yards, six rounds bounced off the Panzer when shot from the front, but six rounds fired at the flank "penetrated both the turret and the hull." On the same Tiger II they experimented with sandbags placed on the Panzer as a protection against the German *Panzerfaust* (German version of a bazooka). After firing that weapon, the result was a smaller hole burned into the armor plating than normally expected where the round hit the sandbag. Night firing tests were also conducted using a searchlight and 6mm flares. The searchlight was impractical but the flares "proved to be the ideal medium."

During the first week of March, Sergeant Nowak noted Welch and another soldier visited him while he was in the hospital with the eye wounds he suffered at La Maison Rouge. That week, Welch's mother wrote him a V-mail dated March 6. Because it was never delivered, it is the only letter of hers that survived and it shows she had received his letter of February 21, 1945:

I do hope you are getting our mail, because I know how I watch the mailman for a letter from you. He now rings the doorbell when he has a letter from you. The last fight you were in must have been a bad one but I am glad you are resting for a few weeks. Does your new APO mean that you are with a different outfit than the Seventh [Army]? Let me know. I guess I worry more, trying to figure out what I don't know, than I do when I think I know where you are. Also do you still have the Great Dane dog? Also you said you would tell me what the medals you received are for. You know we think that it is wonderful all the things you are doing. You are sure you are just resting and not injured?

Unbeknownst to the men of the 601st, March 7 marked the end of tank destroyers as a separate weapons platform. On that day, a tank platoon of the 14th Tank Battalion, 9th Armored Division, equipped with the new M-26 Pershing Tank and armed with the same 90mm gun as the M-36, crossed the Rhine on the Remagen bridge into Germany. Simply put, there was no longer a need for both a tank and a tank destroyer armed with the same 90mm gun to be on the same battlefield.

Nonetheless there were signs in mid-March that the battalion was going into action. On March 8 there was a formal battalion review where General O'Daniel presented medals and, on March 11, there was a battalion equipment inspection during which Welch was presented with an Oak Leaf Cluster to his Silver Star.

Sergeant Larson wrote home on March 10, 1945:

I now have my old crew back on my tank, the same crew that I had all thru France. My gunner, who was shot in the hand came back from the hospital a few days ago and is now ready for the next round. The radio operator who got burned when my tank was hit has not come back nor have we heard anything from him so I guess he was pretty bad. But he wasn't one of my regular men anyway. Guess I told you I've been outfitted with a new tank. Got a gun on it that looks like a telephone pole sticking out front so from here on in the Panzers had better beware. At least the odds won't be so much in their favor as they have been so often in the past. Hope I reach Berlin with this one.

We have learned to admire these French the way they look at things. Their homes and everything they own might be destroyed and they just shrug their shoulder and say *C'est la guerre*. Of course not all are that way but the majority take a plucky attitude. This part of the country I am in now surely had its share of war. Whole cities are completely flattened and everywhere are burned-out hulks of destroyed tanks and other vehicles, both German and American. Dugouts and trenches are everywhere around here, many of them left since World War I. Battles in this war were fought right over large graveyards of American soldiers from the other war and now in some places right across the road from these cemeteries are large new ones with soldiers from this war.

The 601st, newly equipped and trained, was ready for battle. Josowitz wrote about the place that had been their home for almost a month: "There was much wailing and wringing of hands when the 601st moved out of Pont-à-Mousson on the night of March 13th. There were fond goodbyes and wild, soon-to-be-forgotten vows."

"Hang out the washing on the Siegfried Line"

At 2300 on March 13, the battalion moved 68 miles to an assembly area near Rohrbach, France, in preparation for the 3rd Infantry Division's assault on the Siegfried Line. This action was code-named Operation *Earthquake*, part of the Seventh Army's Operation *Undertone*. It would be the first time the 601st took its M-36s into battle.

The Siegfried Line was a gigantic defense installation, a counterpoint to the French Maginot Line. The Germans, who referred to it as the West Wall, started it in the late 1930s as a secret project. Engineers and soldiers working on the line kept its construction secret by wearing civilian clothes. The Siegfried Line was a series of bunkers, tank traps and pre-identified artillery aim points. The line stretched almost 400 miles from Holland to the Swiss border. It was strongest in the Rhineland area of Germany where an invasion from France might be expected. The line, which in some places was several kilometers wide, had more than 18,000 bunkers, forts and reinforced concrete structures, not to mention rows and rows of tank traps, nicknamed "dragon teeth." It was a huge propaganda success and had burned itself into the British psyche. A popular song sung by the 1939 British Expeditionary Force at the beginning of the war had the lyric, "We're going to hang out the washing on the Siegfried Line."[137]

The 3rd Infantry Division was south of Zweibrucken, Germany on March 15 when they launched their attack. They captured the German-held French towns of Ormersviller, Volmunster, Windhof, and Ohrenthal before crossing into Germany. Corporal Borriello wrote this about the attack:

> Now we're facing the city of Zweibrucken and the Siegfried Line with its tank traps, pillboxes, fire trenches and mines. We carried extra TNT to blow up the pillboxes so the Germans couldn't infiltrate back into them. We were trying to bulldoze enough dirt to fill in the tank traps and over the Dragon Teeth of the Siegfried Line.

Private Alfred F. Curatolo (Pittsburg, Pennsylvania) of the 601st was killed in action during the first day attack on the Siegfried Line, March 15.

Clearly HQ was worried the Germans would resort to chemical weapons as the division crossed into Germany. The battalion received Instructions Number 28 from the 3rd Infantry Division Operations on March 15. Paragraph one stated: "Gas masks with protective ointment, eye ointment, eye-shields, protective cover and chemical warfare reference card included in the carrier, will be carried by all personnel forward of corps boundaries or will be kept within immediate reach." The instruction went on to list the protective equipment to be held in unit supply and the admonition that unit gas officers "will be used to the maximum extent possible to insure that protective measures against chemicals are carried out by all individuals and units."

On March 18, B Company approached Dietrichingen, Germany, the last town in front of their section of the Siegfried Line. Here, the company went into action, knocking out two enemy half-tracks and firing at enemy pillboxes and machine-gun nests. Welch, as was his custom before every major battle, wrote home on the eve of the attack:

> This is just a short note. We're cracking the Siegfried line today so I'll be busy for some time. We had a great rest but it wasn't long enough. I'm in Germany now, still with the Seventh Army. It looks the same as France except all of the towns are deserted. The Siegfried Line is quite a thing, very well fortified and will be pretty rough getting thru. It's just like spring here now, warm days and cold nights. I guess this should pretty well clean things up.

On March 19, Sergeant Nowak, now with 2nd Platoon, described the attack this way:

> On the first day the first platoon went out in the open and shot pillboxes, dragon teeth, etc. We brought ammunition to them, and snipers were active. I saw many dead doughs and much abandoned equipment. All around doughs were dug in, and they kept down. Larson's TD was hit in the rear idler and had to come back. The second platoon went out on the second day. My TD was on the right flank. Smoke shells landed about ten yards to my right for about 20 minutes, so I finally moved to another position. I directed my gunner to fire at targets of opportunity. Kraut with machine-guns

kept sniping at us and made us keep our heads down. It was a hot day and we couldn't find out where the Krauts were. We couldn't move forward because of a tank ditch. Big shells dropped in near us. But we kept them guessing by moving around when they got too close. One big shell landed about five yards away and I was about to tell Sgt. Telecky that they were shelling us. I had to go and get more ammunition, so I told the driver via inter-phone to take off and the hell with Telecky, he knew that we were being shelled. We broke through the line in two days and made contact with the US Third Army. Homan [Private First Class Virgil O. Homan, Valentine, Nebraska] was hit by a sniper and KIA. Lt. Linkey [Ernest W., Brooklyn, New York] was also wounded.

Josowitz reports: "the fighting was very tough in some spots and comparatively easy in others. The 601st A and B Companies suffered casualties but all three gun companies inflicted very heavy damage on the enemy." One of those casualties was Staff Sergeant Eugene C. Claytor (Glasgow, Virginia) of A Company; however, the exact circumstances are unknown. Once again B Company was in support of the 15th Infantry Regiment. According to the post-battle examination of the defenses, the 15th Infantry regimental history said:

> The Siegfried Line in this sector had the extra advantage of excellent terrain for defensive positions. The rolling hills of barren farms had been stripped of wooded patches that may have neutralized some of the fields of fire. Pillboxes were placed so that every bit of terrain had been covered by cross fire and the draws and gullies were zeroed in with mortars. In the pillboxes each automatic weapon had before it a panoramic sketch of the land visible from the slits. Each feature, no matter how seemingly insignificant, such as bushes, rocks, and paths, were zeroed in with the ranges marked.[138]

Shortly after the attack, Sergeant Larson wrote his brother a most detailed description of the Siegfried Line and of the foresight and precision of its builders:

> As you can see from the headlines we are now on our last leg of the journey over here. Have one very tough obstacle behind us and that is the Siegfried Line. Wish you could have seen that line, Les, you had to see it in order to understand how formidable it was. It extended several miles in depth and it was just one mass of pillboxes, bunkers, tank traps, etc. It of course was first laid out so that you'd have to cross a long stretch of open terrain, usually uphill, to approach it. This open terrain was naturally covered with every type of gun, with all kinds of cross fires of machine guns as well as the big guns. Nothing was left to chance for we found charts with the big guns showing the exact ranges to the different points on this open terrain so whenever a tank or some other target presented itself all they had to do was set off the range and let fly. They could be sure of a hit.
>
> After crossing the open terrain you first came to about three sets of dragon teeth. They are heavy concrete pillars sticking up out of the ground to stop tanks especially. Each set had about six or eight staggered rows of these dragon teeth. If you got through all of them you next came to deep antitank ditches, most of them a good ten feet deep and just as wide if not more. Now backing all this up were pill-boxes and bunkers with the big guns on every advantageous spot. There wasn't a foot of ground that wasn't well covered by those guns. These pillboxes were so thick that all you had to do was point the gun toward the Siegfried Line and you were almost sure to have one of them in your sight. And they were elaborate affairs, with steel and concrete domes (from where they fired) anywhere from two to six feet thick. I don't think there is a shell made that would penetrate some of them.

Underground were all the stores, living quarters, ammunition rooms, etc. There were three and four stories deep under each pillbox, with 16 to 20 good-sized rooms. And there were all the comforts of home, electric light, running water, fine living quarters, etc. Not even block-buster bombs could get them down there. And of course there were connecting corridors with each pillbox so if one was disabled they could just move into the next one without coming above ground.

The guns in the pill-boxes were fixed up with periscopic sights so the gunners could sit well below ground to do their sighting and firing. And there was 360-degree traverse so they could get you regardless of which way you approached. You can see what a problem all of this presented since all you had to shoot at of this elaborate affairs was the impregnable cupolas or domes that stuck out of the ground only three or four feet. But here's the best part of it, we broke the line on the third day after day and night attacks. Of course we had to pay a price, even my tank was knocked out, but we all got out of my tank OK with only two men very slightly wounded. Makes my fourth tank lost, just about enough I'd say. Can't tempt fate forever and expect to come out of it. When we get together I can give you more details of how this line was cracked. Right now the line is a has-been. Our engineers went to work with demolitions and are blowing this elaborate 12 years of hard labor sky high. It's just a mass of broken concrete and steel when they finish.

McFarland's *History of the 15th Infantry Regiment in World War II* added a couple of details to Larson's closely observed account. The turrets were made of very thick steel and 90mm shells would bounce off or sink ineffectively into several inches of metal. The main part of the pillbox was underground with several large rooms big enough for 30 men each. These rooms looked like the interior of a ship. The fortifications were connected with deep, zigzagging trenches protected by barbed wire and mines. There were rows of dragon teeth of progressive height. Behind them were deep antitank ditches, 30 feet deep and 30 feet wide. Antitank and flak guns protected the entire area and the fortifications were camouflaged into barns, houses and other innocent-looking structures. Most of the trenches facing the 15th Infantry were manned by elite SS troops who fought with everything they could muster.

The battalion's March monthly report explained how the pillboxes were overcome:

> In the assault of the Siegfried Line the HVAP [high-velocity armor-piercing] shell was tested against pillboxes and found to be very successful. It was found that two or three rounds of high-velocity ammunition had the same effect as six or eight rounds of normal velocity ammunition. However, the extreme shortage of this type of ammunition made it impossible to use it as desired. Consequently during the firing of pillboxes the HE (delay fuse) was used and proved to be the second best type of ammunition available for this mission.

"There's a chance I might be able to get home soon"

The battalion had broken through the Siegfried Line with its infantry regiments by March 21. It was now mopping up bypassed enemy resistance. The town of Contwig, Germany, was captured and Welch's sister Betty wrote him a letter. It too, was not delivered but returned:

> There is a radio commentator who broadcasts at two PM every day by the name of Trotter. Unlike other reporters, he mentions all the divisions fighting at the moment in the

news. Consequently today you must be getting your bearings in Zweibrucken. It's nice to finally know where the 3rd is. He mentions all the different divisions because the 4th Armored [Division] of Patton gets all the write ups and he stresses the fact that there are other divisions who get little glory but without whom it would be impossible to operate. So darling now we can follow you day to day. Congratulations to all of you for your splendid work. I wish I could come over there and kiss every one of you. The radio just says that Hitler is resigned to the fact that the Allied Armies and Russians will meet someplace in central Germany. Brilliant deduction that.

It was standard procedure when preparing to send men back to the States to use them as temporary POW guards or at least have them available in rear areas in case of trouble. Welch hadn't received those letters from his mother and sister because, on March 21, he was ordered to report to the 404th Prisoners of War enclosure at Marseille, France by March 24 for Temporary Duty (TDY). The 3rd Infantry Division orders confirmed this, adding: "Upon completion of this TDY they [the men listed] are placed on further TDY with the Reception Station in the US under which their names are listed for forty-five (45) days rest and recuperation at addresses shown."

Welch was scheduled to return to the 601st, but now he was going home! He was going home as part of the troop rotation program which picked men based on recommendations, availability of replacements and transportation. In most cases the order to go home on rotation usually came as a most welcome surprise.[139]

Josowitz might have been referring to Welch when he wrote: "The leading elements were just beyond Zweibrucken when Capt. Richardson dashed up to an M-36 that was actually engaged in a close-range duel with an 88 and dragged the Chief of Section out for a trip to the States."

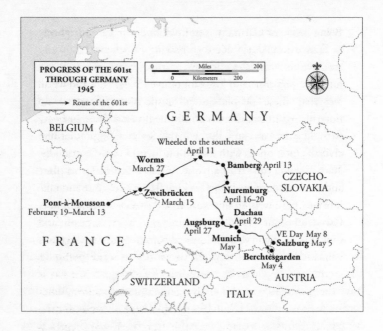

On March 22, B Company was near the towns of Windsberg and Thal when it destroyed an enemy self-propelled gun and assisted the 15th Infantry Regiment in destroying a column of vehicles, capturing 300 Germans racing for the Rhine. To cut off the Germans, 601st vehicles carrying as many 3rd Division soldiers as possible made a mad dash to the Rhine. For most of the battalion this was the third time on the banks of the Rhine: the first after the capture of Strasbourg, the second after the Colmar Pocket.

According to Josowitz, there was a "spectacular take off by 6th Armored Division beyond Zweibrucken and terrible carnage on the road to Ludwigshaven where armor and air annihilated huge German columns. German civilians looted their own dead and white flags were everywhere."

Sergeant Larson wrote to his brother on March 23 noting a change in attitude now the fighting was on German soil:

Being inside of Germany is quite different from our fighting in France and Alsace. Here everything we see is a target and we have no conscience about destroying everything. We've fought a long time and lost a lot of lives to get here and we all feel that these people are all responsible. There is no fraternizing, in fact there is a $50 fine if you are caught being friendly with a German civilian. Some of the German civilians look on us with hatred but many try to be friendly. Naturally you can't trust anyone. When we come into a place and want a house to stay in we kick the civilians out and take it over. As I'm writing this we're in a very nice German home. Came in here at 0500 this morning, put the civilians out and took it over. If you've ever doubted before about the Germans being military minded you won't do so after being in Germany. They just think in terms of fighting. It just seems to be as much a part of their lives and thinking as automobiles are to the Americans. You can see they have no regret for the suffering they've caused with this war. Their only regret is that they're losing the war.

Having beautiful spring weather here in Germany and the country we're in now is surely pretty except where the war has wrecked it. It's rolling country, well-cared for, with beautiful highways and other improvements and modern fine homes. They're an industrious people, these Germans, if only they could live peacefully.

Meanwhile rotation continued. The battalion morning report of March 24 noted Lieutenant Colonel Tardy departed for the States on TDY and Major William R. Harrison, the battalion executive officer, assumed command of the 601st. As things worked out, neither Lieutenant Colonel Tardy nor Welch was to return to the 601st. As Josowitz noted the day after Tardy left the battalion, the 601st was considered to have completed its transition from a prewar professional Army outfit to a unit made up of civilians. Few of its soldiers left in the unit now were from the prewar days.

Prior to shipment all personnel had to be certified they were "free from any communicable, infectious, or venereal disease." The Naples-based 31st Replacement Battalion February history report describes the process that soldiers had to undergo:

> The processing of men returning to the United States is a task. Every man who arrives must be thoroughly processed. This includes the issuance of clothing and equipment to individuals, the processing of service records and all Allied papers, the completion of questionnaires for the proper publishing of orders, orientation lectures, physical examinations and change of currency. The time is short, and it is necessary for the companies to accomplish this immediately. The exchange of currency and physical examination must be accomplished 24 hours before the shipping date.

In Marseille, therefore, Welch had a physical. He waited until he arrived at Marseille on March 26 to send his mother a letter in which he mentioned he might be coming home:

> Well the war news sure does look good. Everyone seems to be going places in a hurry. We managed to break thru the Siegfried line without too much trouble. Spring is here for sure it's even starting to rain and all that stuff. There is a chance that I may be able to get home for a short time before long. I hope so.

The same day he arrived in Marseille, Welch was designated the commander of Group 500-2TD (Temporary Duty) by HQ Delta Base Section,[140] in Movement Orders. His group consisted of 11 men; only one other was from the 601st,

Sergeant Earl E. Thompson (Holcomb, New York). One other 601st man, Tech Five Ralph E. Satterfield (Paces, Virginia), was in Group 500-3TD. Records indicate Welch left the European Theater fifteen days later, on April 10. Although he did not know it, his intense military career was almost over. He was just shy of his 25 birthday.

CHAPTER 16
IT FINALLY ENDS

"Got a little careless and got myself shot"

In war, plans change because the exigencies of battle require them to change. Originally, the supreme Allied commander, General Eisenhower, planned to have American troops follow Field Marshal Montgomery in the race for Berlin. After crossing the Rhine, they were to take off across the northern German plains to the besieged city. Montgomery, cautious as usual, had planned the attack down to the last bullet and had been gathering materiel for weeks. First would be a huge artillery barrage with a paratroop drop just behind enemy lines. He would leave nothing to chance.

But the situation on the ground had altered. US Army and corps commanders were now along the Rhine south of Field Marshal Montgomery, and were ready and eager to cross the river and end the war. They didn't want to wait for a slow attack across Germany to capture the German capital. There wasn't time.

At the end of March, the Soviet Red Army had advanced to within 30 miles of Berlin, and Eisenhower's forces were more than 300 miles away. A rapid linkup with the Russians to the south across the middle of Germany would cut the remaining

German forces in two, which appeared the much better option. Adding pressure to change tactics was the fact that the Germans were moving what industry they could to the southwest of the country. There was a serious concern fanatical Nazis would establish a "National Redoubt" in the Alps south of Munich and stage a long, drawn-out last stand.

There was no practical reason for US troops to go to Berlin now. Furthermore, most of the territory they would have to cover on the way was to be in the designated Soviet sector and so would have to be handed over to the Russians. The political significance of an Allied capture of Berlin was very important to Churchill and the British, who hated the idea of abandoning the German capital to the Soviets. Nevertheless, the Sixth Army Group, under General Devers, and including the 3rd Infantry Division, was given the mission to eliminate any attempt by the Nazis to make a last stand in the Alps. The German defense in this sector was still fierce. Although there was no longer any truly coordinated German resistance, SS units and the Hitler Youth had not given up and continued to fight.

The entire 601st was on the east bank of the Rhine on March 27; B Company and the 15th Infantry were the last to cross. They were south of the ancient cathedral city of Worms and they headed due east. Along the way, tanks and TDs were brought up to neutralize enemy guns placed to stop the Allied advance. The first day, with the Germans in full retreat, the 15th Infantry took four towns and more than 300 prisoners.

By the end of three days, the 3rd Division was 20 miles east of the Rhine. Private First Class John J. Schweizer (Penrose, Colorado) was killed on March 29. The circumstance is unknown. They were on their way to the Main River, which they crossed without much difficulty the night of March 29/30. They continued to capture much equipment and many prisoners as they sped on.

As April began, German villages, towns and cities hastily surrendered to the Allies. Forgotten were their oaths to defend their homes to the last. Now the Germans thought only of staying alive. Nearly every home flew a white flag of capitulation to indicate there were no troops inside. It was a matter of survival that they did. Any structure that didn't hang a white sheet out of the building was blasted by US tanks and TDs. Overwhelming the advancing Allies were the hordes of deserters and stragglers from the Wehrmacht, who posed a huge problem because there were so many of them. McFarland noted:

> The scenes of destruction which greeted the advancing Americans have perhaps never before been surpassed anywhere in the world. Town after town and city after city had completely lost its identity, smashed by our air corps and ripped and torn by our artillery and infantry. Hundreds and thousands of people lived in the ruins and rubble streets of their once immaculate homes, a drab contrast to the proud people who set out to conquer the world.[141]

Resistance was encountered, however, and the brutal fighting continued. According to the unit journal, when 2nd Platoon of B Company entered the small town of Rothenbuch, they knocked out one antitank gun and a truck. The cost was high. Two of their M-36s were shot up, one by antitank fire and the second by a Panzerfaust. Five 601st men were killed: Tech Five William C. Powers (El Dorado Springs, Missouri), Private First Class Verne P. Cardoza (Livingston, California), Private James L. Loper (Homestead, Florida), Sergeant Frank A. Vargo (Detroit, Michigan), and Private Jefferson S. Rogers (Harlan, Kentucky). Lieutenant Bell was also slightly wounded that day during the same engagement.

A larger battle took place near the village of Steinach on April 7. Here A Company engaged 12 German Panzers in what may well have been the last major Panzer attack of the war. The battalion operations report noted they knocked out two Mark V Panzers, one Mark VI, an antitank gun, and killed 15 of the enemy. The report noted "When the enemy company attempted to withdraw they found the road behind them had been cut off by B Company and friendly infantry. Rather than run the gauntlet of tank destroyer fire, the enemy destroyed their tanks and retreated on foot." The cost to the 601st was again high. During this engagement, two M-36s were hit and destroyed by tank and antitank fire. Two men were killed, Private Mason E. Bailey (Birmingham, Alabama) and Corporal Forest P. Powers (Coeburn, Virginia), and five men wounded. All of them were burned in fires caused by the gasoline-powered M-36s.

The Seventh Army made a wheeling movement to the southeast on April 11, the day Staff Sergeant Harper was assigned a brand new, inexperienced second lieutenant to "watch out for." He was Beverly S. Blackburn (Harrisonburg, Virginia). Lieutenant Josowitz told the new lieutenant to listen to Staff Sergeant Harper and he admonished Harper not to get the new lieutenant killed since he was scheduled to take over for him while he (Josowitz) went on a pass to Brussels.

On April 13, B Company captured three "doodlebugs" just outside the city of Bamberg.[142] Then, together with the 15th Infantry, it entered the city itself. Bamberg was a town without any military significance; however, there were two large military hospitals with a handful of American patients. After some initial fighting on the way, the city was quickly taken. The Americans had faced a garrison of SS troops and the local Volksturm (armed civilian) units, but they had been ineffective defenders. The German soldiers were all drunk. More than 150 of them summarily surrendered.

The History of the 15th Infantry Regiment in World War II reports an incident during the capture of Bamberg:

The Kraut was in a very confused state when the battalion moved into the town with their armor support. German military vehicles attempted to flee through the main street, but the tanks blasted them. One enemy truck came skidding around a corner and rammed into the rear of a TD. The surprised gunners swung the turret around and lowered the barrel, poking it through the windshield and fired a round. There wasn't very much left of the German truck.[143]

After Bamberg, the 601st headed to Nuremburg 30 miles to the south, where the famous war crimes trials would be held later. Nuremburg was strongly defended with a ring of antiaircraft defense guns used as tank killers. US troops had to fight for every house and building. It took several days for resistance to crumble.

In a letter dated January 30, 1991, John J. Spear (Duquesne, Pennsylvania) had this to say about Sergeant Larson during the early days in Germany:

He was the bravest man I ever met. He was cool under fire. I remember one time we were behind a house, along a river in Germany and the Krauts were lobbing mortar rounds at us from across the river behind a hill. One round hit the house. We pulled out in the open about 25 yards down the road. They shot another round and it landed about 50 yards in front of us. Rudy took his pipe out, took some tobacco and stuffed it in his pipe and calmly lit his pipe, and told the driver "Huey [unknown] you better back it up a little." We backed up a little and a round hit in the back of our tank. Then he told Huey to haul ass to the town about 500 yards down the road. While all this was going on I was a bit scared, but I knew we had a good tank crew with him running the show. I was with him when he got hit.

Yes, wounded. On the outskirts of Nuremburg, on April 16, Sergeant Larson was severely wounded for the third time. Later he described the skirmish in a letter to his brother with all the details:

> Got a little careless and got myself shot up a little a couple of weeks ago. But I'm doing OK now and it's just a matter of time till I'll be back to normal. After all the fighting we've been thru I surely want to be present with my outfit when the last shot is fired. Oh well, there may still be quite a long battle for the Redoubt so I'll probably be back before that is over. I got shot twice thru my right leg, one thru the thigh and one behind the knee. The latter is probably the one that will trouble me the most. And then a third one cut a groove on the little finger of my right hand. But none of the three bullets hit any bones.
>
> It was while attacking a town near Nuremburg that I got hit. Had knocked out a couple of machine-gun nests on the edge of this town and when I drew near to them I decided to check a dugout alongside them for Krauts. Well I did too, for a Panzerfaust was sitting at the entrance all ready for firing. It was a deep, dark dugout so I hesitated before going into it but I had my gunner with me who talks perfect German so he called in and ordered out anybody in there. I then fired a burst from my tommy gun into it and crawled down into it. As I turned a corner I flashed on my flashlight and there right in front of me was a German SS officer with his Luger pistol pointed right at me. The officer opened up on me right away and hit me with the first three shots before I had time to throw myself around the corner. I managed to get outside a little ways from the entrance before I passed out. For an SS officer he was a very poor shot, I'm thankful to say. He should have gotten me for keeps for he was right on top of me. Even got powder burns on my clothes from his pistol. But that's the way it goes, if your time isn't up it seems you manage to squeeze out of it

someway. Of course I hate to think what would have happened if he or one of the others (for there were at least a couple more with him) would have had one of their machine pistols. Some townspeople told me after I came to again that was the German officer in charge of the garrison defending the town.

Later, he described his trip to a hospital in Verdun to his mother:

I'm in a general hospital at Verdun, France. I was wounded when fighting on the outskirts of Nuremburg, Germany. I was put on a stretcher and hauled by jeep back to our battalion medics. Casualties were pretty heavy that day so I lay for about six hours there before my turn came to be hauled out in an ambulance. Then I had about a 30-minute ride over rough cow trails to an evacuation hospital. Toward morning they put me to sleep and operated on me. I stayed there about three days until my temperature came down near normal, then was again loaded on an ambulance and hauled about 90 more miles to an air evacuation hospital. I was there only a few hours when we were loaded aboard large ambulance planes and were in the air about three hours. We were unloaded near Rheims, France where we spent the night in a hospital there. The next day we were loaded on an ambulance train and rode about six hours until we got to Verdun, where we've been ever since.

The battle for Nuremburg was heavily fought. Enemy soldiers, often SS, hid in cellars, on rooftops and fired out of every window. Between Allied bombing and the battle, Nuremburg had been reduced to rubble. Sergeant Nowak on April 17 described some of the action in and around Nuremburg:

The doughs were stopped all morning by direct dual purpose 88s. I saw one dough fire a bazooka from a window and immediately an 88 hit the house he was in and he got wounded. At one place where we pulled roadblock all night, Eilas [unknown] and I went to investigate a closed door and got 23 prisoners for our curiosity. Later that day eight more came from a cellar next to Telecky's TD.

Staff Sergeant Harper, still in the thick of things, wrote of the need to remain alert:

> As we were advancing down this wide boulevard, an infantry sergeant came and told me that there was an obstacle across the street and wanted me to see if the tanks could get by it. When I got out of the tank, I told Lt. Blackburn [the new platoon leader] to stay in the tank. When we got to the obstacle I found it to be a jettisoned fuel tank from a P-38, which was no problem to get by. As I turned to go back to my tank, there was Lt. Blackburn. He had his carbine slung over his shoulder by the strap and I told him to get the gun off his shoulder and into position to fire. You never knew what might happen and needed to be ready for anything that came your way.[144]

The lieutenant and Staff Sergeant Harper headed back for the tank, about 300 yards away. They went only a short distance when Staff Sergeant Harper saw someone lying in the gutter and bent over to see who it was. The man replied, "*Comrade*" so he knew he was a German. Apparently eight German SS soldiers had infiltrated between the TD and the US infantry. Staff Sergeant Harper pulled the soldier up by the shirt collar and then the shooting started. Harper got off a few rounds before he was hit. Friendly infantry took care of the Germans, but during the melee Lieutenant Blackburn was killed.

The unit journal for April 18, in addition to mentioning Staff Sergeant Harper's injury, listed men from Recon, A, B and C

Companies who had been killed or wounded. Recon was outside Nuremburg, near a village called Heroldsberg. The casualties included First Lieutenant Lewis P. Elliot (New York, New York), who was killed and Private First Class James F. Hadju (Freeport, Illinois), who was burned. From A Company, First Lieutenant Thomas J. Kelly was wounded and from B Company, which captured an enemy hospital that day with 1,500 patients (including a Wehrmacht Brigadier General), Tech Five Richard T. Smith (unknown hometown) was killed and Tech Four Harold R. Summerville (Lilly, Pennsylvania) was wounded.

Captain Richardson, the officer who had taken time to get married in December in Mutzig, was also wounded for the third time. He was leading C Company TDs into the city and while passing an L-shaped building his TD was struck by fire from a well-hidden gun. He was knocked out of the vehicle and although he later recalled all others in the TD killed, the records can confirm only that Tech Five Joseph W. Albensi (Dover, New Jersey) was wounded; he had been clubbed on the head during the attack.[145]

The battle for Nuremburg was officially over by April 20 (Hitler's last birthday). Sergeant Nowak recorded that on April 23, the battalion had taken more than 1,000 prisoners. He added: "their underground city was much to marvel at. It included sleeping quarters, aid rooms, administrative rooms, a printing shop, and mess quarters. Water and Electricity were plentiful."

Captured at Nuremberg was the parade ground sacred to the Nazi party. Albert Speer, Hitler's architect, had designed the stadium in the 1930s; it was also called Zeppelin Stadium. It was here that an incident took place involving Colonel Ralph Smith, the 3rd Division chaplain. General O'Daniel thought it would be a fitting place to present five 3rd Division soldiers with the Medal of Honor. This was a grand ceremony and Chaplain Smith was almost a victim of it. According to Corporal Borriello:

I was instructed to drive to division headquarters where we picked up Lt. Col. Ralph Smith, our Division Chaplain (Father Smith to us). We then drove to the Zeppelin Stadium where the ceremony was held. Col. Petherick [commanding officer, 10th Engineer Battalion] had asked General O'Daniel for permission to blow the swastika off of the stadium after the ceremony and it was granted. As soon as the ceremony was over and the stadium emptied, the charges were set. Col. Petherick suggested that anyone taking pictures could get a better view from across the stadium. I went with Father Smith to the other side. Unfortunately, a piece of shrapnel flew across the stadium and hit Father Smith. Medics arrived immediately and I thought that he had just been knocked down. I found out later from Col. Petherick that Smitty was seriously injured, but he survived.

The new M-36s were still catching on fire. Two soldiers suffered first and second degree burns on April 23 but their injuries were not life threatening.

Resistance was sporadic but, when encountered, it was fierce and costly. Because a bridge across the Danube had been captured intact, the battalion and the 3rd Infantry Division raced from Nuremburg and crossed the river near Dillingen, Germany, on April 25. They had orders to proceed to Munich and then into Austria to halt the reinforcing of the Alpine Redoubt. On the way to Munich, they took the city of Augsburg, a city of 200,000. In its suburbs, the battalion met with perhaps the worst artillery barrages of the war. The remaining Wehrmacht fired everything it had. Tech Five John F. Szczotka (Shinnston, West Virginia)[146] was killed in unknown circumstances. After subduing the artillery, Augsburg fell without further fight on April 27.

That day, Sergeant Nowak had received the good news that he too would be going home as part of the troop rotation program. On April 28, he left the French city of Strasbourg and later described his trip to Marseille:

> We left Strasbourg about eight in the evening on the 28th in a boxcar. There were ten of us in one car and we had 10-in-1 and C rations. [10-in-1 rations were designed to feed groups of men and were modeled after the British 14-in-1 "compo" rations. It contained one day of meals: breakfast, evening supper and midday snack for 10 soldiers.] We built a fire in a big can inside the car and thereby heated water for coffee and rations. At stops in Nancy and Lyon we traded rations for eggs and bread. If we had been in coaches, we wouldn't have been so well off. We traveled down the Rhone Valley and it was to be admired for its beauty. On the 30th we reached Marseilles from where we went to Camp Tee Dee. Before leaving, I sold a whole can [carton] of 10-1 rations for 30 bucks [$30.00] and gave the money to Holstein who was broke. We got assigned to tents, got processed, got interviewed and received shots. I saw Ricci and Sakowski, who were on their way home. [Two of the three soldiers mentioned are likely Sergeant Ernest B. Holstein (Branford, Connecticut) and Tech Five John J. Sakowski (Springfield, Massachusetts). The name Ricci is unknown.][147]

On April 29, somewhere between Augsburg and Munich, the last man to lose his life while in combat with the 601st Tank Destroyer Battalion was killed: Private Jesus V. Covarrubias (Encinitas, California). The exact circumstances are not recorded but the operation report listed all those lost during the month of April: "two officers were KIA and six WIA [wounded in action], ten enlisted men were KIA and 28 enlisted men were WIA." That accounted for more than one-tenth of the battalion's total KIAs during the war; a painful irony with the war drawing to a close.

For men who had seen enough horror in battle, a new and terrible shock was in store for them. Just outside Munich, elements of the battalion entered the horrific Nazi concentration camp at Dachau. For the men who saw the conditions at the camp and breathed in the stench, it was an unforgettable experience. In a US Army Heritage and Education survey, Tech Five James R. Stevens (McKeesport, Pennsylvania) wrote of the "absolute horror as we saw flatcars stacked with dead naked bodies!! Shocked!" Tech Five Jimmie Frank Burrett, B Company (Atlanta, Georgia) recalled he had "nightmares about the German Concentration Camps" and Technical Sergeant Frances E. Miller, (Washington, New Jersey) wrote of his visit to Dachau: "It was pure hell."

Technical Sergeant Phallen may have been the first 601st soldier to see first hand the horrors of Dachau. He was off doing some independent advance reconnaissance for A Company in his jeep when he came upon a series of low buildings behind a fence. Attached to an L-shaped building was an incinerator and he observed two German youths throwing corpses into the flames. Having recently been fired upon by Hitler Youth, Technical Sergeant Phallen was concerned they would turn on him, however, they ran off and he reported back to his company.[148]

"Enjoying teetotaler Hitler's champagne"

By the time the battalion entered Munich on May 1, it found the German people's attitude toward their conquerors had radically changed. The people of Munich welcomed the 3rd Division. Some even showed the US troops where fanatical SS troops and munitions were hidden. In some cases, German civilians beat the SS soldiers before turning them over to the Americans. According to Josowitz, it was nothing for men sent out to find water to return with a couple of hundred German prisoners. Munich's well-developed autobahn network ringed the city and these "highways were jammed with the remnants of the once proud Wehrmacht trudging unbidden to the rear areas."

After Munich, the battalion headed for Salzburg, Austria, which was taken without trouble. *The History of the 15th Infantry Regiment in World War II* states:

> Thousands of prisoners streamed in after the surrender of the Italian Front, which included southern Austria. They seemed to flow from every tiny village, hill and valley. Everywhere there were columns of unarmed Germans carrying their huge packs. One German truck company was captured intact and was utilized in transporting prisoners. Others were grouped into massed thousands and marched on the autobahn guarded by flak wagons and armored cars. They rode in on bicycles, horse, automobiles, trucks, wagons, by foot and even by train. The surplus of vehicles brought in by the prisoners piled up until almost every squad of the 15th Regiment had comfortable transportation for a limited time.
>
> Mixed with this flow were hundreds of thousands of displaced persons (DPs). Every nation in Europe was represented in Germany's slave labor system. Now with their sudden release, they packed their few possessions and began a long trek home. Most of them went to our camps for DPs to await orderly shipment home, but others merely wandered in the general direction of home living by foraging and enduring extreme hardships.[149]

On May 4, a new shakeup was under way. HQ 3rd Infantry Division issued Operations Instruction Number 72, which gave new assignments for each unit. The 7th Infantry Regiment, for example, was to advance and capture Hitler's mountain retreat at Berchtesgaden in the Bavarian Alps. Other components were to begin patrols, guard bridges and set up roadblocks. The war was almost over as is clear from the following:

> Every effort will be made to rehabilitate personnel and equipment with emphasis on haircuts, shaves, clean uniforms, and cleaning of weapons. Vehicles will be washed, painted, and serviced. Helmets will be painted. Messes will be placed in operation without delay, and will be inspected regularly for excellence of hot meals.

According to James Tubman, a member of Love Company, 7th Infantry Regiment, his regiment was the first to enter Hitler's retreat. He wrote, in an undated edition of the 3rd Division newsletter, *The Watch on the Rhine*:

> I can attest that the 7th Regiment was first in Berchtesgaden. We came into the town I believe in the afternoon, and we were on a high road overlooking the streets of the town. I was riding on a tank commanded by Lt. Lebo [Leonard Lebo, Swissvale, Pennsylvania] of the 601st TD Battalion. Riding along one of the streets was a civilian vehicle, about a half-mile away from our vantage point. Lt. Lebo had his machine gunner fire at the vehicle, and we could see the tracers hitting the hooded motor area. The vehicle stopped and out jumped a GI probably scared to death, but he wasn't physically injured. He ran back to where the vehicle had come from. We learned very soon after that the 2nd Battalion had preceded us into the town and the 3rd Battalion was right on their heels in entering. Later that night I was walking guard in the town proper and about 2am the following morning the first French troops arrived, a day or so later the 101st Airborne, and immediately the credits for the occupation were given first to the French and to the 101st. Believe me, and also Capt. Pratt, the 7th Regiment was first into town.

At 1650 on May 5, to avoid any "friendly fire" casualties, the battalion ordered there be no further fighting unless fired upon, according to the unit journal. Three men had been wounded during this first week in May and they were the last.

Victory in Europe (VE) Day was declared May 8, signifying the unconditional surrender of Germany, The long awaited day found half the battalion drinking champagne liberated from Hitler's cellars. According to Josowitz, the 601st ended up at Hitler's Berghof on the Obersalzberg, outside Berchtesgaden, "where they enjoyed teetotaler Hitler's vast stock of champagne." Captain Rydal L. Sanders, A Company was with Captain Pratt (7th Infantry) when they entered Berchtesgaden and wrote in the US Army Heritage and Education survey that he was one of the men who drank Hitler's champagne at Berchtesgaden.

The central German campaign, the last campaign of the war, ended after 54 days of battles marked by increased carnage, suffering and, at last, victory. On May 8, Lieutenant Tommy Welch was already at home in Geneva, New York, and Sergeant Nowak was boarding a Liberty ship for the long voyage home, which he described this way:

> On the 8th we went on board the Liberty Ship John Milledge, about 300 of us. We stayed in port overnight and left Marseilles without escort the next morning for a calm two-day trip to Oran. On the 12th we left in a convoy, which moved slowly. On the 13th about noon we passed by the Rock of Gibraltar. We still had an over two-week trip to the US. About the 15th we were in the vicinity of the Azores, but we did not see the islands. We had many hot, sunny days and fellows were out on the deck getting tans. Inside there was a bunch of fellows who played poker nearly all-day and quit about two or four in the morning. On the 24th the ships stopped at sea and maneuvered into different positions. Those on the south side (on our left) would go to Newport

IT FINALLY ENDS

News, Virginia. We would go to New York Harbor. During the last days at sea there was a seaplane overhead every once in a while. On the 29th we sighted land and as we went up a river, a Quartermaster boat with a WAC [Women's Army Corps] band escorted us to Pier Three of the Port of Entry. Our Liberty Ship was all dressed up. We got off and were greeted by the American Red Cross who gave us sugared donuts and milk. We went on a ferry, which took us to Fort Hamilton (Brooklyn, New York, a US Army Post). We got a special steak dinner with milk and ice cream. The next day we got processed and interviewed and had other details taken care of. Overnight passes to New York City were given to us.

The 601st Tank Destroyer Battalion operations report for the period May 1–10, 1945, dated May 25, mentions that:

At the end of the period the objective which this battalion had begun fighting for at Oran, Algeria, on 8 November 1942 had been achieved: the utter defeat and surrender of all German Military Forces of land, sea, and air. At the close of hostilities in Europe this unit still had more than two hundred and forty of its men and officers who had come overseas with it thirty-three months before, most of them had fought in eight campaigns and had made four D-Day amphibious landings.[150]

There was one final loss. Private First Class Otto J. Bruske (Vandercook Lake, Michigan) died of his wounds on May 12, 1945. He is buried in the American Cemetery at St Avold, Lorraine, France.

Staff Sergeant Benjamin A. Buckley's platoon had a curious experience when C Company was the first armored unit to enter Hallstatt, Austria, high in the lake country of the Austrian Alps. As he explained:

We dismounted the AA guns and pedestals from the destroyers and just squeezed through an old stone arch at the entrance to the town. Those people hadn't seen any armor since the knights used to ride around: they just stood there with their mouths hanging open and their eyes popping. We were still fighting two weeks after the end of the war up in those mountains, and had to turn into cavalry at that. I took the platoon into the hills to round up stray Krauts. The roads were too narrow to turn mounted patrols so we just requisitioned some horses and rode them. We flushed out a few Jerries.[151]

Josowitz sums up the 601st record in *An Informal History of the 601st Tank Destroyer Battalion,* which he wrote while on occupation duty in Salzburg, Austria:

There have been many omissions in the writing of this history, some of them intentional, but that was inevitable; for after all, this could not possibly be anything more than a very brief resume of the highlights in the composite career of the 1,800 men who fought eight campaigns, made four D-Day assaults, spent five hundred forty-six days in actual combat, suffered six hundred eighty-three casualties, had one hundred ten [actually 111] men killed, knocked out at least one hundred fifty-five tanks and self-propelled guns and destroyed a fantastic number of enemy personnel.

He further noted that battalion personnel were awarded the following remarkable array and number of decorations:

One Medal of Honor; four Distinguished Service Crosses; one Soldier's Medal; five Legions of Merit; ten Individual Croix de Guerre; 105 Silver Stars [92 first awards and 13 clusters (for second awards to the same individual); a small oak leaf cluster is worn on the ribbon to denote a second or further awards]; 236 Bronze Stars [210 were first awards, 22 clusters to the same individual and four clusters were third awards to same individual]; 630 Purple Hearts [523 were first awards, 91 clusters to same individual, 13 were third awards to same individual and three were fourth awards to same individual]; in addition the unit was awarded: two Presidential Unit Citations [three since one was added in 2008 for the action at Salerno] and the French Croix de Guerre [unit award].[152]

His leave in Geneva over, Welch reported at Fort Dix, New Jersey on June 14. Originally he was scheduled to return to the 601st, but the war in Germany was over so that was no longer necessary. The war with Japan raged on, however, and preparations for the attack on the Japanese home islands were being made. Because it was predicted that it would cost a million US casualties to defeat the Japanese, no combat veterans like Welch or other members of the 601st were to be immediately released.

As previously mentioned, the development of a new tank with a 90mm gun meant the days of the tank destroyer were numbered. At Camp Butner, North Carolina, the Army had set up a regional reassignment center to find new Army jobs for officers and men no longer essential at their present stations. Welch was sent to Camp Butner for a skill assessment. The War Department required reassessment for men in the following categories: personnel returned from overseas for whom no immediate assignment was available; personnel made surplus temporarily by the reduction, inactivation or reorganization of their units; personnel whose qualifications suggest reassignment would be beneficial.

Welch fit into several of those categories and he stayed there a couple of weeks before being sent back to Camp Hood, Texas.

"The long wait to start the trip home"

Throughout July more men of the 601st started to return home. As the war in Europe ended, combat veterans were being transferred to the States to be ready for further service against Japan. A point system – the Adjusted Service Rating – determined who returned home first. Ratings were developed in reaction to the World War I practice of letting the last men in to be the first men released from active service, which was seen as unfair. The point system was therefore established and was known to be in effect at least as early as May 1945. Under the system, the longest serving and most deserving servicemen were sent home first. Counting points became a ritual for most of the men of the 601st. One point was assigned for every month in the service, one point for every month in combat, five points for every Purple Heart, and five points for every personal decoration (such as a Bronze or Silver Star). At war's end, the first soldiers sent home were those with 85 or more points.

In the meantime, on July 16, Sergeant Larson returned to the battalion from the hospital. It might have been easier to send him back to his unit than to try and process him home for discharge.

When a battle or a war ends there is much to do. Mopping up is exactly that: cleaning up, tying up loose ends, making order as the enormous skein of military fabric unravels. And so, in addition to occupation duty, Fascists and Nazis in hiding had to be hunted down, and Nazi loot had to be identified and prepared for return to rightful owners, a huge undertaking in itself. August of 1945 was about those things.

At this time, Welch's brother-in-law, Reg Bushnell, who himself was tracking down Fascists and Nazis, sent a V-mail letter to Betty Welch Failmezger. Reg was in Italy with Army Counter Intelligence Corps (CIC):

I guess this time you may not look for me back for a while, we arrived here about 10 days ago. I am at present just outside of Naples, Italy and will probably be moving further north soon. The trip over was fine and uneventful, came in the same ship as we started out in the first time. Welch was no doubt all over the same spots I have been in so far, except when he was here, there must have been a lot more excitement than there is now, I can tell that from the many buildings that are no longer standing.

Dispersing the huge military presence in Europe meant redefining, reorganizing, cutting down, cutting out. What had been useful in war was not needed now. And so it was that on August 17, the 601st was inactivated, its brief life over, its usefulness no longer justifiable to a US Army which no longer needed separate tank destroyer units. Since it was such a long-serving unit, however, it was promised that the men of the 601st would be returned to the States by air. That sporadic airlift program was called the "Green Project." The very next day the men departed Salzburg, Austria, at 1000 for the return to the States. The trip to Marseille, France, took three days, and they just missed going by air, so it was back on a slow troop ship. They departed France on September 20, 1945, arriving in New York three weeks later on October 7, 1945. It seemed forever. The unit was now history.

Sergeant Colprit reflected on the voyage home and his homecoming, not without some foreboding:

Then there was the long wait to start the trip home and that did not start till August. We loaded up on boxcars for the long trip to a depot in southern France [from Austria]. It was mid-September before we loaded onto the troop ship *David C. Shanks*. Now we had 14 days to think about returning home after three years. I wondered what my future would be.

I know Dorothy had been writing to me all this time but what were her hopes and plans? We never had any agreement or expressed our feelings toward each other knowing I was off to war and might NOT be coming back and almost didn't. At last we would see the Statue of Liberty there to welcome us home. At camp [New York] the first one I called was Dorothy; and she answered the phone. In a couple of days I was separated from the service and traveled to Winchester, Massachusetts to my Aunt and Uncle's office. Within five minutes my Aunt Vivian complained: "We've had it hard here at home you know, standing in line for butter and meat." I just could not answer her.

Corporal Borriello was sent by truck to France to Camp Phillip Morris (many of the camps were named after cigarette brands). Later he was shipped across the English Channel to Southampton. He was told they were to go home on the fast, well-appointed *Queen Mary*. But that was canceled and they were loaded instead on the USS *William S. Young*, a much slower Liberty ship. The water was choppy causing the screw (propeller) to lift out of the water over the larger waves, sending a shudder throughout the ship. After about a week they were passed by the *Queen Mary*; the *Queen* took four days to make the Atlantic crossing, the *Young* 13. They landed at Hampton Roads, Virginia and were trucked to Camp Patrick Henry.

Welch was back in Texas at North Camp Hood by this point, where he stayed until October 2. He was appointed a first lieutenant in the Officers' Reserve Corps, Army of the United States and given two months and 25 days' leave and eight days' travel time to Geneva, New York. His effective date of release from active duty was January 5, 1946. Welch immediately registered for college at Cornell University for the fall term of 1945. Like other returning soldiers, Welch wanted to make up for lost time. According to Childers; "Like colleges all over the country, Cornell was flooded with men returning from the service, eager to take advantage of the GI Bill. By 1946 more than half the student body and three-quarters of the male students were veterans."[153]

Although now veterans of a deactivated unit, pride of service was still felt and recognized. All the 601st were authorized to wear the World War II Victory Medal (which closely recalled the World War I Victory Medal in appearance), and the European–African–Middle Eastern Campaign Medal. The Victory Medal has President Roosevelt's Four Freedoms inscribed on the reverse (Freedom from Fear, Freedom from Want, Freedom of Speech and Freedom of Religion). The European–African–Middle Eastern Campaign medal has the colors of each of the three nations the Allies fought in this theater during World War II. In the center are the three colors of the French flag (red, white and blue). On the left are the three colors of the Italian flag (green, white and red). On the right side are the white and black colors of the German flag of the time. Each side of the ribbon is trimmed in brown, representing the dry landscape of North Africa and the Middle East, while the green color represents the green fields of Italy, France, and Germany. On the obverse of the medal is displayed a landing craft for the six D-Days of North Africa, Sicily, Salerno, Anzio, Normandy and Southern France.

The 601st had served in 10 campaigns.[154] Each soldier was authorized to wear a small bronze star for each campaign in which he personally participated. If a soldier was in five campaigns he could wear a small silver star to keep the ribbon uncluttered. Welch, for example, was in six campaigns and so could wear one small silver and one bronze star on the ribbon. The places and dates of the battalion's significant actions follow:

Algeria–French Morocco (November 8–11, 1942)
Tunisia (November 17, 1942–May 13, 1943)
Sicily (July 9–August 17, 1943)

Naples–Foggia (August 18, 1943–January 21, 1944)
Anzio (January 26–May 24, 1944)
Rome–Arno (January 22–September 9, 1944)
Southern France (August 15–September 14, 1944)
Rhineland (September 15–March 21, 1945)
Ardennes–Alsace (December 16, 1944–January 25, 1945)
Central Europe (March 22–May 11, 1945)

The speed of the US Army's demobilization was stunning. The author of a *Life Magazine* article of April 22, 1946 called it a disintegration:

> The Army with 6,884,000 of its men demobilized, the greatest military machine in American history has suffered shocking disintegration less than a year after its triumphal entrance into Berlin. It was July of last year when the 2nd Armored (Hell on Wheels) Division, veterans of North Africa, Sicily, France, the crossing of the Rhine, rolled proudly into Berlin. In its ranks were 10,616 men. Last week at Camp Hood, Texas, less than a year later, the remnants of the once great 2nd Armored posed for the picture above. In its ranks were 60 men. Another 100 were off on furlough. The other 10,456 were gone.[155]

The military had, with great precision, turned those millions of civilians into warriors. It had taken time and training. But where was the un-training, the conversion of those warriors back into civilians? For Welch and hundreds of thousands of others their Army life was over, but their war was perhaps still going on. Welch was at Cornell, but was never engrossed in his studies. He did not graduate. It must have been impossible for him and others like him to sit in a classroom after living on a hair trigger for so long. The end of his war had been very abrupt and perhaps he didn't have the transition time he needed before he left the service. He dropped out of Cornell after the first year. He went home.

On May 7, 1947, Loretta (Welch's mother) sent Betty (Welch's sister) a letter in which she talks about having him home:

> It is a little relief (if you know what I mean) to have Tom working. That way he is out of my hair during the day. Nights, I don't know whether I would rather have him out, and worry about him, or have him stay in, and drive us all crazy. Never stays put five minutes at a time. Three men [her husband, Lt. Commander Harry S. Trotter, Welch, and Sgt. Reg Bushnell, her son-in-law] after all these years of just girls around, I can't get used to it.

This was not at all unusual. According to Childers:

> In early 1946, an estimated 1.5 million veterans were living with friends or family, and despite the upbeat prognostications, the situation did not improve in the following year. In 1947 the VA (US Department of Veterans Affairs) revealed that 64 percent of all married veterans and 80 percent of unmarried vets were still squatting with friends or relatives.[156]

Although the story of the 601st ends here, the lives of its soldiers went on. The men whose words have helped to tell this story would each cope in their own ways with a future that held no guarantees and perhaps little glory.

EPILOGUE

The Men

This book has followed the story of the men of the 601st and one engineer during the course of their personal experiences during World War II. Here is the rest of their story.

Joseph F. Borriello

Joseph F. Borriello was born in Meriden, Connecticut in 1923. He graduated from Meriden High in 1942 where he played varsity tennis. He enlisted in the US Army in September 1942. Joe was inducted at Fort Devens, Massachusetts and after a short time was sent to basic training at Fort Croft, South Carolina. After basic training, he stayed there to attend radio school. His Army specialty remained communications, primarily CW (Morse code), but he "strung a lot of wire [telephone], especially at Anzio." He left for Casablanca on board the USS *Hahn*, arriving in Morocco in March of 1943 as a replacement. He returned home in October 1945.

In 1946, Joe attended the Teachers College of Connecticut (now Central Connecticut State University), graduating in 1949 after just three years. His major was elementary education. At the same time he worked on a Masters of Education in secondary education. He taught for a short time, but the Army called him back for the Korean War. By 1951 he was a first lieutenant, and he was stationed in Augsburg, Germany. He even went back to see his sweetheart in Pont-à-Mousson but by this time she was married.

Returning home, he married Evelyn Mary Charest (1926–2013) and they had two children, William and Jo Anne (Picard). They also had four grandchildren (Brandon and Natalie Borriello and Wendy and Neil Picard); and two great-grandchildren (Brianna and Teagan Herdic). Joe taught in an elementary school and for a long time was the first and only male elementary school teacher in Meriden. He was then made the principal of a Meriden elementary school, a position he held for 18 years. He retired in 1989. The author made extensive use of his memoirs in this book and has enjoyed his conversations with him.

Charles W. Colprit

Charles W. Colprit was born on September 17, 1920, the son of Ernest Sprague and Helen Woodman, on a farm in New Hampshire. He graduated high school and joined the Army on August 29, 1942. He was sent to Fort Bragg to train at the Field Artillery Replacement Center and studied instrument and survey. This entailed laying the guns and training in the Fire Direction Center. Without notice he was transferred from the artillery to the newly formed Tank Destroyer Corps. He first went to Camp Gordon outside Augusta, Georgia for training as a replacement. Sent to North Africa, he joined the 601st right after El Guettar in Tunisia. He was wounded on May 24, 1944 on the way into Rome, but was able to rejoin the 601st by ignoring his orders to report to a replacement depot in England for reassignment. During the war he was promoted to sergeant.

He married his wartime sweetheart, Dorothy, in 1946 and they had two daughters: Dr Elaine Colprit (a professor at Bowling Green University, Ohio) and another who is a minister in Estill Springs, Tennessee. He had several grandchildren and at least one great-grandchild. He retired in 1983 after serving as a US Postal Service letter carrier for 30 years. Charles died on May 19, 2004; he was 84 years old. He made his wartime memoirs available to Jeff Danby, who passed them on to the author.

Bill R. Harper

Bill Harper was born on February 1, 1920 on the Smith Farm in Titus County, Texas. He was the son of Henry Allen, Sr and Melinda Josephine McAdams. He was the tenth of eleven children, seven boys and four girls. He joined the Civilian Conservation Corps in April 1937 and enlisted in the US Army on December 5, 1939 in Dallas, Texas. He was sent to Fort Benning, Georgia and on the first day was assigned to D Battery, 5th Artillery Battalion (the Alexander Hamilton Battery, the oldest unit in the US Army). There was no boot camp and training was done by the battalion corporals. He transferred with his entire battery to the 601st Provisional Antitank Battalion, which later became the 601st Tank Destroyer Battalion.

On October 11, 1944, Bill was fortunate enough to be sent home on a furlough as part of the troop rotation program. During the furlough he married his sweetheart, Dorothea Dobbs, in Sculpture Springs, Texas on December 16, 1944. He returned to the battalion on March 7, 1945. He was wounded outside Nuremberg on April 17, 1945. In addition to a Purple Heart he was awarded a Silver Star. He returned to the States on June 6, 1945 on a medical evacuation plane. During the war he was promoted from private to staff sergeant.

After the Army, he worked for many years for the Southland Corporation, retiring at age 55. Later he was a rural mail letter carrier and eventually became a county judge. He also served in the first two terms of the Texas Silver-Haired Legislature.

EPILOGUE

In retirement, he wrote four newsletters a year to men of the 601st and helped organize reunions. He formed post 601 of the Society of the 3rd Infantry Division. In September 2003, at their last reunion, Bill saw to it that they presented their flag to the 3rd Infantry Division Museum at Fort Stewart, Georgia. He and Dorothea adopted two sons, Henry Alan (Hal) and Edward Dobbs (Ned) and had four granddaughters (Laura MacKenzie, Madison Rhea, Jessica Ann and Elizabeth Dobbs). Bill's life story is available for reading at both the 3rd Infantry Division Museum and at the US Army Heritage and Education Center, Carlisle, Pennsylvania. Additionally he was interviewed for the Library of Congress, Veterans Heritage Project and a transcript of that interview is available online. He is deceased.

Edward L. Josowitz

Edward L. Josowitz was born in New York, New York in 1912. He completed at least three years of high school. He enlisted on June 4, 1942 and listed his marital status as single, with dependants. During the war he received a battlefield commission to lieutenant and at the end of the war was the author of the *Informal History*, which has been extensively quoted in this book. Although the circumstances are unknown to the author, he was awarded two Silver Stars, two Bronze Stars, a Purple Heart and an individual *Croix de Guerre*.

After the war he changed his name to Ed Justin and wrote poetry. He presented the poem reproduced at the end of this chapter at a 601st reunion and it was saved by Sergeant Nowak. Josowitz's *Informal History* is available at the US Army Heritage and Education Center, Carlisle, Pennsylvania. Occasionally copies can be found and purchased online.

Rudolph 'Rudy' E. Larson

Rudy Larson was born on a farm near Lansing, Iowa on July 6, 1909. He was the fourth child of Eddie and Ella (Eastman)

Larson in a family of five sons and two daughters. He graduated from Lansing High School in 1928 where he was an athlete. He attended the University of Minnesota for one year. While working in Washington, DC, he met Peggy B. Davis and married her on January 12, 1941. He enlisted in the US Army in August 1942 and, after training, joined the 601st Tank Destroyer Battalion on October 1, 1943 in Italy.

During the campaigns that followed, he had four of his tank destroyers shot out from under him. His personal decorations included the Silver Star (May 30, 1944 action which saved a tank driver's life), the Bronze Star (for assisting in the stopping of the German Panzer attack on February 29, 1944 at Anzio) and a Purple Heart with two Oak Leaf Clusters. Late in the war he was promoted to staff sergeant. He was discharged in November 1945.

After he returned home, Rudy was a government meat inspector in Chicago for the remainder of his working life, retiring in 1979. He died of cancer on December 22, 1990 at Cape Coral, Florida. He and Peggy had no children but were well loved by 18 nieces and nephews. The author is indebted to one of these nephews, Colonel Lars E. Larson, US Army (Retired), for access to Rudy's extensive diaries, letters and notes.

Harold E. Lundquist

Harold Lundquist was born August 9, 1923 in Minneapolis, Minnesota. He was named after his father and was called Junior while he was growing up, although he hated the nickname. He graduated from Senn High School in Chicago, Illinois in 1941 where he studied drafting. He worked for a Chicago firm until joining the Army and meeting his wife, Aili Maria Hannula (1921–2010) in the spring of 1942. They were married on December 19, 1942. Harold was drafted into the Army on January 15, 1943 and he went to basic training at the Tank Destroyer School at Camp Hood, Texas.

At Camp Hood, he attended radio operator school and after crossing the Atlantic to North Africa was later assigned to the 601st Tank Destroyer Battalion, Reconnaissance Company in October 1943. Harold was a half-track radio operator and artillery spotter. He was in Salzburg when the war ended. He was discharged October 31, 1945 and although he had malaria in North Africa, he was never wounded during the two years and four months he was overseas.

After the war Harold returned to Chicago and met his two-year-old son for the first time. He and Aili lived in Chicago, Libertyville, Illinois, West Covina, California and Lakewood, Colorado. He was able to support the family on his income and Aili stayed at home to raise their three sons, Jim, Sven and David, and a daughter, Janet. Harold retired from work in 1986 and traveled with his wife Aili and son David. There were 11 grandchildren and 14 great-grandchildren. He passed away in August 2010, shortly after his beloved Aili. Before he died he made his wartime diary and a short paper he wrote in 1997 called *Random Thoughts* available at the US Army Heritage and Education Center, Carlisle, Pennsylvania; both texts have been extensively quoted in this book.

Thomas E. Morrison

Thomas E. Morrison was born in Brewster, Ohio in 1918, the son of D. P. and Sarah Morrison. He was drafted and inducted in the US Army on April 28, 1942. Initially he trained as a radio operator at Fort Bragg and then was sent to the 1st Infantry Division at Indiantown Gap, Pennsylvania where he was assigned to the 601st. He rode the *Queen Mary* to Scotland and after four months training in England, traveled on HMS *Derbyshire* to Oran.

After the action in North Africa, his request to become a medic was approved on July 10, 1943. He remained with the 601st, landing on September 14 at Salerno and also made the landing at Anzio. Eventually he was transferred out of the 601st after having been diagnosed with battle fatigue and he was returned to the US. Over the course of the war he was wounded twice. His notes, memoirs and drawing are available at the Third Cavalry Museum at Fort Hood, Texas and the US Army Heritage and Education Center, Carlisle, Pennsylvania. There he filled out a questionnaire at the age of 81. When he was 83 he was interviewed for the Library of Congress, Veterans History Project July 29, 2001. A transcript of that interview is available online.

John Nowak

John Nowak was born on August 14, 1918 in Ludlow, Massachusetts. He was the son of Polish immigrants, Michael P. and Anna Nowak and was a lifelong resident of Ludlow. He was a graduate of Ludlow High School and was well known as a high school athlete, starring in baseball, basketball and hockey. He followed his brother who joined the US Army Medical Corps in 1930 by enlisting in the regular army of the United States on October 23, 1940. Among his early assignments was the 32nd Field Artillery Battalion at Fort Devens, Massachusetts. That unit was among the first to be assigned to the 601st Provisional Antitank Battalion, which later became the 601st Tank Destroyer Battalion.

John served with the 601st overseas from the beginning of the war until he departed the European Theater for home leave on May 8, 1945. During the war he received two Silver Stars: the first on July 23, 1943 for action at El Guettar and the second on January 30, 1944 for action during the ranger rescue attempt on the Anzio beachhead. He also was awarded two Purple Hearts: the first during the invasion of southern France on August 20, 1944 and the second on January 23, 1945 during the attack in Alsace, France at La Maison Rouge. He had at least one Good Conduct Medal and all the unit and campaign awards given to the battalion during the war. During the war he was promoted to staff sergeant.

John was discharged from the US Army on June 4, 1945 at Fort Devens, Massachusetts. In 1946 he was employed as a steam and pipefitter by the Monsanto Company in Springfield. He stayed with Monsanto until he retired after 35 years. On June 5, 1948 he married Norma Ella Frennier (September 14, 1925–March 27, 2007). They had three children: Linda Nowak (married name Novak); William Michael Nowak; and Robert John Nowak. There are three grandchildren (Scott, Sarah and Allison). He was an active attendee at many of the battalion's reunions and stayed in touch with many of his World War II comrades. He passed away January 4, 2003 at Ludlow. Engraved on his tombstone are the Tank Destroyer insignia and the shield of the 601st Tank Destroyer Battalion. He preserved his military career in several large albums of correspondence, notes and photographs, all of which contributed enormously to the writing of this book.

Thomas Peter Welch

Thomas Peter Welch was born on May 30, 1920 in Geneva, New York. He was the fourth of five children of Harold J. Welch and Loretta Higgins and the only boy. His father died in an automobile accident in 1929. He graduated from Geneva High School in 1938 and enrolled at Hobart College, also in Geneva. He did not graduate but completed over one year of college. By May 5, 1942 he had enlisted in the US Army. His initial training was at Camp Wheeler, Macon, Georgia. He was selected for officer training and reported to Camp Hood, Texas to the Officer Training School for Tank Destroyers. He departed the States on June 6, 1943 on board the USS *West Point* and arrived in Casablanca, Morocco on June 12, 1943.

He was kept waiting for a combat assignment until September 1943 when he received orders to the 601st Tank Destroyer Battalion. During his time with the battalion he was awarded a Bronze Star and Purple Heart at an action at Presenzano, Italy (southeast of Cassino), a second Purple Heart for wounds suffered during the January 1944 US Army ranger relief effort, a Silver Star for the action on the Anzio beachhead on February 29, 1944, and an Oak Leaf Cluster to his Silver Star for an action in February 1945, north of Colmar, France.

He returned to the States in April 1945 on the Troop Rotation Program and was eventually released from the Army in October 1945. He briefly attended Cornell University and, after a restless time in Geneva, moved to Texas in 1950, where he held a variety of jobs, but never really settled down. He was married twice and had a daughter, Parker, by his first marriage. He died on May 18, 1972. The author's grandmother, Loretta Higgins Welch Trotter, preserved his 150 letters from the war and also his 201 file, which contained official documents no longer required by the Army. These documents were the spark that led the author to write this book.

World War II and Post Traumatic Stress Disorder

Like a lot of veterans, Welch couldn't settle down. Little survives of his postwar correspondence to support this, but according to his mother in April 1949:

> There are times when I think everything will be alright with Tom and then he goes and breaks out, like the measles, staying out all night and I knowing he has only a dollar or less in his pockets and then the check cashing starts. He has not been able to get to the Veteran's Hospital as yet but he has applied. He also promised me that he will not cash any more checks. I think the reason is that they now go to the police station instead of just being turned down at the bank and the people call me. He has done a lot of work in the yard and

other things like scraping the hall floor with a sander and finishing it and he is wonderful that way, until he gets out and then goes haywire.

This letter brings up the question of whether or not Welch and millions of other World War II veterans suffered from what is now called Post Traumatic Stress Disorder (PTSD). During World War II it was called battle fatigue. The short answer is of course they did. Childers' book, *Soldier from the War Returning*, centered on this issue for the soldiers and their families that he followed during the postwar period. It is highly recommended for its insights. Readers are also directed to the US Department of Veterans Affairs website: www.ptsd.va.gov for more information on PTSD.

It is not known if Welch got to the Veterans Administration Hospital or received any help settling down, but he did change his surroundings and moved to Texas. The question remains: what kind of an officer was he? Thanks to Jeff Danby and the interviews of surviving members of B Company 601st, some first-hand observations survive that describe Welch's leadership style:

> Upon hearing this name [Welch], Lt. Col. Tardy chuckled. He was a bit of a character but Lt. Col. Hallett D. Edson, commanding officer of the 15th Infantry Regiment thought very highly of him. Welch was a cowboy and very aggressive on the battlefield, over-aggressive in some instances.

Lieutenant Ambrose G. Salfen, commanding officer, B Company 601st recalled:

> Lt. Welch was another matter. On the battlefield he was known as a daredevil. He would do things that no one else would do or even think of. He was very aggressive; however in my opinion I thought Welch was a rather poor officer.

He would do things off the battlefield that I thought set a bad example; such as playing cards with the enlisted men, etc. He would also pull rank to obtain supplies and did this on a number of occasions. I do not think this was a fair way to treat a supply sergeant. A few times I told Welch that I would treat him like an officer when he acted like one. Yet again, on the battlefield, he was something else. One of the things he would do was to have two or three of the TDs pull out from behind cover and return in a rapid succession so that the shots they fired would happen in rapid succession. It was three-quick shots, before retreating behind cover again.

Sergeant Charles W. Colprit, 1st Platoon B Company 601st noted:

We called him "death after dark" Welch. I heard a story that a 150mm shell hit so close to an M-10 that rivets popped out. Welch is supposed to have drawn his 45 and fired around the corner of a house saying "counter battery." True or not I do not know.

Finally, Private First Class Arnold Petersen, 1st Platoon B Company 601st added:

Welch was a very aggressive leader, if there was a lull in the action Welch would go back to the CP for targets. Welch was a college kid from New York. He was something like a Patton and very aggressive. He carried a pistol on each side of his hips. His aggressiveness made his men a little unhappy with him at times. He was always getting us in trouble. Then he would pull us out of it.

Commenting on Lieutenant Welch, John R. Howard, Lieutenant Colonel, US Army, Special Forces (Retired) of Fredericksburg, Virginia wrote the author that:

EPILOGUE

Lt. Welch's character is revealed slowly through his words and actions as we track his progress through training and deployment to combat in Africa, Italy, and Northern Europe. I was also struck by the number and substantial nature of your Uncle's awards. He was a highly decorated soldier, and exceptionally so for a tanker. It was important that his story not be lost.

In light of the improved understanding we have gained since 9/11 of the psychological and physical impact of intense, sustained combat and combat injuries, Lt. Welch's resilience and courage are remarkable and his later life more understandable. To me, how he handled life after combat was equally as interesting as how he survived his battles during the war.

By the time Welch received his second Purple Heart it becomes evident that he was experiencing serious, heavy combat and probably had sustained multiple concussions. Today he would be treated for possible traumatic brain injury and PTSD. There can be little doubt of the source of any emotional or behavioral issues he had after the war. That he was hardened by combat is shown by his frank discussion in letters of what his job entailed; he was a killer. I gained the impression that his aggressive nature and will to engage in combat was off-putting to peers and superiors who considered him erratic, or even nuts. Thus the multiple decorations without rapid promotion or increased responsibilities; Lieutenant Welch had just committed himself fully to the fight with intensity and to a degree that others did not, and it must have scared them.

In the US Army History and Education Service Experience survey Tech Five Jimmie Frank Burrett was one of the few who courageously admitted to having had "battle shakes" in combat and that after the war he suffered nightmares about the German concentration camps that he helped liberate. Sergeant Max Altschuld also admitted that he suffered flashbacks. Several other soldiers commented on others who suffered from battle fatigue or shell shock. Major James Cahill Grimes (Oklahoma City, Oklahoma) said he observed that two officers suffered shell shock (one was a company commander and the other a platoon leader). He attributed it to Nebelwerfer fire which probably took place in Italy. Staff Sergeant Harper also said that many in his platoon suffered from shell shock and at least three other 601st soldiers commented that their friends and others did as well. Lieutenant Robert A. Maynard (Cleveland Heights, Ohio) said that he had one soldier desert due to battle fatigue and that was after almost two years of continuous service with the battalion.

When they returned from the war several 601st men recalled that they just did not want to talk about the war. Lieutenant Ambrose G. Salfen, B Company summed it up by saying that "There are things that you don't always discuss and war is one of them. The exception is with someone that shared that experience."

Lieutenant Welch was long gone by the time the last gathering of 601st veterans took place. He would have liked to have been there. At one of the reunions, Josowitz (Ed Justin) passed out the poem overleaf.

AN EXTRA PLUS

TIME HAS DIMMED THE HORROR OF
THE WAR WE FOUGHT AND WON;
TELLING NOW, WE MAKE IT SOUND
AS IF OUR WAR WAS FUN.

WE DON'T BEMOAN THE FEARFUL DAYS
WHEN ILL-EQUIPPED AND GREEN,
WE TOOK A MIGHTY BEATING AT
A PASS CALLED KASSERINE.

THAT WAS OUR BAPTISMAL AND,
WE LEARNED OUR LESSON, THEN,
EXCEPT PERHAPS FOR EL GUETTAR,
WE NEVER LOST AGAIN.

FORGOTTEN NOW, SALERNO WITH
THE RAIN, THE COLD, THE MUD;
AND WHEN WE SPEAK OF ANZIO
THERE'S LITTLE TALK OF BLOOD.

WE'VE ALL GOT TALES OF SOUTHERN FRANCE,
THE BATTLES TO THE RHINE;
BY THEN WE WERE UNSTOPPABLE;
WE TOOK THE SIEGFRIED LINE!

GOOD FRIENDS WERE LOST ALONG THE WAY,
SO YOUNG, IT SEEMED A SIN;
WE TOOK NO TIME TO MOURN THEM THEN
WE HAD A WAR TO WIN!

THE BATTLES WON, THE JOB WELL DONE,
THE ARMY SAID, GOODBYE;
I ADD FOR US, AN EXTRA PLUS;
WE DIDN'T COME HOME TO CRY!

ED JUSTIN (Josowitz)

379

601st Roll of Honor

Unfortunately, World War II records, as good as they are, are often incomplete or in error. There are bound to be mistakes in this list (and in the book) and for that the author can only offer his sincere apology. Throughout the book, individual deaths, the missing in action and prisoners of war have been recorded; but there are others known to have made the ultimate sacrifice whose date and place of death, MIA or POW status is not known. They are named here.

KIA: Of the 111 soldiers who died in the 601st during the war, the date and place of death for 12 soldiers is not known:

Pvt. Harold N. Blair, Afton, Iowa
Cpl. Wilson R. Bridges, Laskar, North Carolina
Sgt. Paul A. Chamberlain, Albion, New York
Cpl Robert D. Griffith, Swissdale, Pennsylvania
Cpl. Patsy M. Iovino, Stamford, Connecticut, buried in Connecticut
T/4 Joseph Lopacki, New York, New York, buried in New York
Pvt. Michael E. McDonough, Norwood, Massachusetts, buried in Massachusetts
Pvt. Johnny H. Pennington, Tutwiler, Mississippi, buried in Mississippi
T/4 Alphonse J. Petteruto, Lawrence, Mississippi
Sgt. John S. Sabala, New Salem, Pennsylvania
Sgt. John A. Smith, Chateaugay, New York, buried in New York
Pvt. Dominick Yadaresto, East Haven, Connecticut, buried in Connecticut

EPILOGUE

MIA: Of the four 601st soldiers permanently listed as missing in action and presumed dead, only one is listed but with no known memorial or other details:

Sgt John F. Smith, New York, New York

POW: Of the 36 soldiers in the 601st who were made prisoners of war, all are believed to have returned home safely, but for one; his capture details are not known.

Pfc. Joseph J. Esposito, Brooklyn, New York

APPENDIXES

APPENDIXES

Appendix A: The M-10 Tank Destroyer
Specifications of the M-10 Tank Destroyer*

Crew:	5 (commander, gunner, loader, driver, co-driver (radio operator))
Combat weight:	32.6 tons
Power-to-weight ratio:	12.6 horsepower per ton
Overall length:	22 feet 3 inches
Width:	10 feet
Height:	9.5 feet
Engine:	2 General Motors Corporation 6046 12-cylinder, 2-cycle, diesel engines with 850 cubic inch displacement; 410 horsepower
Transmission:	Synchromesh transmission with five forwards and one reverse gear
Fuel capacity:	165 gallons
Maximum speed (road):	30 miles per hour
Maximum speed (cross-country):	20 miles per hour
Average fuel consumption:	1.2 miles per gallon
Ground clearance:	17 inches
Armament:	3-inch gun (M-7) (Model number 7) in M-5 mount; .50-caliber (M2 HB) machine gun
Ammunition storage:	54 rounds for the 3-inch gun; 1,000 rounds for the .50-caliber machine gun

Projectiles (shells for the 3-inch gun):
APC (armor-piercing capped) projectile: (M-62): muzzle velocity 2,600 feet per second, penetration of 93mm at 500 yards at 30 degrees
HE (high-explosive) projectile
HVAP (high-velocity armor-piercing) projectile: (M-93): muzzle velocity 3,400 feet per second, penetration of 157mm at 500 yards at 30 degrees

Fuses:
HE – Delay fuse (a high-explosive shell with a delay fuse)
HE – Quick fuse (a high-explosive shell with a short fuse)

Maximum effective range: 16,100 yards

Gun depression/elevation angles: -10 to +30 degrees

*   Adapted from Zaloga, M10 and M36 Tank Destroyers 1942–53, p.28

Comments on the M-10 Tank Destroyer by men of the 601st

The following comments are from men who all had extensive experience with their combat-tested M-10. Jeff Danby interviewed them and recorded their comments:

Lieutenant Ambrose G. Salfen: The M-10 had more armor than the M-3 half-tracks that we started out with in North Africa. The 3-inch gun was very dependable but didn't match up to the German 88mm gun, as it did not have its muzzle velocity or penetrating power. The 3-inch barrel was much better than the short barrel 75mm on the Sherman. We really liked the twin GM diesel, as they didn't catch fire the way a gas engine did in combat. We stood a better chance of surviving when a slug hit the TD. I can only recall one time when a TD with a diesel engine blew up upon getting hit. An 88 round had directly hit the ammo storage so even in that case it wasn't the fault of the engine.

Sergeant Charles W. Colprit: I personally liked the M-10 as I thought the gun was super. The motors were diesel and would not explode like the gas engine M-36s we got later. Most of my gunning was on the M-10. We were used for both offensive and defense.

Lieutenant Robert Maynard: The TD had a 360-degree view of things and could react more appropriately to what was occurring all around. Overall I was very happy with the M-10. The TD also proved quite useful as additional artillery and was better equipped in this role than the Sherman tank. It was easier to train artillery officers in the deployment of TDs than to train TD officers all the mathematics involved in proper artillery use. A tank destroyer only had one inch of protection [armor] all around and couldn't stop anything but small-arms fire. The turret was open at the top as if someone had sliced it off with a knife.

Author's note: The turret was open because the 3-inch gun was very loud and the concussion would have been tremendous. Having it enclosed would only have made these conditions worse.

APPENDIXES

Private Arnold Petersen: Because the TD turret was nice and open it allowed the crew to get out in a hurry and I liked it for that reason. The M-10 was easy to maintain and I never remembered having to ever service the thing. I don't know how much diesel they carried but we kept it topped off because we didn't want to run out of fuel in battle. The gun was very good, with a range of about 2,500 yards at least. I am hard of hearing from 2½ years in the TDs, as the gun was very loud. The infantry would call us in to knock off a target and then complain that the gun was too loud.

Comments on M-10 tactics against German armor by men of the 601st

Almost 60 years later, Jeff Danby solicited these comments concerning the tactics they used against German Panzers:

Sergeant Charles W. Colprit: Then came the M-10, these had a chance against the Mark IV, V and VI Tiger tanks. To give you an idea, the 60-ton Tiger tank with the 88mm gun had four inches of steel on the front plus six inches of reinforced concrete, it was impossible to penetrate. A shot from the side was the only possibility.

Lieutenant Robert Maynard: To take out a German tank, we would generally aim first for the tank's suspension system [with both the M-10 and the M-36]. Once immobilized, we would aim squarely for the turret. Although we could not penetrate the armor, just the impact of the slug hitting the steel would cause a great concussion inside the turret, leaving the crew physically damaged or even killed. I recall instances where the German soldiers would scurry out of the turret after being hit in this manner, evidently to surrender; instead they would collapse on the ground with blood flowing from their ears and noses. I thought the concussion was enough to kill them. TDs would never stay clustered but would stay 30 to 100 yards apart. [On one occasion] during a night march we got out in front with about 50 other soldiers. I called in artillery to within 100 yards of our position. It was my most memorable experience of the war.

Colonel Walter E. Tardy: The TDs had the 500 series radios and the tanks had the 600 series (or vice versa). However, there was overlap between the tanks and the TDs and they were able to listen and communicate with each other. When the TDs and tanks were in combat, the radio traffic was cut down severely. Coordinates and such were not usually discussed for fear of them being overheard by the enemy. We would use code words given to us by the division. For a time, my code word was "Sunray TD." Code words would be changed from time to time.

Staff Sergeant Bill R. Harper: In an ideal setup it would be infantry, tanks, then the TDs, but there seemed to be no ideal setups. There were times that we advanced with the infantry without tanks. A few times my platoon was ahead of the infantry. My experience was that we were used for very close support of the infantry and many times without tanks. This all depended on where the tanks or TDs were needed in any situation. When we were in action we were never lined or clustered up. We advanced spread out and the lay of the land and our target dictated how far apart our TDs were. Anytime we were advancing with the infantry in battle we never considered ourselves to be in a defensive reserve line.

Lieutenant Ambrose G. Salfen: I did not feel that the TDs were deployed in a manner too differently than the tanks. Open turrets were not an issue and I cannot recall losing anyone to German airburst artillery. We would not hold back if we had to enter a town [for fear of having something thrown into the turret].

Sergeant Max Altschuld, B Company observed that he never lost a TD he commanded and he attributed that to smoke shells fired for concealment.

Sergeant Allen H. Bowman, Recon Company said that in Recon Company they were so far out in front they were often shelled by their own artillery and bombed by their own planes.

APPENDIXES

Captain Rydal L. Sanders had this advice for those in combat and under an air attack: "Hit the ditch, stay low, keep firing back, cuss like a sailor and pray like a lost sinner at a country revival." He also observed that on one occasion "A platoon of 3rd Recon and another platoon with TDs while on night patrol encountered another American unit on patrol. An improper response to password resulted in killing a soldier of the other patrol."

Author's note: In order not to make these appendixes overly long, I have chosen not to include separate sections on the other US Army World War II tank destroyers used by the 601st: namely, the M-3, M-6, M-18 and the M-36. This basic information is readily available online or in other Osprey Publishing books.

Appendix B: Tank Destroyer Battalion Tables of Organization and Equipment (TO&E)

June 8, 1942

The information for the 601st TD Battalion is good through December 1943 with the exception that 36 M-10 TDs replaced the M-3 and the M-6 TDs.

	HQ	A (B/C)	Recon	Cadre*	Medical	Total
Officers	14	5 (15)	6		3	38
Men	155	181 (543)	139	77	23	937
.45-cal pistol	25	9 (27)	10			62
.30-cal carbine	123	137 (411)	99			633
.30-cal M-1 rifle	21	40 (120)	36			177
.30-cal LMG	2	6 (18)	12			32
.50-cal M2 HMG	27	9 (27)	6			60
M-6 Gun 37mm AT SP** TD		4 (12)				12
M-3 Gun 3in. AT SP TD		8 (24)				24
Armored car light	5	5 (15)	11			31
Ambulance					1	1
Motorcycle solo	8	2 (6)	9			23
Truck small arms repair	1					1
¼-ton truck	8	18 (54)	20			82
¾-ton truck weapons carrier	11	3 (9)	2		1	23
¾-ton truck Com & Recon	3				1	4
2½-ton truck	20	1 (3)	1		1	25
10-ton wrecker	1					1
1-ton trailer	17		4			

March 15, 1944

The 601st came into alignment with this in July 1944, after the liberation of Rome.

	HQ	A(B/C)	Recon	Cadre	Medical	Total
Officers	13	5 (15)	6	0	1	35
Men	109	130 (390)	120	104	15	738
.45-cal pistol	29	13 (39)	11	0	0	79
.30-cal carbine	28	67 (201)	64	0	0	293
.30-cal M-1 rifle	67	55 (165)	51	0	0	283
.30-cal LMG	3	5 (15)	12	0	0	30
.50-cal M2 HMG	7	10 (30)	7	0	0	44
2.36in. bazooka	14	9 (27)	21	0	0	62
81mm mortar	0	1 (3)	0	0	0	3
M-8 armored car	0	0 (0)	6	0	0	6
M-20 armored car	3	8 (24)	3	0	0	30
M-32 TRV*	0	1 (3)	0	0	0	3
M-10 3in./76mm GMC TD	0	12 (36)	0	0	0	36
¼-ton jeep	8	6 (18)	18	0	4	48
¾-ton truck	6	0 (0)	1	0	0	7
1½-ton truck	1	0 (0)	4	0	1	6
2½-ton truck	18	1 (3)	0	0	0	21
Heavy wrecker	1	0 (0)	0	0	0	1
¼-ton trailer	1	1 (3)	2	0	0	6
M-10 ammo trailer	0	3 (9)	0	0	0	9
1-ton trailer	18	0 (0)	0	0	0	18

Appendix C: US Army organization and units

US Army Organization circa 1940

Numbers on the table below are average, and vary by type of unit.

Unit Designation	Number of Men	Commanded By
Squad	12 men	Sergeant
Platoon	50 men	Lieutenant
Company	184 men	Captain
Battalion	900 men	Major/Lieutenant Colonel
Regiment	3,200 men	Colonel
Division	15,000 men	Major General
Corps	75,000 men	Lieutenant General
Field Army	300,000 men	General

Battalion abbreviations

CO: Battalion Commanding Officer (also used for company commanders)

Exec: Executive officer (second in command)

Adjutant: An officer who acts as an administrative assistant to the battalion CO

S-1: Battalion Personnel and Administration Officer

S-2: Battalion Intelligence Officer

S-3: Battalion Operations Officer

S-4: Battalion Supply Officer

HQ: Headquarters Company

Recon: Reconnaissance Company

Battalion Officer Allowance Table

TO&E of June 8, 1942 and TO&E Corrections of March 15, 1944 for 601st Tank Destroyer Battalion.

	HQ		A/B/C		Recon		Medical		Total		
	1942	1944	1942	1944	1942	1944	1942	1944	1942	1943*	1944
Lieutenant Colonel	1	1							1	1	1
Major	1	2							1	1	2
Captain	5	4	1(3)	1(3)	1	1	1	1	10	9	9
First Lieutenant	5	5	2(6)	3(9)	3	3	2		16	16	17
Second Lieutenant	2	1	2(6)	1(3)	2	2			10	17	6
Totals	14	13	5(15)	5(15)	6	6	3	1	38	44	35

601st Command Structure in 1944

Thanks to the Jeff Danby interviews of Lieutenant Colonel Tardy and others, we know the positions of the following officers and NCOs assigned to the 601st at the time of the invasion of Southern France:

Commanding Officer: Lieutenant Colonel Walter E. Tardy
Executive Officer: Major Daniel Hinman
S-2 Intelligence Officer: Captain Coleman D. Asinof
S-3 Operations Officer: Captain Benjamin Fuller
B Company Commander: Lieutenant Ambrose G. Salfen
1st Platoon Leader: First Lieutenant Thomas P. Welch
1st Platoon NCOs: Sergeants Nowak, Larson, Lombardi, Mulcahy
2nd Platoon Leader: First Lieutenant Charles R. Bell
3rd Platoon Leader: First Lieutenant William W. Finley

As a sidenote Sergeant Colprit mentioned that the men gave their officers nicknames. Major Fuller was called "Jungle Jim" and he was described as a very brave man and was fearless. Lieutenant Welch was called "death after dark" Welch. Lieutenant Bell was nicknamed "Fearless Bell" because he was like all the rest of us, scared as anything but talked a good fight. Lieutenant Finley was called "Bones Finley" because he was so tall and thin.

Appendix D: 601st Gun Company (A/B/C) Organization from TO&E of March 15, 1944

B Company (for example): 5 officers and 127 enlisted men, 12 tank destroyers

Company Headquarters: 2 officers and 37 enlisted men

Command Section: 2 officers and 23 enlisted men

Capt. (CO)

2nd Lt. (Exec)

1st Sgt.

S/Sgt. (radio)

S/Sgt. (supply)

Cpl. (company clerk)

Sgt. (reconnaissance)

Cpl. (ammunition)

2 T/5s (armored car drivers)

Pvt. (bugler/driver)

Pvt. (machine gunner)

Pvt. (messenger/jeep driver)

12 Pvts. (used for assorted tasks)

Maintenance Section: 9 enlisted men

T/Sgt. (motor)

T/4 (driver tank recovery vehicle)

T/4 (artillery mechanic)

T/4 (auto mechanic/driver)

2 T/4 (tank mechanics)

T/5 (tank mechanic/jeep driver)

T/5 (tank mechanic)

T/4 (radio repairman)

Kitchen Section: 5 enlisted men
(usually assigned to battalion HQ Company)

S/Sgt. (mess)

2 T/4s (cooks)

T/5 (cook)

Pvt. (cook's helper)

1st TD Platoon: 1 officer, 30 enlisted men, 4 tank destroyers

Platoon Headquarters: 1 officer and 10 enlisted men

1st Lt. (platoon leader)

S/Sgt. (assistant platoon leader)

Sgt. (section leader)

Cpl. (assistant section leader)

2 T/5s (armored car drivers)

2 Pvts. (machine gunners)

3 Pvts. (rifleman/drivers)

1st Section: 10 enlisted men, 2 tank destroyers

1st tank destroyer, 5 enlisted men

Sgt. (TD commander)

Cpl. (gunner)

T/4 (driver)

2 Pvts. (loader and radio operator)

2nd tank destroyer, 5 enlisted men crew

2nd Section: 10 enlisted men, 2 tank destroyers

3rd tank destroyer, 5 enlisted men

4th tank destroyer, 5 enlisted men

2nd TD Platoon: 1 officer, 30 enlisted men, 4 tank destroyers

3rd TD Platoon: 1 officer, 30 enlisted men, 4 tank destroyers

Appendix E: Tank destroyer officer training and Lieutenant Welch's comments

Officer Candidate School covered a wide range of subjects. The instruction was divided into five areas:

General subjects: aircraft identification, command training, company admin-istration and mess management, chemical defense, efficiency reports, map and aerial photo interpretation, medical services, military law, physical training, sanitation, hygiene and first aid, social customs, and tank identification.

Tactics: air-ground liaison, armored force tactics, combat orders, command staff and logistics, current events, defensive combat, offensive combat, reconnaissance, and security.

Weapons: antiaircraft, automatic pistol and revolver, carbine, grenades, machine guns (.30-caliber, .50-caliber, and Thompson submachine gun), 37mm antitank gun (mounted on the M-6), 75mm antitank gun (mounted on the M-3 half-track) and 3-inch guns (mounted on the M-10), and close combat methods.

Automotive: Army maintenance system, motor vehicles inspection, nomenclature and functioning of major assemblies, principal parts and installation, preventive maintenance, formal and informal inspections.

Pioneer: Antitank mines, bridges and roads, camouflage, demolitions, engineer reconnaissance, engineer tools and equipment, and obstacles.

All subjects required the candidates pass tests. There was ceaseless studying and cramming. Welch explained in one of his letters that three flunks and you were "bounced." That meant a candidate was "sent back" to a company not as far along in the syllabus in order to repeat the failed section. Or he was sent to a regular army unit as an enlisted man. Once with an OCS company, the last thing you wanted was to be sent back without your new pals. When he had time, Welch wrote his mother during his transition to a 90-day wonder. Some highlights include:

> This week [week 5 of 13] was pretty tough, lots of rushing until all hours of the night not to mention the days. I haven't flunked any tests yet, so keep your fingers crossed. They have already flunked out about 15 men and will keep it up until graduation, so I'll have to keep on the ball.

> I got my first flunk last week [week 8 of 13]. I found myself daydreaming. Consequently when it came time for the exam, I didn't know the answers. However, on the next quiz, I got an excellent, so I made up for it. They are really pouring on the coal down here; it gets tougher every week. This week we had tests in radio, demolition, camouflage, antitank mines and map reading. If that isn't a schedule, I never saw one.

Christmas 1942 came and went for Welch. He didn't get off the post as he had hoped and he was still frantically busy. According to Lieutenant Colonel Emery A. Dunham, in *The Army Ground Force Tank Destroyer History*, on December 28 there were 2,005 men in training as the 23rd class started. This was the largest number of OCS candidates ever at Camp Hood. There were now 12 OCS classes in progress, also a record. There were 45,000 men at the camp. Quoting from two of Welch's letters:

> Today we had a quiet day [week 10 of 13] all we did was drill for about five hours, then we had a whopping big Sunday dinner of bologna and potatoes. I wonder what the army does with all the meat they buy, and the dogs in camp look pretty well fed. This New Year's Eve promises to be a good one; we have a night problem [exercise] all night long. I guess I'll see the New Year in, out on the Texas plains.

Busy, busy, busy, that's me all over [week 11 of 13]. I'm so damn dizzy; I don't know where I'm going. But, it'll soon be over. This week we're finishing up tactics which is really tough. There are a million different ways to employ your men and vehicles but only one right way. The problem is to find it. The strain is really telling down here. We've had about 25 men tossed out and expect only 2/3 of the original men will be with us at graduation. We also have about 15 men in the hospital. This damn state is the icebox of the country. The wind starts blowing up in Canada, and doesn't stop anywhere until it hits us.

All 77 days of the 13 weeks were filled with instruction and practical exercises. In the field they practiced night reconnaissance, fording streams and ravines and disarming explosive devices among other things. Commando-style training was the rule. Prior to graduation, all officer candidates were evaluated in eight areas: Military Bearing and Neatness, Practical Adaptability, Capacity for Teamwork and Leadership, Acceptability, Attitude, Capacity to Express Himself, Ability to Handle Men, and Reliability. By the end of the course the men felt that they were part of an elite force. They were pumped up.

In keeping with the normal procedure, Welch was honorably discharged from the US Army on January 20, 1943. Candidates were classified as enlisted men during their training. After passing all the requirements, the candidate was discharged from the enlisted ranks and the next day commissioned as an officer by the authority of the President. Welch renewed his oath. A grand parade with dignitaries in attendance and speeches was usual. On January 21, 1943, Welch received his temporary appointment to second lieutenant. The new lieutenant went home on leave.

Appendix F: Wehrmacht Panzers

These summaries have been collected from a variety of sources and reviewed by Dr Rolf Wirtgen of the *Bundesamt für Wehrtechnik und*

Beschaffung. Also see Gill, *Tank Destroyer Forces, World War II*, Appendix IV for a very useful chart entitled Axis Armor, p. 129.

The Panzer Mark III

The Panzer Mark III was classified as a medium-size Panzer and was the main German battle Panzer for the first two and a half years of World War II. This 15-ton Panzer was designed to penetrate enemy armor and was armed with a 50mm gun. It was considered an antitank Panzer.

The Panzer Mark IV

The Panzer Mark IV is sometimes described as having been the mainstay of the Wehrmacht Panzer forces of World War II. Initially, it was a close-in support weapon. Only after it was armed with a long barrel gun in the summer of 1942 did it become a potent tank killer. It slowly replaced the Mark III in 1943. It weighed approximately 25–30 tons and had a 75mm gun.

The Panzer Mark V

The Panzer Mark V commonly called the Panther (Panzerkampfwagen V Panther) was also classified as a medium Panzer and was designed after Hitler ordered the development of a Panzer similar to the Russian T-34 tank. It became available by the summer of 1943. It had a 75mm gun and weighed 50 tons. It served alongside the heavier Tiger until the end of the war. On February 27, 1944, Hitler himself ordered that the Roman numeral V be deleted from the designation. It is frequently regarded as the best Panzer or tank design of World War II and was cheaper to produce than the Tiger.

The Panzer Mark VI or Tiger I

The Panzer Mark VI or Tiger I is the common name for the Wehrmacht's heavy Panzer used in World War II. Like the Panther, it was developed in 1942 as an answer to the Russian T-34 tank. It was the first Panzer to mount the 88mm gun, which had previously demonstrated its effectiveness as an antiaircraft gun. Weighing in at 62 tons, it has been described as over-engineered and too expensive and was too time-consuming to produce. The Tiger II superseded it in the fall of 1944.

The Tiger II

The Tiger II is the common name for a German heavy World War II Panzer, although the Germans called it the Panzerkampfwagen Tiger B, often shortened to Tiger B. It is also known as the Königstiger (German for Bengal Tiger) and translated as King Tiger or Royal Tiger. It was similar to the Tiger I but had the sloping armor of the Panther medium Panzer. It weighed about 75 tons and had the long barrel 88mm guns. It was the basis for the Jägdtiger tank destroyer.

The Jägdtiger

The Jägdtiger or hunting tiger is a turret-less tank destroyer that saw service from late 1944 until the end of the war. It weighed in at 70 tons. Because it was so heavy it was continuously plagued with mechanical problems. It was equipped with the 128mm gun.

The Jägdpanther

The Jägdpanther, which means hunting panther in German, was a tank destroyer built on the Panther chassis. It entered the war late in 1944 and some consider it the best German Panzer of World War II. It was equipped with the long barrel version of the 88mm gun found on the Tiger II. It weighed in at about 46 tons.

The men of the 601st had this to say about German Panzers to Jeff Danby:

Liuetenant Robert Maynard: None of the three large US tank-mounted guns, the 75mm, 76mm and 3-inch naval gun could match the German 88mm gun, which was far superior. The turret [of the 88mm] did not move more than 20 degrees in either direction. It had to be square to any target. Our biggest advantage against German Panzers was that for every one encountered we had five or six tanks or tank destroyers to match them. American strength came in numbers.

APPENDIXES

Sergeant Charles W. Colprit: The German Mark VI, called a Tiger, had an 88-mm gun with a [muzzle] velocity of 3,300 feet per second, the front had four inches of steel armor plus six inches of reinforced concrete. You had to hit them on the side.

Private Arnold Petersen: I remember one time the platoon observed some German Panzers traveling across a road in the distance. Welch opened up fire on them and missed. The German Panzer simply stopped quickly and turned around 180 degrees on one track and went in the opposite direction down the road. This illustrated one example of German armor superiority. The M-10s had to turn around by a series of back and forth maneuvers. I thought that the German gunners weren't quite as good as the American gunners. After 540 days of combat there were several times that the German gunners should have got me but missed. I always wondered why and I just concluded that the gunner wasn't that good.

BIBLIOGRAPHY

Books

Allen, William L., *Anzio: Edge of Disaster* (E. P. Dutton, New York, 1978)

Ardagh, John, (ed.), *The Collins Guide to France* (Wm. Collins Sons & Co Ltd., London, 1985)

Astor, Gerald, *Terrible Terry Allen* (the Ballantine Publishing Group, New York, 2003)

Atkinson, Rick, *An Army at Dawn* (Henry Holt and Company, Inc., New York, 2002)

Atkinson, Rick, *The Day of Battle* (Henry Holt and Company, Inc., New York, 2007)

Atkinson, Rick, *The Guns at Last Light* (Henry Holt and Company, Inc., New York, 2013)

Baker, Hershel D., *TD Combat in Tunisia* (prepared and published at the Tank Destroyer School for distribution to Tank Destroyer units within the continental United States January 1944: part two, El Guettar, Fort Hood, Texas, 1944)

Black, Robert W., Col., *The Ranger Force, Darby's Rangers in World War II* (Stackpole Books, Mechanicsburg, Pennsylvania, 2009)

Boles, Terry C., *Germantown to Germany, the Military Service and Civilian Life of Clifton Hartgrove Boles, 1940–1949* (Self-published, 2007)

Breuer, William B., *Operation Dragoon, the Allied Invasion of Southern France* (Presidio Press, Novato, California, 1987)

Burn, W. P. Col., US Army, *Salerno, The American Operations from the Beaches to the Volturno,* third in a series called "American Forces in Action," (War Department Military Intelligence Division, Washington DC, August 26, 1944)

BIBLIOGRAPHY

Bykofsky, Joseph and Larson, Harold, *The United States Army in WW II, the Technical Services, Transportation Corps, Operations Overseas* (Washington DC, 1954)

Carmichael, Thomas N., *The Ninety Days, Five Battles that Changed the World* (Konecky and Konecky, Old Saybrook, Connecticut, 1971)

Champagne, Daniel R., *Dogface Soldiers, the Story of B Company, 15th Regiment, 3rd Infantry Division* (Merriam Press, Bennington, Vermont, 2008)

Childers, Thomas, *Soldier from the War Returning* (Mariner Books, Houghton Mifflin Harcourt, New York, 2009)

Churchill, Winston S., *The Second World War Volume II* (Time Incorporated, New York 1960)

Clarke, Jeffrey J. and Smith, Robert Ross, *Riviera to the Rhine: United States Army in World War II, The European Theater of Operations* (Washington DC, US Army, Center for Military History, 1993)

Clark, Lloyd, *Anzio, Italy and the Battle for Rome – 1944* (Grove Press, New York, 2006)

Danby, Jeff, *The Day of the Panzer* (Casemate, Drexel Hill, Pennsylvania, 2006)

Darby, William O. and Baumer, William H., *Darby's Rangers, We Led the Way* (Presidio Press, San Rafael, California, 1980)

Dunham, Lieutenant Colonel Emory A., *The Army Ground Force Tank Destroyer History* (Study No. 29, 1946)

Edwards, Roger, *Panzer, A Revolution in Warfare, 1939–1945* (Arms and Armour Press, London, 1989)

Eisenhower, Dwight D., *Crusade in Europe* (Doubleday & Company, Garden City, New York, 1948)

Failmezger, Victor "Tory", *An American Knight, A Tank Destroyer Story* (National Media Services, Front Royal Virginia, 2012)

Fifth Army History, 9 vols (Florence, Italy & Washington, DC, 1945)

Fisher, Ernest F., *The U.S. Army in World War II: Cassino to the Alps – The Mediterranean Theatre* (Center for Military History, Washington DC, 1989)

Gawne, Jonathan, *Finding Your Father's War* (Casemate, Drexel Hill, Pennsylvania, 2006)

Gill, Lonnie, *Tank Destroyer Forces, World War II* (Turner Publishing Company, Paducah, Kentucky, 1992)

Grover, Kathryn, *Geneva & World War II* (Geneva Historical Society, Geneva, New York, 2002)

Hart, B. H. Liddell, *The German Generals Talk* (William Morrow & Co, New York, 1948)

Hartstern, Carl J., *Memoirs of a Dogface Soldier* (Xlibris Corporation, USA, 2011)

Hapgood, David and Richardson, David, *Monte Cassino* (Congdon & Weed, NY 1984)

Haupt, Werner, *Kriegsschauplatz Italien* (Motorbuch Verlag, Stuttgart, 1977)

Heffner, Wilson A., *Dogface Soldier, the Life of General Lucian K. Truscott, Jr* (University of Missouri Press, Columbia, Missouri, 2010)

Hibbert, Christopher, *Anzio the Bid for Rome* (Ballantine Books, New York, 1970)

Holland, James, *Italy's Sorrow* (St. Martin's Press, New York, 2008)

Ingersoll, Ralph, *The Battle is the Payoff* (Harcourt, Brace and Company, New York, 1943)

Jeffers, H. Paul, *Onward we charge* (NAL Caliber, New York, 2007)

Josowitz, First Lieutenant Edward L., *An Informal History of the 601st Tank Destroyer Battalion* (Pustet, Salzburg, Austria 1945)

Katz, Robert, *Death in Rome* (Macmillan, New York, 1967)

Katz, Robert, *The Battle for Rome* (Simon & Schuster, New York, 2003)

Kahn, Lawrence H., *The Tank Destroyers* (Pocket Books, New York, 1952)

Knapp, Ronald A., Major, *The Operations of the 3D Infantry Division in the First Crossing of the Volturno River 12–14 Oct 1943* (Advanced Infantry Officer Class NO II, 1950)

Life's Picture History of World War II (Time Incorporated, New York, 1950)

Lewis, Norman, *Naples '44* (Pantheon Books, Random House, New York, 1978)

MacCloskey, Monro, Brigadier General, USAF (Retired), *Torch and the Twelfth Air Force* (Richard Rosen Press, New York, 1971)

Macksey, Kenneth and Bachelor, John H., *The Tank, a History of the Armored Fighting Vehicle* (Ballantine Books, New York, 1971)

Mauldin, Bill, *Mud, Mules, and Mountains, Cartoons of the A.E.F. In Italy* (published by the US Army, January 1944)

Mauldin, Bill, *Up Front* (Henry Holt and Company, Inc. New York, 1944)

McFarland, Robert C. (ed.), *The History of the 15th Infantry Regiment in World War II* (Glenn A. Rathbun, Boise, Idaho, 1990)

Memen, Aubrey, *Four Days of Naples* (Simon and Schuster, New York, 1979)

Mogavero, Giuseppe and Parisella, Antonio, *Memorie di Quartiere, Frammenti di Storie di Guerra e di Resistenza nell' Appio Latino e Tuscolano 1943–1944* (Edilazio, Roma, 2007)

Morton, H. V., *A Traveler in Rome* (Dodd, Mead & Company, New York 1957)

Murphy, Audie, *To Hell and Back* (Bantam Edition, New York, 1983)

Norfleet, George, *A Pilot's Journey* (Rebnor Publishing LLC, Washington, DC, 2007)

BIBLIOGRAPHY

Pogue, Forrest C., *Organizer of Victory, 1943–1945, George C. Marshall* (Viking Press, New York, 1973)

Porch, Douglas, *The Path to Victory* (Farra, Straus and Giroux, New York, 2004)

Pictorial History of the Second World War, Volume 2 (Wh. H. Wise and Co. Inc., New York, 1944)

Pictorial History of the Second World War, Volume 3 (Wh. H. Wise and Co. Inc., New York, 1946)

Rand McNally Ready-Reference Atlas of the World (Rand McNally & Company, New York, 1941)

Salmaggi, Cesare and Pallavisini, Alfredo (compilers), *2194 Days of War* (Windward, New York, 1977)

Schneider, Wolfgang, *Tigers in Combat I* (Stackpole Books, Mechanicsburg, Pennsylvania 2004)

Stein, Barry Jason, *U.S. Army Patches, Flashes and Ovals, An Illustrated Encyclopedia of Cloth Units Insignia* (Donohue Group, Inc., 1997)

Strawson, John, *The Battle for North Africa* (Scribners, New York, 1969)

Taggart, Donald G. Editor, *History of the Third Infantry Division in World War II* (the Battery Press, Nashville, Tennessee, 1987)

Whiting, Charles, *The Other Battle of the Bulge, Operation Northwind* (Avon Books, New York, 1990)

Whiting, Charles, *West Wall, the Battle for Hitler's Siegfried Line* (Spellmount, Staplehurst, Kent, United Kingdom, 1999)

Yeide, Harry, *The Tank Killers* (Casemate, Havertown, Pennsylvania, 2004)

Zaloga, S. J., *Anzio 1944, The Beleaguered Beachhead* (Osprey, Oxford, United Kingdom, 2005)

Zaloga, S. J., *M-10 and M36 Tank Destroyers 1942–53* (Osprey, Oxford, United Kingdom, 2002)

Zaloga, S. J., *M-18 Hellcat Tank Destroyer 1943–97* (Osprey, Oxford, United Kingdom, 2004)

Zaloga, S. J., *Operation Nordwind 1945, Hitler's Last Offensive in the West* (Osprey, Oxford, United Kingdom, 2010)

Zaloga, S. J., *US Tank and Tank Destroyer Battalions in the ETO 1944–45* (Osprey, Oxford, United Kingdom, 2005)

Unpublished memoirs, diaries and letters

Borriello, Joseph, Meriden, CT, 10th Engineer Battalion, 3rd Infantry Division, *World War II, My Way*, courtesy of the author

Colprit, Charles W., Dover, DE, 601st Tank Destroyer Battalion, unnamed notes, courtesy of Jeff Danby

Harper, Bill, R. courtesy of 3rd Infantry Museum, Fort Steward, Georgia

Larson, Rudolph E., Chicago, Illinois, courtesy Colonel Lars Larson

Lundquist, Harold E., Chicago, Illinois, diary, US Army Heritage and Education

Morrison, Thomas E., Brewster, Ohio, notes on The 601st Tank Destroyers in Tunisia 1942–1943, Third Cavalry Museum, Fort Hood

Nowak, John, Ludlow, Massachusetts, 601st Tank Destroyer Battalion, unnamed memoirs, courtesy of Jeff Danby

Tardy, Walter E., letters to family

Welch, Thomas P., letters to family

Poems

Justin, Ed (formerly Ed Josowitz), *AN EXTRA PLUS* (unpublished, Sgt. Nowak collection)

Articles from periodicals

Beckman, Joy, "Half-track Brings Back Memoirs," unidentified publication and unknown date, from Sergeant Nowak collection (remembrances of Ambrose Salfen)

Bracker, Milton, "What to Write the Soldier Overseas," *The New York Times Magazine* (October 3, 1943)

Burtt, John D., "The Battle that Won't End: Operation Anvil/Dragoon, August 1944," *World at War, the Strategy & Tactics of World War II*, (Decision Games, Bakersfield, California, April–May 2011)

Hailey, Foster, "The Foe That Is Worse than the Japs," *The New York Times Magazine* (October 3, 1943)

Martin, Sgt. Ralph G., "For Them the Men Will Go Through Hell," *The New York Times Magazine*, (October 10, 1943)

Raymond, Edward J. Major, "Brassing off Kraut," *US Army Field Artillery Journal* (European edition) (October 1944)

Raymond, Edward J. Major, "Slugging it Out," *US Army Field Artillery Journal* (European edition) (January 1944)

Sullivan, Patricia, "Tardy, Walter E., Col. USA: Obituary," *The Washington Post* (January 21, 2006)

Unknown author, "A Tale of Two Towns," *Time Magazine* (September 7, 1942)

Vannoy, Allyn, "Operation Grandslam, Counter Attack Blunted at Colmar," *WWII History Magazine* (January 2012)

BIBLIOGRAPHY

US Army publications/booklets

Fall In (produced and presented by the American Legion, circa 1942)

Fifth Army Antiaircraft Artillery, Salerno to Florence, 9 September 1943–8 September 1944 (prepared by the Antiaircraft Artillery Section, Headquarters, Fifth Army)

If you should be CAPTURED these are your rights, War Department Pamphlet No 21-7, 16 May 1944 (US Government Printing Office, Washington, 1944)

IRTC, I am a Doughboy (US Army Office of War Information, circa 1943)

M-18 Tank Destroyer (HQ Seventh Army, Training Memorandum: No 10, 14 December 1944)

Military House Keeping, the Armored School (TL-13459-H-Knox-2-4-45-5M, Fort Knox, KY, 1945)

Naples, A Soldier's Guide (compiled and published by Information & Education Section, HQ, MTOUSA, circa November 1944)

Road to Rome, Salerno, Naples, Volturno, Cassino, Anzio, Rome (issued by Lt. General Mark Clark, USA)

Rome, A Soldier's Guide (compiled and published by Information & Education Section, HQ, MTOUSA, circa March 1945)

Tank Destroyer Notes (HQ European Theater of Operations, US Army Battle Experiences, July 1944 to April 1945)

When you are Overseas, these facts are vital (War Department Pamphlet No 21-1, July 29, 1943, US Government Printing Office, Washington, 1943)

Welcome Home, (War Department Pamphlet No 20-10, March 15, 1944, US Government Printing Office, Washington, 1944)

Newspaper clippings

NB: Not all had headlines or published newspaper so the author has given them some to better identify the subject.

1943

"Major Earle Tardy Active in Allied Move into Naples, Area," Whitehead Don, unidentified newspaper (September 13, 1943)

"Lt. Welch Describes Tank Fighting on Italian Front," unidentified newspaper (November 1943)

1944

Foisik, Sergeant Jack, "Tank 'Buffer Battle' Fought on the Beachhead,"
The Stars and Stripes (January or February 1944)

De Luce, Daniel, "Wichita Falls Officer Answers Call for Artillery
Assistance" (February 6, 1944)

"Lt. Welch Picked off a Half-Dozen Germans," *Geneva Daily Times*
(D. Max Henry Insurance clipping) (February 1944)

"Lt. Welch awarded Silver Star," unidentified Geneva newspaper, undated

Lehman, Sergeant Milton, "Dead Tigers Brought Back into Play by
Cunning Foe," *The Stars and Stripes* (April 1944)

"Genevan Helps 'Get' Nazi Tanks," unidentified newspaper (May or June
1944)

"Mentioned for Good Work on Via Casilina," *Geneva Daily Times* (May
or June 1944)

"Americans Seize Alban Ridge, Stand within Sight of Rome; US Flyers
Blast Nazis' Wall," *Democrat and Chronicle*, Rochester, NY (June 2,
1944), p.1

"Broken Leg Puts Genevan in Hospital," *Geneva Daily Times* (D. Max
Henry Insurance Clipping) (June 21, 1944)

"Lt. Thomas Welch of Geneva Awarded Bronze Star Medal," *Syracuse
Herald-Journal* (October 9, 1944) also *Geneva Daily Times* (D. Max
Henry Insurance Clipping) (October 1944) and another unidentified
clipping

"Take Last Strasbourg Forts," *New York Daily News* (early December 1944)

"Lt. Welch Somewhere in France, Unknown (Boys in the Service)," *Geneva
Daily Times* (D. Max Henry Insurance Clipping) (late 1944)

"Lt. Welch is Commended for Coolness, Though Greatly Outnumbered He
Directed Attack on Germans," *Syracuse Herald-Journal* (December 11,
1944), p.2

"Close-In Support and How!" *The Beachhead News* (December 17, 1944)

1945

"Geneva Lieutenant Aids in Rescue of 2 Wounded GIs," *Catholic Courier*,
Rochester, New York (February 1945), p.9

"Boys in the Service, (Rescue of 2 Wounded GIs)," *Geneva Daily Times*
(D. Max Henry Insurance Clipping) (February 3, 1945), p.7

"Lt. Thomas P. Welch Awarded Silver Star in Italy (Boys in the Service),"
Geneva Daily Times (D. Max Henry Insurance Clipping)
(March 12, 1945)

BIBLIOGRAPHY

"News of Our Men and Women in Uniform," (Welch comments on surrender of Germany) unidentified newspaper, (May 8, 1945)
"5 Uniformed Men Guests of Rotary Today," *Geneva Daily Times* (May 9, 1945), p.9

Postwar years
Kindrick, Sam "Offbeat: A Last Goodbye to Peter Welch," *San Antonio Express*, (around May 20, 1972)
"A Campaign in France to Remember Allies, John Kelly's Washington," *The Washington Post* (August 11, 2010)
Balestra, Katie "Operation Dragoon, Ceremony Hails Veterans of the 'Other' D-Day," *The Washington Post* (September 2010)
Tubman, James, "First to Berchtesgaden? Yes, The Watch on the Rhine," *3rd Infantry Division Society Newsletter* (undated)

Newsletters
Hobart Alumni New, Hobart College, Geneva, NY (April 1945), p.5. (Oak Leaf Cluster to Silver Star)
Keeping in Touch, Elks, Geneva Lodge No. 1054 (February 5, 1945) (Rescuing two GIs)
Off the Wind, Seneca Yacht Club (Geneva NY) (October 1943) (Getting shot at while sailing)

Army associated newspapers/sheets
The Stars and Stripes Mediterranean, Vol. I, No. 174, Tuesday, June 6, 1944, Italy Edition
Headquarters 3rd Infantry Division, *Daily News* Sheet: the Italy Edition Vol. III:
   No. 3 of Tuesday, January 25, 1944
   No. 24 of Tuesday, February 15, 1944
   No. 25 of Wednesday, February 16, 1944
   No. 26 of Thursday, February 17, 1944
   No. 38 of Tuesday, February 29, 1944
   No. 39 of Wednesday, March 1, 1944
   No. 41 of Friday, March, 3, 1944
   No. 130 of Thursday, June 1, 1944
   No. 134 of Monday, June 5, 1944

Headquarters 3rd Infantry Division *Daily News* Sheet, France Vol. V:
No. 4 of Wednesday August 16, 1944

The Beachhead News, VI Corps, Vol. I:
No 15, Monday, May 29, 1944
No 18, Thursday, June 1, 1944
No 92, Friday, October 6, 1944
No 100, Sunday, October 15, 1944
No 125, Thursday, November 9, 1944

Written correspondence of 601st Veterans with Jeff Danby

Harper, Bill R., December 20, 2001
Maynard, Robert, January 30, 2002
Petersen, Arnold, February 8, 2002

Telephone interviews of 601st Veterans with Jeff Danby

Ashe, William C., February 22, 2002
Donaldson, Albert, February 19, 2002
Maynard, Robert, February 12, 2002
Petersen, Arnold, January 30, 2002
Salfen, Ambrose G., January 2, 2001
Tardy, Walter, January 3, 2001
Tardy, Walter, December 16, 2001

US Army Heritage Project survey of 601st veterans

The US Army Heritage and Education Center, Army Service Experience survey for World War II veterans contains a great deal of information. The survey is an ongoing project to get veterans from all wars to fill out forms detailing their service. They are grouped for research by unit. There are approximately 84 questionnaires filled out by World War II tank destroyer men; 23 men of the 601st Tank Destroyer Battalion filled them out due to the urging of Staff Sergeant Harper. It should be noted that some filled out the forms more extensively than others did and most importantly these forms were filled more than 50–60 years after the fact.

BIBLIOGRAPHY

Documents produced at Stateside US Army camps or by the War Department

Camp Bowie, Texas

Pictorial Review of Camp Bowie, with sketches by Bill Mauldin (Universal Press, San Antonio, Texas, November 1941)

Tank Destroyer School, Camp Hood, Texas

Handbook for Officer Candidates, TDS 110 (May 1943)

Officer Candidate Characteristics, revised s-143 TD School – 8-25-43- 5000 Instruction (Third Cavalry Museum, Fort Hood)

Master Schedule OCS (TD School, July 8, 1942)

Recapitulation Officer Candidate Course (July 8, 1942) (Third Cavalry Museum, Fort Hood)

Tank Destroyer Replacement Training Center, Camp Hood, Texas

Greeting from Camp Hood Texas (Curt Teich & Co, Inc., circa 1943)

Major Thomas Denny, *Tank Destroyer Men, the Song of the Tank Destroyers*, Official Song of the Tank Destroyers (Copyrighted 1943–44 Carl Fisher, NY Publisher)

Tech Five John Cross, *Under the Hood, A Souvenir Cartoon Book of Camp Hood* (circa 1943)

Welcome Booklet (Presented by Southwestern Bell Telephone Company, undated circa 1944)

Welcome to the Tank Destroyer Replacement Training Center (North Camp, Camp Hood, Texas, 1945, 7799-TD School-1-30-45-2500)

Camp Kilmer, New Jersey

Welcome booklet (summer 1945)

Camp Wheeler, Georgia

Camp Wheeler and Cochran Field (Souvenir Military Folder, Color Picture Publication, Cambridge, MA, circa 1942)

AMERICAN KNIGHTS

War Department, the Adjutant General's Office, Washington
Heraldic Section, Office of the Quartermaster general US Army,
    November 5, 1942
Instructions Applicable to Casual Officers Ordered Overseas, January 18, 1943
Manual Transportation Rules Military Railway Service, Technical Manual
    No. 5-415, Washington 1942

US Army Numbered Unit Documents
1st Provisional Antitank Battalion (later the 601st Tank Destroyer Battalion)
General Order Number 5
General Order Number 7

3rd Infantry Division and Major General O'Daniel memos/orders
Fighting To Be Done, September 26, 1944 (Officers are not tired memo)
General Orders Number 139, June 27, 1944 (Welch Bronze Star)
General Orders Number 252, November 5, 1944 (Welch's first Silver Star)
La Maison Rouge, the Story of an Engagement 23–24 January 1945, Lasky,
    Melvin J., Second Lieutenant
Message, Questionnaire on Replacements, January 26, 1945
Operations Instructions Number 33, June 4, 1944 (Special instructions for the
    occupation of Rome)
Operations Instructions Number 106, Orientation on forthcoming operations,
    December 22, 1944 (Colmar Pocket)
General Orders Number 83, March 3, 1945 (Welch and Audie Murphy Oak
    Leaf Clusters to Silver Star)
Operations Instructions Number 28, March 15, 1945 (gas masks)
Operations Instructions Number 72, May 5, 1945 (disposition of the division)
Tank Destroyers, 3rd ID Poop Sheet, March 16, 1944
Special Orders Number 79, March 21, 1945 (Welch gets to go home)

7th Replacement Depot
General Orders Number 10, Reorganization of the 7th Replacement Depot,
    3 November 1943
General Orders Number 12, Activation of Companies, 4 November 1943
History of the 7th Replacement Depot, 10 December 1942–31 May 1944
Monthly Narrative Report
    Period July 1–27, 1944

BIBLIOGRAPHY

Period July 28–August 27, 1944
Monthly Historical Report
  March 1–31, 1945
  April 3, 1945
Special Orders Number 203, October 1, 1943

15th Infantry Regiment

Unit Journal, May 28, 1944
Unit Journal, May 29, 1944

29th Replacement Battalion

Welcome Booklet (printed by the Battalion Information and Education
  Section, June or July 1945)

601st Tank Destroyer Battalion

B Company Personnel September 9, 1943–May 15, 1945 (single sheet)
B Company Statistics, August 17, 1945
Battle Operations Report, [El Guettar] March 28, 1943
  Reconnaissance Company Statements, undated
  A Company Statements, March 26, 1944
  B Company Statements, March 27, 1944
  C Company Statements, March 27, 1944
Battalion Commander–Company Commanders Meeting
  June 19, 1944
  June 25, 1944
  July 24, 1944
  October 13, 1944

Battalion Report of Operations for period (only written for combat periods):
  Ousseltia Valley, 18 April 1943
  October 1–31, November 5, 1943
  October 20–26, 1943, B and Recon Companies, Paulick, Michael
  November 1–30, December 3, 1943
  January 22–31, February 4, 1944
  February 1–29, March 6, 1944
  March 1–31, April 3, 1944
  March 16–19, April 16, 1945
  April 1–30, May 4, 1944
  May 1–31, June 3, 1944

411

June 1–30, July 2–3, 1944
August 1–31, August 31, 1944
September 1–30, October 2, 1944
October 1–31, October 31, 1944
November 1–30, December 3, 1944
December 1–31, January 2, 1944
January 1–31, February 2, 1945
February 1–28, March 4, 1945
March 15–31, April 1, 1945
April 1–30, May 3, 1945
May 1–10, May 25, 1945

Recommendation for Retaining Equipment, June 25, 1944

Grimes, James C. First Lieutenant Adjutant, *Battle Report of the Operation Avalanche* (September 25, 1943)

Battalion Roster, B Company, September 22, 1944

Comments and Lessons Learned, December 2, 1944

Corps Tank Destroyer Reports (various dates, April–May 1945)

Miner, Frederick C., Captain, BN S-3, *Lessons Learned in Combat* (August 15–October 15, 1944)

List of Casualties, January 22–January 25, 1945

Morning Reports (multiple days as noted in the text)

S-3 Reports:

Perry, John C., February 29, 1944
Perry, John C., March 1, 1944
Perry, John C., March 2, 1944
Perry, John C., March 3, 1944

Special Order Number 134, October 6, 1943

Unit Journals (multiple days as noted in the text)

Period maps

Brigadier General William Carey Crane Battle Map of Italy South of Rome: produced by the Chief of Engineers US Army, 1943, from the Italian Touring Club Map no. 17, 1:200,000. Revised 1943 by A.M.S. from the Istituto Geografico Militare, Italy 1:100,000,1923-28; G.S.G.S. 4164; Italy 1:100,000 1941; TCI (Touring Club Italia) Road Maps of Italy 1:250,000; 1939; Esso Road Map of Italy, 1939; and intelligence Reports.

Brigadier General William Carey Crane Battle Map of Rome, drawn by C.I.U. and War Office, photo lithographed by War Office, 3rd Edition, 1943 December

BIBLIOGRAPHY

Brigadier General William Carey Crane Battle Map of Naples, drawn by
    C.I.U. and War Office, photo lithographed by War Office, 3rd Edition,
    1943 December
War Map II, ESSO, General Drafting Company, NY, circa 1943

Photo collections

Author's collection
Third Cavalry Museum, Fort Hood, Texas
Geneva Historical Society, Geneva, New York
Hinman, Daniel S. T., General Photo Collection, Third Cavalry Museum,
    Fort Hood Texas
Larson, Rudy, Sergeant, personal photo collection
Nowak, John, Sergeant, personal photo collection
Toomey, William J., online collection from a five-man crew of
    photographers (William Heller, John Cole, Robert Seesock and
    Howard Nickelson), 3rd Signal Company, 3rd ID
The National Archives (NARA), Maryland Branch
US Army Military Heritage and Education Center, Carlisle, PA

Videos

Desert-The War in North Africa, the World at War Series Volume 8,
    (Thames Television, 1981)
Love Behind the Lines, MacWhirter, Pat, (2013, go to www.vimeo.com)
Tunisian Victory (Department of the Army, 1943)
The Battle of San Pietro (US Department of War, 1945)

NOTES

Chapter 1

1.   The Maginot Line was named after the French Minister of Defense, André Maginot. It consisted of a line of concrete fortifications, tank obstacles, artillery casements, and machine-gun posts constructed along France's border with Germany in the 1930s. These static defensive fortifications, based on World War I experiences, were built to buy time for the French Army to mobilize in the event of attack.

2.   168 artillery-trained men came from batteries of the 1st Division's 7th, 32nd, and 33rd Artillery Battalions. This is according to the October 7, 1941 General Order number 5, First Provisional Antitank Battalion, Fort Devens, Massachusetts. According to the October 20, 1941 General Order Number 7, First Provisional Antitank Battalion, Fort Bragg, North Carolina, an additional 61 men were transferred to the battalion from the 16th, 18th, and 26th Infantry Regiments of the 1st Infantry Division.

3.   Welch's number started with 1, which meant that he had enlisted. Draftees were given serial numbers that started with a 3. His second digit was a 2: that meant that he was from the New York area, which included the states of New York, New Jersey and Delaware. If a soldier became a commissioned officer he was given a new number preceded by the letter O.

4.   These camps, often named after US Civil War generals, were built with astonishing speed. Where wooden floors and tents had been the order of the day for the temporary camps built to train soldiers for World War I, steel-reinforced concrete foundations topped with wooden buildings were the new standard. Camps with the capacity to train tens of thousands of men at one time were built on a huge scale all over the country. Construction at Camp Wheeler eventually included a 1,000-bed hospital and even facilities to house prisoners of war. Troops were trained in virtually all types of small arms used by the military. Men thus trained could be sent anywhere they were needed.

5.   The SS *America*, for example, was converted by the Newport News shipyard into a troop transport in only 15 days; it was rechristened USS *West Point*.

6.   On September 4, 2007 Private Luigi Bagnato wrote this description of shipboard life on the USS *West Point*.

Chapter 2

7.   Thomas N. Carmichael, *The Ninety Days, Five Battles that Changed the World* (Konecky & Konecky, Old Saybrook, Connecticut, 1971), p.203.

8.   Brigadier General Monro MacCloskey, USAF, Retired, *Torch and the Twelfth Air Force* (Richard Rosen Press, New York, NY, 1971), p.78.

9.   Since the French left Algeria in 1962, the village has been renamed Zahanda.

10.   "Obituary Headlines" *Dallas Morning News* (November 1, 2013), see www.dallasnews.com.

11.   The normal rail route was from Casablanca to Tunis via Fes, Oujda, Oran, Algiers, and Constantine (Kasantina).

12.   The Silver Star is the third highest US military award for valor; only the Medal of Honor and the Distinguished Service Cross have precedence over it.

13.   General Orders: Department of the Army, General Orders Number 65 (September 24, 1948).

14. Later, on March 6, Rommel would attack the British in a blinding sandstorm and lose 55 of his remaining 150 Panzers. He had confronted a mass of 500 British guns. Shortly thereafter Rommel was recalled to Germany. Ill, he was never to return to Africa.

15. HQ 601st TD BN General Order Number 3, dated April 1, 1943.

Chapter 3

16. For a minute-by-minute recounting of the ranger attack see Ralph Ingersoll, *The Battle is the Pay-off* (Harcourt, Brace and Company, New York, 1943).

17. General Orders: Headquarters, 1st Infantry Division, General Orders Number 21 (1943).

18. Much of the El Guettar story was taken from *TD Combat in Tunisia*, prepared and published at the Tank Destroyer School for distribution to tank destroyer units within the continental United States with the approval of the commanding general, Army Ground Forces, TDS-117, January 1944: part two, *El Guettar, the push from Fériana through Gafsa and El Guettar,* was written by Lieutenant Colonel Baker. The report annotates Lieutenant Colonel Baker's remarks with quotes from official tank destroyer employment doctrine thus proving their doctrine was sound and this was the classic use envisioned for tank destroyers. It was the only occasion during the entire war when the combat situation met the criteria. A copy of the report is held at the US Army Heritage and Education Center, Carlisle, Pennsylvania.

19. Because there was an urgent need for the rapid resupply of men and materiel for the Allies in Western Tunisia, the motor and rail experts demanded additional equipment. Initial planning called for the Allies to augment the equipment that was on site. This included bringing more than 50 additional locomotives and more than 1,000 railway cars and other rolling stock. A special railway supply convoy was organized in the States, which arrived in Oran in March 1943. Materiel supplies were generally sent direct to Oran while

replacement personnel were sent on a shorter voyage to Casablanca. Railway cars and even engines were usually sent in pieces and assembled on site to conserve valuable shipboard cargo space. Overall the system was under the authority of the French Military Railroad Service run by French civilians with US officers supervising. By April 1943, 48 trains a day passed through Constantine and during that month over 31,000,000 tons of supplies were moved.

20.   Detailed specifications on the M-10 are listed in Appendix A.

Chapter 4

21.   At least two 601st men, Tech Five James and Captain Rydal L. Sanders got to see the Bob Hope, Dorothy Lamour and boxer Joe Louis USO Show in North Africa.

22.   V-mail stood for Victory Mail and was the fastest way to communicate with servicemen during World War II. The idea originally came from a British mail system called Airgraph. Both systems employed a photographic process to speed the mail and lighten the load by using microfilm (16mm) to reduce the letter to thumbnail size. These reels were then shipped by air to specific destinations where they were enlarged, printed on photographic paper and sent on to the destination. The letter that arrived was about quarter the original size and was folded so that the address was visible through a window in the envelope. Mail sent from servicemen was free, while that from the States required postage. According to the National Postal Museum (Washington, DC) it would have required 37 mailbags to carry 150,000 one-page letters and V-mail used one bag. That meant that 2,575 pounds of mail could be reduced to 45 pounds, saving about 98% of the weight and cargo space. The Army reported 1.25 billion V-mail letters were sent between June 15, 1942 and November 1, 1945 when the program ended.

23.   Paestum was founded in the 7th century BC and has the three best-preserved Greek temples in mainland Italy. Miraculously the

24. Tech Five James R. Stevens felt that the battleship HMS *King George* provided great support at Salerno.

25. According to the Department of the Army Permanent Orders 065-10, dated March 5, 2008, Companies A and B of the 601st TD BN were retroactively included in this award for their support to Darby's Rangers, September 10–18, 1943.

26. The 3rd Division entered the war in North Africa on November 8, 1942 and was in combat until the end of the war in May 1945. Along the way it was the only US division to earn ten battle stars and had over 34,000 casualties, more than any other US Army division. It spent a total of 531 days in combat and took over 175,000 prisoners of war. Men in various units under its command earned 41 US Medals of Honor. German Field Marshal Albert Kesselring, commanding general of German troops in Italy, declared that in his experience the 3rd Infantry Division was the most effective US division. At this time the 3rd included the 7th, 15th, and 30th Infantry Regiments plus supporting units such as the 10th Engineer Battalion. Corporal Borriello recalled that in the 3rd Infantry Division: "We learned how to do the 'Truscott Trot' as the General thought of a way to move the troops faster than a forced march. He marched us for ten minutes, trotted us for ten minutes, marched ten minutes, trotted ten minutes, etc. We did this for fifty minutes then rested ten minutes each hour."

27. Lloyd Clark, *Anzio, Italy and the Battle for Rome – 1944* (Grove Press, New York, 2006), p.33.

28. A terrible battle had been fought at Avellino, which resulted in hundreds of civilians killed and many, many GIs. It was to become the site of the first US military cemetery on mainland Italy. This cemetery was later moved to the seaside town of Nettuno and is now known as the Sicily-Rome American Cemetery.

29. Sergeant Ralph, G. Martin, "For Them the Men Will Go Through Hell," *The New York Times Magazine* (October 10, 1943), p.5. The article was sent by wireless from Algiers.

NOTES

30. The term "shave-tail" came from the old US Cavalry practice of placing a new officer on a horse with a shaved tail, and, until the horse's tail grew back, the men took special notice of the young officer to try to keep him out of trouble.

31. Upon receiving this note, his mother wrote on it in pencil the things she was going to send him: two pipes, three packs of tobacco, one carton of cigarettes, and one pair of socks.

32. Robert C. McFarland, *The History of the 15th Infantry Regiment in World War II* (Glenn A. Rathburn, Boise, Idaho, 1990), p.71.

33. As told to the author by Charles Phallen on August 2, 2014.

34. The men of the 601st had a lot to say about the M-4 Sherman tank. Their comments included this from Lieutenant Robert Maynard: "The tank was like a submarine on the sea. The men were locked up inside with a limited view of the battlefield and most information came from a tiny periscope. Our tank destroyers were designed to make up for the inability of the Sherman to go up against German tanks." Private Arnold Petersen added, "the Sherman was better going up against a machine-gun nest than our tank destroyers."

35. The unit journals were minute-by-minute recordings of comings and goings and significant events. It very much depended on the battalion clerk what was recorded. Some things now considered insignificant were recorded and other things that should have been recorded were not.

36. Welch's comment about sleeping in the tank destroyer is of interest. According to Staff Sergeant Harper five men could sleep in a destroyer by arranging themselves in a star pattern inside the hull. They all had to keep their feet pointing toward the center. To sleep, most of the men were on two or three different levels at once, each with a sharp edge. It was often cold and rarely quiet for more than a few minutes or so. For other living functions, a small dugout was scooped out beneath the M-10. Staff Sergeant Harper pointed out there was a trapdoor under the radio operator's seat (passenger side) and they used that to put the trash out.

37. Martin, *New York Times Magazine* (October 10, 1943).

Chapter 5

38. According to Gawne, *Finding Your Father's War* (Casemate, Drexel Hill, Pennsylvania, 2006), p.179, "A 1947 decision was made to award Bronze Stars to every combat infantryman so many veterans were surprised to learn they were due a Bronze Star for no apparent reason." The thinking was that everyone who was in combat and had the Combat Infantry Badge must have done something that was heroic although it had probably gone unnoticed. In the author's view, the thinking was correct.

39. This snippet of an article comes from *The Watch on the Rhine*, the 3rd Division newsletter. Mr Byke also mentioned that there appeared to be two or three of these rocket units in front of them at Monte Cassino.

40. There is some family lore that during the war Welch wore his father's ruby pinky finger ring and on one occasion it was damaged as he was pulled out of a destroyer by his sergeant, probably Sergeant Nowak. As he was unconscious his arm banged against the side of the tank and one of the two side diamonds was chipped. The author cannot verify the story, but the author's wife has this ring complete with chip.

41. Martin, *New York Times Magazine*, p.5.

42. The Paulicks were to have six children. He stayed in the Army and served a tour in Vietnam retiring as a brigadier general. He is buried in Arlington National Cemetery.

43. According to Dr Rolf Wirtgen, curator for the German Armed Forces Weapons Collection (*Wehrtechnische Studiensammlung* at the *Bundesamt für Wehrtechnik und Beschaffung*) at Koblenz, Germany, flak is a German term, derived from *Flugabwehrkanone*, which translates as aircraft defense cannon. The German weapons firm Krupp developed an 88mm Flakwagen, which became one of the most famous artillery pieces in history and proved to be one of the best antiaircraft guns in the world, as well as particularly deadly against light and medium tanks.

44. The Naples that Sergeant Nowak and others visited during the war must have presented an amazing spectacle. German writer Johann

NOTES

Wolfgang von Goethe visited Naples in the 18th century and is reported to have said the city was so beautiful that everyone should see it before dying. Although still chaotic, Naples has a vibrancy that is unique and has always been a special place. After the unification of Italy in the 1870s the government in Rome abandoned it, but not before removing the gold bullion from the Royal Treasury of the Kings of Naples.

45.   The famous Hollywood actor and director, John Huston, made a film documentary called *The Battle of San Pietro*. This film is considered one of the best made documentary films of World War II and gives a good idea of what Fifth Army units were up against. It won an Oscar for best documentary, but because it showed dead American soldiers, it was not widely shown.

46.   The DUKW, popularly pronounced duck, is a six-wheel-drive amphibious vehicle. It was designed by General Motors Corporation during World War II for transporting goods and troops over land and water and for use approaching and crossing beaches. The DUKW designation is not a military acronym; the name comes from the model naming terminology used by GMC. The D indicated a vehicle designed in 1942, the U meant utility (amphibious), the K indicated all-wheel drive and the W indicated two powered rear axles.

Chapter 6

47.   The Tuskegee Airmen were the first black pilots trained by the United States Air Corps. Many of these groundbreaking men fought in the 99th Fighter Squadron, nicknamed the Red Tails because the aircraft tails were painted red. The squadron proved that they were the equal of any other World War II fighter squadron.

48.   Major Edward J. Raymond, F. A., "Brassing Off Kraut," *The Field Artillery Journal* (October 1944, Overseas Edition), p.695.

49.   George Norfleet, *A Pilot's Journey* (Robnor Publishing, LLC, Washington, DC, 2007), p.140.

50. While in Sicily Lieutenant Colonel Darby felt that the Rangers
     suffered from a lack of integral antitank capability so he created an
     antitank platoon within Cannon Company, 1st Battalion.
     It consisted of four M-3 half-tracks, and rangers with artillery
     experience were recruited. The four half-tracks were christened Ace
     of Diamonds, Ace of Hearts, Ace of Spades and Ace of Clubs.

51. At least two other 601st men, Staff Sergeant Max Altschuld and
     Private First Class Mack I. Latz (Brooklyn, New York) also saw Ernie
     Pyle, the famous WWII war correspondent, and they remembered
     the event 60 years later.

52. The bombing incident that Borriello witnessed may be the one that
     occurred on February 8. A German bomber aircraft was being chased
     across the beachhead by a British spitfire. In order to gain altitude
     and increase speed, the bomber punched off its bombs. Regrettably
     the bombs landed in the middle of the hospital and killed or
     wounded nearly 100 soldiers. Later that morning, the German pilot
     was shot down and treated in that same hospital.

Chapter 7

53. Raymond, as quoted by Gill, *Tank Destroyer Forces, World War II*
     (Turner Publishing Company, Paducah, Kentucky, 1992) p.49.

54. "Tank Buffer Battle fought on Beachhead," *The Stars and Stripes*
     (early February 1944).

55. Schneider noted that January 14–24, the 508th took delivery of
     28 new Tiger Is, bringing their total number of Panzers to 45. On
     February 4, they boarded a military train from Metz, Germany to
     Arezzo, Italy. By February 12, the 508th unloaded around 12 miles
     north of the town of Orvieto, Italy. They then proceeded via road
     to Rome and camped at the Forte Tiburtina, an Italian military base
     on the city's outskirts. From Rome, the 508th's First Company drove
     to the Anzio beachhead. Their route took them over mountainous
     roads with serpentine curves. One Panzer under the command of
     Corporal (Feldwebel) Nagel caught fire and exploded. On

February 16, four of the 508th's Panzers participated in an attack on the British sector. It was unsuccessful. They had to keep to the narrow roads just like their Allied counterparts and did not achieve their objective.

56. This stateside rotation started in the summer of 1943. The purpose was to provide some relief to troops who had unusually long or arduous overseas assignments. The theater commander set the period for the rotation and typically replacements had to be available before anyone was allowed to depart on temporary duty for rest, recuperation and rehabilitation. In 1944 a total of 260,000 men in the European Theater were sent home. Staff Sergeant Harper noted, "Typically these men spent 30 days in the States on leave and then rejoined their units. The leave plus travel time could mean the men were away from their units for as long as 90 days."

57. The Anzio Express was a German 218-ton railway artillery cannon that fired 280mm shells. The cannon fired from a siding in the outskirts of Rome. There was also a second gun that was similar, nicknamed Anzio Annie, German name Leopold. After being captured, Anzio Annie was brought to the States for evaluation. Today it sits abandoned on a disused railroad siding at Fort Lee, Virginia.

58. Technical Sergeant Phallen told this story to the author on August 2, 2014. Over the years Phallen has visited Tech Five Brooks' grave at the Sicily Rome Cemetery and has attempted to contact the Brooks family without success.

59. Long after the war, Colonel Tardy commented: "The 3rd Infantry Division was very fortunate to have General O'Daniel and General Truscott as commanding generals. General O'Daniel was known to show up unannounced on the front lines. He liked to do it for morale and would say encouraging things like 'Go soldier' when he would see someone sitting as he made his unannounced visits. I once lost a number of officers and had to find a way to quickly replace them and I did so without the customary divisional procedures. I got called to General O'Daniel and thought I was about to be relieved of command, instead I was given a Bronze Star."

60. German forces consisted of two infantry divisions (the 362nd and 715th Infantry Divisions); two panzer divisions (the 26th and the Hermann Göring Panzer Divisions); the 29th Panzer Grenadier Division; the 114th Jäger Division; the 1028th Grenadier Regiment; and the 26th V7 (a battalion-sized unit).

61. Sunday supplement of *The Beachhead News* (December 17, 1944). Author's collection, as sent by Welch to his mother at the time. *The Beachhead News* was founded on May 1, 1944, by a former 601st Officer, Captain James C. Grimes, previously the 601st BN S-1. He had been transferred as OIC VI Corps Beachhead News and this may explain the great coverage. The unit journal records that he visited the battalion HQ on December 11, 1944.

62. Raymond, as quoted by Gill, *Tank Destroyer Forces*, p.49.

63. Adapted from S. J. Zaloga, *Anzio 1944, The Beleaguered Beachhead* (Osprey, Oxford, United Kingdom, 2005), pp.73–74.

64. From the 0830 attack Tech Five Otto Aimone, Private Frank F. Brown, Jr, Tech Five Orville W. Freed, Corporal Henry E. Godlewski, and Private William E. Alexander all received Bronze Stars. From the second action, Lieutenant Welch and his tank commander, Sergeant Robert A. Hawks, each were awarded a Silver Star. The Bronze Stars were awarded to: Sergeant Rudolph E. Larson (then Corporal); Tech Five Donald G. Lees, Corporal Peter Dykstra (then Private); Sergeant Antony J. Mello; Sergeant Benjamin Gelade, (then Corporal); Private First Class Joseph J. Carey (then Private). Because two of the men already had Bronze Stars, they were awarded Oak Leaf Clusters; they were Tech Five Joseph W. Monahan and Tech Five John C. O'Donnell. It is not known whether Sergeants Ritchie or Christian received any recognition for this action; if not, they probably should have.

65. Clark, *Anzio, Italy and the Battle for Rome*, p.216.

Chapter 8

66. By March 1944, Anzio had emerged as the fourth-largest port in the world according to Clark, *Anzio, Italy and the Battle for Rome*, p.231.

67.   Some sources say 700 men a day left the beachhead for the rest camp at Caserta.

68.   Staff Sergeant Benjamin A. Buckley (Lowell, Indiana) enlisted in the 1st Signal Company of the 1st Division in 1939 and joined the 601st Tank Destroyer Battalion in February 1942.

69.   This was the same day as the partisan attack on the Via Rasella in Rome when a German column marching through the city was attacked. Thirty-two soldiers were killed and the Nazis retaliated with the murder of 335 Italian men at the Ardeatine Caves. See Robert Katz, *Death in Rome* (Macmillan, New York, 1967), for full details.

70.   Lieutenant Colonel Howard, US Army (Retired) provided the following comments on the Ferdinand, later known as Elefant: It was a Ferdinand Porsche design that began as a Tiger variant (Tiger P) but was never put into production. Eighty-five of the chassis were fitted with new superstructure, more armor, and the long-barreled 88mm Pak 43/2 L/71 antitank gun. The gun was mounted on a large, fixed (won't traverse) turret set back at the rear of the chassis. The original Porsche engines were replaced by two standard Maybach HL 120 TRM tank engines and a new heavy tank destroyer was born. Ferdinand/Elefant weighed 71.1 tons and possessed 200mm of frontal armor.
      It is doubtful that Welch's 3-inch gun could penetrate the Ferdinand/Elefant's armor at the ranges discussed in the book, although such a large and slow target might have been readily hit, even at long ranges.

71.   Bill Mauldin, *Up Front* (Henry Holt and Company, Inc., New York, 1944), pp.96–97.

72.   Rita Luisa Zucca (born 1912) was one of two American expatriates given the nickname "Axis Sally" (the other broadcasted from Berlin). Zucca was an Italian-American who broadcast Axis propaganda to Allied forces, first in North Africa and later in Italy. She had returned to Italy in 1938 and renounced her American citizenship to save her family's property from expropriation by Mussolini's government. In the summer of 1943, the Italian National Radio Network in Rome hired Zucca and teamed her with German broadcaster Charles Gödel in the

program "Jerry's Front Radio Calling." When Rome fell, Zucca retreated
north with the Germans and resumed broadcasting from Milan. Her
final broadcast was in April 1945 and she was arrested that June.
American attempts to prosecute Zucca for treason broke down when it
became clear that she had renounced her American citizenship before
she had started broadcasting. Zucca was tried by an Italian military
tribunal on charges of collaboration and was sentenced to four and a
half years in prison. She was barred from returning to the United States.

73. William L. Allen, *Anzio: Edge of Disaster* (E. P. Dutton, New York,
1978), p.51.

74. Clark, *Anzio, Italy and the Battle for Rome – 1944*, p.239.

75. Zaloga, *Anzio 1944*, pp.82–83.

Chapter 9

76. Clark, *Anzio, Italy and the Battle for Rome*, p.287. Allen put the figure
even higher at 1,626 casualties, p.151.

77. Staff Sergeant Harper probably saw a 15-meter-deep complex called
the Cisterna Caetani Caves. There were many such caves built under
the town over the millennia. They were cut into the natural rock and
used as cisterns, stables and other storage areas. During the war, the
civilian population took refuge in these caves until forcibly removed
by the Germans on March 19, 1944. German soldiers then moved
in.

78. McFarland, *The History of the 15th Infantry*, p.141.

79. Hamilton H. Howze (1902–92) was a famous American World War II
tank commander who very successfully fought all over Italy.

80. See Robert Katz, *The Battle for Rome* (Simon & Schuster, New York,
2003), for the long sad story of the occupation.

81. On June 4, 1984, the author served as the US Assistant Naval
Attaché, Rome and attended the celebration of the 40th anniversary
of the liberation of Rome. During this event, he met many veterans
of General Frederick's 1st Special Service Force who were among the
first to enter Rome. The mayor of Rome presented a commemorative

medal to each of the participants, including the author. That day, the author was also pleased to meet Sergeant Bill Mauldin, the famous World War II GI cartoonist. The author, who was in full dress naval uniform, fittingly wore the naval sword of Lieutenant Commander Harry N. Trotter, Welch's stepfather.

82.   After some difficulty, and with the help of the curator of the National Museum of the Liberation, Via Tasso, Rome, the author was able to find the exact spot where the picture was taken. This was because visible in the photo is a preserved ancient Roman water storage pressure tank for the Aqua Felice Aqueduct just inside the Porta Furba.

83.   H.V. Morton, *A Traveler in Rome* (Dodd, Mead & Company, New York 1957), p.203.

Chapter 10

84.   Many years later, Colonel Walter Tardy was also buried at Arlington National Cemetery, in 2006.

85.   Norman Lewis, *Naples '44* (Pantheon Books, Random House, New York, 1978), pp.153–154.

86.   Adapted from Lewis, *Naples '44*, pp.94, 95, 101 and 115.

87.   Lewis, *Naples '44*, p.100.

88.   7th Replacement Depot, Monthly Narrative Report, Period July 28–August 27, 1944, p.1.

89.   7th Replacement Depot, Monthly Narrative Report, Period July 1–27, 1944, p.1

90.   7th Replacement Depot, Monthly Narrative Report, Period July 28–August 27, 1944, p.5.

91.   The author, a Vietnam-era veteran, was unaware that this derogatory term was used during World War II. However, he has since learned that it was first used by US soldiers in the Philippines in the late 1890s and was thereafter applied to any foe or local inhabitant.

92.   William B. Breuer, *Operation Dragoon* (Presidio Press, Novato, California, 1987).

93.   McFarland, *History of the 15th Infantry*, p.145.

Chapter 11

94. Mauldin, *Up Front*, pp.196–197.

95. McFarland, *History of the 15th Infantry*, p.146.

96. McFarland, *History of the 15th Infantry*, p.152.

97. Lieutenant Henry Anderson, C Company 601st Tank Destroyer Battalion, undated one-page paper, US Army Military Heritage and Education Center.

98. Two of the over 5,000 American and some British paratroopers who had landed just before the invasion.

99. The 3rd Reconnaissance Troop, at that time assigned to the 3rd Infantry Division.

100. On September 25, 1944 French Army B was re-designated the French First Army. It was the French who liberated the southern area of the Vosges Mountains and the 3rd Infantry Division was often in support of this force. They were on the right flank of the Allied Southern Group of Armies, adjacent to Switzerland. This army, composed of over 280,000 men, was made up of two corps, the French I and II Corps.

101. HQ 3rd Infantry Division Secret Memo dated August 21, 1944.

102. Captain Rydal L. Sanders described the FFI "as carefree, romantic, daring and although they didn't destroy a lot of the enemy they appeared to have had a lot of fun." His criticism may have been a little harsh.

103. This story has been told in Jeff Danby, *The Day of the Panzer* (Casemate, Drexel Hill, Pennsylvania, 2006). It is a truly remarkable story. The author is indebted to Jeff for providing many documents and interviews with surviving members of the 601st, which would not have otherwise been available. Jeff spent six years researching the story of his grandfather, First Lieutenant Edgar Danby, who was killed on his first day of combat (August 26) with B Company 756th Tank Battalion. Jeff has painstakingly put together the story of this action in the small village of Allan, about 10 kilometers south of Montélimar. Arguably this was the place where the invasion of southern France got tough. Although his platoon was involved, Welch missed this action

because on that same day he was flown to Naples with recurring malaria. In his absence, an unidentified lieutenant from the 756th Tank Battalion took charge of Welch's platoon.

104. Sanders, Rydal L., Captain, member of Recon Company, memoir written January 29, 1993 (US Army Military Heritage and Education Center).

105. Gill, *Tank Destroyer Forces*, p.67.

106. While certainly some of the women mentioned had provided comfort to the enemy, a certain percentage had courted favor with the Germans in order to obtain information to pass on to the FFI. The local citizenry of course did not know of this clandestine activity and these women were unjustly punished.

107. Harry Yeide, *The Tank Killers* (Casemate, Havertown, Pennsylvania, 2004), p.162.

108. Quoted in *Lowell Tribune* (August 30, 1945), p.4, columns 1–4.

109. The lack of a steel cover that allowed snipers to fire down from a height into the open tops of the TDs would eventually injure crewmen. Fitting collapsible steel covers to protect the crew solved this problem, but it was a hard won lesson.

110. Four of the five men from the first TD (Prauman, Childers, Brown and Corthell) share a single grave at the Zachary Taylor National Cemetery in Louisville, Kentucky. They were returned to the US and reburied together on February 23, 1947.

111. Danby, *The Day of the Panzer*, p.viii.

Chapter 12

112. The author has attempted to verify this episode but with no success. If Welch spent a night in Cannes, which was possible, it might have been after transporting paratroopers to that city from their drop zone at Le Muy as any available transportation, including tank destroyers, was used.

113. McFarland, *History of the 15th Infantry*, pp.195–96

114. Ibid., p.201.

115. Armistice Day, now called Veterans Day, originally honored the armistice that ended World War I on the eleventh hour of the eleventh day of the eleventh month.

116. Efforts to identify the sentry were unsuccessful.

117. McFarland, *History of the 15th Infantry*, p.212.

Chapter 13

118. In addition to Sergeant Nowak's comment on looting, four other men acknowledged that the men of the 601st did their share of looting. On their US Army Heritage and Education Center survey forms Sergeant Allen H. Bowman said "there was some of course, but mostly looked for booze"; First Sergeant William Duke Hill (Cliffside, North Carolina) recalled "much looting" but didn't elaborate; Lieutenant Robert A. Maynard mentioned that the "only looting [he] saw was for food;" and Captain Rydal L. Sanders noted that there was "little looting from civilians, most everything from enemy soldiers – chocolate candy, women's hosiery and cameras."

119. Film buffs may remember a scene in Rick's Café in the 1942 movie *Casablanca* when the Germans sing this song and the French, led by Victor Laszlo, respond and drown them out by singing *La Marseillaise*. The refrain, in German, goes like this: *Lieb' Vaterland, magst ruhig sein* (repeat); *Fest steht und treu die Wacht, die Wacht am Rhein!* (repeat); the English translation is: "Dear Fatherland, no fear be thine (repeat), firm and true stands the watch, the watch on the Rhine" (repeat). According to Lieutenant Colonel Stoy, this was also the name of the 3rd Division's mission as occupation troops at Andernach and Koblenz after World War I and thus the name of the Division Society newsletter since 1919.

120. MacWhirter, Pat, *Love Behind the Lines* (2013, see www.vimeo.com).

121. On the back of one photo of Martha Schneider there is an inscription in German and on another one in French. Both can be translated as: "A little souvenir from an Alsatian." Looks like she was ready for both sides; maybe that's why she wanted to learn English.

122. Lieutenant Colonel John R. Howard, US Army (Retired) casts some light on "the utility of the loafers Lt. Welch was so keen to obtain. Welch had boots, perhaps even a spare pair, but you simply have to get your feet out of boots at least once every 24 hours to maintain healthy feet over the long haul, particularly in a cold-wet environment. Clean loafers inside the tank would be preferable to muddy boots. Nobody wants a filthy turret. Also, loafers would be ideal when nature called at night or if you have to bail out or run for your life in an emergency. Soldiers today might substitute a pair of running shoes or Croc sandals."

123. Lieutenant Colonel Howard also commented on Lieutenant Welch turning down a promotion. "He may have been offered the position of Company Executive Officer (XO), and advancement in responsibility if not rank and a likely fast track to company command. Platoon leader is a better job than XO, which is a non-fighting job primarily concerned with logistics and maintenance. I don't blame him for avoiding the opportunity."

124. McFarland, *History of the 15th Infantry*, p.233.

125. Ibid., p.238.

126. It is worth mentioning that three Medals of Honor were awarded to 15th Infantry Regiment men in the fighting in this area. During the attack on Bennwihr on December 23–24, one was awarded to Technical Sergeant Kefurt; another on December 26 to Lieutenant Colonel Ware at Hill 351; and one at Sigolsheim on December 27 to First Lieutenant Whitely. There is also a *Place de 15th Infantry Regiment* in Sigolsheim, a parking lot near the old town hall.

127. It is not known what happened to the dog, but he did not bring him back to the States.

Chapter 14

128. Second Lieutenant Melvin J. Lasky, *La Maison Rouge the Story of an Engagement 23–24 January 1945*, p.7. Lasky noted that this small-unit action was part of 3rd Infantry Division's Operation

Grand Slam in the Colmar Pocket. In a cover sheet Lasky further described the action as "Attack, panic, and withdrawal at La Maison Rouge..." The Welch quote comes directly from Lieutenant Lasky's debriefing of Welch on February 18, 1945 and the words are his.

129. Lasky, *La Maison Rouge,* p.21.

130. Ibid., p.28.

131. One of the things that Sergeant Larson lost was a diary he had been keeping and that was an irreplaceable loss to this story.

132. Today there is a memorial to Audie Murphy, the most decorated US soldier of World War II, and this action, on the site where it happened in the woods just outside of Riedwihr. It depicts Murphy on an M-10 tank destroyer. The 3rd Division Museum at Fort Stewart, Georgia has a plaque with a piece of that tank destroyer found on site. The TD had been blown up when the ammunition exploded and pieces were scattered about. When the movie, *To Hell and Back*, starring Audie Murphy as himself was in production, Lieutenant Colonel Paulick, formerly a captain in the 601st and Audie Murphy's battalion commander in the 15th, served as the technical adviser to the movie company.

133. The author is indebted to Lieutenant Colonel Tim Stoy, USA 15th Infantry historian, who provided the name of the village.

Chapter 15

134. *The US Army in World War II, European Theater of Operation, Chapter XXIX,* The Colmar Pocket, p.552.

135. As an example of how bad the weather in the Vosges Mountains can be, the author and his wife traced this route in the mid-morning on July 22, 2011. It was only 10 degrees Celsius with fog and drizzle.

136. The 776th Tank Destroyer Battalion had served in North Africa and Italy and in October 1944 had been shipped to France. It had received the M-36 in November 1944, several months before the 601st. See S.J. Zaloga, *US Tank and Tank Destroyer Battalions in the ETO 1944–45* (Osprey, Oxford, United Kingdom, 2005), p.89.

137. This song is still well known in the UK today and was written by Jimmy Kennedy who was a captain in the British Expeditionary Force at the start of World War II.

138. McFarland, *History of the 15th Infantry*, p.375.

139. The 7th Replacement Depot's Monthly Historical Report for March 1945 noted that soldiers, called TDRs (Temporary Duty Returning), were returned to their units in Europe after their time in the States. For example their report noted that: "The [troop ship] USS *General Richardson* arrived on 3 March with 202 officers, 15 nurses, and 1718 enlisted men returning from temporary duty in the States. Of these, a total of 1537 were ground forces personnel and were officially registered into the depot for return to their units." The report also notes that 148 soldiers were to be shipped on to France to rejoin their units.

140. Delta Base Section was one of several European sections, like Normandy and Channel. It was responsible for administration and supplies at various ports and was run by the US Army Transportation Corps. The earlier name for these operations was SOS (Service of Supply). Delta Base Section included the French Mediterranean ports of Marseille, De Bouc, Toulon and Nice.

Chapter 16

141. McFarland, *History of the 15th Infantry*, p.289.

142. The doodlebugs were also called "buzz bombs" by the British. They were the German V-1 rockets that resembled a flying jet engine with a suspended bomb load. The last doodlebug launch was March 29, 1945, so these were captured later. (B Company 601st Tank Destroyer Battalion memo of August 17, 1945, company statistics, probably for the history, p.2, paragraph 4.(b).)

143. McFarland, *History of the 15th Infantry*, p.294.

144. Harper likely was in error when he wrote in his memoirs that First Lieutenant Tolbert Hays, Jr was the officer killed during this action. Lieutenant Hays is buried in Golden Gate National Cemetery and

his date of death is listed as October 23, 1944. On the other hand
Second Lieutenant Beverly S. Blackburn is listed as KIA in Germany
on April 17, 1944. The author therefore has taken the responsibility
to change the names in Staff Sergeant Harper's account.

145. MacWhirter, *Love Behind the Lines* (2013, www.vimeo.com.)

146. This was the second man listed as killed this month for whom
Josowitz did not list a hometown. Although speculative, it might
have been that the men were not in the unit long enough for such
details to be recorded. Replacements, because of their inexperience,
were often the first men killed in an attack.

147. The men really liked the 10-in-1 ration as there were a lot of different
things in them. Captain Rydal L. Sanders said he had "only one
complaint, someone in quartermaster had a nasty habit of removing
the plum pudding from the 10-in-1 rations – the dirty bastards."

148. As told to the author, August 2014.

149. McFarland, *History of the 15th Infantry*, p.299.

150. The amphibious landings were: North Africa (Oran), Salerno, Anzio,
and Southern France. They did not get credit for Sicily since they
were there for POW guard duty and were not part of the invasion.

151. Quoted in *Lowell Tribune* (August 30, 1945), p.4, columns 1–4.

152. According to a B Company memo, the company with the 601st and
3rd Infantry Division received two citations from the French
Government:
Croix de Guerre with palm for action in the Vosges Mountains,
France (Oct–Dec 1944)
Croix de Guerre with palm for action at Colmar, France (Jan 1945)
The French *fourragère* is pending authorization, in lieu of the above
two awards.
This is the only notation known to the author that the unit may have
been awarded two *Croix de Guerre*. (B Company, 601st TD BN
Memo of August 17, 1945, company statistics, probably for the
history, p. 2, paragraph 4 .(d).)

153. The GI Bill was passed by Congress to provide funds for service
members to go to college and to obtain low-cost housing loans

among other things. Welch was out of the Army, back in college and now a member of the Delta Kappa Epsilon (Deke) Fraternity at Cornell University.

154. At the time of the operation report of May 25, 1945, it was expected that the unit would be credited with eight campaigns; however, the official US Army listing of campaigns listed ten.

155. *Life Magazine* (April 22, 1946), p.29. By "gone," *Life* meant out of the service.

156. Thomas Childers, *Soldier from the War Returning* (Mariner Books, Houghton Mifflin Harcourt, New York, 2009), p.211.

INDEX